# Sheffield

RUTH HARMAN

JOHN MINNIS

with contributions by

ROGER HARPER

PEVSNER ARCHITECTURAL GUIDES

YALE UNIVERSITY PRESS

NEW HAVEN & LONDON

*For Graham Hague and Tom Wesley*
*and the bus drivers of Sheffield, who helped us know the city*

YALE UNIVERSITY PRESS
NEW HAVEN AND LONDON
302 Temple Street, New Haven
47 Bedford Square, London WC1B

www.pevsner.co.uk
www.lookingatbuildings.org
www.yalebooks.co.uk
www.yalebooks.com

Published 2004
10  9  8  7  6  5  4  3  2  1

Set in Adobe Minion by SNP Best-set Typesetter Ltd., Hong Kong
Printed in Singapore by CS Graphics

Library of Congress Cataloging-in-Publication Data

Harman, Ruth.
Sheffield / Ruth Harman John Minnis.
    p. cm. – (Pevsner architectural guides)
    Includes bibliographical references and index.
    ISBN 0–300–10585–1 (pbk. : alk. paper)
    1. Architecture – England – Sheffield – Guidebooks. 2. Sheffield
(England) – Buildings, structures, etc. – Guidebooks. I. Minnis, John.
II. Title. III. Series.
    NA971.S5H37  2004
    720´.9428´21–dc22
                                                2004012273

# Contents

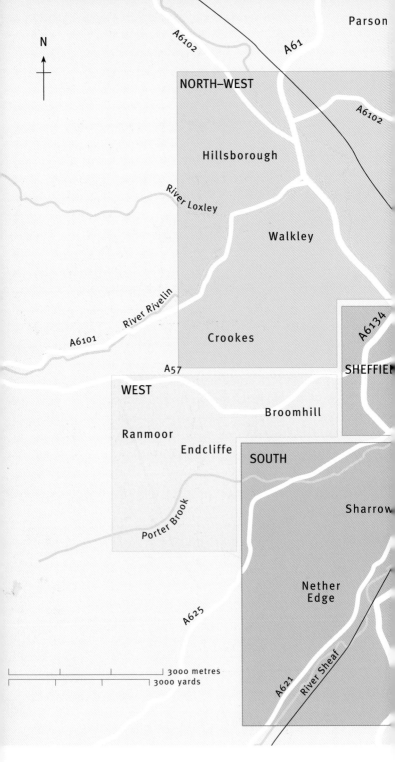

1. Sheffield, showing areas covered by walks

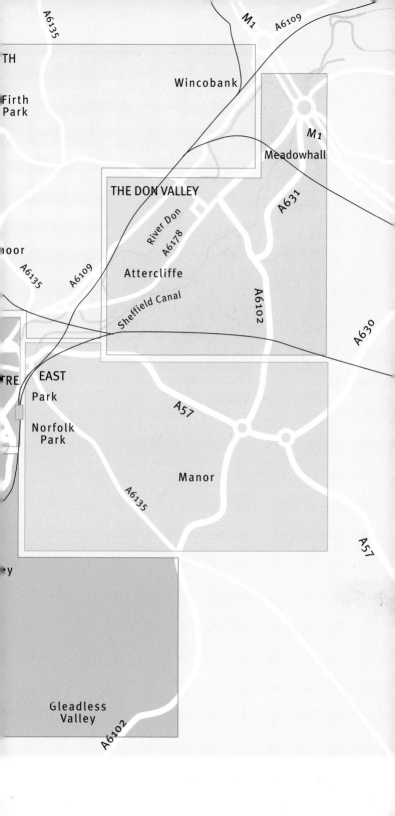

2. Sheffield, view from Meersbrook Park

# How to use this book

This book is designed as a practical guide for exploring the buildings of Sheffield city centre and most of its surrounding suburbs. The divisions between the sections are shown on the map on pp. vi–vii. After a historical Introduction, the gazetteer begins on p. 45 with entries on seven Major Buildings, all of which can be found in the city centre. A separate section follows, covering the buildings of the University of Sheffield and the central campus of Sheffield Hallam University. The city centre, broadly defined as the area within the Inner Ring Road, is covered in a series of six walks, each provided with its own street map. Arrows on the maps are intended to aid navigation and to indicate detours from the principal route of each tour. The selection of suburbs is divided geographically into North, East, South, West and North-West, with a separate section for the Don valley. Each suburban area has its own introduction and maps, followed by either walks or lists of individual buildings of note. Readers should note that the description of the interior of a building does not indicate that it is open to the public.

In addition certain buildings topics and themes have been singled out for attention:

*Architects:* Sheffield Architects p. 24, J. L. Womersley p. 32, W. J. Hale p. 277

*Cathedral and Churches:* St Paul, Wordsworth Avenue p. 37, The Shrewsbury Monuments p. 51, The Gerente Window p. 55

*Education:* The Board Schools p. 20–1

*History:* Sheffield's Population p. 9, Smoke and Soot p. 17, Patronage p. 22, Ruskin and Sheffield p. 74, The Heart of the City p. 96, Paradise Square p. 114, Sheffield Castle p. 148, Wincobank Camp and the Roman Rig p. 185

*Housing:* Bylaw terraced Housing p. 18, The Cottage Estates p. 29, Streets in the Sky p. 211, Freehold Land Societies p. 282

*Industry:* Little Mesters p. 6, Abbeydale Industrial Hamlet p. 10–11, Cutlery Workshops p. 126, Steelmaking: The Cementation Process p. 165, Steelmaking: The Crucible Process p. 166, Steelmaking: The Bessemer, Open-hearth and Electric Arc processes p. 193

*Sculpture:* The Town Hall's Sculpture p. 63, Frank Tory and Sons, Architectural Sculptors p. 110

*Styles:* Brutalism p. 209

# Acknowledgements

Our first debt is to those who pioneered the study of Sheffield's often underrated buildings: principally Nikolaus Pevsner, whose original account of Sheffield was largely re-written in 1966, with the assistance of Enid Radcliffe, for the 2nd edition of *Yorkshire: The West Riding*; also the late Steven Welsh, Professor of Architecture at Sheffield University whose typescript notes on the city's Victorian and Edwardian architects have greatly aided our research, and Canon William Odom, whose book on Sheffield's Anglican churches is a mine of information.

This volume would not have been possible without generous funding from the Heritage Lottery Fund and support from the Buildings Books Trust, and our thanks are also due to English Heritage, who helped by providing many of the photographs, and to their photographer, Keith Buck. We are also very grateful to Roger Harper, who wrote the Cutlers' Hall entry and gave help with Sheffield University and much support and encouragement generally. Tom Wesley volunteered enthusiastically to try out the various walks and made many helpful and perceptive comments. Special thanks go to Graham Hague, formerly of the Planning Department, who read the text and made available the work he undertook for the List review and over many years studying Sheffield's history. Derek Bayliss read the entries relating to industrial buildings and made many useful suggestions and Peter Machan also gave much assistance, especially with John Watts' building, Lambert Street.

Several Sheffield City Council officers assisted us – Les Sturch, Simon Ogden, Craig Broadwith and James Arnold of Planning, Transport and Highways, and Jim Breakey of Sheffield Design & Property. Jim McNeill and Dinah Saich at the South Yorkshire Archaeology Service read through the entries relating to archaeological matters. Heather Hillon, Tracey Nation and Andy Barker of the Design Team were helpful in providing photographs. In addition Graham Williams, Secretary of Sheffield DAC gave much help with recent developments affecting Anglican churches.

Eva Wilkinson generously made her research on Broomhill available and commented on a draft, as did Dr Nyra M. Wilson who kindly gave access to her work on the development of the w suburbs. For information on Ranmoor we particularly thank Gerald Eveleigh and Peter Warr. We are also very grateful to others who gave us help and information on individual buildings, architects, areas and subjects: Joan Flett (Nether Edge), Nancy Greenwood and Daphne Gabbertas (W. J. Hale), Professor Clyde Binfield (W. J. Hale and the nonconformist connexions of Sheffield architects), Audrey Rowe and Monica Slater (NADFAS surveys), Diane Gascoyne (war memorials), Dr Martin Purdy, Canon Nick Howe, Alan Cottam, Margaret Garner and Gill MacGregor (Sheffield Cathedral), Dr Paul Walker and Peter Howell (St Marie's), Julie MacDonald and Joan Unwin (the Cutlers' Hall), Fiona MacCarthy (Broom Hall and No. 1 Park Lane), Michael Kerney (superb summaries of C19 stained glass), Martin Olive ( Freehold Land Societies), Elain Harwood (postwar buildings), and Joan Sewell (the gardens at The Towers).

We also thank Andrew Lines of ARCUS, The Ven. Dr. Tim Ellis for help on Leslie Moore and much encouragement generally, Roger Allum, Public Relations Director at Sheffield University, Andrew Shepherd of Elden Minns & Co. Ltd and Andy Travis of Hadfield Cawkwell Davidson. Also all those who allowed us to view their buildings and answered our questions, including the clergy of Sheffield's churches, staff at the Town Hall and other public buildings, headteachers, and other custodians and private householders, as well as everyone who allowed us to take photographs or provided photographs for us.

The staff at Sheffield Local Studies Library, especially Doug Hindmarch, Sylvia Pybus and Mike Spick, and colleagues at Sheffield Archives, the Conservation Unit, and the Arts and Sports Reference Library were always exceptionally helpful.

For general help and encouragement, we thank Valerie Bayliss, Judy Hague, Tanya Schmoller and other members of the South Yorkshire Group of the Victorian Society. Also Terry Cooper, Sue Blundell, Clare Hartwell, Jean Moulson, Sue Wrathmell, and, especially, Kate Minnis and the neglected but understanding Harman family.

Our special thanks are due to the editorial team at Yale University Press. Firstly we owe a huge debt to our editor, Charles O'Brien, who was a constant and patient source of advice and encouragement. Simon Bradley and Bridget Cherry made helpful comments on parts of the text and Emily Winter, Assistant Editor, steered the book through the production stages with good-humoured professionalism. Emily Lees was our diligent picture researcher, Touchmedia produced the maps and Alan Fagan drew the plans. Sue Vaughan was a meticulous copy editor and indexer, while Rosamund Howe read the proofs. Sally Salvesen, as Commissioning Editor, oversaw the whole project with enthusiasm, and Gavin Watson provided invaluable administrative support.

Any errors or omissions are our own and in the long tradition of this series we appeal to readers to send corrections to us at the publishers.

# Introduction

# Introduction

'None of the big cities of England has such majestic surroundings as Sheffield' wrote Pevsner in 1959. The River Don flows down a broad valley from the NW and is joined by the Sheaf, which, like the Porter, the Loxley and the Rivelin has carved out its own steep-sided valley. The undulating hills are the city's greatest natural asset, accompanied by green corridors that penetrate down to the very edge of the city centre, which stands on a low hill, dwarfed by the surrounding landscape. No better introduction can be made to Sheffield's topography than the prospect from Skye Edge on the eastern side of the city. From here views extend to the western suburbs with their mansions dotted amid the greenery on the SW-facing slopes, and on to the high country of the Mayfield Valley and Ringinglow. Visible on the horizon are the heather clad moors that mark the edge of the Peak District.

Sheffield's buildings have been less well-appreciated. Pevsner considered the pre-war city 'architecturally a miserable disappointment, the layout of the centre confused, the buildings – certainly before the late C19 – of no distinction'. Ian Nairn's assessment* was even harsher: 'The old buildings are something of a joke. In style after style there is the demure and the second rate.' It is true that Sheffield's staple industries of steel and cutlery neither required palatial warehouses to display their

* Ian Nairn, *Britain's Changing Towns*, 1967

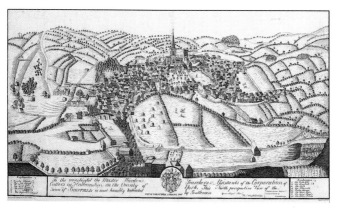

3. Sheffield at night
4. View of Sheffield by Thomas Oughtibridge (1737)

wares nor produced, until the late C19, the wealth to support grand architecture. The town was bypassed by main roads and, initially, by the railways. This led to an insular conservatism expressed by a distaste for excessive display and a slow response to changing architectural fashion. Sheffield's buildings are mainly the work of local men, outsiders contributing little until the C20, but their work from churches to schools, and workshops to housing, deserves recognition alongside the justly famous developments of the mid-C20 which provoked the enthusiasm of the planners, architects and architectural press in postwar England. Those developments too must now be set in context and Pevsner's view, that 'if an architectural traveller stops at Sheffield, he can only be in search of mid-C20 buildings', properly reassessed.

Although Sheffield is the largest city in Yorkshire in area (second largest in population behind Leeds, with 513,230 in 2001) and the fifth in England, its inhabitants are fond of its description as 'the biggest village in the world'. The city centre is modest when compared even with smaller cities such as Nottingham, let alone with Leeds or Manchester. Indeed, the principal shopping area takes a linear form, scarcely more than one street deep, from Waingate in the E, along High Street, Fargate, Pinstone Street and The Moor. This guide therefore looks beyond the centre (defined as the area within the ring road to the s and w and bounded by the former Midland and Great Central Railway lines to the E and N) to the inner suburbs within a two-mile radius. It also covers two areas outside this inner zone: one extending north-eastwards along the Don Valley and the heartland of Sheffield's steel industry, the other south-westwards to the districts inhabited by those who prospered from the city's industries and trades. The remaining suburbs will receive full treatment in the forthcoming revision of *Yorkshire: The West Riding*.

## Early History to the Seventeenth Century

The earliest physical evidence of habitation in Sheffield dates from the pre-Roman period (*see* topic box, p. 185). The district was known by the Anglo-Saxons as Hallamshire, a large parish including Sheffield, Ecclesfield and Bradfield with its church at Ecclesfield. The medieval town grew up around the C12 castle (*see* topic box, p. 148) sited defensively at the confluence of the Don and the Sheaf. This was the seat of William de Lovetot, Lord of Hallamshire. The lordship has passed unbroken to the present day (*see* topic box, p. 22). On high ground to the SE was the manor's hunting park (where Manor Lodge became an alternative residence to the castle in the C16). A timber bridge crossed the Don close to Castle Hill and the stone Lady's Bridge that replaced it in 1486 survives, albeit much widened. The Town Mill was sited a little upstream and weekly markets, first referred to in 1296, were established in Haymarket, not far from their present location. Houses extended to Fargate and the burgage plots on High Street were still evident well into the C19. Indeed, the city centre retains its medieval complexity, unaltered by the addition of Leopold Street and Pinstone Street after 1875.

5. The Old Queen's Head, Pond Hill, c15

Although there was a thriving town by the late C13, when the burgesses were given a charter setting out their privileges and Town Trustees assumed responsibility for some local government functions, **early buildings** are few. In the central area and inner suburbs the only pre-C18 survivals are parts of the parish church of St Peter and St Paul (now the Anglican cathedral, much extended and rebuilt in the C18–C20), the Old Queen's Head (the Hall-in-the-Ponds, associated with the Manor), the ruins of the Manor Lodge and the Turret House in the former hunting park, the so-called Bishops' House and parts of Broom Hall, together with Lady's Bridge.

Most of the medieval town centre was built of timber and several timber-framed buildings survived in High Street and Snig Hill until the beginning of the C20. South Yorkshire is significant as the point where the cruck frame and the kingpost truss forms of timber construction coincide and both types appear indiscriminately across Sheffield: kingpost trusses are found in the higher-status houses, e.g. the Old Queen's Head [5], Broom Hall [150] and Bishops' House [140], which also share close studding, coved eaves and bay windows, and posts set diagonally for decorative effect; cruck frames in lesser buildings, e.g. the barn in Wilson Place, Heeley. The frontier between the two major roof types found in South Yorkshire, the principal rafter truss and common rafter types, also runs through Sheffield. It is perhaps no coincidence that two of the earliest students of vernacular architecture, *S.O. Addy* and *C.F. Innocent,* were Sheffield men and used local examples to illustrate their arguments.

From the second quarter of the C17, stone largely replaced timber. The local building stone was sandstone available from quarries at Crookes, Woodseats and Brincliffe, with a superior pink sandstone coming from the Duke of Norfolk's quarries at Treeton Bolehills. In the N and W parts, millstone grit was also employed. By the C19, Hollington stone from Staffordshire was being imported for decorative work on public buildings.

The town became notable for **cutlery** very early; the first reference to a Sheffield cutler is in 1297 and Sheffield knives were sufficiently well known for Chaucer to allude to one in '*The Reeve's Tale*'. During the C16 the power of the fast-flowing rivers was harnessed to drive grinding wheels and Leland in about 1540 mentions 'many Smithes and Cuttelars in Halamshire'. The trade thrived to the extent that, by the late C16, Sheffield had the most specialized workforce in England with three out of four men employed in the cutlery trade. By 1578, about sixty hall-

## Little Mesters

The 'little mester' is a concept unique to Sheffield. It arose directly from the highly specialized nature of the Sheffield cutlery and tool trades, and blurs the usual distinction between masters and men. Prior to the mid C18, the cutlery trade was entirely in the hands of highly skilled craftsmen (it is not known when the term 'little mester' was first applied) who made cutlery, carrying out the processes of forging, grinding and finishing, working perhaps with a handful of apprentices or journeymen.

With the rise of water-powered wheels in the C18, craftsmen tended to specialize in a particular type of work. They were totally flexible in the way they carried out the work. They could either work for themselves, sometimes employing one or two people or sub-contracting work to outworkers, or they could contract to work for factors who would provide capital, sell the finished goods and rent workshops to the 'little mesters' within their factories. Physical evidence of their existence can be seen in the distinctive design of Sheffield workshops (*see* topic box, p. 126), divided into small rooms, often with separate external access. The system allowed manufacturers to cope with sudden demand for their products; it also enabled the craftsmen to be independent, not reliant on the fortunes of a single firm. But there were disadvantages to their role: as independent craftsmen, they were themselves outworkers, their working hours and conditions were unregulated and when trade was slack, they were often in a poor bargaining position when dealing with the larger manufacturers.

As partnerships and then, by the C19, limited companies took over quantity production, many craftsmen continued to work in the traditional way. The numbers of 'little mesters' declined dramatically from the 1950s but in 2004 there are a handful still at work. The best known is the penknife maker Stan Shaw.

marks are recorded. But the cutlers were not rich men and there was no proud guildhall or town hall to reflect the prosperity of the town, nor were there any fine mansions. There was, however, the Cutlers' Company (formed in 1624) with its own hall from 1638, which together with the Town Trust, the main instrument of local government, became one of the principal institutions in the town.

## 1650–1750

The independence the 'little mesters' (*see* topic box, p. 6) enjoyed in their working situation influenced their religious and political attitudes. Staunchly Puritan in the Civil War, Sheffield maintained a strong **dissenting tradition** thereafter. The first Nonconformist chapel to be built was Upper Chapel, Norfolk Street [57], in 1700. Its brick side walls survive, the earliest example of the material that characterized the development of the Georgian town. Although **brick** had been used in the 1570s to face the grand entrance towers at the Manor Lodge, the first brick house in the town, built about 1696, was 'viewed by the inhabitants with wonder and ridicule'. It proved more durable than they anticipated, however, and the Earl of Oxford's chaplain, visiting in 1725, remarked on the rebuilding in brick of the older wooden houses. The earliest surviving brick house, of 1728, in Hartshead, was part of the

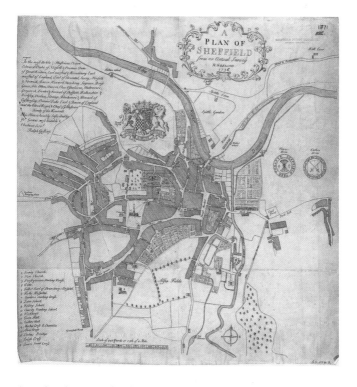

6. Map by Ralph Gosling (1736)

modest growth of Sheffield in the early C18, and its owner, Nicholas Broadbent, built the first five houses of Paradise Square [62] nearby in Hickstile Field in 1736. Gradually the gardens and orchards of existing houses were built over. As new streets were formed in the fields and meadows on the NW edge of the town, houses and workshops were built in these 'crofts' or lanes around Scotland Street and West Bar Green, while more substantial houses appeared across the Don at Bridgehouses. To the s of the town Norfolk Street was created along the w edge of the manorial deer park, which was converted to farmland. Building plots were let along the new street by the Duke of Norfolk in the 1740s, a few years after the Church Burgesses had started granting 800-year leases on their land to the w of the new church of St Paul [7].

The finest of all the **new buildings** of the late C17 and early C18, St Paul's (dem.) was built by public subscription in 1720–1 as a chapel of ease to the parish church. An unfortunate dispute over patronage delayed its opening until 1740 and the dome on its elegant Baroque tower was not added until 1769. Both the new Cutlers' Hall of 1725, replacing the 1638 hall, and the Town Trustees' new Town Hall at the corner of the parish churchyard, were modest buildings. The latter has the distinction, however, of being the first building in Sheffield by a named architect, the obscure *William Renny*, who was paid £2 3s. for a 'draught' in 1699 and £200 as builder the following year. The new three-storey brick workhouse of the 1720s at West Bar was more substantial but surpassed by the two almshouses provided by charitable individuals, the Shrewsbury Hospital of 1666, just E of the Sheaf, and Thomas

7. St Paul, Pinstone Street (dem.). Engraving, by E. Blore, from Hunter's *Hallamshire*, 1819

| | | | |
|---|---|---|---|
| 1600 | 3000 | 1871 | 239,900 |
| 1700 | 5000 | 1891 | 324,200 |
| 1736 | 10,000 | 1901 | 391,600 |
| 1750 | 20,000 | 1921 | 512,000 |
| 1801 | 46,000 | 1981 | 537,600 |
| 1831 | 91,700 | 2001 | 513,200 |
| 1851 | 135,300 | | |

Sheffield's population grew rapidly in the C18 and early C19, in common with other northern industrial towns, almost trebling in the fifty years up to 1851. Growth was especially strong in the 1820s when the cutlery trade and related industries expanded in the boom after the Napoleonic Wars. The C20 figures are distorted by the various boundary extensions referred to in the Introduction but reveal that the population was declining by the start of the C21. The statistics are rounded, those pre-census derived from Poll Tax returns, parish registers and surveys.*

* Source: D.L. Linton (ed.), *Sheffield and its Region*, 1956

Hollis' Hospital and school founded in 1703 in the existing New Hall at the bottom of Snig Hill (all dem.). Such private benefactions were rare in a town where the vast majority of the population were artisans or labourers and only a very few had substantial wealth. Fine houses such as the Steades' elegant remodelling of Burrowlee House [171] at Hillsborough in 1711 and the handsome five-bay pedimented house (dem.) built for the Duke of Norfolk's agent in Fargate in the same year were exceptional.

Most houses were modest buildings of one to three bays and many had a workshop or smithy attached or in a yard behind. The Hearth Tax returns of 1672 list 494 households in the town with 224 smithies in use among them.

Despite the increase in population in the C18 the high proportion of those employed in the cutlery and toolmaking trades continued, as demand for their products grew. The number of water-powered sites on Sheffield's rivers rose from forty-nine in 1660 to ninety in 1740. While more than half were used for grinding cutlery and edge tools, others powered ironworks which also increased their capacity to meet local demand, taking advantage of plentiful supplies of local coal as coke replaced charcoal as fuel. By 1700 some South Yorkshire ironmasters were also venturing into steelmaking using cementation furnaces (*see* topic box, p. 165), and a furnace had been built within the town, at Balm Green, by 1716. Two more existed near West Bar by 1737. These were the precursors of far-reaching changes affecting Sheffield's industrial development that were to follow in the next few years.

# Abbeydale Industrial Hamlet

8. Abbeydale Industrial Hamlet, forge, 1785, and grinding hull, 1817

Abbeydale works is the most important example of early metalworking premises in the city and demonstrates the semi-rural nature of Sheffield's early water-powered industry better than any other site. One of the principal steel and scythe works to be built on the Sheaf, the precise date of its foundation is unclear but it is known to have been in existence by 1714. It may well date back to 1676 when a cutler's wheel was built for Sir John Bright in Ecclesall. The works differed from many in that it carried out a range of processes, starting with the raw materials and producing finished goods, rather than concentrating on a single process. Agricultural blades were the mainstay of production. The works passed through a number of tenancies before being leased in 1848 to Tyzacks who remained there until 1933. In 1935 it was sold to the philanthropist J.G. Graves who presented it to the city for use as an industrial museum, one of the earliest examples of the preservation of a complete works. It finally opened as a museum in 1970 and underwent further restoration in 2000–2.

Although the works was developed piecemeal over several decades, the various buildings form a harmonious and picturesque group. To the s is the four-acre dam, created to form a reservoir to supply the wheels that powered the works. The buildings form a loose quadrangle to the N. All are of humble appearance and built of coursed rubble with stone slate roofs. Steel was made in the crucible shop, built in 1829 with five melting holes and a substantial brick crucible stack secured with iron ties to resist the excessive heat. The melting shop floor is raised up over a brick vaulted cellar, access given by external steps. Two-

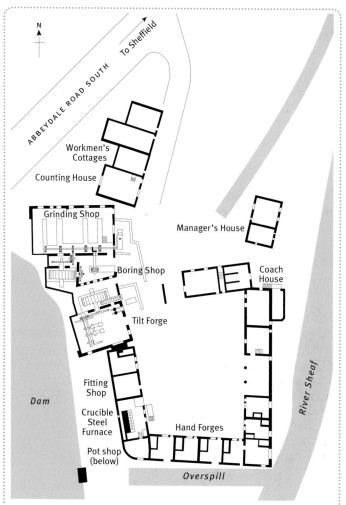

9. Abbeydale Industrial Hamlet, plan

light unglazed openings provide ventilation. The two-storey tilt forge was built in 1785, the grinding hull in 1817. Both have gables facing the courtyard with tripartite Venetian windows. Serving these are four water wheels which power the tilt hammers, a two-cylinder blowing engine, grindstones and horizontal boring machines, all preserved. Secondary power is supplied by an 1855 single-cylinder horizontal steam engine outside the grinding hull. On the SE side of the yard is a row of five hand forges, each with a door and two-light windows under a shared lintel to light the benches. The workmen's cottages which, like the other buildings, have large casement windows, were there by 1793, the manager's house is of 1838 and coach house and stabling were added c. 1840.

## 1750–1840

The next century saw the beginning of significant expansion of Sheffield as developments in industrial technology and improvements in communications promoted trade and the population increased tenfold. In 1751 Benjamin Huntsman perfected his secret invention of the crucible process (*see* topic box, p. 166) and set up his first steelworks at Attercliffe. The growth of the **steel industry** was, initially, slow, and until the early C19 the number of producers was small. Mostly operating on sites within the town their output was predominantly blister steel, and in 1774 only a handful of firms such as Marshall's at Millsands had both cementation and crucible furnaces. Raw materials, principally Swedish and Russian bar iron, were imported via Hull and the River Don Navigation, which reached Tinsley in 1751. As much of the steel produced was used locally for cutlery and tools it was the phenomenal increase in these trades that stimulated the first major expansion of the steel industry. In the economic recovery that followed the end of the Napoleonic wars trade with Sheffield's overseas markets soared and in 1823 the first of a new type of steam-powered **integrated works** producing steel, tools and cutlery on one site was opened. The Sheaf Works, Maltravers Street, with its imposing classical office block beside the newly extended canal (*see* below), was followed in 1825 by the Globe Works, Penistone Road [101], whose long pedimented front hides the utilitarian buildings around the courtyard behind. Similarly impressive ranges were built for the new, large-scale works of the major cutlery firms which established themselves in the midst of the more typical small workshops around the town, the names of Wostenholm's Washington Works (dem.) and Columbia Works, Suffolk Road, *c.* 1836, reflecting the importance of American demand for Sheffield goods in this period.

In contrast with the gradual growth of crucible steelmaking, Joseph Hancock and other manufacturers were quick to exploit Thomas Boulsover's new process of fusing a thin layer of silver onto copper to make Old Sheffield Plate. From the 1750s a highly profitable industry producing coffee pots, candlesticks and other household items in both plate and solid silver was established. By 1800 the use of another local invention, James Vickers' White or Britannia Metal, was creating a parallel market for similar but cheaper goods in 'poor man's silver'. The new type of purpose-built works housing all the different processes was a forerunner of the large sites developed by the major manufacturers of hollow ware and table cutlery a generation later, the best example being James Dixon & Sons' factory at Cornish Place [100] which accommodated every stage of production from design to showroom display.

The successful creation of a navigable waterway to within four miles of the town was a significant spur to economic development. The improvement of the roads also needed to convey an ever-increasing range of goods out of the town began in 1756 with the Act to turnpike the road s to Chesterfield and London, and continued into the 1780s. Later Acts of 1805 and 1808 enabled the building of new turnpike roads to Langsett and Glossop. Despite strenuous opposition from the Duke of Norfolk, who feared an influx of cheap South Yorkshire coal to undercut his Sheffield collieries, the **canal** was eventually extended from Tinsley to the edge of the town in 1819. The benefits of the new waterway and its magnificent four-storey brick terminal warehouse were, however, short-lived, for within twenty years the Sheffield and Rotherham Railway, linking the town to the North Midland Railway and London, was opened. Its effect on the NE side of Sheffield, which had remained largely undeveloped, would be unprecedented.

The **late C18 expansion** of the town had been mainly to the s and w, continuing outwards from the modest development of the early C18, and was initiated by the principal landowners, particularly the Duke of Norfolk and the Church Burgesses. The 9th Duke commissioned plans for a grid of new streets to be laid out in Alsop Fields, SE of the newly built area around St Paul's Church (*see* Walk 4, p. 135), and in about 1775 engaged first James Paine and then Thomas Atkinson to prepare schemes for an elegant residential quarter. The proposals were never realized, however, as Sheffield lacked the prosperous professional and merchant classes who sustained similar schemes in Bath and Liverpool. During a period of forty years from the 1780s the area was developed in a piecemeal fashion with ninety-nine-year leases of modest plots for mixed housing and industry. Examples of the simpler three-storey houses of the 1780s–90s survive in Charles Street and Howard Street,

10. Doorcase, Norfolk Row, early C19

with three more substantial, pleasingly proportioned houses of 1791 remaining in Arundel Street [77]. s and w of the town streets were laid out either side of The Moor and as far as Rockingham Street by 1797, on land belonging to owners including Earl Fitzwilliam, who was Lord of the Manor of Ecclesall, and the Church Burgesses. Building beyond this was stimulated by the new turnpike road to Glossop and from the 1820s mixed development on ninety-nine-year leases, mainly from the Burgesses, took place. Unlike the Norfolk estate the Burgesses imposed specific planning controls, and while the blindback houses of *c.* 1830 that survive in Canning Street [70] were acceptable in side streets, properties of higher value were demanded on the principal streets. Taking advantage of the access to capital that the new banks provided and the design skills of local architects such as *William Flockton* (*see* topic box, p. 24), speculative builders completed handsome brick houses along Glossop Road. Further out and uphill the more substantial villas of Broomhall and Broomhill [147] mark the beginning of the middle classes' move to the western suburbs where they could enjoy cleaner air and water, the higher land values of the s-facing slopes being reflected in the quality of development.

At the bottom of the town, either side of the Don, and to the N and NW industry and poor-quality **housing** sprang up side-by-side. These densely packed courts of brick back-to-back houses of two- or three-storeys were the first candidates for slum clearance in the 1930s and only where they have been absorbed into neighbouring works have any survived. Early recognizable examples are those of *c.* 1800 in Snow Lane [93], which have typically irregular bricks and small casements without sills. Other early c19 houses survive nearby as part of the Well Meadow Steel Works, and at John Watts and Co.'s premises in Lambert Street which extended over five courts.

The spiritual and educational needs of the larger population were supplied by new **churches, chapels** and **voluntary schools**. Many of these disappeared or changed use in the c20 as the housing around them was demolished. The strength of Nonconformity in the town, especially in the poorer areas, ensured the building of a range of chapels to suit all religious tastes. The imposing Wesleyan Methodist Chapel in Carver Street (1804) and *J.G. Weightman's* Brunswick Chapel on The Moor (1834, dem.) were typically classical in style, with big galleried interiors accommodating nearly 2,000 people. The notable exception in style is *Joseph Botham's* boldly castellated Gothick Ebenezer Chapel of 1823 at Shalesmoor. The Anglicans countered with four 'Million Pound' Act churches to augment the limited space available at the parish church, whose nave was rebuilt in 1802–5 to provide a galleried preaching box, and at St Paul's and St James' (1788, dem.). St George's (1825), St Philip's (1828, dem.), St Mary's (1830) [128] and Christ Church at Attercliffe (dem.) were in typical Commissioners' Gothic, with vast naves and big square towers. All had associated schools which supplemented the National Schools, two of which survive with new uses, in

11. East Parade, early c19 houses

Carver Street and Garden Street. The Wesleyans produced the grandest of all the educational buildings of this period: the monumental Corinthian front of their Proprietary Grammar School at Broomhill [146], opened 1838, outclasses *Hurst*'s castellated Gothic Grammar School of 1824–5 (dem.), *Woodhead & Hurst*'s austerely classical Boys' Charity School of 1826 on East Parade and *Weightman*'s Perp-style Collegiate School of 1835–6, in Collegiate Crescent, Broomhall.

In the absence of a borough corporation **public buildings** needed to meet the increasingly complex civic, commercial and social needs of the town were provided by private, public or institutional enterprise. The Town Trustees, whose powers and means were very limited, built the new Town Hall [82] in Waingate in 1807–8 for visiting West Riding magistrates sitting in Petty and Quarter Sessions as well as for their own use. The other principal public buildings were the Cutlers' Hall, rebuilt 1832–3, and the markets, none of which survives. Exercising their rights for the manor of Sheffield the Dukes of Norfolk built a new market hall and shambles in 1786–90 and *Hurst*'s large classical Corn Exchange in 1830 (dem.), its central semi-circular projection defined by giant columns. Earl Fitzwilliam's attempt to provide a rival attraction for Ecclesall Manor, with *Watson, Pritchet & Watson*'s 1828 Bazaar on The Moor was short-lived but *William Lindley*'s manor court and gaol of 1791 nearby were in use until 1847. Facilities for entertainment were limited until the Assembly Rooms and Playhouse were built in 1762–3, with *Hurst*'s Surrey Street Music Hall the principal venue for concerts from 1824 (both dem.). Like them, the Botanical Gardens, where *Robert Marnock*'s landscape and the impressive glasshouses [152] by *B.B. Taylor* still fulfil the original intention of providing a health-giving and educational ornament to the town, were funded by public subscription. Local charities provided **hospitals** for the sick and the old. *John Rawstorne*'s Infirmary [165], planned on the model of Northampton's hospital, offered medical care from 1797 in a refined building of country house proportions. Hollis's Hospital, rebuilt plainly in brick by *Carr* in 1769–76 (dem.) and *Woodhead & Hurst*'s new Tudor Gothic Shrewsbury Hospital of 1825 on Norfolk Road, housed a lucky few of the elderly. After 1837 the less fortunate were dependent on the workhouses provided by the new Poor Law Unions, *Flockton*'s Tudor block [136] of 1842–3 for Ecclesall at Nether Edge (now converted to housing) offering more attractive accommodation than Sheffield Union's converted cotton mill at Kelham.

## 1840–1900

Sheffield became a municipal borough in 1843 but the Town Council had little effect on its appearance before the 1880s–90s when a vigorous street widening programme stimulated new development in the centre, the magnificent new Town Hall was built and expansion of the tramway system enabled further suburban development. In the middle of the C19, just as in the 1740s–50s, it was improvements in **communications and industry** that brought the greatest changes. In 1837, before the Sheffield and Rotherham Railway was even completed, Spear and Jackson moved NE to their new Aetna Works to make saws among the fields on Savile Street East. Charles Cammell followed in 1845, setting up the Cyclops Iron and Steel Works next door, the most ambitious and grandly conceived industrial project of the time. From 1851 first Thomas Firth & Sons and then John Brown moved to their new Norfolk and Atlas Works, also on Savile Street East. These were large-scale versions of their town centre sites, with two- or three-storey offices in a simple classical style fronting the street, and a courtyard behind with crucible and cementation furnaces and steam-powered forges, mills and workshops. These produced steel for an expanding national and international market, first for the railways and then for armaments. In 1860 John Brown was the first to adopt the new process Bessemer had brought to Sheffield in 1858 (*see* topic box, p. 193); other firms soon followed and by 1870 production had overtaken the output of crucible steel. Soon after, the Siemens open-hearth process gained acceptance, gradually replacing other methods for most bulk steel production. Armaments became the mainstay of the five largest firms, Brown and Cammell dominating the armour-plate industry while Firths, Hadfield and Vickers concentrated on guns and shells. The scale of their operations saw the replacement of the ranges of gabled brick forges and foundries by the massive black steel-clad sheds that characterized the industrial landscape of the Don Valley in the C20.

12. South-East View of Sheffield by William Ibbitt (1855). Lithograph

Sheffield had a reputation as a smoky place as early as 1608, when Sir John Bentley expected to be 'half choked with town smoke' while visiting the Earl of Shrewsbury. Industrial development and the use of coal for the fires and furnaces needed to melt, soften, mould and shape metal inevitably produced vast quantities of smoke and soot. The problem was exacerbated as steam engines replaced water power and by 1897 the number of industrial chimneys was counted in thousands. Visitor after visitor acknowledged the beauty of Sheffield's natural surroundings, the skill of its workers and the value of its products, but universally condemned it for the 'thick pulverous haze' spread over it and the 'murky clouds' that blotted out the sun and made a 'foggy twilight' in the streets. The difficulties of keeping clean were spelt out in 1848 when it was calculated that the townspeople would make an annual saving of £7,600 on soap and over £56,000 on labour for clothes washing if the air was cleaner.

The inevitability of buildings quickly turning black did not deter architects although it must have influenced some in choosing new materials such as 'self-cleaning' faience, which made the White Building in Fitzalan Square a startling anomaly in 1908. In the Don Valley, where the sulphurous pollution was worst, C20 architects used hard, smooth-faced bricks, slate and stainless steel to withstand it.

While other towns used the earlier Smoke Acts to curb smoke from domestic fires, similar attempts in Sheffield proved futile until the 1956 Clean Air Act was implemented and 'sooty Sheffield' finally lost its smoke.

Both there and elsewhere in the town a wide range of other, smaller, firms continued production of crucible steel, the unique survival of the furnaces at Darnall Works showing the scale of production possible. By the 1880s traditional crucible steel for the specialized markets was

## Bylaw Terraced Housing

13. Houses in Ruth Square, late C19

Sheffield developed a distinctive type of terraced housing after the intro-duction of bylaws in 1864 which forebade back-to-back housing. Decoration was sparse with none of the ornamental brickwork found, for example, in Leeds. From the 1890s, a shaped timber shaft to the window dividing two lights was frequently found on the ground floor, with bay windows as an alternative on the larger houses. Bays were constructed entirely of timber above a brick base with ornate carved brackets below the eaves. Sheffield houses had highly distinctive moulded timber guttering, supported on small brackets, usually attached to a fascia board. When, as frequently happened, houses were on a slope, they rose in steps. The practice, commonly employed in the northern West Riding and Lancashire, of a continuous sloping roof was never seen in Sheffield.

In plan, there were usually two rooms on the ground floor, separated by steep stairs placed across the width of the house, two rooms on the first floor and a single attic room lit by skylight, dormer or gable-end window. Back extensions were rare until towards the end of the C19. Groups of houses, usually four, sometimes up to eight, would share a broad open yard, the privies grouped in blocks along the back wall at a considerable distance from the houses. Access to the yard both for ser-vices and to the houses was gained via a tunnel known locally as the 'entry'. Narrow service lanes of the type found in Lancashire were unknown, all refuse and the contents of the privies going out through the entries. The front doors to the houses, most of which opened straight on to the street, were seldom used. Most visitors, even to the present day, were received via the yard.

supplemented by the development of special steels for tools and engineering as Sir Robert Hadfield's experiments with alloys helped maintain Sheffield's position as the world's leading steel producer.

The traditional 'light trades' of cutlery and edge tools and the manufacture of silver and silver plate were still predominant in the town centre. A few large four- and five-storey works for the biggest firms such as Joseph Rodgers & Sons and Mappin Bros., which each employed hundreds of people, towered above the mass of small workshops and yards around them. Apart from Dixons' Cornish Place Works [100] the big factories have gone, but Butcher's Wheel on Arundel Street [78] gives some sense of their scale. It is, however, more utilitarian than most works, which generally used a restrained classical vocabulary for the ornament of the their main façade. Henry Hoole's Green Lane Works [98], built in 1860 as a stove grate manufactory, is uniquely grand with a triumphal arch gateway. On either side bronze relief panels depicting Hephaestus and Athene, possibly by *Alfred Stevens* who was a designer there in 1850–2, celebrate industry and art.

Like the metalworking trades, most of the other industries and trades in Victorian Sheffield – such as the breweries, flour mills, builders, printers and the suppliers of food and coal – were dependent on efficient transport. The canal continued as a useful link to the Humber and a

14. Hephaestus, Green Lane Works, attributed to Alfred Stevens, 1860

## The Board Schools

Sheffield has one of the best surviving collections of Board Schools in England, unparalleled outside London. Prior to the 1870 Education Act, Sheffield had the usual mixture of private (194 in 1851), denominational, workhouse and charity schools. Following the Act, Sheffield's newly elected School Board vigorously set about constructing new schools, completing thirty-nine before its demise in 1903. *C.J. Innocent* was appointed architect to the Board and his firm was responsible for nineteen of the twenty-two schools built between 1873 and 1881. While it has been suggested that Board Schools, particularly in London, used a secular architectural style to dissociate themselves from the Church Schools, in Sheffield *Innocent & Brown*'s use of what they called 'English Domestic Gothic' was unchallenged. The first of the new schools and, it was claimed by the architects, the first commenced under the 1870 Act, was Newhall School, Sanderson Street, opened 1873 (dem.). By 1877, attendance had reached 31,000 (70 per cent).

As with all Board Schools, there was separate access and playgrounds for girls, boys and infants. Most of Innocent's schools share identical forms of planning, based on the 'Prussian' hall plan in which classrooms are grouped around a central school hall. This allowed efficient circulation and, in recognition of the shortage of trained schoolteachers, allowed the headmaster to supervise several classes through the glazed partitions. In the multi-storey schools, infants were on the ground floor, older children above. The most innovative of the schools, *Innocent*'s Huntsman's Gardens, Attercliffe, of 1884 (dem.), had its classrooms arranged in a semicircle around a single central hall. Lighting was evenly diffused through large windows with as little shadow as possible. Innovations included covered play sheds for wet weather which were placed on the ground floor to avoid steps, leaving 'abundant space for marching'.

While all Innocent's schools were constructed in rock-faced stone and were similar in plan, great care was taken to vary the elevations which ranged from one to three storeys, most having two. Innocent stated that he 'attempted to obtain effect by the picturesque grouping of parts rather than by a redundance of ornament or enrichments and to give all these buildings such distinctive external features as should express the purposes and the means of their erection'. Elevations were broken up by the end bays being brought forward and the central bays given large gables. Internal arrangements were sometimes expressed externally e.g. the rounded staircase turrets at Netherthorpe (*see* p. 285). Boldly modelled buttresses at Pye Bank (*see* p. 178), provided a strong vertical emphasis. Bellcotes, disguised as flèches, gave Innocent much scope for inventiveness. The schools were widely publicized, perspectives and plans appearing in the architectural press. A collected volume was published in 1874.

15. Springfield School, by Innocent & Brown, 1875

The lavishness of schools' provision and the quality of construction was not always appreciated. When invited to open Park School in 1875, the Liberal M.P. David Chadwick wondered 'How in the name of fortune the School Board have persuaded the ratepayers of Sheffield to tolerate their extravagance in spending £100,000 in the building of fourteen or fifteen schools as substantial as so many castles!'

Innocent continued to design Board Schools until his death but from 1875 the scale of the programme meant that other local architects were involved including *Holmes & Watson, Hemsoll & Paterson* and *W. J. Hale*. Through his personal friendship with J.F. Moss, Secretary to the School Board, *E.R. Robson*, the best-known school architect in the country, responsible for many of the London Board Schools and author of *School Architecture* (1874), designed the schools at Jenkin Road and Myrtle Road in 1880. He exchanged the brick of the London schools for coursed stonework but retained his favoured domestic 'Queen Anne' style.

large brick warehouse was built at the basin in 1889, with the steel-framed and concrete Straddle warehouse as the last addition in 1895–8. More important for goods and passengers were the **railways**. In 1845 the Sheffield, Ashton-under-Lyne and Manchester Railway reached Bridgehouses, before the line was extended across the Don Valley in 1848 and into Lincolnshire as the Manchester, Sheffield and Lincolnshire Railway, later (1897) the Great Central. The monumental stone viaduct of forty arches, by the local engineer *Sir John Fowler* and architects *Weightman & Hadfield* [88], is one of the great engineering feats of the century. Victoria Station (dem.), built on the viaduct and opened in 1851, had extensive facilities on its platforms, the central section being covered by a great glass roof 400 ft long and 84 ft wide. The Midland Railway Station, in Sheaf Street, which eventually opened in 1870 to provide a direct route s to London, also had a glass roof over the tracks, removed in later rebuilding. All the stables for the dray horses transporting goods to and from the stations and around the town have gone, except for the multi-storey block in the unusual complex of flats, veterinary surgery and dogs' home built in 1899–1900 for a local vet at Lady's Bridge. More conventional stabling for the horse trams survives at the Heeley depot of 1877, which closed in 1901. Stables at the first tram depot, opened in 1874 at Tinsley, were demolished in 1899 when the sheds were extended to house ninety-five new electric cars.

Availability of public transport, first from horse buses and especially from trams after 1873, led to a boom in house building to create lower-middle- and working-class suburbs in the areas they served. This was mostly two-, or occasionally three-storeyed terrace housing built by

## Patronage

After the death of the 7th Earl of Shrewsbury in 1616 Sheffield no longer had a resident noble patron whose wealth and influence could benefit the town. The lordship of the manor of Sheffield descended to the Howard Dukes of Norfolk whose absenteeism and Catholicism prevented them from having any real influence while their receipt of substantial rental income from their property has been seen as a permanent haemorrhage from the local economy. The 9th Duke's grand development scheme for Alsop Fields was never realized and it was only in the mid C19 that their general attitude of *laissez-faire* changed. The 15th Duke promoted the development of the estate and was a generous benefactor of local charities and Catholic churches and schools; he rebuilt the Corn Exchange, restored the Turret House and Shrewsbury tombs and became Sheffield's first Lord Mayor in 1897.

As a manufacturing town whose inhabitants were almost entirely artisans and labourers, Sheffield had few other wealthy patrons until the late C19 when local men who made their fortunes in steel or cutlery commissioned buildings to support religion, health and education.

speculative builders for rent. The cheaper houses, particularly those serving the new steelworks, were in brick; stone was used only where it was readily available, e.g. Walkley and Crookes. As back-to-backs were prohibited after the 1864 bylaws (*see* topic box, p. 18), Sheffield's housing was generally of a higher standard than in other towns which still allowed them. The formation of Land Societies (*see* topic box, p. 282), mainly in Walkley and Nether Edge, produced an even better standard of detached and semi-detached houses with gardens.

The **western suburbs** are one of Sheffield's main attractions, with their mix of villas in classical and Gothic styles, invariably in stone. Only two large-scale planned residential developments exist: the Broomhall estate, which was laid out *c.* 1840 and mostly built by 1853, and at Nether Edge, where *Robert Marnock* created a picturesque road layout in 1851–61 for George Wostenholm of Kenwood. Most of the houses were built by the 1890s, usually in Gothic with decorative bargeboards. The largest houses were built by the wealthiest manufacturers in Ranmoor. The most palatial are Endcliffe Hall [155], John Brown's Italianate mansion of 1863–5, designed by *Flockton & Abbott*, and the earlier Oakbrook [157], by *Flockton & Son* for Mark Firth. These aspired to ballrooms, libraries, conservatories and stables; more unusual is the rare example of a private theatre, the small Lantern Theatre built next to his house at Nether Edge by a cutlery manufacturer *c.* 1893.

At the other end of the social scale the older housing in the town centre and areas like Park, built in the first half of the C19, was increasingly unhealthy. Surrounded by industry, it lacked fresh air, clean water and proper sanitation, and in 1894 the Council obtained powers under the Housing of the Working Classes Act 1890 to demolish the worst slums, which were in the Crofts area around Campo Lane and Lee Croft. The replacement buildings included the Townhead Street flats, completed in 1903 and one of the earliest of many public housing schemes.

Public provision of elementary education after 1870 created a distinctive group of Board Schools (*see* topic box, p. 20) while strong support for adult and further education produced a variety of institutions, including the Romanesque-style School of Art (*Manning and Mew*, 1857), and the Mechanics Institute's handsome Italianate palazzo (*George Alexander*, 1847–8) with artwork by *Godfrey Sykes* (both dem.). The Church of England chose a simple Gothic style for their Educational Institute of 1860, while *E.R. Robson* and *Flockton & Abbott* drew inspiration from Clare College, Cambridge, in their design for the college founded by Mark Firth [64] to accommodate the Cambridge University Extension lectures in 1879.

Scholarly study of medieval precedent also informed the design of some of the best **Victorian churches**. *M.E. Hadfield*'s debt to St Andrew, Heckington is evident in the rich Decorated style of St Marie [32], whose interior is enhanced with work by Pugin, Bentley and Westlake (*see* Major Buildings, p. 57). Of the Anglican churches only *E.M. Gibbs*'s E.E. St John, Ranmoor [16], with Sheffield's wealthiest parishioners as

# Sheffield Architects

Major commissions in C19 Sheffield were in the hands of a limited number of firms. Those associated with the Flockton and Hadfield families were the most prominent and included several generations. The broad stages of their development are set out below, together with other important Sheffield practices. Dates of changes in partnerships are approximate.

The Flockton firm: William Flockton (1804–64); 1845–9 Flockton, Lee & (Thomas James) Flockton (1846–99); 1849–64 Flockton & Son; 1864–78 Flockton & (G.L.) Abbott (c. 1823–84); 1878–95 Flockton & (Edward Mitchell) Gibbs (1847–1935); 1895–9 Flockton, Gibbs & (Charles Burrows) Flockton (1867–1945); 1899–1910 Gibbs & (C.B.) Flockton; 1910–21 Gibbs, Flockton & (J.C.A.) Teather (1874–1957)

The Hadfield firm: John Grey Weightman (1801–72); 1838–50 Weightman & (Matthew Ellison) Hadfield (1812–85); 1850–60 George Goldie (1828–87), a partner in the practice; 1864–90 M.E. Hadfield & Son (Charles Hadfield (1840–1916); 1890–9 Hadfield Son & Garland; 1899–1916 C. & Charles Matthew Ellison Hadfield (1867–1949); 1916–24 C.M.E. Hadfield; 1924–35 C.M.E. Hadfield & Robert Cawkwell (1894–1968); 1946–63 Hadfield Cawkwell & Davidson; since 1963 Hadfield Cawkwell Davidson & Partners

The Hemsoll Firm: 1881–91 (William Frederick) Hemsoll (1846–1903) & (Joseph) Smith (1850–1921); 1893–1902 Hemsoll & (Henry Leslie) Paterson (1861–1926); 1902–10 Hemsoll & (Frank W.) Chapman (1869–1933); 1910–48 Chapman & (John Mansell) Jenkinson (1883–1965); subsequently J. Mansell Jenkinson & Son and from 1964, Mansell Jenkinson & Partners

Holmes & Watson: Samuel Francis Holmes (1821–82) whose son, Edward Holmes (1859–1921) was in partnership, 1893–1908, with Adam Francis Watson (1856–1932)

Innocent & Brown 1870–81 Charles John Innocent (1839–1901) and Thomas Brown (c. 1845–81); subsequently practised on own account. In 1901 C.J. Innocent was joined in partnership by his son Charles Frederick Innocent (1874–1923), author of *The Development of English Building Construction* (1916)

John Brightmore Mitchell-Withers (1838–94) succeeded in 1894 by his son (same name) (1865–1920)

John Dodsley Webster (1840–1913), joined by his son John Douglas Webster (d. 1933) in 1900

Pupilages and assistantships reveal close links between many of the Sheffield architects. J.B. Mitchell-Withers the elder and J.D. Webster had both served pupilages with Samuel Worth; C.J. Innocent and Thomas Brown trained with M.E. Hadfield. Experience outside Sheffield was less common although T.J. Flockton and E.M. Gibbs had worked in London as assistants: Flockton to G.G. Scott c. 1840 and Gibbs to Alfred Waterhouse for two years in the 1860s. J.D. Webster had worked for Mallinson & Healey in Halifax. The formation of the Sheffield Society of Architects in 1887 at the instigation of T.J. Flockton helped encourage a broader outlook; visiting speakers included W.H. Bidlake, J.M. Brydon, Beresford Pite and Reginald Blomfield.*

* Based on research by Dr Roger Harper.

16. St John, Ranmoor, Fulwood Road, by E.M. Gibbs, 1879–88

its donors, can match its architectural quality. Most of the thirty-odd
other new parish churches were competent essays in a variety of Gothic
styles by local architects working to tight budgets, notably the *Flocktons*
and *J.D. Webster*, who was York Diocesan Surveyor for Sheffield. The
different strands of Nonconformity were both more prolific and more
eclectic in their styles. Wicker Congregational Church, 1855 (dem.),
designed rather surprisingly by the Catholic *M.E. Hadfield*, had a simple Dec exterior and pairs of cast-iron columns with Byzantine capitals
supporting its 1,000 seat galleried interior, while the Baptists on
Cemetery Road, Sharrow (1859), chose an unconventional Romanesque.
Among the Methodists Primitive Methodism had a particular appeal
for Sheffield's respectable, independent and liberal-minded artisan
classes and went from strength to strength in the second half of the century, outgrowing the first chapel of 1819 in Cambridge Street to fill
another thirty in the city by 1897. Their loyalty to the classical tradition
is seen in their huge, pedimented Ebenezer Chapel at Walkley [163].

Sheffield became a city in 1893. Though traditionally a manufacturing town and not a commercial centre to the same extent as Leeds or Birmingham, by 1900 its centre had the wide range of shops, offices, banks, theatres and institutions characteristic of the major Victorian cities. *E.W. Mountford*'s long-awaited Town Hall [35] was built in 1893–7 as the splendid focus of the new city centre created by the ambitious programme of improvements begun by the Council in 1875. Eleven major streets were widened and three new streets made, including Leopold Street, to create an unusually long linear commercial area stretching from the old Town Hall and markets at Waingate up High Street, Fargate and Church Street and down Pinstone Street to The Moor. Extensive demolition (including the entire s side of High Street) provided opportunities for rebuilding on an appropriately grand scale, mostly by Sheffield architects but with a handful of notable contributions from outsiders, including *Waterhouse & Son*'s Prudential offices and *Perkin & Bulmer*'s Yorkshire Penny Bank. Despite war damage and demolition the prolific versatility of the Flocktons' practice and the high-quality designs of the Hadfields are especially evident, both in the centre and beyond. *Flockton & Gibbs* achieved simple Italianate elegance with Channing Hall and turreted Gothic on High Street, while *M.E. Hadfield & Son*'s richly decorated palazzo style Gas Company offices [83] in Commercial Street bear comparison with offices in Leeds or Manchester. Equally accomplished examples in Charles Hadfield's favourite Tudor style are Parade Chambers [60] on High Street and Cairn's Chambers [63] nearby.

For some buildings the specialized skills offered by outside architects were needed. The four principal Victorian theatres, which included Matcham's exuberantly oriental Empire Palace, are now represented by Sprague's Lyceum [55], but in other cases, such as the Jessop Hospital and the Royal Infirmary Outpatients' Department, both by *J.D. Webster*, and *Flockton & Gibbs*'s imposing Greek Revival Mappin Art Gallery [167], local architects were chosen. While this partly reflects the rather conservative and insular outlook of local patrons (*see* topic box, p. 22) it also demonstrates the professional skill and competence of Sheffield's architects.

## The Early Twentieth Century

Boundary extensions to the N at Hillsborough, to the NE at Tinsley and to the s at Meersbrook recognized the rapid growth of Sheffield at the turn of the C20, stimulated by the electrification of the tramway network. This suburban expansion, much of which comprised small terraced artisans' houses [13], decently built but of dull appearance and set out unimaginatively, dismayed many. The first terraced Council housing was built at Walkley in 1903, while flats were developed in the overcrowded city centre. A more considered approach was promoted by progressive elements in the Council who encouraged the York and North Midland Cottage Exhibition at Wincobank in 1907 as the foundation of a garden suburb. Sheffield also made an early response to the

Housing and Town Planning Act of 1909 when, in 1911, *E.M. Gibbs* was nominated by the Sheffield Society of Architects to the newly formed planning committee. He proposed a grand, but unrealized, expansion plan for the city on garden city principles with radiating main roads linked by a ring road with suburban settlements at the junctions.

*J.D. Webster* continued to build large **churches** in the growing suburbs; St Cuthbert, Firvale (1901–5), was still in the style he had favoured since the 1870s but at St Timothy, Crookes (1910), he adopted the more fashionable Perp. Rich church furnishings are uncommon but exceptions are the Arts and Crafts work by *H.I. Potter* at St Matthew, Carver Street, in similar vein to that carried out earlier by *Henry Wilson* [69] and the fine stained glass by *Archibald Davies* of the Bromsgrove Guild at St Cuthbert, Firvale [106]. By far the most original work both in planning and design is that by *W.J. Hale* (*see* topic box, p. 277) who developed free Arts and Crafts Gothic into a powerful personal style at the Methodist St Luke, Crookes (1900) [161], Crookes Congregational (1905) and Wesley Hall, Crookes (1907) [162]. His reworking of *Waddington Son & Dunkerley*'s Victoria Hall [17] with the addition of a mighty tower demonstrates an equal versatility in handling the Baroque. *John Wills*, the prolific Nonconformist church architect, contributed several churches: Victoria Methodist, Norfolk Park (1899–1901), with a handsome broach spire, is among his most striking works.

Free styles were increasingly favoured for **public buildings**. *Hemsoll & Paterson* freely mixed Tudor and classical detailing in their Walkley Library of 1905. *Joseph Norton* achieved grandeur on a relatively small canvas in his deft handling of Georgian motifs at the Meersbrook Vestry Hall (1903–4) [139]. The Common Lodging House [92], West Bar, by *J.R. Truelove* (1912) is the most striking expression of the new found freedom, relying on variety of surface treatment rather than mouldings to achieve a rare slickness. Glossop Road Baths were extended in a flamboyant Wrenaissance style (1908–10) by *Arthur Nunweek*. By contrast, *E.W. Mountford*'s extensions of 1899–1904 to the Northern General Hospital were almost domestic in treatment, Ernest Newton writ large. **Public sculpture** is notable for its absence with the major exceptions of *Alfred Drury*'s magisterial memorial to Edward VII (1913) in Fitzalan Square and that to Queen Victoria (1904) by *Alfred Turner* now in Endcliffe Park.

The appointment of *E.M. Gibbs* by the newly founded University of Sheffield resulted in the handsome red brick buildings of Firth Court (1903–5) [46] at Western Bank, in a Neo-Tudor aping of the style of Cambridge colleges. At St George's Square he used a Wrenaissance style for the Sir Frederick Mappin Building (1902–13) [48]. Fewer schools were built during this period than in the three decades after 1870 but the architectural stock remained high: notably *W.J. Hale*'s Art Nouveau-inspired Lydgate Lane School (1907; outside the area of this guide) and *A.F. Watson*'s Porter Croft School, Pomona Street (1900), with its original adoption of Artisan Mannerism.

**Commercial buildings** showed the increasing use of faience and other glazed materials in an attempt to combat Sheffield's appalling pollution (*see* topic box, p. 17). *Flockton, Gibbs & Flockton*'s use of glazed bricks in two shades of brown in Royal Exchange Buildings (1899–1900) [87], Lady's Bridge, makes a striking contribution. The White Building, Fitzalan Square, by *Gibbs & Flockton* (*c.* 1908) combined original use of faience with charming sculpture of the Sheffield trades by *Alfred & William Tory* [84]. Faience was again used to good effect in one of Sheffield's principal landmarks, Kemsley House (1913–16) by *Gibbs, Flockton & Teather*. Faience was much favoured in commercial redevelopment in West Street, following widening for tramways. A move to Baroque is to be seen on a small scale in *Goddard & Co.*'s Alliance Assurance offices (1913) and more loosely applied in the imposing central Post Office (1910) by *Walter Pott*. Restraint was a keynote of two banks: the former York City & County Bank of 1904 by *Walter Brierley* and HSBC Bank, Glossop Road (1911), by *A.F. Watson* with its convincing Mannerist detailing. A number of early cinemas survive: *W.G. Buck*'s engagingly Moorish Lansdowne Cinema, Highfield of 1914 and the mighty Abbeydale Cinema (1920) by *Dixon & Stienlet* which retains much of its coarse but exuberant interior decoration.

**Industrial buildings** became increasingly utilitarian with great steel-framed sheds, the key buildings of the Don Valley. These were a

18. Manor Estate, c. 1932

A total of 25,000 council houses were built by the Council between 1919 and 1939. Most of these were erected on massive estates at the Manor, Woodthorpe, Arbourthorne, Shiregreen and Parson Cross which in the NE of the city made up one of the largest concentrations of council housing in the country. They favour formal geometrical plans based on intersecting circles, that derive from pre-war garden suburb planning but their layout paid little regard to Sheffield's natural contours and the effect is bleak. The style for the cottages is a minimal Neo-Georgian, best seen in its unaltered state at Wisewood, but the Council also built houses for sale on the fringes of the estates marked out by embellishments such as bay windows. They were accompanied by Neo-Georgian shops, pubs and primary schools, the latter designed on open-air principles with sliding partitions opening onto courtyards.

response to industrial expansion encouraged by the demand for heavy armaments before and during the First World War. Offices such as *A.F. Watson*'s for Vickers, Brightside Lane (1906) [114], with its marble boardroom [115] were still intended to impress. In the cutlery and tool-making works, architectural embellishment continued to be reserved for the offices and cart entrances, e.g. *Holmes & Watson*'s Alpha Works, Carver Street (1900).

Early C20 **suburban housing** reflected the national shift towards the lighter style of the late Arts and Crafts movement. White-painted woodwork, leaded windows, roughcast upper storeys and tile-hung gables are common in the better houses. The best examples are unsurprisingly in the salubrious western suburbs, e.g. *W.J. Hale*'s Tainby, Snaithing Lane [158] (1909) and Rydal, Snaithing Park Road (1921), and above all in the two handsome houses in the Carsick Hill area, the Croft and Snaithing Croft [159], built in 1909–10 by *Briggs, Wolstenholme & Thornely*. The work of non-native architects was still rare although *Edgar Wood* designed a billiard room for a house in Tapton Crescent Road in 1908.

## The Interwar Years

Sheffield emerged prosperous from the First World War, for which it had supplied much of the heavy armaments, but this wealth was not reflected in its appearance: George Orwell described it in 1936 as 'one of the most appalling places I have ever seen . . . you can smell the sulphur in the air'. The Corporation was still concerned that people in the inner city were living in slums close to industry and in 1919 commissioned *Patrick Abercrombie* to prepare a **Civic Survey and Plan** for their separation and the improvement of the city's image. He later described this as the foundation of all his town and regional planning work. Submitted in 1924, the plan was of national significance in its proposals for zoning of housing and industry, recommendations for an average density of twelve houses per acre and the creation of satellite towns within a green belt – a concept with major implications for the reconstruction of Britain after 1945. In practice, little was done other than clearance of houses from the industrial areas of the city centre. Of greater significance was the attempt to create a civic centre focussed around the city's major **public buildings**. Foremost amongst these were two recently completed buildings: *Vincent Harris*'s City Hall (planned in 1920; built 1928–32) [38] and the imposing Central Library and Graves Art Gallery by the City Architect, *W.G. Davies*, 1929–34. Both buildings are in an appropriately monumental classical style and clothed in traditional stone dress but with radically different interior treatments; a subdued Art Deco at the Library contrasts with *George Kruger Gray*'s highly coloured medieval entrance hall at the City Hall [39]. Steel City House, the Telephone Exchange of 1927 by *H.T. Rees*, also suggested a monumental scale and style appropriate to a major city but little in the same vein followed. Other public architecture is typified by the bloodless Neo-Georgian of Division Street's Fire Station (*W.G. Davies*, 1928) and YWCA (*J. Mansell Jenkinson*, 1939). Neo-Georgian too were smaller public buildings such as branch libraries, e.g. Firth Park, sometimes carried out with panache, as at the Portland stone-fronted Hillsborough Baths (1926) by *F.E.P. Edwards*. Enthusiasm for newer styles in architecture was limited before 1945, discouraged by the absence of large-scale building in the city centre. Several of the most prominent new buildings such as the Brightside & Carbrook Co-operative store, Angel Street, and the Art Deco C&A Modes in the High Street were destroyed by bombs in 1940. Jazzier was Burton's, Attercliffe Road (1931), but only the Express Dairy, Broadfield Road (1939) comes close to the radical style of the Modern Movement.

19. City Hall, apse, by Vincent Harris, 1928–32

It is in **church architecture** that avowedly modern styles come to the fore, e.g. *C.M.E. Hadfield*'s R.C. Church of the Sacred Heart, Hillsborough (1936) [169], whose bold, blocky form ably recalls the work of Cachemaille-Day. Other church building was more traditional. The most important, if abortive, scheme was that of *Sir Charles Nicholson* to enlarge the parish church to a size commensurate with its newly acquired cathedral status. Of his 1936 proposals, only the late Perp-style chapter house and the Chapel of the Holy Spirit [30] were completed. In the suburbs, *Leslie Moore*'s St Hilda, Wincobank (1935) [110], exploited its site to provide an undercroft and exemplifies Moore's command of lighting interiors. Elsewhere, early Christian styles predominated, Italian at St Catherine's R.C. Church (1925–6) by *Charles Edward Fox & Son*, Burngreave Road; slightly Byzantine at St Polycarp, Malin Bridge (1933–4), by *H.I. Potter*. Even some very traditional Gothic churches were still being built, e.g. *Flockton & Son*'s St Aidan, City Road in 1932–3.

In 1926 Labour took power in Sheffield for the first time and embarked on a major council **house-building** programme, principally for cottage estates (*see* topic box, p. 29), which consumed land at an appalling rate. This was partly countered by the designation of a green belt in 1938, the culmination of a programme that had begun with the creation of a linear park from Endcliffe Park to the open Derbyshire moorland. This continued the C19 Sheffield tradition of large open spaces for public parks and included Graves Park, the largest in the city, given by the indefatigable philanthropist Alderman J.G. Graves in 1926.

Sheffield's **interwar private housing** is particularly undistinguished, many estates of semi-detached houses lacking even the mock-Tudor half-timbering and leaded lights found elsewhere in Britain. Only *Robert Cawkwell*'s restrained Neo-Georgian detached villas and *J. Mansell Jenkinson*'s Cotswold vernacular found in the exclusive w suburbs rise above the general level of mediocrity. But the precepts of Continental Modernism make a surprising appearance in private flats at Regent Court, Hillsborough (1936), by *Edgar Gardham*. These are on a considerable scale and highly unusual in being intended for working-class tenants at a time when few multi-storey flats were being erected by the Council. A second block at Duke Street, Park, was demolished after the war.

## The Postwar Years

Sheffield's role as a leading centre for armaments production led to it being singled out as a bombing target in the Second World War. Damage in the centres of production along the Don Valley was slight  but both the High Street area and The Moor were left as bomb sites in 1945.

Sheffield responded quickly to the 1944 Town and Country Planning Act, producing *Sheffield Replanned* in 1945: a plan for **reconstruction** which envisaged total rebuilding of the city centre with little other than the Central Library, Town Hall and City Hall retained, grouped around a newly created civic square and flanked by buildings in an austere stripped classical style. Road schemes included a tightly drawn inner ring road, the Civic Circle, around the principal shopping streets. An outer ring was included on the advice, according to Lord Esher, of Herbert Manzoni, Birmingham's notoriously pro-car Chief Engineer. Only parts of these ring roads were eventually built. Zoning was proposed but paramount was the need to replace the dilapidated housing stock.

An attempt to extend the city's boundaries failed in 1951. This limited expansion of the cottage estates although Sheffield occupied 39,486

## J.L. Womersley

The appointment in 1953 of *J. Lewis Womersley*, as City Architect, was of profound significance for the city. Previously Borough Architect at Northampton where he was responsible for the town's first ten-storey point block, Womersley's radical vision of how Sheffield might look was shared by its Labour councillors. Although most pronounced in housing, it extended to all areas of public architecture: schools, colleges, bus garages, markets, fire stations and libraries were all designed in a crisp and beguiling modern style.

acres, much of this was green belt or moorland. Parson Cross, left uncompleted at the outbreak of war, was finished, and while new estates at Ballifield, Birley, Stradbroke and Hackenthorpe (outside the city boundary) and extensions of existing ones at Woodthorpe and the Manor were constructed. They followed conventional pre-war cottage estate designs but more ambitious **housing** was to follow. Little building other than housing took place well into the 1950s, the temporary single-storey shops on The Moor seeming like a fixture until they finally went at the end of the decade.

The publication of *Ten Years of Housing in Sheffield* in 1962 in English, French and Russian indicates the widespread sense of a 'massive achievement', as Pevsner saw it, after a decade of work. Under J.L. Womersley, City Architect from 1953 (*see* topic box, p. 32), Sheffield's housing would grow upwards. Schemes for comprehensive redevelopment in the inner areas were drawn up in the early 1950s. The most notable of course were Park Hill (1955–61) and Hyde Park (1955–64) which attracted unprecedented national and international attention. Inspired by Le Corbusier's Unité d'Habitation, Marsailles, their concept was revolutionary in combining for the first time deck access – the famous 'streets in the sky' – with extensive social facilities. Also novel was the layout of massive blocks linked at angles and the high density (160 persons per acre). They were

20. Park Hill, by J.L. Womersley, 1955–61

21. Netherthorpe, during redevelopment, looking across to Woodside, *c.* 1965

intended by their young designers *Ivor Smith* and *Jack Lynn* to repli-
cate the modes of working-class life but the brutal sublimity of their
design repelled as many as it excited. In contrast were the more usual
schemes: mixed estates of low-, medium- and high-rise, reflecting
the needs of different groups of people. All exploited the opportunities for picturesque planning provided by Sheffield's hills and followed in the tradition established by the London County Council's
Alton Estate East at Roehampton (planned from 1951). The late 1950s
saw greater use of high-rise flats following the increase in grants
available for blocks over six storeys.

The first major scheme under Womersley was Low Edges (1953–9), much of which followed the principles of 'Radburn' planning for separating pedestrians from traffic, an early example in Britain. Three tower blocks and low-rise flats gave a seventy person per acre density (more than twice that of the pre-war cottage estates). There followed in quick succession Netherthorpe (1959–72) [21], where tower blocks replaced tight streets of terraces and a great swathe of cleared land was transformed into a park, and Woodside (1960–2), perhaps the most sculptural of the estates (now mostly demolished). It was described by Harold Lambert, Chairman of the Housing Development Committee, as having 'something of the fascination of the Italian hill towns'. Exceptionally, it used the Wimpey 'no-fines' system building method for some of the maisonettes, Sheffield otherwise employing bespoke schemes. The supreme, but often overlooked, achievement of Womersley's time is the Gleadless Valley estate (1955–62) [142] which combined urban housing types and the natural landscape so effectively that it still looks stunning, especially on a bright winter's day. Tower blocks were carefully placed to act as landmarks across the city and even from the Peak District. Equally significant was the visual relationship of one development to another. In all these schemes, Womersley applied his favourite maxim from Capability Brown: 'Flood the valleys, plant the tops'. The towers of Netherthorpe, described surprisingly by John Betjeman in 1961 as 'well-proportioned and even noble . . . super-human additions to a new landscape' looked NE across the valley to Woodside which in turn faced the 'castle keep' of Hyde Park on the eastern hill. Such dramatic townscape has been lost with the demolitions of the 1990s.

Womersley also placed Sheffield at the forefront of the postwar **Schools Building** programme. Almost all of such schools are in the outer suburbs, outside the scope of this guide but should be mentioned as part of the city's contribution (*see* the forthcoming *Yorkshire: West Riding South* for further details). Womersley commissioned leading young practices including the *Architects Co-Partnership*; *Gollins, Melvin, Ward & Partners; Basil Spence & Partners;* and *Lyons Israel & Ellis. Womersley's* own schemes such as Granville College, Norfolk Park (1958–61) were of equal quality.

The city's **architectural renaissance** was not just led by Womersley. The University's competition held in 1953 was a seminal point in postwar British architecture: the first time that a competition for a major architectural project had a commitment to modern architecture as a prerequisite and as a focus for a debate about the form that architecture should take. The deck-access designs of the *Smithsons* [45], echoing their entry for the Golden Lane Estate, London, and a powerful entry by *James Stirling* were both in the late Corbusian tradition. *Gollins, Melvin & Ward*'s successful entries for the Arts Tower (1961–5) and Library (1955–9) [47] looked instead to America and the functionalism of Mies van der Rohe and Skidmore, Owings & Merrill. The theme was continued for the Sheffield Polytechnic (now Sheffield Hallam University) in

1953–68. Further confident expressions of Modernism were made not only by tall slab-like student residences by *Hadfield Cawkwell & Davidson* for the University and by *Womersley* for the Polytechnic, but also by later residences such as *Tom Mellor & Partners'* Earnshaw Hall (1960–5) [154]. By the beginning of the next decade, Sheffield University had also completed *William Whitfield*'s Geography Building (1968–71), and the emphatically red brick Alfred Denny Building (1971) by *Gollins, Melvin, Ward & Partners*. *Bradshaw, Rouse & Harker*'s heavily modelled College of Art (1970) at Brincliffe is among the few significant educational buildings of the decade.

**Churches** too reflected new ideas. The influence of the Liturgical Movement, which encouraged greater participation in the service by the congregation, is evident at Holy Cross, Gleadless (1964–5), by *Braddock & Martin-Smith*. Liturgically more traditional are two of Basil Spence's finest small suburban churches (both outside the area covered by this guide): the minimalist St Paul, Parson Cross (*see* topic box, p. 37), and St Catherine of Siena (1958–60), Richmond. The influence of *George Pace* as Diocesan Surveyor was felt in the many fittings by him in Sheffield churches, in both Gothic and Georgian styles and in his masterpiece at St Mark Broomhill (1958–63) [145] which paid homage to Le Corbusier at Ronchamp. *Pace* prepared plans for the completion of the Cathedral extensions but these were replaced by a modern Gothic scheme carried out by *Ansell & Bailey* in the mid 1960s.

In redeveloping the **city centre** Sheffield sought, like other British cities, to separate cars from pedestrians. In practice, only part of an inner ring road (a revival of the Civic Circle of the 1945 plan), comprising Arundel Gate, Eyre Street and Charter Row, was built and St Mary's Road and Hanover Street were upgraded to form an outer ring. A new focal point was created for the city centre with Castle Square and its shops at subway level (opened in 1968, now removed). The Moor was rebuilt as a principal shopping street in the 1950s–60s but the uniform designs with Portland stone facings and canted corners display little panache. A more radical approach was taken only in a handful of **commercial buildings** notably *Yorke, Rosenberg & Mardall*'s white-tiled Cole Brothers store (1961–5), providing a strong foil to the City Hall in Barker's Pool; the granite-clad Castle House, Castle Street (1959–64) by *G.S. Hay* of the Co-operative Wholesale Society [23]; and *Andrew Darbyshire*'s Castle Market (1960–5), a bold attempt to exploit the falling site with entry at various levels. The similarly ingenious handling of *Jefferson Sheard*'s Epic Development (1968) was characteristic of its period, and so too their remarkable Brutalist electricity substation (1965–8) [75] in Moore Street, though neither has gained popular affection.

*J.L. Womersley* was succeeded as City Architect in 1964 by *W.L. Clunie*, who oversaw the last two major housing schemes: Kelvin and Broomhall (by the Yorkshire Development Group of which Sheffield was a member authority). Both proved unsuccessful and were demolished after a short life. Broomhall's flats were of prefabricated

22. St Paul, Wordsworth Avenue, by Basil Spence & Partners, 1958–9

Built to a limited budget to serve the vast council estate at Parson Cross, St Paul's is deceptively simple and comprises two unadorned brick walls joined by a shallow barrel vault with diagonal steel bracing. Detached campanile of just two brick walls linked by concrete ties to keep them up safely and together. It is connected to the body of the church by open roofed passages. Both end walls glass, following Spence's experiments at St Oswald, Tile Hill, Coventry in the previous year, but internally the nave walls are slightly zigzag and the placing of side windows in strips at the top of the walls gives the roof a floating quality. A vertical slatted afrormosia screen behind the altar and the placing of the organ on a bridge, a visually very successful motif, combine to emphasise the transparency of the building. Spence was responsible for the altar, priest's stall, seating and other furnishings, including his personal gift of altar ornaments in hammered iron, their simplicity matching that of the church.

construction, something that Sheffield had been much involved with since the 5M houses, Gloucester Street, of 1962–3, built by the *Ministry of Housing and Local Government* as an experiment in economy and named after the five-metre module around which they were built. Other system-built designs, developed in association with Vic Hallam Ltd, appeared across the city in the late 1960s, including the well-landscaped

23. Castle House, Angel Street, detail of cantilevered staircase, by G.S. Hay, 1964

Norfolk Park estate. High-density development virtually came to an end following boundary changes in 1967 which meant that the city was at last able to expand southeastwards. In 1974 Sheffield became part of the new county of South Yorkshire and continued to construct large numbers of council houses but moved away from monolithic estates to housing based on traditional street patterns, e.g. the sensitively designed Bressingham Close scheme of 1977 at Burngreave or, less imaginatively, long rows of semi-detached housing. Sheffield's hilly terrain continued to provide inspiration, however, and enabled ingenious small schemes of deck-access flats, first at Netherthorpe in 1976 and later at Derby Place, Heeley. By the end of the decade, Sheffield Council owned 37 per cent of the city's housing, one of the highest proportions of any city in Great Britain. Private housing in the suburbs also produced some surprises, including *Patric Guest*'s Miesian No. 1 Park Lane (1961) [151] and *Peter F. Smith*'s houses of 1968–9 at Endcliffe. Also in the suburbs, the Merlin Theatre, Nether Edge [135], an expressionist design of 1965–9 by *Black Bayes & Gibbs* was inspired by Rudolf Steiner's Goetheanum, with echoes of eastern European Cubism.

Sheffield's confidence in its continued industrial prosperity throughout the 1960s and into the 1970s was reflected in the publication of *City on the Move* in 1972, which trumpeted new architecture as the city's major attraction: 'This, then, is modern Sheffield. A city that has removed the scars of the Industrial Revolution, and replaced them with all the excitement of the 21st century. Gone is the smoke; gone are the dirty old buildings. In their place, clean air, sparkling new developments . . . This is the city where the good things happen'. The absence of more far-reaching road schemes distinguished Sheffield's centre from many other British cities in sparing it the *cordon sanitaire* of car parks, retail parks and meaningless open space separating it from its suburbs. Even today, the majority of the principal roads out of the city are lined with C19 shops and houses.

But besides housing, new building was limited in the **1970s**. The most distinguished public building was the Crucible Theatre with its octagonal auditorium (1969–71) [56] by *Renton Howard Wood Associates*, the most prominent and least popular the Town Hall extension (popularly known as the Egg Box), demolished in 2001 for the Winter Garden (*see* p. 75). The major office development, the Manpower Services Commission building (1978) by the *Property Services Agency,* impresses by its sheer scale and position at Moorfoot. The Royal Hallamshire Hospital was finally completed in 1977 but its bulky mass fails to enhance the city's skyline. The enthusiasm for Modernism in the postwar decades has also had a negative effect in creating an antipathy towards C19 buildings and a lack of sympathy with the city's industrial past. The early C17 Norwood Hall (regrettably demolished by the Council in 1976), *Flockton & Abbott*'s All Saints, Brightside and a host of C18 and C19 industrial premises were among the casualties while hospital and university expansion also claimed many early C19 suburban villas. In the city centre the Lyceum Theatre, Leader House, the Education Offices and Gladstone Buildings all came under threat. Although the city was quick to designate its first Conservation Areas, Sheffield came to value its architectural past relatively late (the Hallamshire Historic Buildings Society was founded in 1970 and a local group of the Victorian Society in 1977), just as the city was about to enter its first period of serious economic and industrial decline.

## The Late Twentieth Century Onwards

In the 1980s Sheffield's traditional steel and engineering industries were hard hit by recession. In the Don Valley the number of jobs dropped from 40,000 to 13,000 as works like Firth Brown's and Hadfield's were closed and demolished. Paradoxically the city is still a world leader in special steels and continues to produce high-value products, but with a fraction of the workforce the industry once needed. The consistent theme of the last twenty-five years has been the need for economic **regeneration**, which has often meant that opportunities for new development promising jobs have been seized, however mediocre the quality of new building and irrespective of the price paid in loss of irreplaceable fabric of historic interest.

In most of the Don Valley the **Sheffield Development Corporation** had responsibility for economic and physical regeneration from 1988 to 1997, overseeing reclamation of derelict industrial sites and redevelopment. The Meadowhall shopping centre, already under construction in 1988, the restoration and re-use of the West Gun Works and Abbey National's new offices at Carbrook are schemes that stand out among the unexceptional industrial units. More important are the sports facilities that have brought buildings of a new type and grand scale to the area. *Sheffield City Council's Design and Building Services'* Don Valley Stadium [116], built for the World Student Games in 1991, set an architectural standard that has been maintained with the English Institute of Sport [117] by *FaulknerBrowns* and *BDP*'s iceSheffield, while on the edge of the city centre *FaulknerBrowns'* swimming pool complex at Ponds Forge [85], also built for the Games, provides a striking landmark.

The needs of students, though on a more permanent basis, have also been the impetus for extensive building at the city's two **universities** and in nearby areas. At Sheffield University existing buildings at Western Bank have been extended or re-formed, while at St George's Square *BDP*'s small but sophisticated red brick library stands out among other new buildings' clumsy references to the distinctive red brick and stone of the older Mappin Building. At Sheffield Hallam an atrium [50] has been skilfully integrated with the original 1950s–60s buildings alongside the dramatically cascading roofs of *FaulknerBrowns'* Adsett's Centre [51]. **Conversion** to student flats has brought a fresh use to buildings as diverse as Truro Works and the Unity Church, Crookesmoor,

24. Persistence Works, Brown Street, interior, by Feilden Clegg Bradley, 1998–2001

and blocks of flats for students have sprung up, especially in the area around West Street. Here and elsewhere in the city centre there are new bars and restaurants, some in existing buildings such as banks and the old fire station. More recently conversion and new apartment blocks such as *Carey Jones*'s overbearing west.one and Riverside Exchange have brought residents back to the centre and a different scale to the townscape. Since the 1990s residential conversion has rescued several important industrial buildings, following the successful scheme by *Axis Architecture* for Gleeson's at Cornish Place in 1998.

The importance of the **conservation** of Sheffield's unique industrial heritage has not been universally recognized and significant losses continue. The pioneering efforts of specialist groups in the city, supported by English Heritage, have raised awareness but in Sheffield's efforts to reinvent itself as a bright, modern European city some see its past as a grimy embarrassment. As with Park Hill, whose listing as a building of special architectural and historical interest in 1998 caused great controversy, the interest and importance of the city's buildings is often appreciated more by outsiders than its own citizens.

Sheffield's tendency to think of itself as a collection of villages rather than a city has not helped it to develop a strong sense of civic consciousness. The renewal of the city centre, starting with the Lottery Funded 'Heart of the City' project (*see* topic box, p. 96) in 1995 and the immensely successful and popular re-creation of the Peace Gardens [53], has, however, fostered a new sense of pride and ownership. The proposed regeneration of other parts of the city centre was set out in *Koetter Kim & Associates*' **Masterplan** of 2000, which developed the idea of ten Quarters and proposes further redevelopment including a new Retail Quarter between Barker's Pool, Carver Street and Pinstone Street. Enhancement of other public spaces and the improvement of pedestrian access into and around the centre are also envisaged. In the **Cultural Industries Quarter**, the first to be designated, where development has focused on the arts, media and communications, two new buildings have attracted widespread attention. Persistence Works [80], by *Feilden Clegg Bradley* is an outstanding and innovative block of studios for a co-operative of artists and craftspeople. Nearby *Branson Coates*'s four eye-catching stainless steel-clad drums for the former National Centre for Popular Music [79] have found a new use by students. The principal development has been *Pringle Richards Sharratt*'s Millennium Galleries [42] and Winter Garden [43] which have set a high standard for the future – whether the projected office, retail and hotel developments of the new century will match that and the best of previous centuries remains to be seen.

# Major Buildings

N

Cathedral Church of
St Peter and St Paul

Parade
Chambers

HIGH STREET

CHURCH STREET

Cutlers' Hall

Former Firth College

Former School
Board Offices

LEOPOLD STREET

Former Central
Schools

FARGATE

Victoria Hall

Cathedral Church
of St Marie

NORFOLK STREET

Crucible
Theatre

City Hall

Upper Chapel

TUDOR
SQUARE

Odeon
Cinema

POND STREET

BARKER'S
POOL

PINSTONE STREET

Town Hall

SURREY STREET

Lyceum
Theatre

Peace
Gardens

Winter Garden

Central
Library &
Graves Art
Gallery

SHEFFIELD
HALLAM
UNIVERSITY

Millennium
Galleries

ARUNDEL GATE

HOWARD STREET

Howden House

Sheffield Hallam
University

200 metres

500 feet

25. Major Buildings

# Cathedral Church of St Peter and St Paul

Church Street

Sheffield's medieval parish church became the cathedral of the new Anglican diocese in 1914. Despite the inevitable alterations and additions that had taken place over the centuries it was not an especially large or grand building and in the next half-century ambitious schemes to make it more 'cathedral like' were proposed. These were only partly carried through and the present complex arrangement is the result. Though lacking the scale and grandeur that were intended, it presents a beguiling mix of different periods and offers an altogether different architectural tangle from those of the great medieval cathedrals.

## History

Little is known of the earliest churches in Sheffield. None is mentioned in Domesday, and it seems likely that the first post-Conquest building was contemporary with the castle built by William de Lovetot after 1116 and probably destroyed in 1266; fragments incorporated in the chancel interior are thought to be its only survivors. The dedication of another, equally elusive, church is recorded in the 1280s; this was replaced *c*. 1430 by the church whose Perp chancel and splendid crossing tower and crocketed spire are visible today. The original cruciform plan of the church began to disappear when the Shrewsbury Chapel was added to the SE *c*. 1520 by the 4th Earl (d.1538) and there is further evidence for other changes to the church at this time.

By 1771 much of the fabric was in a ruinous condition and *John Carr* was engaged to remedy matters, refacing part of the chancel in a sympathetic and surprisingly convincing Gothic and supervising other repairs. *Thomas Atkinson* filled the NE corner in 1777 with a small vestry with the Church Burgesses' room above, and after the N and S walls of the nave were rebuilt to match the chancel under the direction of *William Lindley* (Carr's former assistant) in 1790–3, the transformation to a rectangular plan was complete. Next the higgledy-piggledy accumulation of C18 private pews and galleries was swept away in a further rebuilding by *Charles Watson* (Lindley's former partner), 1802–5. The chancel and its aisles were walled off from the nave and the nave arcades heightened to accommodate new galleries on all four sides. Minor alterations were made 1855–6 by *Flockton & Son* who removed the screen under the crossing tower.

A major **restoration** of the church was undertaken in 1878–80 by *Flockton & Gibbs*, with advice from *Sir George Gilbert Scott*. They added

26. Proposed extensions to the Cathedral, by Sir Charles Nicholson, 1936. Perspective view from the SE (1938)

the N and S transepts and another bay, with porches, at the W end and built new vestries on the NE side. The galleries in the nave and the screen walls blocking the earlier transepts were taken down and plaster and paint removed from walls and roofs.

This was, essentially, the church that *Sir Charles Nicholson* was engaged in 1919 to transform. His first proposal, approved in 1921, was to build a new nave and choir N of the existing church, changing the existing nave and chancel into a S aisle to be balanced by a corresponding N aisle with a matching steeple. Lack of funds put any immediate start out of reach, and in 1936 Nicholson changed his plans to a more radical N–S reorientation of the building, which proposed the demolition of the nave, and the creation of a new chancel with a large nave extending S across the churchyard towards the Cutlers' Hall. The existing chancel was to become a (ritual or liturgical) 's' transept, with the tower and spire replicated on the W (ritual N) side of the new nave [26].

Work began in April 1937 and the new vestries, offices and Chapter House, together with a chapel linking them to the existing N transept, were completed the following year. Foundations of the new nave were begun in the churchyard but the contract was suspended at the outbreak of war, although work continued N of the existing nave. The 's' choir aisle, crypt and adjacent passages were consecrated in 1942 and although work on the Chapel of The Holy Spirit [30], which was to form the 'E' end of the new cathedral, was interrupted, it was eventually dedicated in 1948. At this stage no part of the existing church had been demolished except to create new openings. In the 1950s the plans were revived under Nicholson's successor, *Steven Dykes-Bower,* and from 1956 with new designs by *George Pace.* Constrained by cost, both resigned. The work of resolving Nicholson's incomplete scheme fell to *Arthur Bailey* of *Ansell*

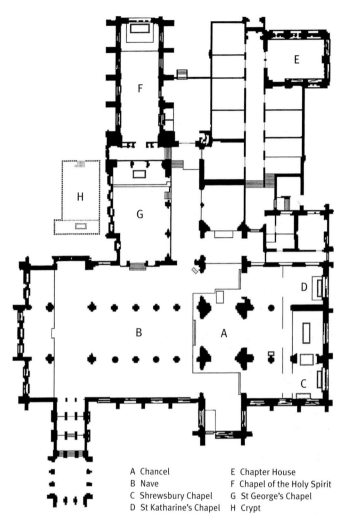

A Chancel      E Chapter House
B Nave      F Chapel of the Holy Spirit
C Shrewsbury Chapel      G St George's Chapel
D St Katharine's Chapel      H Crypt

27. Plan of the Cathedral

*& Bailey*, with a return to the old orientation, the replacement of Flockton & Gibbs's w end of the nave with a new w crossing entered through a towered porch and narthex, and transformation of the unfinished chancel into a chapel. Dedication took place in 1966. In 2004 plans by *Martin Purdy* of APEC Architects propose a new Community Resources Centre at the NW.

## Churchyard

The churchyard originally extended further s, but was reduced in 1866–7 and 1891 for the widening of Church Street, and again in 1994. The overcrowded burial ground with its jumble of monuments was closed in 1856. Some headstones were used as paving in a series of landscaping schemes which created the open forecourt to the s, the most recent by *Martin Purdy*

28. Cathedral Church of St Peter and St Paul, from the sw, c15–c20

of *APEC* in 1996. This resolved some of the variations of level across the site with a gently sloping paved area embraced at the w end by a diminishing flight of curved steps. On the e side a granite **monument** to James Montgomery (1771–1854) with bronze statue by *John Bell*, moved from the General Cemetery (*see* p. 226) in 1971, and the four gabled and crocketed stone piers of the gates set up in 1890 at the Church Street entrance.

## Exterior

Although of several phases, the s side of the cathedral, facing Church Street, is consistent in its greyish gritstone ashlar. We start with the wall of the **s aisle** to the right of the porch. Four bays, rebuilt by Lindley, 1790–3, set higher and slightly further out than the old wall in order to line up with the chancel. Pointed arched windows of three lights with single transoms and panel tracery. Buttresses with details copied from Carr's work on the chancel (*see* below) and crocketed pinnacles restored *c.* 2000. The nave clerestory, rebuilt 1805, has five two-light windows and can just be seen above the crenellated aisle parapet. Next the gabled **s transept** of 1880, the stone carefully matched with the older work, but the details clearly Victorian, with flowing tracery in the big five-light s window and the smaller windows to e and w. Gabled angle buttresses, and narrower crenellation to the parapet, giving a more jagged effect than the C18 work. Behind the transept the superb C15 **tower and spire** rise above the crossing. Square tower, with large bell-openings, each of four lights with transom and flowing tracery. Above, the crocketed broach spire rises behind a crenellated parapet with corner pinnacles.

The three bays of the s **chancel aisle** and its E wall (i.e. the E wall of the Shrewsbury Chapel) are as rebuilt by *Carr* in 1772–4. He seems to have left untouched (except for the parapet?) the wall of the adjoining **chancel**, which had been restored in 1704 by Thomas Howard, the 8th Duke of Norfolk. The differences in the stonework of the walls, the tracery and the plinths of the two bays are plain, even without the evidence of Howard's initials on the older work and those of Edward, the 9th Duke (d.1777), on the later. Carr replaced the 'very decay'd' E window of the chapel with a careful copy of the chancel window, which has flowing Dec tracery. Was this in its turn copied from an original C15 window in 1704? The hood moulds of both windows have classical imposts. These and other details such as the little cusped arches and squat obelisks on pedestals carved on the buttresses are clues that the work is not the genuine Gothic it first appears. The illusion is maintained by *Atkinson*'s copy of Carr's work in the vestry added in 1777 at the end of the **chancel N aisle**. Rainwater heads dated 1806, marking the completion of the rebuilding and alterations begun in 1772.

The single-storey **vestry** and **Church Burgesses' room**, added in 1878–80 in the manner of a chantry chapel, bring us to the junction with the northward extensions, so from here the exterior is almost entirely C20 work. *Nicholson*'s additions of 1937–48 are heavy, rather sombre, late Gothic in plain ashlar blocks of buff sandstone. Deep moulded plinths and massive buttresses, with sloping parapets hiding flat roofs. The rectangular **Chapter House** at the NE corner of a two-storey range of offices has two-light pointed arched windows set high up in deep recesses, except on the w wall which has a single large window with Dec tracery. Beyond a narrow gap the walls of the **Chapel of the Holy Spirit** rise high above Campo Lane, its big gabled buttresses embracing the finely traceried five-light window at the N end. Aisleless, it has four slender two-light windows on each side.

Now we reach *Arthur Bailey*'s completion of Nicholson's scheme and his w extensions, which Pevsner thought 'depressingly traditional' for their date, but now seem perfectly acceptable and considerate. Free Gothic, with minimal tracery and closely-set buttresses ending squarely above the roof-line. The **ambulatory** and the four bays of the **Chapel of St George** link the Chapel of the Holy Spirit to the nave. Their tall windows rise above the flat roof of the unlovely concrete **hall** 1966–7, and match those along the w end of the nave. The 1880 w window, with Dec tracery, was reset in the N wall of the w extension. Finally, at the sw corner of the Cathedral the towered **porch** projects confidently, skilfully acknowledging its Gothic context in a modern idiom. Behind it, *Bailey*'s striking octagonal lantern sits above the w crossing.

## Interior

The entrance through the porch steps down to the narthex which leads into the spacious W **crossing**. The lantern's lower structure forms an eight-pointed star, the dark Opepe hardwood mullions of the upper glazing descending into the space below as a 'Crown of Thorns'. Lantern reconstructed 1998–9 with new abstract glazing by *Amber Hiscott* with *David Pearl*, symbolizing darkness and light. It replaced the original glass between the points of the star by *Keith New*. The proposed reordering by *Martin Purdy* will place a baptismal pool directly beneath it. The concrete and painted brick of the extension sit unobtrusively beside the original **nave**. The concrete piers match the nave's octagonal piers of 1802–5 with their embattled capitals, which in turn are copies of the C15 chancel arcade (*see* below). Shields above the nave piers display the arms of the Lords of the Manor of Sheffield on the N side and the owners of the advowson since the Reformation on the S. Somewhat oddly, Watson retained the original arrangement of five bays in his rebuilding of the nave arcades and clerestory, even though the then newly-rebuilt aisle walls have only four bays. The discrepancy must surely have been determined by a wish to retain the existing nave **roof**. This is a simple double-framed structure with billeted tie-beams which have carved and gilded bosses. Its low-pitched profile is matched exactly by the line of the later of the two earlier and lower roofs on the tower wall, suggesting it may have succeeded the original roof and was then raised in the C19.

The **crossing piers** are early C15. They have three orders of concave mouldings to the jambs and arches, with vestigial embattled capitals. The roof-lines of the original transepts can be seen on the N and S faces of the tower, and the S springer of the old N aisle survives on the NW crossing pier. Behind a doorway in the NE pier is the circular staircase to the rood loft, removed in 1570. The inner faces of the **chancel** walls and its two-bay aisles are also early C15. Octagonal piers and responds with embattled capitals, and double-chamfered arches. The N aisle N wall and chancel E wall contain fragments of Norman masonry with chevron ornaments. The two tiers of blind arcading with cusped arches on the chancel N wall are by *Robert Potter*, 1841; other work of this date by him has gone. The chancel has a steeply-pitched hammerbeam roof, thought to be an early C16 replacement of the original. Moulded arched braces and collar-beams and gilded angels. Their delicately outstretched wings were the gift of Arthur Bailey to mark the completion of the cathedral extensions in 1966.

The **Shrewsbury Chapel**, built *c.* 1520, forms the E end of the chancel S aisle and contains the magnificent tombs of the 4th and 6th Earls (*see* topic box, p. 51). The oak screen separating it from the aisle was removed after the Duke of Norfolk gave the chapel to the Cathedral in 1933, and placed in the N transept (*see* below). Both chapel and aisle

29. Monument of the 4th Earl of Shrewsbury (d.1538), with the monument of the 6th Earl (d.1590) behind

The monuments of the 4th and 6th Earls of Shrewsbury demonstrate the power and wealth of the Talbot family in the C16 and are exceptionally fine examples of Tudor monumental sculpture.

The 4th Earl (d.1538) lies in effigy between his two wives, under a flat-topped, panelled arch with a heavy pendant and straight cresting. The alabaster figures are exquisitely carved, probably by Italian craftsmen or by Nottingham alabaster workers in the Italian style, and the richness of their robes and other clothing is shown in detail. Lying with their hands folded in prayer, the two Countesses rest their feet on angels, while the Earl's are supported by a talbot, the heraldic dog on the family's badge. The Purbeck marble tomb-chest has panelled sides with shields in quatrefoils and a twisted shaft at each corner.

On the s wall is the alabaster monument to the 6th Earl (d.1590). His armour-clad effigy lies on a straw mat under a very large, but not very imaginative architectural surround, with a big heraldic achievement on top. His feet, too, rest on a talbot, and above the columns on either side talbots flourish small banners. The marble panel in the centre of the monument bears a lengthy inscription in Latin by John Foxe, author of *The Book of Martyrs*, reciting the Earls' family connections, honours and virtues. It refers to his long and loyal service as gaoler of Mary Queen of Scots in Sheffield, but omits any mention of his estranged second wife, the formidable Bess of Hardwick.

have a common roof, of similar style and pitch to the nave, although with more elaborately carved bosses. Similar roofs in the former transepts and the chancel N aisle, suggesting all are early C16. The chapel and aisle were restored as the **Lady Chapel** in 1935 by *W.H. Randoll Blacking.*

At the same time *Blacking* supervised the alteration of the chancel N aisle and its eastward extension of 1777 to create **St Katharine's Chapel** as a memorial to Mrs Burrows, wife of the first Bishop of Sheffield. The cusped piscina in the S wall of the chapel originally served the pre-Reformation altar against the E wall, which was taken down in 1878–80. The tracery of its blocked five-light window was inserted in the E wall of the new N transept. Thought to be original C15, but its panel tracery matches that in the chancel S aisle windows so perhaps dates from Carr's restoration, even if copied at that date from surviving C15 work.

The **N transept** of 1878–80 now forms part of the passage to Nicholson's extensions, with the C16 oak screen from the Shrewsbury Chapel dividing it from the N tower aisle on its S side. The screen has Tudor flower tracery in the heads of its narrow openings. The corridor continues NE of the transept to the Chapter House, beyond the sacristy, vestries and offices on either side. The space N of the transept has a pretty painted panelled ceiling and was originally built as the sanctuary of the Chapel of Chivalry, completed in 1938.

Adjoining to the W is the **Burrows Memorial transept**. This would have been the 's' choir aisle to the High Sanctuary, which was only partly built when work stopped in 1942. The triple arcades in Nicholson's conventional Gothic on the N and E sides of the sanctuary were eventually completed with Bailey's W wall of four bays and three high-arched openings on the S, giving access from the nave. It became the **Chapel of St George** in 1966, the Memorial Chapel of the York and Lancaster regiment. The flat-panelled wood ceiling with painted borders and gilded bosses is *c.* 1985. From the chapel there is an unexpected view through the N arcade to the upper part of the Chapel of the Holy Spirit. Nicholson intended this as the Lady Chapel of his Cathedral, visible yet separate from its functional 'E' end and set at a lower level.

From the Burrows Transept, steps lead down to the **ambulatory**. On the S side, under the Chapel of St George, is the **crypt** or **columbarium**, a tiny stone vaulted chapel four-bays long and three-bays wide. On the N side a doorway in a low screen wall under a high open arch flanked by narrow pointed arches leads into the **Chapel of the Holy Spirit** [30]. Chastely Gothic, it is tall and aisleless, with a quadripartite vault, the simply-moulded stonework of the slender wall-shafts and ribs and bosses set off against the white plastered walls. The clear-glazed windows to E and W are set high up. At once light and tranquil the chapel provides a setting for the richly coloured 'E' window and the furnishings by *Temple Moore* and *Comper*.

30. Chapel of the Holy Spirit, by Sir Charles Nicholson, 1936–48

## Furnishings

After the 1880 restoration the interior was enriched with new furnishings and stained glass windows. Many of these and other fittings were altered and moved to new positions in the c20. Furnishings are described in the same order as the interior.

w crossing: **font** of polished grey granite, given by the Freemasons in 1881. By *Charles Green*, who modelled the bronze figures and other ornament. **Royal Coat of Arms** above the sw door, 1805. – Nave: richly carved octagonal oak **pulpit** of 1887, with figures in canopied niches. – Chancel: oak **canons' stalls** by *Temple Moore*, 1918, given by the Freemasons in 1920 as part of their war memorial. The **Bishop's throne** by *Sir Charles Nicholson*, 1937, is English oak with colour and gilding, its tall Perp spirelet terminating with a pelican. Almost hidden in the se corner wall a small and badly defaced medieval figure thought to be of the Virgin Mary. – The Shrewsbury Chapel **altar** is the restored stone mensa of a pre-Reformation altar, discovered in 1864 in two pieces.

Painted alabaster **reredos,** 1935 by *W.H. Randoll Blacking*, the Crucifixion and figures of saints representing the seven altars of the medieval church. – St Katharine's Chapel: **reredos** in the form of a triptych by *Christopher Webb,* 1935. Painted and gilded mahogany panels surmounted by a figure of the Risen Christ carved by *W. Allen*. Fine C15 canopied oak **sedilia** with cusped arcading on the back panels. Pretty painted and gilded Baroque **screen,** 1937 by *W.H. Randoll Blacking.* – Chapel of St George: painted and gilded stone figures of St Michael, St George, St Oswald and St Martin carved by *Esmond Burton,* 1937. On the E side an unusual **screen,** *c.* 1969, of alternate swords and bayonets, the swords with points upwards, the bayonets downwards. – Burrows Memorial Transept: Small bronze **sculpture** by *Stephen Broadbent,* 2000, portraying Christ as a ship's figurehead, its shape symbolic both of an anchor and a sword becoming a ploughshare. Cast from the maquette for an unexecuted work commemorating the special relationship between the city and ships named HMS *Sheffield.* – Chapel of the Holy Spirit: richly gilded and painted **reredos** by *Temple Moore,* originally part of the chancel fittings given in 1920. Figure of Christ in the centre, with the apostles on either side, all carved in half-relief and standing behind a low battlemented parapet. Masonic symbols on the lower end panels. The canopied **screen** and **oak stalls** by *Sir Ninian Comper* came from the Missionary College at Burgh. Delicately stencilled decoration in green and grey on the screen and a vivid blue under the canopy.

## Stained Glass

W crossing, N wall: the former six-light W window of 1880, with most of its original glass, by *W.F. Dixon,* 1881. In the upper lights an animated depiction of St Peter preaching to Cornelius, the figures with swirling drapery in sumptuous colours. Smaller scenes from the lives of St Peter and St Paul below. The bottom six lights, with Christ with the Disciples in the Cornfield set beside the Presentation in the Temple (the Nunc Dimittis window), were originally in two tiers in the easternmost window of the nave N aisle, *c.* 1900. – Nave: N aisle window, scenes from the life of Joseph by *Thomas Baillie,* 1862; S aisle, four windows of the 1880s by *Dixon.* – In the S transept a fine series by *Clayton & Bell,* 1880, showing scenes of healing. – The chancel S aisle now has only *Powell & Sons'* striking Vision of the New Jerusalem 1928, its colours set off by pale gold and clear glass. – Shrewsbury Chapel E window 1871 by *Clayton & Bell.* – Despite its earlier inscription the chancel E window, by *W.F. Dixon,* is J.N. Mappin's 1880 replacement for the window he gave in memory of James Montgomery in 1857. – St Katharine's Chapel, E window, 1935; one of sixteen by *Christopher Webb.* In the N wall *Harry Harvey*'s gentle scenes of works of charity, 1967, is less sentimental. The windows by *Webb* in the N transept, Chapter House and Cathedral offices all relate to Sheffield's history and include a lively depiction of Chaucer's '*Reeve's Tale*'. – In the Crypt a small window by *Keith New* 1971, with pieces of clear glass rods set against a geometric pattern of

31. Tree of Jesse window, by Henry and Alfred Gérente, 1853

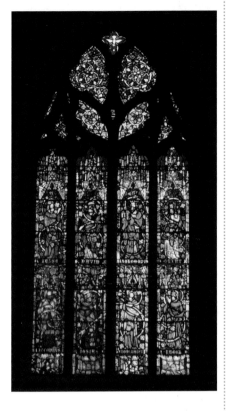

The intriguing four-light window at the N end of the Burrows Memorial transept was installed in 1946, having been removed from the redundant church of St Luke, Hollis Croft. An incomplete Tree of Jesse with eight robed figures, each with a canopy and entwined by part of the stem. Extensive grisaille and vivid colours of green, yellow, red and blue. Previously thought to be genuinely medieval, with C14 Spanish glass, it has now been identified as part of the original W window of Butterfield's All Saints, Margaret Street, London. In accordance with the principles of the Ecclesiological Society, the French artist Henry Gérente was commissioned to make a correctly 'medieval' window based on the C14 Tree of Jesse window at Wells Cathedral. After his death it was completed by his brother Alfred and installed in 1853. Universally condemned for its 'disagreeable colour', however, it was taken out in 1877. The vicar of St Luke's acquired eight of the panels c. 1880 and in time the true origin of the glass was forgotten.*

* *See* Brian Sprakes 'The Tree of Jesse Window in Sheffield Cathedral', *Sheffield Art Report*, 1980

coloured glass, giving a jewel-like effect. – The great Te Deum window in the Chapel of the Holy Spirit [30] is *Webb*'s best work in the Cathedral, its brilliant colours dominating the N end of the lofty space.

## Monuments

The most important monuments in the cathedral are those in the Shrewsbury Chapel (*see* topic box, p. 51).

w end: busts of Archbishop Thomson, d.1890, by *W.D. Keyworth*, and Archdeacon Blakeney, d.1895, by *Onslow Ford*. Medallion portrait of John Greaves d.1828, and bust of Thomas Watson d.1832, both by *Edward Law*. – s aisle. Thomas and Elizabeth Harrison of Weston by *Sir Francis Chantrey* – a weeping figure seated by two draped urns, 1823. – s transept: the Rev. Alexander Mackenzie, d.1816. Moved here from St Paul's. Standing figures of Faith and Mourning either side of the inscription with a bust on top, carved in marble by *Chantrey*. – By the tower SE pier, centenary memorial with medallion portrait of the composer Sir William Sterndale Bennett, born 1816, carved by *Frank Tory & Sons,* 1920. – Chancel s aisle, bust of George Bamforth, d.1739, against the foot of a tall obelisk. – Chancel s wall: memorial to Lady Elizabeth Butler d.1510, the earliest of numerous small brass plates on the walls, piers and floor of the E end. In the arcade on the N wall busts of three vicars. In the centre, James Wilkinson, d.1805, set against a pyramid draped with a pall. This is the first work in marble by *Chantrey*, who was born at Norton. Thomas Sutton (left), d.1851, by *Edwin Smith*, and Canon Sale (right), d.1873, by *William Ellis*. – St Katharine's Chapel: a fine marble memorial to William Jessop of Broomhall, d.1734, the inscription framed by Corinthian columns and broken pediment. – Two finely lettered tablets: to Bishop Burrows, d.1940, by *George Pace* and *David Kindersley* (Burrows Memorial transept); to Bishop Heaslett, d.1947, by *George Pace* (ambulatory).

# Cathedral Church of St Marie (R.C.)

Norfolk Row

Built 1847–50 by *Weightman & Hadfield*. The Church of St Marie has been the seat of the Bishop of Hallam since the new Roman Catholic diocese was created in 1980. There had been a small Catholic community in the town since the Reformation and after 1712, when the Duke of Norfolk completed a new house for his agent in Fargate, Catholics were able to use the private chapel there. Following the demolition of the Lord's House in 1814, part of its grounds was taken for a small, unassuming chapel, opened 1816, with a graveyard along Norfolk Row. The last restrictions on Catholic worship were removed in 1829, and as the congregation was joined first by Italians, and then by increasing numbers of Irish immigrants in the 1840s, proposals for a larger and more impressive church were put forward.

*Weightman & Hadfield*'s designs, in accordance with Pugin's principles, were preceded by a scholarly study of C14 churches in Yorkshire and Lincolnshire. The style they used is a rich and fluent Decorated, strongly influenced by St Andrew, Heckington, and the building is justifiably considered the finest Gothic Revival church in the city. It is cruciform in plan, skilfully contrived to fit the confined site, and comprises a nave with clerestory, side aisles, s porch, transepts and chancel flanked by side chapels. A mortuary chapel opens off the N aisle. In 1878–9 a chapel by *M.E. Hadfield & Son* was added and at the same time the sacristies at the SE corner were extended. Small private crypt by *Vincente Stienlet* under the N transept completed in 1992.

The church can only be viewed properly from Tudor Square to the SE. It presents a dignified and compact composition of high gables and steeply pitched slate roofs, with the slender stone spire, which is its chief glory, crowning the imposing square tower at the sw corner [32]. The stone is coursed sandstone with ashlar dressings. In his *History of the Gothic Revival* (1872), Eastlake commented favourably on the stonework, praising the delicacy and sharpness of the mouldings and the chiselled finish which gives the walls an attractive texture. The octagonal tower of the Lady Chapel, sprouting rather awkwardly from the s transept aisle, has a little spire with herringbone leadwork. Above the door at the Norfolk Street corner is a **sculpture** of the Annunciation, set in a niche with graceful ogee canopies, from *Thomas Earp*'s studio. To Norfolk Row gates and railings by *Maria Hanson*, 1997.

32. Cathedral Church of St Marie, Norfolk Row, by Weightman & Hadfield, 1847–50

The **interior** is subdued and spacious, with an uninterrupted view from the nave through the chancel to the great E window. Lofty **nave** of six bays with panelled wagon roof. Seven clerestory windows were added in 1889 by *Charles Hadfield*, distinguished from the originals by their quatrefoil tracery. Plain arcades with clustered quatrefoil piers and chamfered arches – the hoodmould stops are carved heads of male saints (S side) and female saints (N side) by *Charles James*. The narrow mortuary chapel opens off two bays in the N aisle, the capital of the massive central pier carved with a choir of heavenly angels. Unusual tiled **dado**, *c.* 1886: a memorial to several priests with one shown at death with his angelic escort to heaven. Short N transept with Chapel of the Blessed Sacrament to the E.

The **chancel** [33] is now more open than was originally intended. The rood screen and choir stalls that enclosed its w side were removed in the major reordering of 1970–2. At the same time the Minton tiled floor was replaced with polished marble. Magnificent painted and gilded arch-braced hammerbeam roof with ogee wind-braces and traceried spandrels. The angels are by *Arthur Hayball*. The stonework is more richly detailed here, mostly by *Charles James*, including the finely carved angel stops to the chancel arch and the lusciously crocketed gables of the sedilia. The debt to Heckington is even more obvious in the e window's gloriously flowing tracery.

Enclosed by screens, the small **Chapel of St Joseph** s of the chancel was originally the Norfolk Chantry Chapel; the Minton floor tiles include the ducal emblem and motto. Overlooking it is the tiny Lady Chapel, built as the Munster Memorial Chapel by *M.E. Hadfield & Son* 1878–9, and now used by Sheffield's Polish community. It is reached from the s transept by a winding stone stair. The open arcade of its octagonal shrine is supported on two piers of green Pyrenean marble, the other sides have richly sculpted blind arcades. These and the exquisite little lierne vault above were carved by *Thomas Earp*.

Until the reordering this was one of the most completely and artistically furnished and decorated Catholic churches in the country. Much has gone but the quality of the surviving **furnishings** reflects the fact that they are by the leading designers and craftsmen of the day. Chancel **reredos** (detached), 1850, designed by *Pugin*, sculptor *Theodore Phyffers*. (The High Altar by them was replaced in 1921.) The **reredos** in St Joseph's Chapel, 1872, designed by *Charles Hadfield* in early c14 style and sculpted in Caen stone by *Thomas Earp*. The relievo of St Joseph's death is by *Theodore Phyffers*. Marble **altar** in the Lady Chapel by *Boulton* of Cheltenham, *c.* 1878. The **rood** of 1850 (now suspended), decorated by *Henry Taylor Bulmer*, with figures by *Arthur Hayball*. In the n transept two richly decorated **shrines** by *M.E. Hadfield & Son*. The Shrine of Our Lady has a statue by *Johann Petz* of Munich, *c.* 1850, with a base including Frosterley marble columns, 1866, and a carved and gilded oak canopy, 1872, with paintings by *Westlake*. Also the Shrine of the Sacred Heart, 1879, the statue and the marble work of the base by *Boulton*, the oak reredos carved by *Thomas Earp* and gilded and decorated by *Lavers, Barraud & Westlake*. **Organ case**, 1875, designed by *J.F. Bentley*, Charles Hadfield's friend and mentor, and carved in Austrian oak by *J.E. Knox*. The wrought-iron entrance **screen** to the Chapel of the Blessed Sacrament and the **screen** between the chapel's eastern bay and the chancel, 1850, by *J. & C. Ellis*. The crypt has **gates** by *Giuseppe Lund* and **crucifix** and **mosaic** by *Fenwick Lawson*.

**Stained glass**: e window, 1850, designed by *George Goldie*, made by *Wailes*. w window, 1850, designed by *Pugin*, made by *Hardman*. Both have sacred events in several tiers, but the superior quality of Pugin's design is patent. Other windows of the 1850s–60s by *Hardman* and *Wailes*. e windows of the Chapel of St Joseph, 1872, by *Lavers, Barraud &*

33. St Marie, chancel, with organ case by J.F. Bentley, 1875, and E window by George Goldie, 1850

*Westlake* who also made the two windows on the Lady Chapel staircase to designs by *J.F. Bentley*, 1879 and 1884. s transept w window by *Patrick Reyntiens*, 1982, to commemorate the new diocese, depicting the Virgin Mary as patroness and the Padley Martyrs executed in 1588.

**Monuments**: (Mortuary Chapel) Effigy of Fr Charles Pratt, d.1849, holding a model of the church, by *Thomas Earp* as assistant to George Myers. Originally in the chancel. (N transept) Matthew Hadfield, d.1885, by *Charles Hadfield*, with alabaster Pietà sculpted by *Frank Tory*, the design from a cast supplied to Matthew Hadfield by Pugin.

# Town Hall

Pinstone Street

Built 1890–7 by *E.W. Mountford*, extended 1914–23 by *F.E.P. Edwards*, the City Architect. Sheffield's grandest civic building, the Town Hall provided the city with a long-awaited municipal showpiece. For over fifty years the Council's officers and members had endured the inconvenience of working from offices scattered round the town and holding meetings in the Cutlers' Hall, Assembly Rooms and Public Library. Proposals to build a proper Town Hall were invariably defeated on the grounds of cost and it was not until 1889 that the decision was finally made, despite arguments that ratepayers' money was better applied to street improvements and housing for the poor.

The site had been purchased three years earlier as part of a general improvement scheme and was crammed with dilapidated properties either side of New Church Street, which was extinguished when the area was cleared for the new building. The awkward triangular site, with its shortest side facing Pinstone Street, presented a challenge but 178 architects entered the **competition**, which was held in 1889–90 with Alfred Waterhouse as judge. Mountford was successful despite strong protests from Flockton & Gibbs who claimed that their 'patent' design

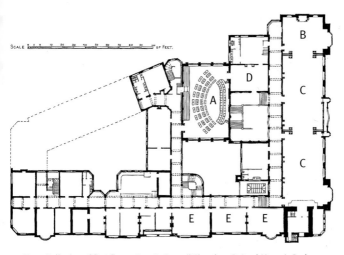

34. Town Hall, plan of first floor, 1897. A, Council Chamber; B, Lord Mayor's Parlour; C, Reception Rooms; D, Ante Room; E, Committee Rooms

35. Town Hall, Pinstone Street, by E.W. Mountford, 1890–7

for municipal buildings had been incorporated into the additional instructions for the finalists and used in Mountford's scheme. Mountford responded to the difficulties of the site by placing all the principal rooms on the first floor, with the grand staircase hall in the centre. The ceremonial rooms face w to Pinstone Street, with Committee Rooms on the N side of the building and the Council Chamber to the E of the staircase. Ground-floor offices face outwards or into two small internal courtyards separated by N–S corridors across the middle of the plan. The building contract was awarded in 1890 to Edmund Gabbutt of Liverpool whose tender amounted to £83,945. Over the next six years Mountford produced over 500 working drawings detailing not only the design of the building but all the interior fixtures and fittings, many of which were supplied by local firms. The building was lit by electricity from the beginning and Mountford's decorative electroliers survive in the principal rooms. The final cost of the building, excluding the site, was over £134,000.

## The Town Hall's Sculpture

The rich decorative scheme of **stone carving**, both externally and internally, was devised by *Mountford* and *F.W. Pomeroy*, the principal sculptor, and expresses a particular local pride in Sheffield's history and the art and skill of its workforce. At first-floor level either side of the main entrance a frieze of figures represents the arts and industries of Sheffield, the left side including architects, sculptors and artists together with workers in the fine trades – electroplaters, buffer girls, ivory turners and cutlers, preceded by the goddess of light and knowledge. To the right a procession of smiths, grinders, hammermen, smelters and miners follows the goddess of plenty bearing a cornucopia. In the spandrels of the doorway are graceful female figures symbolizing the power of steam and electricity, while above the balcony arch heroic figures of Thor and Vulcan support the city's coat of arms. Above them all at the top of the central gable is a life-size statue of Queen Victoria surrounded by symbols of her dominion of the seas. On Surrey Street are figures of Peace and War and in the gable above the Council Chamber facing Cheney Row, Justice. Elsewhere heads of animals represent the Empire, with an owl for Wisdom and roses and sheaves of corn as the emblems of Yorkshire and Sheffield.

The **exterior** is a lively interpretation of Northern Renaissance architecture. Mullioned and transomed windows, with small-paned casements, and a profusion of dormers, gables, pinnacles, turrets and chimneys, form a picturesque composition which is enhanced by the tall asymmetrically placed angle tower at the junction of Pinstone and Surrey Streets. The exterior is faced in Derbyshire sandstone from Stoke Hall quarry, the steeply pitched roofs are covered in green Westmorland slates laid in diminishing courses and the turrets roofed in copper.

The symmetry and skilful articulation of the two-storey main front to Pinstone Street, raised on a semi-basement, gives a fitting dignity to the principal entrance, which takes the form of a gatehouse with first-floor balcony under a deep arch. A strong vertical emphasis is provided by the gabled central and end bays; the latter have elegant canted oriels with glazing bars typical of the late C17. At the N corner the clock tower, 210 ft (64 metres) high and topped by the figure of Vulcan, is set slightly back in deference to the main façade and leads into the long elevation on Surrey Street. This rises to five storeys in the gables and is enlivened by the projecting porch, oriel windows and the two-bay loggia on the second floor. The corner of the Norfolk Street return is marked by an octagonal tower with a turret and lantern, with a nearly identical tower at the southern end on Cheney Row, part of the L-shaped extension of 1923. This is a sensitive addition in matching style and materials, which provided much-needed accommodation, including the members'

36. Electrolier in the staircase hall, by F.W. Pomeroy, *c.* 1896

library, a conference room and a new rates hall with a glass-domed roof. (The 1977 extension on Norfolk Street was demolished in 2001–2.)

The entrance **vestibule** is secured by decorative wrought-iron gates, designed by *Mountford* and made by *J.W. Singer & Sons* of Frome. The walls are lined with polished Hopton Wood stone with Ionic columns of Irish marble on pedestals between the bays. The figures carved on the panels within the six blind arches depict 'civic' and 'eternal' virtues – Religion, Labour and Patriotism on the left, and Knowledge, Charity and Prudence on the right (*see also* topic box, p. 63). The vestibule's sombre tone provides a dramatic contrast with the main **Staircase Hall** which is flooded with light from the lantern above. Here the lower walls are lined with Barrow-in-Furness limestone, the blind arcade above

37. The Council Chamber

faced with a sumptuous confection of grey Derbyshire marble banded with red and black Devonshire marbles. Rising from the N wall the half-turn staircase has balusters of Derbyshire spar and a handrail and plinth of green Connemara marble, with steps of white Sicilian marble to match the floor. All the marblework was executed by *E.E. Twigg & Co.* of the Ashford Marble Works, Derbyshire. On the inner face of the entrance arcade a carving of the local legend of the Dragon of Wantley shows Sir Thomas More despatching the monster on the left while its hapless victims struggle in the tangled branches on the right. Further carving, displaying the city's manufactures, arts and crafts, enlivens the frieze below the richly panelled plasterwork of the deep-coved cornice. The magnificent bronze electrolier suspended in the centre of the hall has four graceful winged figures, designed and modelled by *Pomeroy*, standing on a globe encircled with the signs of the zodiac [36]. Each originally held a lamp, symbolically lighting the four corners of the world. On the staircase are two sculptures in white marble by *E. Onslow Ford*. On the first landing a statue of the 15th Duke of Norfolk, Sheffield's first Lord Mayor, 1897, sitting in reflective pose, 1900. On the s landing a bust of Queen Victoria on a pedestal, 1898.

Opening s of the stair is the Ante-Room, with oak-panelled dado and chimneypiece with segmental top, the grate of hammered and raised copper. It leads to the **Council Chamber** [37], which is decorated in Northern Renaissance style with elaborate plaster ceiling with pendant bosses and delicate flowers and foliage in the panels. The half-height oak panelling, the Ionic aedicule for the Lord Mayor's chair and the exquisite floral carving on the Aldermanic bench, were all executed by *Johnson & Appleyard* of Sheffield. The chamber was lit on three sides until the 1920s extension was built, when a new public gallery replaced the windows on the E wall. The members' library and the conference room in the extension both have marble chimneypieces, the latter room with early examples of stainless steel fireplaces.

The principal suite of three reception rooms extends along the main w front, opening off the marble-lined grand corridor. They all have carved oak panelling and were designed with oak dividing screens that ingeniously disappear into the roof space to create a single room. At the s end, the **Lord Mayor's Parlour,** with an elaborate stone and alabaster chimneypiece standing on four columns of polished green Irish marble. Carved panels represent Wisdom and Valour guarding the gates of the city and illustrate Psalm 127, 'Except the Lord build the house, their labour is but lost that build it; except the Lord keep the city, the watchman waketh but in vain'. The grate is from a design by *Alfred Stevens*. The other two rooms, which form a suite 150 ft long, have elaborately carved arched niches with columns in the oak panelling and a musicians' gallery at the N end. The three Committee Rooms on the N corridor have oak dados and decorative ceilings and fireplaces.

# City Hall

Barker's Pool

Sheffield's monumental City Hall, built 1928–32 by *E. Vincent Harris*, ranks among the finest civic buildings of the interwar period and displays Harris' masterly handling of form and style on a grand scale. In the C19 the town's need for a large hall for concerts, meetings and lectures was recognized, but from 1873 the new Albert Hall, on the s side of Barker's Pool, provided a suitable venue as a commercial venture, and so a public hall was not included in the specification for the Town Hall in 1889. A proposal in 1916 that the City Council might buy the Albert Hall was rejected in favour of a new building and in 1918 the scheme gathered momentum after agreement that the hall would be the city's war memorial. The site opposite the Albert Hall was purchased and in 1920 a competition was held for a 'simple and dignified design'. *Harris*'s winning entry, in a contemporary Classical Revival style, was less austere than the designs used for the completed building, whose

38. City Hall, by E. Vincent Harris, 1920–32

construction was repeatedly delayed by the fragile state of public finances during the Depression. The final cost was £443,000, for a building containing a large hall seating 2,300 and the smaller Memorial Hall for 550. Ballroom, bars and smaller function rooms in the basement were added to the brief in 1925.

The impressive massing of the building is achieved by large, compactly composed blocks of unrelieved outline, constructed in reinforced concrete and brick and faced with Darley Dale stone. The two concrete beams supporting the entire roof were, at the time, among the largest ever made, using 25 tons of local steel reinforcing bars.

At the **front** the entrance portico of eight giant Corinthian columns *in antis* is flanked by the severe blank walling of the main elevation. There is no pediment. The decoration of the entablature originally proposed was omitted from the final design, leaving only the simple dentil cornice and narrow frieze of the central block. This and the other stone carving is the work of *Frank Tory & Sons*. The apsidal N end (*see* topic box, p. 110), which contains the semi-circular Memorial Hall, has rusticated stonework and the surprising feature of giant square pillars rising several feet higher than the wall and carrying a heavy entablature on Corinthian capitals [19].

Three arched doorways with splendidly crested wrought-iron gates lead into the galleried **entrance hall**. Above walls lined with bands of Hopton Wood stone the vaulted ceiling has three saucer domes and brightly coloured painted and gilded decoration by *George Kruger Gray*. Incorporating heraldic devices, this has a slightly 'Merrie England' quality that is unexpected after the classical solemnity of the exterior. The inner doorways and the balustrades of the little vaulted gallery are of veined black Ashburton marble. The great domed **Oval Hall** fills the centre of the building and has two sweeping balconies at the S end. It is lit by a magnificent elliptical roof-light set in an elaborate radiating coffered ceiling, with a huge polyhedral lantern suspended from the centre. Behind the stage, decorative iron grilles painted in scarlet and gold and set between Corinthian columns screen the Willis concert organ. Two Assyrian lions carved by *John Hodge*, which originally flanked the central stage entrance, were removed in 1962. The **Memorial Hall** has a small curved balcony and a coffered ceiling. In the basement is a grand Ballroom with columned arcades and richly decorated beamed ceiling. The adjoining vestibule also has giant Doric columns and painted decoration.

39. Entrance hall, with decoration by George Kruger Gray, c. 1931

# Cutlers' Hall

Church Street

Built 1832 by *Samuel Worth* and *Benjamin Broomhead Taylor*, extended 1865–7 by *Flockton & Abbott*, and 1888 by *J.B. Mitchell-Withers*. One of Sheffield's finest buildings, it presents a handsome dignified Grecian exterior; internally, an unexpectedly opulent and extensive sequence of rooms, a showcase for assembly, display, feasting and entertainment – the annual Cutlers' Feast is the opportunity for local business to meet and influence the wider political and commercial world.

Cutlery has been manufactured in Sheffield for over 700 years. Chaucer mentions a Sheffield thwitel (knife) in the '*Reeve's Tale*'. The London Cutlers' Company dates from the C12; in Sheffield the Company of Cutlers in Hallamshire was founded in 1624, and it became the leading Company in the C18. A guild of craftsmen, it safeguarded and controlled its trading interests, apprenticeships and the trademark '*Sheffield*'. By the C18, Sheffield's administration was represented in three neighbouring buildings – the parish church (*see* p. 45), the old Town Hall (dem.), and the Cutlers' Hall. From 1860 the Company incorporated the steel manufacturers and thereby became a larger and more powerful body, still regulating its own trades but additionally promoting wider social, educational and transport initiatives.

The present hall is the third: the first (1638) was possibly, and the second (1725) certainly, on the same site. Hemmed in by adjacent properties, the site is awkwardly shaped and there are no other publicly visible elevations. Daylight penetration into the depths of the building is limited so, except for the rooms facing the street, only skylights, clerestories and obscured glazing permit subdued illumination of the inner reaches. Three halls dominate the interior; offices, kitchens and service spaces taking second place. Successive Masters Cutler have commemorated their reign by donating improvements or additions – and frequent redecoration over the years means that the interior is now a complicated architectural palimpsest.

Seen from Church Street, the flat-headed archway to the left and the front door, embracing two giant Corinthian columns, *distyle in antis*, in Derbyshire sandstone ashlar, define the extent of the original 1832 building. Its design was won in competition in 1831, predating by just three months Henry Roberts's similar design for the central part of the eastern front of the Fishmongers' Hall, London. To the right, two further identical columns front an extension of 1888, won in

40. Cutlers' Hall, Church Street, by S. Worth & B.B. Taylor, 1831–2, extended by J.B. Mitchell-Withers, 1888

competition by Worth's pupil, *J.B. Mitchell-Withers*. This addition altered the balance of the original design: the main door now appears to be central, with the archway as an appendage. Above, lurking behind the coats of arms, the attic storey, an unfortunate excrescence by *Alfred E. Turnell*, 1928.

The original plan form, still identifiable, is based on a tripartite schema which is three bays wide (narrow, wide, narrow), corresponding to archway, giant order and entrance door, by, in depth, three (wide) bays. This is similar to the grander c18 London town houses or early c19 clubs: three bays wide by three bays deep, with a staircase in the centre giving access to a circuit of reception rooms on the first floor, but here the circuit is broken (because of planning problems with neighbouring access) and the Old Banqueting Hall is turned through almost 90 degrees, to project into the rear of the site.

The **entrance lobby** and **hall**, with Doric columns heralding the main imperial staircase (doubled in size 1865–7), leads to a **vestibule** on the first floor. Its sycamore and mahogany panelling and electroliers, from the former White Star liner *RMS Olympic*, were installed here in 1936. This opens into a handsome **Reception Room**, with bay windows at either end, both with pairs of Ionic columns. Across the vestibule is the **Old Banqueting Hall**, 70 ft by 25 ft (21.3 by 7.6 metres). Giant

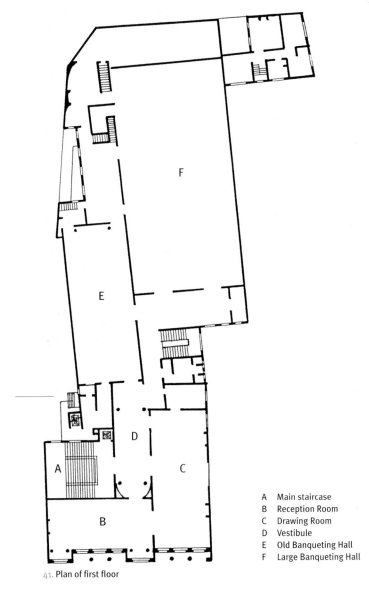

41. Plan of first floor

A   Main staircase
B   Reception Room
C   Drawing Room
D   Vestibule
E   Old Banqueting Hall
F   Large Banqueting Hall

Corinthian pilasters define three bays, the narrower end ones with shallow segmented glazed vaults above, the wider central one with dome on pendentives and lantern light. At the far end, a musicians' gallery, framed by a Palladian archway with Corinthian columns supporting entablatures either side of an uncomfortable depressed arch.

*Flockton & Abbott's* **Large Banqueting Hall**, 100 ft by 50 ft (30.4 by 15.2 metres), with ladies' and minstrels' galleries, was built on land to the w in 1865–7. Strident Italian Renaissance-style interior. A high black

Belgian marble dado, incorporating pedestals supporting pairs of engaged Scagliola Corinthian columns, single columns at the ends, dividing the large area of windowless walling into panels. On the frieze of a continuous entablature are key dates in the company's history, the quotation from Chaucer's 'Reeve's Tale' and words from Ruskin in praise of Sheffield's workmanship. Above are clerestory lunettes in a coved ceiling. The effect is unexpectedly overpowering and contrasts harshly with the softer treatment of the Old Banqueting Hall. Connected by further vestibules is the **Drawing Room** in the 1888 extension, with gilded and impressive Grecian decoration; this room in turn connects with the Reception Room (q.v.), both rooms overlooking Church Street.

On the ground floor, the undercroft below the Large Banqueting Hall forms the **Hadfield Hall** (formerly the Workmen's Hall), with eight free-standing Doric columns and limited, plain decoration. Two murals by *Jean Clark*, 1954: one celebrating the industrialist Sir Robert Hadfield, the other, entitled Joy, commemorating the accession of Elizabeth II. Then the small but dignified **Muniment Room** and, opposite, the **Hughes Room** – long, narrow and elegantly proportioned, entered at the narrower end, with at the far end, a Corinthian segmental pedimented mantelpiece, under an arch spanning the width of the room. Next, in the 1888 extension, the Master and Mistress Cutlers' Rooms, as a suite either side of a spacious panelled foyer, 1956–8, by *Hadfield Cawkwell & Davidson*. The foyer connects via sliding doors with the entrance hall, directly opposite the foot of the main staircase. The **Master Cutler's Room** has a richly-carved oak mantelpiece, with cartouches and strapwork, dated 1623. Originally in Norton Hall, Derbyshire, it was rescued from Derwent Hall in 1919 and installed here in 1928. Outside and beyond, in the far depths of the site, are various service rooms and, in very cramped quarters, the kitchens and a house (*c.* 1888), originally for the Beadle.

Roger Harper

# Millennium Galleries and Winter Garden

Arundel Gate and Surrey Street

A pair of inspirational, landmark buildings by *Pringle Richards Sharratt* who won the commission in competition in 1995. The galleries were completed in 2001, the Winter Garden in 2002. They were conceived as the most important elements of the Heart of the City Project (*see* topic box, p. 96) and as covered links in a new pedestrian route between the station and city centre, helping restore part of the urban fabric that had been unravelled by postwar road schemes and redevelopment.

The **Millennium Galleries** provide 1,900 square metres of temporary exhibition space as well as permanent displays of the Ruskin Collection (*see* topic box) and the city's fine metalwork and silverware collections. The building eschews ostentation, presenting an elegant and quietly understated front to Arundel Gate, and is set into the slope of the hill

## Ruskin and Sheffield

In 1871 the Victorian writer and art critic John Ruskin (1819–1900) founded the Guild of St George, a body of Companions under his personal leadership as Master, who were to help him achieve a variety of social reforms. He published his ideas on the ways the Guild would relieve the misery and ignorance inflicted by a capitalist, industrialized society in a series of letters addressed to working people, proposing to improve their lives by buying land to provide agricultural employment and setting up schools and museums to develop their minds. Impressed by the skill and craftsmanship of its metalworkers and the beauty of the countryside around it, he chose Sheffield as the place to start his reforms and the St George's Museum was opened in a small house at Walkley in 1875. The collections included original paintings as well as specially commissioned copies of great works of art, illuminated manuscripts, rare books in fine bindings, drawings and photographs of buildings in Italy and France, plaster casts of architectural details from the Doge's Palace in Venice, minerals and precious stones, and exquisite studies of plants and birds, some by Ruskin himself.

The collection, which remains the property of the Guild, is now displayed in the Millennium Galleries where it continues to stimulate appreciation of the beauty of art and nature and to attract admirers of Ruskin from all over the world.

42. Millennium Galleries, Arundel Gate, by Pringle Richards Sharratt, 1995–2001

with the galleries on the upper level over a service undercroft. The glazed front is set within a slender modular frame of white concrete and reveals the ground-floor café to the bustle of Arundel Gate. Long silver louvres screen the Long Gallery above. Inside, a light and spacious entrance hall has escalators to the first-floor 'avenue' which both serves as an indoor street to the Winter Garden and gives access to the five galleries on its left side. The roof comprises a series of lateral barrel vaults, only partly visible externally, of fine white pre-cast concrete with columns and beams of the same material, giving a cool tranquillity to the interior. This ethereal quality is enhanced by diffused natural light, created by the imaginative use of glass blocks in the avenue's roof vaults and N wall and cleverly reflected light from clerestories. The largest gallery is flexibly planned with movable full-height screens that run parallel with the vaults. The last of the other three exhibition galleries, containing the Ruskin Collection (*see* topic box, p. 74), is separated from the adjacent Winter Garden by a glazed wall. This has glass panels by *Keiko Mukaide* symbolizing water and clouds, creating an appropriate and stunning juxtaposition of art and nature.

The soaring arches and curved glass roof of the exotically planted **Winter Garden** is a skilful blend of the traditions of glass-roofed public spaces established in the C19 by glasshouses, shopping arcades and railway stations. Spanning a space 230 ft by 72 ft (70 by 22 metres) its frame is formed from twenty-one parabolic arches of laminated strips of untreated larch, which are gradually weathering to a silvery grey.

43. Winter Garden, Tudor Square, by Pringle Richards Sharratt, 1995–2002

Slender timber purlins and glazing bars create a fine framework between the arches to hold over 2,000 square metres of glass. The primary arches are supported at ground level on sculptural steel cradles, while the intermediate arches finish at wall height and sit on elegant wooden raking struts. From the arches at each end, which lean outward to create canopies over the street entrances, they step up to the 72 ft (22 metre) high central section. This will allow the taller species of trees, including Norfolk Island pine and eucalyptus, to reach an impressive maturity, creating a luxuriant canopy above the paving and planting below.

# The Universities

# University of Sheffield

The University of Sheffield began as Firth College in 1879, founded by the steelmaker and philanthropist Mark Firth, who was inspired by lectures held in Sheffield by the Cambridge University Extension Movement from 1875. The original building survives in Leopold Street (*see* p. 117), close to the Medical School, with which it, and the Technical School in St George's Square, were amalgamated in 1895. *E.M. Gibbs of Flockton & Gibbs* was retained as architect to the fledgeling University, founded 1905, an association that was to last almost until his death in 1935. Initial plans drawn up in 1900 envisaged the entire University based at St George's Square, but by 1902 approval for the purchase of a site on Western Bank was given, with buildings by Gibbs for administration, library, Faculties of Arts and Pure Sciences and the Medical School, completed by 1909. Only technical departments remained at St George's Square. Thus the split campus was a feature of the University from its earliest days.

Plans to extend the buildings at Western Bank in the 1930s by *Lanchester & Lodge*, who also carried out work at Leeds University during this period, were only partly realized. The University campus

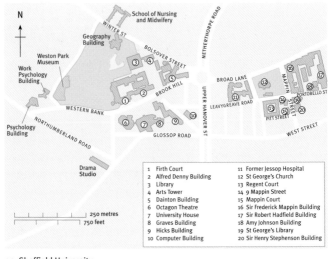

44. **Sheffield University**

developed no further until the postwar era, first with minor additions by *J. W. Beaumont & Sons* but then from 1953 with major extensions (for new library, arts building and students' union), won in competition by the youthful *Gollins, Melvin, Ward & Partners* whose overtly modern design was what the judges, who included F.R.S. Yorke, were seeking. The scheme was subject to many detail changes but the essentials of it are still recognizable. The subsequent growth of the firm had much to do with their success in Sheffield, beating ninety-eight other entries including a radical one from *Peter & Alison Smithson* [45]. Following on from the linear plan of their entry in the City of London's Golden Lane competition of 1952, they designed a continuous structure incorporating a pedestrian deck that angled round the contours of the site much as the Park Hill flats (*see* p. 207) were shortly to do. *James Stirling* proposed a tough slab for the arts building with no attempt to disguise service ducts and plant and the forms of the lecture theatres expressed externally, a characteristic later realized in his Engineering Building, Leicester University (1959–63).

The historic division of the Western Bank and St George's sites was complicated by the building of the inner ring road in the early 1970s. Plans by *Arup Associates* in 1970 to unite the two sites with a covered

45. The Smithson entry in the 1952 University competition

46. Firth Court, by E.M. Gibbs, 1903–5

pedestrian route were unrealized and remain unresolved in spite of a central campus masterplan of 1995 by *HLM Architects* and the *University Estates Department*. The campus today lacks architectural coherence, partly through the piecemeal acquisition of much of the site and partly through the variety of styles represented although, by the end of the C20 the application of red brick was seen as a unifying element. The boldness of the 1950s is noticeably lacking in some of the most recent buildings which have more in common with speculative office blocks than with their distinguished predecessors.

## Western Bank

The heart of the University is **Firth Court** [46] of 1903–5 by *E.M. Gibbs*. It, together with the quadrangle behind, is Tudor style in hard Accrington red brick. Large mullioned and transomed windows, with an oriel in the centre, indicate the grandeur of the rooms on the first floor. Towers, placed well back, rise at both ends of the building; the taller one on the left serves as a visible link with the rear ranges. Internally, there is a plain stair hall of yellow brickwork banded in fine ashlar sandstone (recovered from the early C19 Western House formerly on the site). The planning is simple with a central corridor on both floors decorated in the same style. The name Firth Hall was given to the central room on the first floor above the entrance. It has a fine scissor-braced oak roof with substantial pendants hanging from the trusses but much of this work is now hidden by a suspended ceiling. Also on the first floor is the **War Memorial**, 1926, by *H. St John Harrison*, a canopied shrine whose pillars support an internally-illuminated alabaster bowl that casts light on the names of the fallen. Three rooms have decorated plaster ceilings. Those in the former Professors' common-room and the Norfolk Room are genuine C17, much restored and the gift of the Duke of Norfolk. The ceiling in the Chancellor's Room is of 1905.

Connected at the w end of the main façade by a single-storey link, originally open but subsequently glazed, is the octagonal former **Library** of 1909 also by *Gibbs*, a little like a chapter house, in matching Tudor style with battlements and windows grouped in fours, the fenestration extending the full height of the building. Gibbs made an extensive study of library design, visiting a number of North American universities including Harvard, Columbia, MIT and Montreal. The Library was the gift (£10,000) of the steelmaker William Edgar Allen who argued with Gibbs over the plans on grounds of cost and style. He went so far as to have the elderly *Jean-Louis Pascal* prepare an alternative, characteristically Beaux-Arts-influenced, design but kept the octagonal form. The University sought a second opinion from *Aston Webb* who favoured a rectangular plan. Gibbs held his ground, the only casualty being the original lantern roof which was replaced by a pyramidal roof with roof-lights. Internally, radiating perimeter bays on two floors surrounded a double-height space with a central issue desk. The upper floor is galleried. Arched arcading over the bays with carved heads by *Frank Tory & Sons* of Mark Firth, Sir Henry Stephenson, W.M. Hicks, Charles Harding Firth, George Franklin, H.K. Stephenson, Edgar Allen and E.M. Gibbs. Now occupied by the University's senior officers.

Behind Firth Court is a 154 ft by 110 ft quadrangle, in homage to the ancient universities on which it was modelled, with ranges of 1905 originally for the Faculties of Arts and Pure Sciences (w) and the Medical School (N). Like Firth Court, they are Tudor in style but much modified to meet C20 requirements, the decoration simplified, the windows enlarged and with glazing for laboratories above the parapet. Particularly impressive N elevation of closely spaced buttresses and deep windows with arched heads. This was extended in 1914 by *Gibbs* with the intention of completing the quadrangle with an E range but this was only achieved in 2002–4 with the addition of science laboratories by *Bond Bryan Partnership*, which contain no reference to historical styles. A fully glazed top floor was angled to avoid obscuring a fine oriel on the 1914 building, which is continued E to Winter Street, with an extension of 1938–41 by *Lanchester & Lodge* all in matching red brick, still nominally Tudor but less decorative than Gibbs's work.

Facing Western Bank, set back, the **Finance Department**, 1962, by *Gollins, Melvin, Ward & Partners*, originally black glass curtain-walled, but clad in brick in 1992 and given a cornice and a slated mansard roof, destroying the architects' intention of providing a neutral link between its red brick neighbours, Firth Court and the **Alfred Denny Building**, 1971, a very large slab by *Gollins, Melvin, Ward & Partners*. Shown as a curtain-walled design in their 1953 competition entry but built with brick cladding to harmonize with Firth Court and with the ground floor recessed behind rectangular pilotis. The numerous identical square windows punched out of the walls, their frames slightly recessed and barely visible, recall Alvar Aalto's Baker House at MIT (1947–8), but without its sinuous curves the effect of such treatment to seven floors is overpowering.

To the NE, we come to the University's two set-piece buildings by *Gollins, Melvin, Ward & Partners*: the Library and the Arts Tower [47], the view of which from the lake in Weston Park is justly famous. Linked by a bridge at first-floor level, they are intended to be read together in a manner similar to the block and the podium of Skidmore Owings & Merrill's Lever House, New York (1950–2). The **Library**, built in 1955–9, was the first important modern building to be completed by any English university, and Pevsner's view that it 'deserves the prize for the best individual twentieth-century building in Sheffield' is still tenable today. A low square block given strong horizontal emphasis by bands of glazing and Portland stone on a base of blue brick. The Reading Room faces the park, its function indicated by the much higher bands of glazing. The building is entered from the E side and the route to the Reading Room enables one to experience fully the building's spatial qualities. Ascent by a broad staircase to a mezzanine floor, used for exhibition purposes, is followed by a 180-degree turn to the Catalogue Hall and a final 90-degree turn into the handsome open space of the Reading Room with its views over Weston Park, an experience, in spite of contrasts of style and scale, as enjoyable as the sublime entrance to Champneys' John Rylands Library, Manchester. The Catalogue Hall has a 40 ft by 8 ft embroidered wall hanging based on the colours of academic dress, Graduation, 1988, by *Diana Springall*. The Reading Room has two floors of bookstacks (which incorporate ducts for par-tial air-conditioning) along the internal wall, with four further floors of bookstacks below, partly underground, which are accessible to readers. The library is little altered since construction, only the upper bookstack floor within the reading room has been extended, and therein lies a problem for the present. Built for a student population of 2,000 and to hold one million books, it lacks the space to cope with vastly increased demand.

Linked to the Library by a bridge at first-floor level, the twenty-one-storey **Arts Tower**, built 1961–5, acts as the climax of the University and

still dominates both it and the skyline of Sheffield today. Concrete-framed, with an open ground floor, the frame exposed at ground level as sixteen columns supporting a 5 ft thick concrete slab with a bush-hammered surface. This, together with the reinforced concrete central core containing lifts and services, carries the weight of all the nineteen floors above. The tower is sheathed in glass curtain-walling of rigid modular pattern based on the unit of the window bay with narrow corner bays. At the top, slender reinforced concrete mullions extend to form a louvred screen around the motor room and plant. This provides a crisp termination and equates to an attic storey, completing a classical tripartite form. The tower's open ground floor, the strong vertical emphasis of the mullions and the screening of services owes much to Mies van der Rohe and Philip Johnson's Seagram Building, New York (1958) – developed more faithfully by Gollins, Melvin, Ward & Partners at the Commercial Union tower in the City of London (1963–9). The Arts Tower is, however, entirely concrete-framed, unlike its American forerunner. Gollins, Melvin & Ward's original plans were for a twelve-storey block. The brief was changed quite late and the proposed arrangement of four lifts, inadequate to deal with the flow of students at peak times, was replaced by a paternoster lift and two conventional lifts. The lifts open onto a mezzanine floor within an open space compromised somewhat by later bridges and stairs. These circulation areas on the entrance and lower floors are extremely generous in space with white Sicilian marble and Danish wood panelling together with locally produced stainless steel handrails. Two underground floors contain nine lecture theatres. The open space in front of the Arts Tower, used as a car park since its construction, cries out for imaginative landscaping.

To the NW on the edge of Weston Park in Winter Street is the **Geography Building** by *William Whitfield*, 1968–71, exemplifying the move from the formalist planning by Gollins, Melvin, Ward & Partners to a looser, more organic approach. The need to incorporate large cartographic drawing offices produced a group of interlinked hexagons of varying heights, clustered around a central lift and stair-tower, framed by a close-knit grid of exposed concrete beams with brick and glass infill. Inside, triangulated coffered ceilings. Opposite, across Winter Street behind tall walls, the **School of Nursing and Midwifery** built as the Borough Hospital for Infectious Diseases in 1877–81 by *S.L. Swann*. An open-ended quadrangle of central administration buildings with a spired tower and four ward blocks in bright red brick Ruskinian Gothic. The blocks, with lavatory turrets angled at the ends, are linked by glass-walled additions by *Race Cottam Associates*, 1995–6. Flat roofs with shallow pierced parapets and railings above. Porter's lodge, 1884. Flemish Renaissance style isolation block added to the E in 1892.

Retracing one's steps to Brook Hill, next is the **Dainton Building** (chemistry laboratories) of 1950–3, by *J.W. Beaumont & Sons*, in a depressingly institutional stripped classicism, surrounded by extensions by *Gollins, Melvin, Ward & Partners*. Those to the w, of 1960–4, are clad in blue glass, grey brick and small tiles with a neutral black-glazed link to the earlier building. The large E block is of 1955–64, remodelled in 2002 by *CPMG Architects Ltd* with a strikingly angled glass façade.

Moving now to the s side of Western Bank, one can cross by means of *Arup Associates'* underpass, the **Concourse** of 1968–9, a highly successful unification of the two halves of the Western Bank campus. The separate carriageways of the road are supported on four-branched piers, gaining just sufficient height to enable a generous and informal pedestrian space to be created. The earliest building on site was *Stephen Welsh*'s **Graves Building** (originally the Student Union) of 1935–6, built of small Maltby bricks in refined but timid Neo-Georgian and now almost overwhelmed by more recent additions. The first of these was **University House** of 1962–3 by *Gollins, Melvin, Ward & Partners,* built on a sloping site and broad rather than high. Very well composed with much glass and grey brick cladding but altered to its detriment with an additional storey in 1978–9, new lift tower in 1992 and the removal of the principal access bridge at first-floor level. The area between the entrance and the Graves Building was filled in quite a spectacular manner in 1996 by *Ward McHugh Associates* who created further offices and a coffee shop linked to the existing building by an atrium with much display of its structural elements. The external curved glass wall of the addition contrasts uncomfortably with the rectangularity of the unaltered parts of the Gollins, Melvin & Ward building. The **Octagon**, also by *Gollins, Melvin, Ward & Partners*, 1982, is a multi-purpose convocation hall. Brick-clad with a quaint pyramidal roof topped by a finial and somewhat self-effacing.

Returning to Western Bank, to the E of the Graves Building is the **Hicks Building**, a 1962 nine-storey slab by *Gollins, Melvin, Ward & Partners* re-clad in brick with a pseudo-classical cornice added, although the lower laboratory block retains its original glass curtain-walling. A free-standing bush-hammered five-storey lecture theatre block lies to the w. Opposite in Hounsfield Road, the **Computer Building**, 1974–6, by *Arup Associates,* the only building from the 1970 plan to be built. Box-like with blockwork chamfered to look like rustication. To the N and E, a few houses give an idea of the area before University expansion, notably two former **Vicarages** by *Flockton & Abbott*, St Paul's (No. 197 Brook Hill) of 1863 and St George's in Favell Road of 1874, both Gothic in brick.

To the w beyond the City Museum (*see* p. 286) are a few outliers. In Western Bank, the **Psychology Building**, 1972–4, by *Renton Howard Wood Levin Partnership*, in the firm's favoured concrete blockwork (cf. the Crucible Theatre, p. 103). V-shaped plan, its form determined by the need for a quiet interior, with the main entrance and lecture room set in the angle and much of the accommodation on the quieter N side. Adjacent to the NE is the **Work Psychology Building** of 1987–8 by the *Architectural Consultancy Service: David Bannister* and *Professor Ken Murta.*

48. Sir Frederick Mappin Building, by Flockton & Gibbs, 1902–13

Steel-framed with two wings meeting at an oblique angle. While the strip glazing echoes its predecessor, a move to vernacular is evident in the buff brick cladding and the hipped roof. The former **Unity Church**, Crookesmoor Road (now student accommodation), 1915, by *J.R. Wigfull*, is Free Gothic red brick with a gabled front. The last big Gothic church to be built for the Unitarians in Britain, it had fine stained glass by *Holiday*. Also in Crookesmoor Road, the **Crookesmoor Building** (Law Department), 1977 by *William Whitfield*. A group of seven octagonal brick pavilions on a sharply sloping site linked at different levels by a cloister-like concrete passage, part glazed, part open, to a taller block with common-room facilities. Effective landscaping of the central courtyard.

## St George's Square and Neighbourhood

The other part of the University developed around the Technical School, founded in 1884 by Sir Frederick Mappin in the former Grammar School (*Woodhead & Hurst*, 1824) in Mappin Street. Extensions were immediately made (*see* below) and the Grammar School subsequently demolished for the **Sir Frederick Mappin Building** [48] (originally the Department of Applied Science). Planned as a single entity but built in three phases, in 1902–13 by *Flockton & Gibbs* (*Gibbs, Flockton & Teather* after 1910).

The style is a robust Wrenaissance, deriving its proportions and use of segmental-headed windows from Gibbs's earlier Technical School (*see* below) but treated much more elaborately with pilasters and prominent quoins. The central three bays are brought forward and embellished with a balustraded parapet with urns, and an open pediment over the central bay, enclosing a circular window, below which is a huge swag. Along the tops of the pilasters, lions' heads hold festoons in their mouths. Three double-height Venetian windows are set within rusticated pilasters and the principal doorway has a round chamfered arch and fine iron gates. The overall effect is busy but not disagreeably so. The wings are plainer with a mixture of segmental and triangular open pediments. The interior has a restrained staircase hall; to the left on the ground floor, is the **John Carr Library**, a handsome room fitted out by *Allinson Ltd*, and, on the first floor, the **Mappin Hall**, oak-panelled with a good plaster ceiling in the Renaissance style, and carving by *Frank Tory & Sons*. Especially fine are the Neo-Baroque door surrounds with big consoles and the carved open pediment at the N end of the room.

Immediately behind, and connected by a bridge at first-floor level, the former **Technical School** of 1885–6 by *Flockton & Gibbs*, the oldest purpose-built building still used by the University. Neo-Georgian, the central bay projecting slightly and given a parapet. Decorative iron circular air vents run around the building, a feature found in most of Gibbs's subsequent work for the University. *Gibbs* designed the **Mining Department Building** in 1926 (extended 1951–7) in a virtually identical style and the plainer **Amy Johnson Building** (formerly the Safety in Mines Research Station) in 1928. N of these buildings along Broad Lane, the utilitarian **Engineering Building** by *J.W. Beaumont & Sons*, 1952–5, and the same firm's equally dull ten-storey **Sir Robert Hadfield Building** (Metallurgy Department), 1961–2, on Portobello Street.

There has been much new building by the University around St George's Square since 1985, replacing several early industrial buildings noted by Pevsner in 1959. The new work takes its cues from the Mappin Building in the use of bright red brick, stone dressings and classical references but much of it is unconvincing. On the s side of the square, in Portobello, **Regent Court** of 1990–2 by *HLM Architects* is an example of this style. If anything even less subtle, two buildings on the w side of Mappin Street, s of Portobello: the **Management School** (*HLM* 1993), taller with stone quoins, and **Mappin Court** (*HLM* 1991), student flats. Opposite these and in contrast to their hackneyed classical detailing, the University's **St George's Library** by *Building Design Partnership*, 1990–1, red brick and box-like but very sophisticated. Minimal classical references point to the influence of Aldo Rossi and Italian Neo-Rationalism. The Reading Room and bookstacks on the first floor are lit by small square windows just below the eaves. At the top of the main stairs, an outstanding engraved glass panel by *David Peace* and *Sally Scott*, depicting images of engineering and two glass slabs or stelae, also by *Peace*, intended to be viewed in three dimensions, the designs changing their relationship as one walks round the library. On the ground floor, built into the wall, is a sculpted keystone of Hercules wearing the head of the Nemean Lion. Removed from the Caledonia Works (1873) formerly on the site. Next the **Sir Henry Stephenson Building**, also by *BDP*, 1987–8, another plain box containing three lecture theatres, seminar rooms and laboratories with a deeply recessed entrance and small windows, its austerity only relieved by a full-height staircase window on the NW corner.

In the centre of St George's Square is the former **Church of St George**, 1821–5, by *Woodhead & Hurst*, an ambitious Commissioners' church, built with a fine ashlar facing in the Perp style. 140 ft W tower with pinnacles and ogee arches to openings and doors, long nave, short chancel, aisles and tall clerestory. Crenellated parapet with very slender pinnacles. It originally had three galleries. A 1994 conversion, by *Peter Wright & Martin Phelps*, placed a lecture theatre in the nave with seating in the former W gallery. A dais was set in the chancel and three floors of student flats built in the aisles. The interior retains its spaciousness and the front panels of the side and rear galleries were reused, although the partial loss of what was a little-altered interior is to be regretted. **Stained glass** back-lit panel by the W door by *Wendy Turner*, 1994, eight brightly coloured squares representing the University faculties. The former **Vestry Hall**, 1965, by *John Needham & R.J. Claridge* has the concrete cross-beams supporting its flat roof cutting through the side wall and is ingeniously built into the raised churchyard.

To the W along the N side of Leavygreave Road, the former **Jessop Hospital for Women**, opened in 1878 and designed by *J.D. Webster* in a rather forbidding late Gothic style with some strange detailing. These include oddly elongated and flattened ogee hoodmouldings over the ground-floor windows and a two-storey oriel at the E corner of the building, with its elaborately carved base bisected by a plain buttress. The central tower lost its top stage during the Second World War. Additional wards to the N added in 1902, also by *Webster*. Extension along St George's Terrace in a simple brick-clad modern style of 1939–40 by *J.M. Jenkinson*. Currently awaiting conversion for University use.

The University has expanded to take in many buildings in Glossop Road. For these and University residences, *see* Broomhill (p. 247) and Broomhall (p. 255); and Endcliffe and Ranmoor (p. 263).*

* We are grateful to Dr Roger Harper for making available his draft text of an architectural history of the University: the opinions expressed here are, however, those of the present authors alone.

# Sheffield Hallam University

Sheaf Street

Sheffield Hallam University has its origins in the College of Technology, planned in 1948 by the City Council as part of its obligations under the 1944 Education Act. It was established in 1950 and temporarily occupied a number of sites in the city. A central college was envisaged from the outset and constructed on the present site to designs by *Gollins, Melvin, Ward & Partners,* 1953–68. It joined with the College of Art in Psalter Lane (*see* p. 236) in 1969 to form Sheffield Polytechnic and with the College of Education at Collegiate Crescent in 1976 (*see* p. 260). This institution became Sheffield City Polytechnic until University status was granted in 1992. Prior to this, it had been agreed to concentrate activities at the city centre and Collegiate Crescent sites only.

The site for the central college, rising steeply above Pond Street, was a difficult one for which *Gollins, Melvin, Ward & Partners* designed an impressively simple and well-related group of three blocks. The focus is the twelve-storey **Owen Building** with the concrete frame exposed and

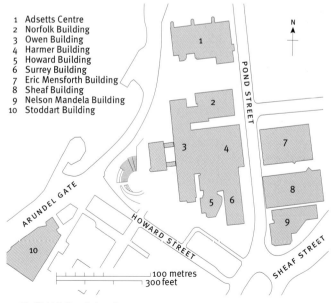

1  Adsetts Centre
2  Norfolk Building
3  Owen Building
4  Harmer Building
5  Howard Building
6  Surrey Building
7  Eric Mensforth Building
8  Sheaf Building
9  Nelson Mandela Building
10 Stoddart Building

100 metres
300 feet

49. Sheffield Hallam University

prominent stair-towers, approached from Arundel Gate by a pedestrian bridge and flanked by a lower meeting hall. On the E side, two spurs: one five-storeyed (**Surrey Building**), the other of eight (**Norfolk Building**) with its lower two storeys recessed behind pilotis, linked to the main block at first-floor level with access from Pond Street by stairs to a deck. Low workshop ranges, stepped up in terraces, stood to the N. Additions were made in the 1970s E of Pond Street, emphasizing the awkward relationship of the blocks to the surrounding streets, something subsequent changes have tried to address.

A limited architectural competition held in 1990 to produce a masterplan for the site was won by the *Bond Bryan Partnership* whose aim was to provide a recognizable heart to the new University with prominent entrances at E and W and a clearly defined route through the campus. The first phase of the development, carried out in 1992–3, has resulted in three new blocks, two of which are dovetailed with the existing buildings and linked by a central atrium, and a concourse over Pond Street joining the two halves of the site. The architects of the new work were *Shepherd Design and Build* and *Building Design Partnership*. There have been few external changes to the existing blocks other than the re-cladding of the main hall on the W side of the Owen Building and part of the Norfolk Building in 1999.

The principal entrance to the site from the SE is now from Sheaf Street. To the W, the impressive mass of the original buildings block the view but the confused foreground reflects the piecemeal development of the site. To the left, the **Nelson Mandela Building** (Student Union), 1977, by *J. Winter*, Director of Planning and Design, is a featureless brick box (due for demolition). Access to the campus is through curved and perforated stainless-steel **gates**, of 1995 by *Amanda King & Christine Twiss* via steps rising alongside the **Eric Mensforth Building**, the former library of 1973 by *Bernard Warren*, City Planning Officer and Architect. Shallow window strips and deep concrete bands relieving the boxy brick exterior give it a pronounced horizontal emphasis. Faced on its S side in red and brown brick to harmonize with its 1990s neighbour, the **Sheaf Building**, a pitched-roofed teaching block, clad in powder-coated metal on the upper floor. Across the pedestrian bridge over Pond Street to the main part of the campus and the **Harmer Building**, also of the 1990s and similarly treated, but with mono-pitch roofs falling towards the E. Five-bay façade on Pond Street with the ground floor set back behind columns that continue at first-floor level as buttresses (a feeble echo of the treatment of the ground floor of the Norfolk Building). Sandwiched between the Owen and Surrey Buildings is the **Howard Building** by *Building Design Partnership*, clad in grey powder-coated panels and stepped down at the S end, providing lecture theatre and academic accommodation. On the S wall, visible from Surrey Lane, a stainless-steel **sculpture** Elements Fire-Steel by *Brian Asquith*, 1965, symbolizing steel making. Originally commissioned for the Westminster Bank in High Street.

50. Atrium, by Shepherd Design & Build and Building Design Partnership, 1992–3

Linking the old and new elements, and a successful focus for the campus, is the **atrium** [50] entered between the Surrey and the Harmer Buildings beneath a glass roof which steps down through five storeys. Inside, at right angles, is a bright and airy quad covered by a space-framed mono-pitch roof. Its exposed structure of complicated tree-like struts is supported by large columns which also carry the access galleries that wrap around three sides of the atrium at each level. Serving these at the s end, a staircase with a single central column and circular landings. This is the strongest element of the composition and mirrored at the N end by an identical feature with curved seating

51. Adsetts Centre, by FaulknerBrowns, 1997

areas at each level. On the E side, the wall surface is animated by teaching rooms (contained within the Harmer Building) cantilevering into the space. At first-floor level one can cross N to the **Adsetts Centre** [51], a library and media resources centre, by *FaulknerBrowns,* 1997 on the site of the original terraced workshops. Their stepped foundations now form a series of bleak and uninviting gardens, enlivened a little by *Laura White's* **Trilogy** of 1995 – three enigmatic sculpted stone blocks. Attention is drawn, however, to the s front of the Centre dramatically falling away below, its face almost entirely concealed by solar shades and four cascading aluminium roofs shaped like aerofoils. This splendid screen hides something altogether more conventional: a concrete frame, partly clad in brick on the exterior but fully exposed within, on which the trusses of the roof are artfully supported. At each level, the open-plan floors are cantilevered out for study areas, gradually receding at the highest level for a double-height space.

A short distance along Arundel Gate to the s on a large triangular site, the **Stoddart Building** business and technology centre, 1994–7, by *Shepherd Design and Build* and *HLM Architects.* A nearly but not quite symmetrical façade on a slight curve, five storeys, mainly clad in buff brick but with the central portion, clad in grey metal panels, brought forward and oversailing the ground floor. What are in effect wings at each end are almost entirely glazed with delicate sun shades.

# City Centre

Walk 1.

# The Town Hall Area

This walk covers most of the area around the Town Hall (*see* Major Buildings, p. 61), now officially the Heart of the City (*see* topic box, p. 96), and the commercial area to the w, s and e. It takes in the three principal public spaces in the city centre – the Peace Gardens, Barker's Pool and Tudor Square, the last now the focus of Sheffield's cultural life. Until the c18 this area was on the fringe of the town, providing fields and rough grazing land crossed only by Pinstone Lane, which formed a route southwards out of town, leading down to Little Sheffield Moor and then on to Chesterfield and London. The natural expansion of the town was accelerated here from the mid-c18 by the laying out of the partly surviving grid of streets in Burgess Street and the nearer part of Alsop Fields. A few three-storey brick Georgian houses remain but much was swept away in the frenzy of redevelopment that followed the street-widening programme begun in 1875. This transformed Pinstone Street from a miserable lane to a bustling 60 ft (18 metre) wide thoroughfare, while the opening of the new Town Hall in 1897 shifted the focus of administrative

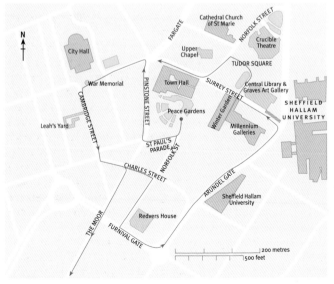

52. Walk 1

53. The Peace Gardens, Pinstone Street, by Sheffield City Council Design & Property Services, 1997–8

and commercial activities away from the markets (*see* Walk 5, p. 144) and reinforced the pace of redevelopment.

The walk begins to the s of the Town Hall in the **Peace Gardens**, one of the city's most impressive and popular civic spaces, which are seen to best advantage with the Hall's long and picturesque s elevation as a backdrop. The gardens occupy the site of St Paul's Church (1720–1) [7], which closed in 1937 after slum clearance in the area had depleted the parish's population. Both it and the churchyard were cleared to make a public open space commemorating the peace promised by the Munich agreement in 1938. Redesigned in 1997–8 as part of the Heart of the City project (*see* topic box, p. 96), by the city's *Design and Property Services* and incorporating artwork by *Brian Asquith* (metalworker), *Tracey Heyes* (ceramicist) and *Richard Perry* (stone carver), which celebrates the natural and industrial aspects of the city's development. Flanked by a large paved area towards Pinstone Street, the lower, walled garden is focused on a spectacular circular fountain embraced by paving and lawns. On each side of the four main approaches water pours from giant bronze vessels and flows down tiled cascades, representing both Sheffield's rivers, the traditional sources of power, and the pouring of molten metals. The surrounding balustrades and walls are made of the same Stoke Hall sandstone as the Town Hall, and have carved decoration inspired by plant forms, continuing the theme of the natural and the man made.

The gardens' E side is bounded by a pedestrianized section of **Norfolk Street**. The site on the E side is vacant in 2004, following demolition of the 1970s extension to the Town Hall, allowing views to the Winter Garden (*see* Major Buildings, p. 75) and the hills to the SE. Whether the proposed offices will retain these views and respect the pre-eminence of the Town Hall remains to be seen. The height and scale of the six-storey hotel (*Weintraub Associates*, 2003) to be built immediately next to the Town Hall sets an unfortunate precedent.

The buildings on the S and W sides of the gardens were all built in the 1890s in similar styles and materials, creating a harmonious group that defers appropriately to the Town Hall. Clockwise, first the SE corner block, built in two phases between 1898 and 1901, by *J.D. Webster*. Warm-coloured brick with red sandstone dressings, an unusual combination for Sheffield where the buff Yorkshire and Derbyshire sandstones are much more common. The earlier part, with a decorative arched entrance of 1900 to Norfolk Street, was built as the Central Hall for the Sheffield Workmen's Mission. It has a claim to be the first cinema in the city, being adapted in 1907 for regular film shows given by Jasper Redfern, one of Sheffield's cinema pioneers. The auditorium was destroyed in the 1940 blitz. The block on **St Paul's Parade**, which comprised shops, tenements, galleries and a studio, has been redeveloped behind the façade but retains its attractively arcaded shopfronts with carved stone piers and arches. The faces of rather glum lions and rose, thistle and shamrock emblems decorate the spandrels. To the right, the distinctive deep pink brick and terracotta of the former **Prudential Assurance Company Offices** by *Waterhouse & Son*, 1895, creates an

## Heart of the City

The Heart of the City project was initiated in 1994 to regenerate the city centre with new and improved public spaces, new public buildings and the redevelopment of the site of the Town Hall Extension. The Peace Gardens, Town Hall Square and Hallam Square provide landscaped areas linked to the new Millennium Galleries and the Winter Garden (*see* Major Buildings, p. 74) and the project has succeeded in attracting both residents and visitors to the city centre. Funding has been provided by a £20.5 million grant from the Millennium Commission and over £100 million from the private sector and other sources. The commercial developments of new offices and a hotel between the Winter Garden and the Peace Gardens remain controversial, with fears that they will not match the quality of design seen in the public works and in the redesign of other regional city centres.

imposing corner to Pinstone Street. Four storeys plus attic with gables, in Northern Renaissance style, it is embellished with the firm's favoured decorative terracotta from J.C. Edwards of Ruabon. Windows with chunky square mullions and transoms have been retained in the exemplary ground-floor shop conversion.

On the w side of **Pinstone Street**, on the lower corner of Cross Burgess Street, **Laycock House** is an unusual block combining shops with what were described at the time as 'better class dwellings'. Developed in 1896 to designs by *Flockton & Gibbs* (E.M. Gibbs was one of the site's owners). Above the shops, which have mezzanine display windows, is what is effectively a terrace of five houses, each of two storeys plus attic, with a canted bay window and a 'front' door opening onto a shared balcony at the rear, accessed by a stone staircase with decorative iron balusters. The corresponding corner block incorporates, on Cross Burgess Street, the former **Salvation Army Citadel**, designed in the usual castellated style with crenellated parapets and machicolations by *William Gilbee Scott* in 1892. The Salvation Army started its mission in Sheffield in 1878 and within three years had four halls attracting attendances of over 4,000 people. This was the movement's largest building in the town, with a theatre-like galleried hall, offices and meeting rooms. The rest of the block, on Pinstone Street, was developed by the Army as shops and offices and retains its original lively roof-line crowded with decorative gables, turrets, dormers and chimneys.

The other developments N along Pinstone Street's w side were, as was hoped, complete by the opening of the Town Hall. Nos. 30–42 is red brick with stone dressings and sash windows with decorative cast-iron balconies on the three upper floors. Fifteen bays, developed in two phases, 1893–4 and 1896, by Reuben Thompson, a horse bus and coach and cab proprietor who introduced the city's first taxi service in 1905. The building incorporated shops and offices with flats above and access to the stabling and carriage sheds of his City Mews, which ran through to Burgess Street, at the back. To the right **Palatine Chambers** by *Flockton & Gibbs*, 1895, is carefully matched but maintains a distinctive identity with its tall casements, projecting end bays and high roof which give it a decidedly French character. Both ranges were remodelled behind the frontages in the 1970s with some unfortunate additions at attic level and pedestrian shopfronts.

Lastly, opposite the Town Hall, is **Town Hall Chambers**, a worthy but slightly dull five-storey block of shops and offices by *J.B. Mitchell-Withers,* built *c.* 1885 as part of the redevelopment following the street improvements here. Ashlar-faced, with a sympathetic modern shopfront, the building turns into Barker's Pool with a canted corner, contrasted opposite in the broad curve of the four-storey **Yorkshire House** by *Flockton & Gibbs*, 1883–4, which has a mixture of giant Ionic and stubby Doric pilasters on its first and second floors, giving weight to the design. Top floor and attic added in 1892. The sculpted panel above the central window contains the Prince of Wales' coat of arms and advertises the royal patronage enjoyed by the building's original occupants, the cabinetmakers Johnson & Appleyard, who made the oak fittings of the Town Hall's Council Chamber. On the left **New Oxford House** by *Hadfield Cawkwell Davidson & Partners* in the standard 'International Modern' of the 1960s. Beside it is a tiny formal **garden** given by Alderman J.G. Graves in 1937 expressly to enhance the setting of the City Hall (*see* Major Buildings, p. 67) and preserve the view of it from the Town Hall. Set back behind the garden is the **Fountain Precinct**, nine-storey offices clad in buff and brown tiles by *Sidney Kaye, Firmin & Partners*, 1976. The open ground floor which extends the entrance piazza under the wing of offices along Balm Green contrasts with the solid monumentality of the City Hall and allows glimpses of the Hall between its supporting pillars. At the front of the piazza is *David Wynne*'s delicately exultant Horse and Rider, 1978, in stainless steel.

**Barker's Pool** was a small enclosed reservoir created by Mr Barker in the C15 which supplemented the town's wells until 1793, when it was filled in. The occasional release of its contents was the signal for communal cleaning of yards and paths as the deluge swept rubbish from the streets into the Don. Its site is now one of the city's principal spaces for public ceremony as well as rallies and demonstrations, with the City Hall providing a dignified backdrop to the civic **War Memorial** to the 5,000 men killed in the 1914–18 war. A competition for its design was instituted in 1924 (with *E. Vincent Harris*, the architect for the proposed City Hall, as adviser) and won by *C.D. Carus Wilson*, head of the University's School of Architecture. His highly unconventional design, unveiled in October 1925, was for a 90 ft (27 metre) steel mast rising from an octagonal bronze base 18 ft (5.5 metre) high. Around it, four almost life-sized figures of soldiers sculpted by *George Alexander*, stand with heads bowed and rifles reversed, above insignia and other military emblems. Ironically, the mast was not made in Sheffield but by Earle's Shipbuilders, Hull. On the s side of Barker's Pool, the scale of the City Hall is well matched by *Yorke, Rosenberg & Mardall*'s coolly confident department store for **Cole Brothers** (now John Lewis), 1961–5, which replaced the drapery firm's long-established premises at the bottom of Fargate. It was innovative for its date in the incorporation at the rear of a ramped multi-storey car park communicating at each level with the store. Clad in the architects' hallmark white tiles with panels of brown mosaic to the window bays. Against this the bright red structural framework and mirror glass cladding of the former **Odeon** by *Hadfield Cawkwell Davidson & Partners*, 1987, seems brash. (For buildings w of Barker's Pool *see* Walk 3, p. 122.)

We turn s down **Cambridge Street**, whose older name of Coalpit Lane came from the small-scale surface workings that once existed on this side of town. On the right, Nos. 16–18 incorporates the two-storey decorative cast-iron framework of a small works designed in 1878 for a firm of coachbuilders. In the building immediately below this a carriage archway marks the entrance to **Leah's Yard**, which was known in the 1880s as the Cambridge Street Horn Works, but takes its current name from Henry Leah, who was in business here from 1892 as a manufacturer of die stamps for silverware. From the street the narrow carriageway leads into the small courtyard which is surrounded by two- and three-storey brick workshops dating from the mid to late C19. Barely one room deep, they have external wooden staircases to give access to the upper floors and long ranges of casements to cast as much natural light as possible on the workbenches that run immediately behind them. By 1905 they were shared by eighteen 'little mesters' (*see* topic box, p. 6) including a dram flask manufacturer, hollow ware and

54. Leah's Yard, Cambridge Street, mid- to late C19

silver buffers, a palette knife hafter, a steel fork manufacturer, a silver ferrule maker, brass and german silver turners, an electroplate manufacturer and a cutler. The site has been disused for over fifteen years and badly needs a sensitive scheme for its restoration and reuse.

Cambridge Street was traditionally one of the centres of the bone-and horn-working trades in the town. Imported ox, buffalo and stag horn were used not only in the cutlery industry for knife and fork handles and pen and pocket-knife scales, but also for the manufacture of a wide variety of other articles such as parasol and umbrella handles, doorknobs, combs, spectacle frames, snuff and tobacco boxes, drinking cups, buttons and jewellery. In the c20 synthetic plastics such as bakelite, celluloid and ivorine gradually replaced horn and its use in the city is now confined to the cutlery trades.

Further down the hill is the narrow gabled front of the former **Bethel Chapel Sunday School** of 1852. Three storeys, brick with ashlar dressings and sash windows, the interior altered. Primitive Methodism, which tried to follow Wesley's original guidance, was introduced to Sheffield in 1819. The first congregation used a former Independent chapel on this site until 1835 when they built a new chapel (part of which survives behind the c20 shop frontage) on the other side of Bethel Walk. The schoolrooms could accommodate over 500 scholars and were the means of educating and influencing thousands of children in the area.

Now left down Charles Street to the s end of Pinstone Street, whose line sweeps downhill to the s across Furnival Gate to **The Moor**, one of Sheffield's principal shopping streets since the mid c19. Badly damaged in the Blitz, it was completely redeveloped in the 1950–60s with large three- and four-storey, flat-roofed blocks of shops, many of them for national chains. Uniformly faced in Portland stone and sparsely detailed: marble panels, splayed corners and stripped classical forms, though No. 64 has a jollier corner with folded window. The street's potentially attractive coherence is impossible to appreciate with all the clutter of kiosks and street furniture that block the view down to **Moorfoot** where vast stepped red brick government offices of 1978 by the *Property Services Agency* fill the horizon.

Continue down Charles Street to **Union Street**, and a cluster of office blocks built since the early 1970s. First **Howden House**, council offices completed in 2001 by *HLM Architects* severely clad in pale brick, cool green-grey panels and green glass. Behind it, the taller **Redvers House** by *Newman Doncaster Associates* 1972, and the former **Amalgamated Engineering Union House** by *Jefferson Sheard & Partners*, 1971, on the corner of Furnival Gate, its unusual octagonal form prominent in dark brown tile cladding.

**Arundel Gate** was one of the worst results of the car-orientated inner-city road schemes of the 1960s and once severed the city centre from the Sheaf Valley, but it is now much improved by a reduction in width and the reintroduction of surface crossings. Turning left, one comes to the

**Novotel**, 1991, by *John Seifert Architects*, on an awkwardly triangular plan. It withdraws unsociably behind blank blockwork walls and black glazing, in complete contrast to the welcoming elegance of the adjacent **Millennium Galleries** (*see* Major Buildings, p. 74).

A ramp leads up to **Surrey Street**. First on the left, a rare survivor of Georgian Sheffield: **Leader House**, *c.* 1780, brick with pedimented Doric doorcase and a big canted bay window added in the early C19. Built for Thomas Leader, one of the first Sheffield plate manufacturers, shortly before the area to the s, Alsop Fields, was developed as a grid of streets (for which *see* Walk 4, p. 135). Another vestige is in Surrey Place, at No. 2 (the Central Deaf Club). At the corner is the former **Masonic Hall** (now pub and health club), built 1875–7 of well-cut ashlar in a restrained Italianate style. It replaced the old Savings Bank of 1832, adapted by the Freemasons in 1861 after the new bank on Norfolk Street opened (*see* below). The high ground-floor windows and blank first floor, pierced only by lunettes set high up under the deep modillion eaves, reinforce its solidity and secretiveness. Pretty, rather delicate foliated capitals between paired arched windows that have Masonic symbols carved in the spandrels. Extended to the right in 1888 and 1909–12 by six bays, absorbing three-storey Georgian houses, now stuccoed and with a new entrance with flamboyant doorcase with a big shell hood on scroll brackets. Masonic symbols in the tympanum.

Opposite is the dignified Beaux-Arts front of the **Central Library and Graves Art Gallery** by *W.G. Davies*, 1929–34. Originally intended to form one side of a grand civic square, first proposed in 1924 by *Patrick Abercrombie*'s Civic Survey as the setting for civic offices, law courts and a college. The abandonment of the scheme after the Second World War left the building in what Pevsner called 'an incomprehensibly insignificant position' and never really seen to best advantage. Steel-framed, faced with Portland stone, with giant Ionic pilasters and a high parapet wall around the top-lit galleries on the third floor. Fine decorative carving by *Alfred and William Tory* – around the main entrance medallions representing Literature, Music, Drama, Architecture, Sculpture, Painting, Mathematics, Chemistry and Astronomy. High up on the splayed corner a figure of Knowledge holds the ankh and asp to represent the choice between good and evil. The building is planned round a large central light well above the ground-floor Lending Library, with the main reading rooms facing Surrey Street and Tudor Square on the ground and first floors. High-ceilinged, they are lit by tall windows and have oak fittings with restrained Art Deco details, seen throughout the building. From the marble-lined entrance hall the main staircase rises to the third-floor Gallery. This was donated by Alderman J.G. Graves, local philanthropist, whose fortune was made by his pioneering mail order business. His gift of nearly 400 pictures forms the nucleus of the city's outstanding art collection. The w side of the Library and Gallery overlooks **Tudor Square**. Created in 1991 to form the centre of Sheffield's cultural area, it is enclosed by the Winter Garden (*see* Major

Buildings, p. 75) on the s and by the Crucible and Lyceum theatres to N and E. Carvings on the low wall around the central lawn, metalwork, and mosaics set into the paving, all by *Paul Mason*, represent the signs and symbols that developed into the alphabets and languages of different cultures.

The **Lyceum** [55] was opened in 1893 as the City Theatre, designed by the theatre specialist *Walter Emden* with *Holmes & Watson*. Only four years later it was substantially remodelled by *W.G.R. Sprague*, who created an enchanting interior that bears comparison with those of his most beautiful London theatres. The only survivor of the four Victorian theatres in the city centre (and Sprague's only remaining theatre outside London), the Lyceum was restored in 1989–90 under the direction of *Renton Howard Wood Levin Partnership*, who reinstated the restrained exterior stucco decoration and the figure of Mercury on the corner dome. Inside, the original multiplicity of separate entrances and staircases, which segregated patrons of different social status and seat price, were replaced, and the cramped front-of-house spaces supplemented, by a simple modern extension overlooking Tudor Square. This contains a staircase sweeping up to circle and balcony levels and spacious bars and circulation areas. The rear was rebuilt with an enlarged stage and a new flytower, dressing rooms and rehearsal space. Above the stage door on Arundel Gate is an abstract **stained glass** window by *Catrin Jones*, inspired by backstage activities. The jewel in this new setting is the original **auditorium**, where the stalls and cantilevered circle and balcony are flanked by three tiers of boxes on either side, the whole space embellished by a glorious profusion of delicately gilded and painted Rococo plasterwork created by *De Jong & Co*. Garlands, swags, drapery, scrolls and shells decorate the sweeping curved fronts of the circle and balcony and frame the proscenium arch and boxes, rising up to the coved and panelled ceiling with its prettily painted details of foliage and musical instruments.

The stripped angularity of the **Crucible Theatre** [56] by *Renton Howard Wood Associates*, 1969–71, is startlingly different. It sits low to the Square, its height increasing to four storeys as the ground drops away behind it to Arundel Gate, filling the irregular site with the subtly complicated geometry of its octagonal form. At the front stepped painted red bands below the shallow pyramidal roof and the black fascia of the entrance canopy contrast with stark white blockwork walls to give a strong horizontal emphasis, which is continued in the fenestration of the bars and rear offices and dressing rooms. Inside, we are drawn upwards in a route that spirals through an enticing series of spaces, with an almost disorientating interplay of levels and angles, into the octagonal auditorium at the heart of the building. Its design was directly influenced by the ideas of 'theatre in the round' developed by the director Tyrone Guthrie, whose associate *Tanya Moiseiwitsch*

55. Lyceum Theatre, Tudor Square, by W.G.R. Sprague, 1897

worked with the architects, and it remains one of the most exciting theatrical spaces in the country. A central thrust stage is embraced on five sides by a steeply raked bank of seating for 1,000 people, the furthest seat no more than 60 ft (18 metres) from the centre of the stage. A pair of diagonal ramped vomitories reinforces the audience's involvement in the action, while the unique feature of an unseen rear stage area adds a further dramatic dimension. Mobile stage towers for flying scenery were also a key innovation. Compared with the Chichester Festival Theatre of 1965, the first experiment with the thrust stage, the Crucible is much more successful in achieving the intimacy, immediacy and flexibility which Guthrie advocated. The Studio Theatre seats 400 entirely in the round, providing an intimate space for small-scale productions and chamber music. Alterations in 1994 provided an additional exit with a new glazed canopy which has compromised the angular solidity of the building's exterior, while changes inside have eroded the original concept of bare white walls as a foil for bold blocks of colour provided by its furnishings.

On the w side of the Square, a three-storey block, 2002, by *Race Cottam Associates* with richly grained sandstone ashlar facing and a modish corner feature in the form of a glazed 'lighthouse' stair-tower. Its proportions spoilt by the addition of a utilitarian ground-floor canopy.

Now into **Norfolk Street**, w of Tudor Square. First on the left, a handsome building designed by *Flockton & Abbott* in 1876 for Hay's Wine Merchants. It housed the Ruskin Gallery from 1985 to 2002 (*see* Millennium Galleries, p. 74). Next door, the carefully composed façade of the former **Sheffield and Hallamshire Savings Bank** (now a bar) is one of the city's most accomplished pieces of mid-C19 classical revival.

56. Crucible
Theatre, Tudor
Square, by
Renton Howard
Wood Associates,
1969–71

57. Upper Chapel,
Norfolk Street,
1700, remodelled
by John Frith,
1847–8, furnish-
ings by E.M.
Gibbs, 1882–1907

By *Flockton & Son*, the design was selected in competition in 1858, after the bank outgrew its previous building in Surrey Street (*see* above). Established in 1819, originally in the Cutlers' Hall, as a philanthropic venture for working people whose savings were too small to be accepted by other banks. Though small – a two-storey cube of three bays flanked by single-storey entrance wings with projecting porticoes – its rusticated stone front is skilfully articulated with round and square Corinthian columns on the ground floor and enriched with finely carved cornices, balustrades and urns. Splendid masks on the keystones above the ground-floor openings and the three first-floor lunettes. Rear extension to Tudor Square, by *Mansell Jenkinson & Partners,* 1973, for the TSB. (For buildings at the N end of Norfolk Street *see* Walk 5, p. 144.)

On the W side, set well back in its landscaped graveyard, is **Upper Chapel** [57], Sheffield's oldest Nonconformist chapel. Now Unitarian. Its origins lie in that independence of mind and spirit that is a recurring theme in Sheffield's history. The congregation was formed by those who followed James Fisher, the Vicar of Sheffield during the Commonwealth, after he was ejected in 1662 for refusing to subscribe to the Act of Uniformity; by 1676 it was estimated that 10 per cent of the town's inhabitants were Dissenters. The brick side-walls of the first chapel, opened in 1700, are still discernible. They were heightened in 1847–8 when the chapel was extensively remodelled by *John Frith* who reversed the building to face Norfolk Street and extended the E end to create a vestibule behind the handsome new pedimented stone front with its Ionic porch. The five arched upper windows are flanked by Corinthian pilasters in the style of Barry's Travellers' Club. The lofty interior with its three-sided oval gallery has been enhanced by later additions and fittings (pews 1882, vestry 1900, organ console and central

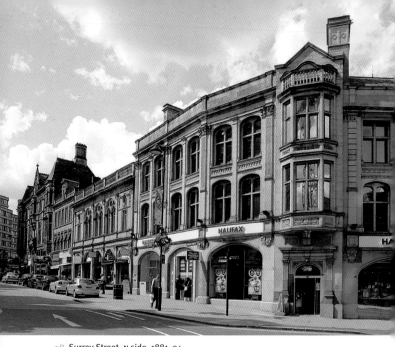

58. Surrey Street, N side, 1881–94

pulpit elevated on Doric columns 1907, all by *E.M. Gibbs*) to create an atmosphere of established respectability and comfort. Several fine C18 and C19 marble memorials, including one to John Bagshawe, (d.1721), with cherubs and winged skull. Excellent stained glass by *Henry Holiday,* 1899 and 1917–20, and by *Hugh Easton, c.* 1940. In the chapelyard are three bronze sculptures by *George Fullard,* cast after his death. Mother and Child is attractively reposed in contrast to the starkly frenzied Angry Woman and Running Woman.

Back on the E side of Norfolk Street, No. 109, a plain three-storeyed brick pub with pedimented doorcase, is the earliest surviving brick house in the area, referred to as 'lately erected' in 1745. To the right, on the corner of Surrey Street, No. 117 Norfolk Street is late Georgian with typical tall twelve-pane sash windows on the first floor. Attractive late C19 wooden shopfront with decorative pilasters and a carved fascia with elaborate brackets, for Hibbert Bros, carvers and gilders, picture framers and suppliers of artists' materials. They inserted the large studio window which breaks through the eaves. Among their customers were many of Sheffield's native artists who gained a national reputation, including Frank Saltfleet, Harry Allen and Stanley Royle.

On the opposite corner with **Surrey Street** the substantial **Halifax Bank**, designed by *J.D. Webster* in 1893–4 as shops, offices and a children's shelter, for Emerson Bainbridge, a local M.P., businessman and philanthropist. Prominent corner with a two-storey oriel window over the entrance. The offices facing Surrey Street have giant, partly fluted Corinthian pilasters dividing the façade into bays of two deeply set mullioned and transomed windows, each with a secondary system of minor bays marked by pilasters with plain capitals. On the simpler front to the shelter in Norfolk Street the flutes are replaced with channelled rustication, a favourite device of Webster's. The shelter was named in memory of Mr Bainbridge's wife, Jeffie, whose initials and the letters 'CS' are emblazoned on two decorative corbels. Others have faces and emblems including the rose, thistle and shamrock (cf. *Webster*'s St Paul's Parade, p. 96), and are set on panels of finely cut oak and acanthus leaves. The upper floors had a dining room and dormitories, together with offices for the NSPCC. Carved panel over the entrance doorway. Rebuilt behind the façade in 1977–8.

To the w is **Channing Hall**, an elegant Italianate palazzo by *Flockton & Gibbs*, built in 1881–2 at a cost of £7,000 by the congregation of the Norfolk Street Unitarian Chapel (which lies behind). Named in honour of William Ellery Channing (1810–84) the American theologian who served briefly at Upper Chapel in 1875. Faced in fine ashlar, it has five bays separated by Ionic pilasters on each floor and an open balustrade above the deep dentil cornice. Three large and boldly traceried windows at front and rear light the spacious first-floor hall, which has a fine open timber roof and walls lined with coloured glazed bricks. Arcaded shopfronts. To its left, a modest building designed as a business training college in 1887 by *T.H. Wilson* for Seth Whiteley, a writing master. Stone-faced, its balustraded parapet is the only concession to ornamentation. There were classrooms for teaching penmanship, shorthand and bookkeeping, a separate Ladies Room on the first floor and a top-floor lecture hall.

The walk ends with **Montgomery Hall**, which has a powerful presence, projecting forwards and upwards with its oriels and gables as if its site can barely contain it and reflecting the earnest endeavour that inspired it. Built in 1884–6 as the headquarters of the Sheffield Sunday School Union (now the Sheffield Christian Education Council) and named in memory of one of its founders, the local poet, journalist and reformer James Montgomery. *C.J. Innocent*, the Union's Honorary Secretary, was the architect and his experience of planning the Sheffield Board Schools stood him in good stead here. Behind the ground-floor shops and strongly modelled stone front with its sober decoration he fitted in not only a large galleried hall (remodelled after a fire in 1971) seating 1,000 people and a smaller hall for 350, but several committee and classrooms, a library, reading rooms, a reception room, anterooms, cloakrooms, kitchens and caretaker's accommodation. When the hall was built 108 Sunday Schools with over 27,000 scholars were affiliated to the Union.

Walk 2.

# The Cathedral Area

This walk takes in the areas immediately N and S of the Anglican Cathedral. The first half, to the N, covers the part of the city centre that was least affected by the great civic improvement scheme of the late C19 and so retains its older street pattern and significant numbers of late C18 and early C19 domestic buildings. In contrast, the area to the S was almost completely redeveloped after 1875 when the street-widening programme began, changing its character with taller, larger buildings in a variety of styles and materials. Fortunately, it escaped serious war damage, and still includes some of the best examples of the city's Victorian and Edwardian shops, offices and banks, mostly designed by local architects.

## Church Street and North

The tour begins on the N side of **Church Street** in the Cathedral forecourt (*see* Major Buildings, p. 45), which is overlooked on three sides by buildings that represent the town's development in the C19 as Georgian housing was replaced by substantial commercial and institutional buildings. First, on the W side, No. 1 **St James' Row**, formerly Gladstone Buildings.

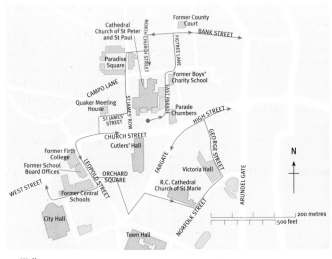

59. Walk 2

60. Parade Chambers, High Street, by M.E. Hadfield & Son, 1883–5. Perspective view (*c*. 1885)

A tall late Gothic block in red brick with stone dressings, designed as the Reform Club and offices in 1885 by *Hemsoll & Smith*. Steep slate roof with a fine array of dormers and spiky turrets with wrought-iron finials and cresting. Above arcaded ground-floor openings for shops, two floors with double-height mullioned and transomed windows for the principal clubrooms – dining room, library and members lounge. Saved from demolition in 1976 and rebuilt as offices behind the façade by *Hadfield Cawkwell Davidson & Partners*.

On the s side of **Church Street** is the Cutlers' Hall (*see* Major Buildings, p. 70), adjoined to its right by the former Sheffield and Hallamshire Bank (HSBC), also by *Samuel Worth*, 1838. Neo-Grecian in fine ashlar. Imposing façade of eight giant Ionic columns on a plinth, with plain frieze and cornice, anthemion panels over the doors at either end and Greek key above the lower windows. Originally five bays with four giant Ionic columns between plain pilasters, duplicated on the left in 1878 by *H.D. Lomas*, who also added the Renaissance gateway. Splendid banking hall with Corinthian pilasters and ornate plaster ceiling. On the left of the Cutlers' Hall is the **Royal Bank of Scotland**, a sober mid-Victorian interpretation of the palazzo style by *Flockton & Abbott*, 1866–7. Rusticated five-bay front with paired Doric columns of polished Aberdeen granite framing the doorways in the projecting end bays.

E of the Cathedral forecourt, **Parade Chambers** [60, 61] answers No. 1 St James' Row, and presents Fargate with one of the most impressive Victorian commercial buildings in the city. Designed for Pawson and

## Frank Tory and Sons, Architectural Sculptors

61. Parade Chambers, sculpture of Geoffrey Chaucer and William Caxton, by Frank Tory, *c.* 1885

The Tory family were exceptionally talented sculptors and architectural carvers whose work enhances some of Sheffield's finest late C19 and early C20 buildings. Frank Tory (1848–1939) trained at Lambeth School of Art and came to Sheffield in 1880 to undertake the decorative stone carving on the Corn Exchange (dem.). His twin sons, Alfred Herbert (1881–1971) and William Frank (1881–1968), trained under their father, who also taught at Sheffield School of Art. Working in stone, wood, marble and bronze, they designed and executed a wide range of architectural decoration, church furnishings and memorials with the liveliness, delicacy and sometimes humour of the medieval work that inspired them. Some of Frank Tory's best carving can be seen at St John, Ranmoor (*see* p. 267) and on Parade Chambers, High Street. His sons' work includes the sculptural decoration on the City Hall [19] and Central Library as well as Leeds' Civic Building and Chesterfield Town Hall, and the ten figures of Sheffield tradesmen on the White Building, Fitzalan Square, reproduced in white faience from their models [84].

Brailsford, printers and stationers, 1883–5, by *M.E. Hadfield & Son* in Charles Hadfield's favourite Tudor Gothic style. Five storeys, its two principal elevations are a lively mix of mullioned and transomed windows, three-storey stone oriels and double gables, crowned with tall chimneys and two picturesque turrets with ornate leadwork. A wealth of delightful decorative stone carving by *Frank Tory*, including richly detailed panels with garlanded portraits of Chaucer and Caxton and a fearsome array of grimacing gargoyles and mythical beasts looking down from the elaborately moulded string course below the gable windows. Gutted in 1988, only the stone staircase has survived the reconstruction.

N of here we are immediately transported into the tranquillity of what was Sheffield's fashionable residential quarter in the late C18 and early C19. **East Parade** [11] was created as a thoroughfare in the 1790s and has a pleasing variety of C19 three- and four-storey buildings in brick and stone. Nos. 4–8 (The Cathedral Bookshop) is restrained Tudor Gothic with especially fine brickwork but a touch of Renaissance detail in the Doric pilasters to its second floor. On the left the miniature Neoclassical grandeur of Nos. 9–10, *c.* 1820, with its rusticated plinth and bays squeezed between four giant Doric pilasters. Rendered attic storey added *c.* 1950. Then, the light-hearted Gothick No. 11 has big ashlar blocks ornamented with slender clustered columns dividing the four ground-floor bays below a panel of quatrefoils in lozenges. Gothick tracery. Next door, the three-storey No. 12 is a conventional five-bay brick Georgian town house of *c.* 1800. Originally two storeys, distinguished by an elegant wooden pedimented doorcase with engaged Corinthian columns and an especially pretty fanlight. The air of comfortable domesticity changes abruptly at the end of the Parade with the strict institutional demeanour of the former **Boys' Charity School** (or Bluecoat School), now offices. By *Woodhead & Hurst*, 1826, replacing an earlier building erected for the charity set up in 1706 to house and educate fifty-four poor boys aged eight to thirteen. The present building accommodated a hundred boys. Correctly classical seven-bay front, built in a greyish gritstone ashlar, with a severely rusticated ground floor and lugged architraves to the windows in the projecting centre bays. Ungainly upper attic storey with dumpy Doric pilasters.

Turn right into **Hartshead** to face **Old Bank House**, the oldest surviving brick house in the city centre, dated 1728 on a rainwater head. Built by Nicholas Broadbent, a local Quaker merchant, whose grandson Thomas ran a private bank here from 1771 to 1782 (*see* below and p. 184). Substantial, three storeys and five bays, with bold stone window dressings and string courses, and more strikingly, giant pilasters at the angles and either side of the central bay. The latter pair rusticated, frame the pedimented doorcase and, rather curiously, break through the cornice to the ramped coped parapet. Inside, rooms have plain panelling and plasterwork, one with an elaborate carved wooden chimneypiece, restored when the building was refurbished as offices in 1978–9 by *Hadfield Cawkwell Davidson & Partners*.

In **Fig Tree Lane**, No. 14 is a rather grand house of *c.* 1800; now offices. Plain three-bay stuccoed front with Ionic doorcase but an imposing N elevation which is set up on a high stone plinth on account of the steeply sloping site. Four bays faced in ashlar, with a rusticated ground floor and giant fluted Ionic pilasters on the two upper storeys. At the rear a domed octagonal turret contains the elegant circular stone stair-case. The Sheffield Hospital for Women (*see* p. 88) was founded here in 1864 by Dr Aveling. At the bottom of the lane turn right into **Bank Street**, laid out in 1791. On the N side, the former **County Court** (now offices), in a quietly dignified and restrained palazzo style by *Charles Reeves*, architect to the County Courts in England and Wales. Dated 1854 on the inscription below the painted Coade stone Royal Arms. Two storeys in a fine ashlar with rusticated quoins and surrounds to the arcaded ground-floor windows and slightly projecting doorways either side. The central window above is pedimented, the other four have plain cornices, all on nicely carved scroll brackets. Simpler w elevation. The courtroom was placed on the first floor to leave room for offices below, a novelty for its date. Inside, the original cantilevered stone staircase survives. The court moved to West Bar in 1996 (*see* p. 162).

Further E is **Wharncliffe House** of *c.* 1885, a ponderous palazzo with an insensitive metal-clad fourth storey added in 1980. The central door-case is extravagantly decorated with masks, brackets and garlands, while imperious bearded heads form the keystones of the two windows either side and on the left return, all below a deep bracketed cornice. Delicate wrought-iron railings to the little balconies above the door-way. To its right a nice group of late C18 and early C19 three-storey houses in brick with simple stone details and wooden doorcases, including Nos. 38 and 40–42 with voluptuous scroll brackets. Beyond, at Nos. 18–20, a bold and tall Italianate stone front of 1861 by *John Frith* to offices for the *Sheffield Independent* (founded 1819), the voice of liberalism and Liberal politics in the town. Big decorated keystones and cornucopia round a coat of arms embellish its rusticated first floor, with shapely balusters and festooned pilasters above. Marred by a modern shopfront and a C20 heightening of the parapet.

Returning w along Bank Street, continue into Queen Street, turning left into **North Church Street** and steeply up to the tall gabled brick front of the former **synagogue** of 1872. Sheffield's Jewish community, always much smaller than those of Leeds or Manchester, numbered less than a hundred in the 1840s, but was considerably increased by Russian and eastern European immigrants and refugees in the second half of the C19, when two separate congregations formed. One of them moved here from Fig Tree Lane and, despite its Christian associations, chose a simple Gothic style with narrow lancet windows. In 1930 the synagogue and adjoining three storeys of offices and meeting rooms were con-verted to warehouses and more recently to offices, the only indication of their original use the Hebrew inscription over the doorway.

Opposite, No. 17, a small town house with a nicely proportioned ashlar front of *c.* 1830 with a vermiculated plinth which wriggles enthu-siastically below the rusticated ground floor. Above a plain string course and sillband the three first-floor windows have moulded sur-rounds with cornices, the middle one distinguished by a segmental pediment. The attic above the cornice has its own more modest cornice.

62. Paradise Square, SE corner, 1736–*c.* 1790

Immediately below, facing the narrow **Wheats Lane**, is a considerably grander house in an Egypto-Greek style, comparable with Samuel Worth's villas in the western suburbs (*see* Broomhill, p. 247). An elegant front with projecting end bays framed by angle pilasters and Egyptian architraves with pediments to the doorcase and ground-floor windows. Rusticated base and a deep curving cornice with blocking course. The blackened stone dressings contrast dramatically with the red brick walls.

Wheats Lane emerges at the NE corner of **Paradise Square** [62], the most elegant survival of Sheffield's Georgian townscape. Despite its seeming coherence, the red brick houses date from two separate building periods and their present appearance largely results from a comprehensive scheme of restoration of 1963–6 directed by *Hadfield Cawkwell Davidson & Partners*. Both Nos. 18 and 26 were virtually rebuilt and details such as doorcases and rainwater heads salvaged from demolitions elsewhere were reused to create the delightful, if not wholly authentic, square we see now. The earliest development was in 1736, when Nicholas Broadbent, of Old Bank House (*see* above), built the terrace of three-storey, three- and four-bay houses stepping down the hill on the E side, on land belonging to the Shrewsbury Hospital estate. The houses fronted on Workhouse Croft (now Paradise Street), which ran down to West Bar through the fields and orchards below Campo Lane. The two at the top, Nos. 4 and 6, retain the most convincing original appearance with their segmental-headed doorcases, minimal reveals to the twelve-pane sashes, moulded cornices and parapets. Below them Nos. 8 and 12 display C19 and early C20 changes in the form of lengthened window openings with plain sashes and a balustraded parapet. Between these No. 10 has a Neo-Georgian front of *c.* 1985 in ill-chosen brick, which replaced early C19 Gothic stucco and a crenellated parapet.

## Paradise Square

The square and its occupants have played an important part in Sheffield's history. The painter and sculptor Francis Chantrey had rooms at No. 24 in 1802, and Dr Davis, the physician who attended the birth of Queen Victoria, lived at No. 12 from 1803 to 1812. No. 18 was the Freemasons Lodge in the early C19, and the House of Help for Women and Girls was set up at No. 1 in 1885 to rescue those 'in moral danger and from miserable surroundings'. Used for a time as a market place, the square's size and slope made it an ideal venue for meetings – in 1779 John Wesley preached to a vast crowd from the balcony of No. 18, and to the alarm of the authorities thousands gathered here to support the Chartists' cause in the 1830s and 1840s. Through the later C19, as its middle-class residents moved out, the square slipped down the social scale and eventually into a state of dereliction and decay.

From 1771 to *c.* 1790 Thomas Broadbent, banker (*see* above and p. 184), laid out the other three sides of the square with an agreeable variety of houses with twelve-pane sashes, ashlar sills and flat brick heads, and moulded cornices or brick dentil eaves below plain or ramped parapets. They range from the modest two bays at No. 24 in the NW corner to the imposing five-bay front of No. 18 in the centre of the N side, projecting slightly forward of its neighbours. It has a first-floor balcony with French windows framed by columns and an open pediment, and more elaborate detailing to set it apart. Opposite, the higher S side has three two-bay houses in the centre, Nos. 5–9, also projecting slightly forward but plainer, their elegant doorcases displaying a variety of details that are repeated round the square – lugged architraves, reeded friezes, semi-pediments and cornices.

SE of the square across Campo Lane, **St James' Row** has handsome three-storey brick houses overlooking the Cathedral. For centuries the land on the right was Vicarage Croft, the gardens and orchards surrounding the parish church vicarage and forming part of its glebe land. To the S some of this ground was taken for St James' Street and the new church (dem. 1950) built at its head in 1786–9. The **Girls' Charity School** (now offices) was built N of the vicarage in 1786, funded by voluntary subscriptions to educate sixty poor girls between the ages of eight and sixteen and train them for domestic service. More homely than the Boys' School (*see* p. 111) which it faced across the churchyard, its foundation is recorded in the semicircular tablet set in the pediment above the three central bays, which project slightly forward of the single flanking bays. The blank fanlight over the doorway is matched by the blank arches framing the windows either side, each with a fine rubbed brick head. To the left are four houses of *c.* 1790, all with smart doorcases, flat brick window heads and bracketed eaves. At the S end of the Row are a pair of plain ashlar and brick houses and a former auction room which were built after the old vicarage was pulled down in 1854. The main elevation of the auction house is to St James' Street. Behind its blind arcade with odd pilasters and high parapet is a spacious saleroom with decorative plaster cornice, generously lit by a big lantern.

On **St James' Street** No. 4 (to the left) was originally the Church of England Educational Institute of 1860 by *Flockton & Son*, founded in 1839 for the education of young working adults, partly in reaction to the secularism of the recently opened Owenite Hall of Science. Reassuringly Gothic, double-gabled front in red brick with stone dressings, with Geometric tracery in the big windows to the main lecture rooms on the first floor. The other floors have simple two- and three-light windows with cusped heads in square-headed openings. Two small but utterly inappropriate windows were inserted when the building was converted to a pub in 1981.

At the junction with Vicar Lane, the **Quaker Meeting House** by *Abel, Sykes Partnership*, 1989, is characteristically unostentatious but confidently Postmodern in a soft, pleasingly-varied pinkish brick with dark brown window frames and quirky stone details that hint at classical forms. The entrance is set back behind a tiny courtyard on the right, while the main elevation projects forward to the street.

Now back to **Church Street**, where a few steps downhill on the s side is the **Stonehouse** pub, successor to Thomas Aldam's wine shop of 1795. Its two-storey painted front dates from *c.* 1840, showing modest aspirations to the Neoclassical details of its grander neighbours with banded rustication to the slightly projecting central and end bays, and simple anthemion details on the shaped blocking course above the eaves cornice. Modern doorway. **Orchard Chambers** is a cheerful Edwardian Baroque essay in red brick and stone. Designed as shops and offices by *Gibbs & Flockton* in 1904, it is another example of that practice's enviable talent for devising buildings in an infinite variety of styles with versatility and flair. A bland modern fascia and shopfronts obscure the skilfully articulated proportions of the central block and two-bay wings but are no competition for the visual attraction of the generous ornamentation of pediments, balustrades and urns above. Ingeniously, the angle pilasters on the projecting central bays, dressed in banded rustication, disguise the chimneystacks, which carry on upwards above the cornice.

On the N side, at the corner of Vicar Lane, No. 20, the handsome three-bay, red brick former solicitors' offices, originally **Cairns Chambers** [63], are by *Charles Hadfield* of *M.E. Hadfield, Son & Garland*, 1894–6, in a scholarly Tudor style. The stone carving, by *Frank Tory*, is more restrained than that on Parade Chambers (q.v.) and has a richness and delicacy of detail unmatched by the decoration on Sheffield's other commercial buildings of the period. The ogee gable over the central doorway and the traceried crest of the little first-floor oriel on the corner are particularly fine, so too the heads along the string course at the same level. The more realistic heads below the upper string course portray Edward, Prince of Wales, and Princess Alexandra, while the imposingly robed statue in the canopied niche in the central oriel is the 1st Earl Cairns, Lord Chancellor in Disraeli's ministries. It was said that Tory hired a set of robes from London to ensure that they were shown correctly. The lively roof-line of tall chimneys, square gable and crenellation survived bomb damage to the rear of the building in 1940.

## South of Church Street

**Leopold Street** was created in the 1870s, replacing the inconveniently narrow Orchard Street as the link between Church Street and Barker's Pool. On the broadly curving corner is the expansive Neo-Elizabethan front of **Leopold Chambers**, solicitors' offices of 1894 by *Holmes & Watson*, in mellow golden sandstone divided by precise lines of string courses, sillbands and pilasters. Striking shaped gables topped with spiky finials reflect the uneven rhythm of the bays, the three wider ones

63. Cairns Chambers, Church Street, statue of Earl Cairns, by Frank Tory, *c.* 1895

distinguished by double-height canted oriels decorated with strap-work. To the right, a more solemn front, designed as the Sheffield Medical Institution in 1888 by *J.D. Webster*. Northern Renaissance style with sturdy rusticated and banded pilasters and strongly modelled cornices above each floor to give horizontal emphasis. The Institution, founded in Surrey Street in 1828, was the third provincial medical school. The new building could accommodate a hundred students and provided a dissecting room, pathological museum and physiological laboratory in addition to class and lecture rooms. The school moved to Western Bank as the Faculty of Medicine at the new University of Sheffield in 1905 (*see* The Universities, p. 78).

The history of the Medical School is inextricably linked with that of Firth College, part of a distinguished education complex built 1876–99 on the large, sloping site bounded by Leopold Street, Orchard Lane, Holly Street and West Street. In 1876 *Flockton & Abbott* and *E.R. Robson*, architect to the London School Board, were commissioned to design offices for the School Board on Leopold Street, then under construction, and Central Schools on Orchard Lane. The following year the Board sold the adjoining site on West Street to Mark Firth, the steel magnate, to provide a home for the Cambridge University Extension lectures. The architects' brief was extended to include Firth College and they succeeded in accommodating these three very different needs in a lively and harmonious composition in a free Renaissance style, using Huddersfield stone. **Firth College** was completed in 1879 and became part of the new university at Western Bank (*see* p. 78) in 1905. Originally of two storeys (the third added 1891–2 by *Flockton & Gibbs*), its design was inspired by Clare College, Cambridge. The entrance on West Street is closely modelled on the College's E gateway, but here the doorway below the little semicircular oriel is flanked by *Onslow Ford*'s figures of Art and Science languidly draping themselves in the spandrels. The other decorative detail on the building, mainly in the form of pretty festoons, is by *J. McCulloch*. Inside, the oak-panelled boardroom and galleried lecture theatre survive. On **Leopold Street** [64] the former **School Board offices** of 1880 form the centrepiece of a long and impressive elevation. They are set up on a rusticated basement storey, with a prominent central doorway framed by Ionic columns and a broken pediment which embraces the moulded corbel of the slender semicircular oriel above. This has a pretty frieze with festoons. The later mansard roof with big gabled dormers and gabled end spoils the original roof-line with its elegant balustrade. To maintain continuity single-storey balustraded links originally joined the offices to Firth College on the right, and, as an arcade, which survives, to the **Central Schools** on the left. The schools end at the corner of Orchard Lane in two blocks, each of three bays, either side of a little bow-fronted link set back between them. The blank wall of the canted block on the corner is relieved by arched niches and delicately carved panels, which include lilies and oak leaves and the emblem of the School Board.

64. Former Central Schools (left), School Board Offices (centre) and Firth College (right), Leopold Street, by Flockton & Abbott and E.R. Robson, 1876–80

Towering behind is the big chimneyed gable of the top floor of the schools which face **Orchard Lane**. Built of tooled ashlar, their main front is set back to allow the basement at the lower end and the two generously windowed floors above to capture as much light as possible in the still narrow lane, oppressively overshadowed by the Fountain Precinct (*see* Walk 1, p. 98). Above the classrooms a lofty open-roofed assembly hall extends the full length of the building, the long clerestory either side divided by shaped buttresses rising from curly bases and topped with urns. At the top of the lane, extensions of 1893–5, by *J.B. Mitchell-Withers Jun.*: an eight-bay block and a buttressed four-storey range which runs back from it across the rear courtyard, displaying a prominent pedimented gable flanked by ramped coping with scrolls and urns to West Street. The carved lintel below the be-ribboned initials of the Board at the entrance announces the new Science School where physics and chemistry as well as other practical subjects were taught.

At the corner of **Holly Street**, the former Pupil Teachers Centre, by *H.W. Lockwood*, 1896, has a rather busy front with two little stair-turrets. Then at the junction with **West Street**, the former **Bow Street School** opened in 1894. A big rectangular block, its reliance on rather flat Ionic pilasters to enliven it indicates a more subdued interpretation of the earlier buildings' Renaissance style, not helped by the removal of its balustraded parapet. From 1969 to 2001 the entire group was the Education Department offices. In 2004 a mixed-use redevelopment scheme by *Axis Architecture* has been approved for flats, restaurants and shops, with the intention of retaining all the c19 buildings.

**Orchard Lane**, E of Leopold Street, has on the left a crisply detailed office block by *Ronald Ward & Partners*, 1962. Grey marble panels to the five upper floors and rich green marble facing to the ground floor.

65. Orchard Square, by Chapman Taylor Partners, 1985–7

Ahead is the entrance to **Orchard Square** [65], a successful extension to the central shopping area by *Chapman Taylor Partners*, completed in 1987. One of the first of the new style of developments more sympathetic to existing urban grain, it takes the form of an open rectangular courtyard, surrounded by a lively mix of new and old buildings, faced in red or yellow brick, and with consciously traditional features such as pitched roofs, casements and weather-boarded oriels. The focal point is the square clock tower with its chimes and moving figures. A short covered arcade through the higher office block on the s side links the square with the top of Fargate; here the development rises more grandly to five storeys and is faced in stone to match its Victorian neighbours.

Opposite, on the corner of **Fargate** and Surrey Street is the long curved front of the **Yorkshire Bank**, 1888–9 by *Perkin & Bulmer* of Leeds for the Yorkshire Penny Bank. The five-storey building also had a temperance restaurant with hotel above. Late Gothic in Holmfirth stone. The bank, to the left, is more ornately decorated, with elaborately carved winged lions and majestically medieval figures above and below a balustraded balcony. To the right, panels carved with lions and shields above the ground-floor arcading, and moulded shafts draw the eye up to fantastic gargoyles leaping from the cornice. The gabled dormers, lofty chimneys and crenellated parapet were sacrificed in the conversion of the hotel to offices after 1965. The handsome building to the left, also in late Gothic style with gabled roof-line and long frontage curving round into Norfolk Row, was built for the **YMCA** in 1889–92 by *H.W. Lockwood*. On the three floors above the shops it provided facilities for over 900 members, including a gym and library. Carving by *Frank Tory* includes six arched panels depicting the days of Creation and four to their right showing the progress of Divine Law.

66. St Marie's
Presbytery,
Norfolk Street,
1903. Carved
head of the
architect
Charles Hadfield
(1840–1916)

On the w side of **Fargate**, the former National Provincial Bank, 1902, by *W.W. Gwyther* of London. It has a muscular metropolitan character with boldly rusticated end bays and a weighty stone dome on its octagonal Baroque turret. Below it, Nos. 38–40 displays *J.D. Webster*'s economic handling of a late Gothic style decorated with carved panels above the first-floor windows and open quatrefoils in the parapets either side of the central gable. Built for Arthur Davy in 1881–2, it was claimed to be the largest provision store in the country, the carved heads of the sheep, cow, pig and ox high above the third floor advertising the hams, potted meats and pork pies for which it was famous.

Turn right down **Norfolk Row**, dominated by the Cathedral Church of St Marie (*see* Major Buildings, p. 57) on the left and with a row of late C18 and early C19 houses, now offices, on the right. Nos. 10–16 have reeded doorcases [10]. At the end turn left into **Norfolk Street** where St Marie's **Presbytery**, by *C. & C.M.E. Hadfield*, 1903, in soft pink brick, has Gothic stone details which sit oddly with its sash windows. The carved label stop on the right of the big canted bay is a portrait head of the architect Charles Hadfield [66] by *Frank Tory* who also carved the graceful statue of the Virgin Mary in the niche over the hooded doorway. Below, the boxy **United Reformed Church**, 1970, re-clad with stone in 2002 by *Hadfield Cawkwell Davidson & Partners*. Tall, fragile looking glazing now encloses the external staircase and makes a self-effacing new entrance in Chapel Walk. The big red brick and stone front of the Methodists' **Victoria Hall** [17] next door is much more assertive, its mix of Gothic and Arts and Crafts styles less the product of *Waddington Son & Dunkerley*'s original design of 1906 than *W.J. Hale*'s reworking of 1908, particularly the massive Baroque top to the landmark tower. Carved decoration by *Alfred and William Tory*, including portraits of the Wesley brothers in the gable.

We turn left up **George Street** to the small paved square. On the right are the former **Alliance Assurance** offices, 1913 by *Goddard & Co.*, a model of ingenuity in fitting a prestigious building onto a tiny site. Dignified and refined Baroque, in Portland stone, its single-bay front enhanced by exaggerated details which give it a monumental character. The **Cutlers Hotel** beyond, by *Mansell Jenkinson & Partners*, 1961–4, was built for the Sheffield Club. Four storeys, gradually diminishing in height, its steel and concrete structure expressed unusually creatively. Opposite, the former **Bank** (currently vacant) was built as George's Coffee House in 1793. The successive alterations and additions made after it was acquired by the Sheffield Banking Company in 1831 can be traced in the changes in the brickwork. Left extension in Portland stone, by *C. & C.M.E. Hadfield*, 1906. The three-storey offices to the right (Nos. 12–14) are one of the rare instances of Venetian Gothic in the city. Big, prickly acanthus leaf capitals to the carriage arch pilasters, with unfriendly-looking griffins doing handstands on top.

At the N end of the street we emerge into **High Street**. On the N side *J.B. Mitchell-Withers Junior*'s handsome classical stone block of 1899–1900 s of High Court survived the 1940 blitz but much of the area down to Fitzalan Square was destroyed and rebuilt after the war with shops and offices, some of their undistinguished concrete livened up recently with new glass façades. The upper end escaped, and **Kemsley House**, by *Gibbs, Flockton & Teather* for the *Sheffield Daily Telegraph*, 1913–16, dominates the N side. White faience, now painted, with two tiers of giant arched window openings, Baroque details and a central square tower with light-hearted domed top. Dwarfed by its neighbours, the former **Bank** across York Street by *Holmes & Watson, c.* 1895, compensates for its smaller size with a front crammed with Renaissance details. On the s side, **Foster's Buildings** of 1896, designed in French domestic Gothic style by *Flockton, Gibbs & Flockton* for a gentlemen's outfitters. Offices on the four upper floors were reached by the first American elevator in the city. Built in Huddersfield stone, its roof-line bristles with crocketed gables and spires above a parapet with Gothic tracery. The window heads too have cusped tracery.

Finally at the junction with **Fargate** one of *Flockton, Gibbs & Flockton*'s more exuberant *fin-de-siècle* essays with high mansard roof, designed as an auction house in 1895. In Fargate itself their versatility is shown by buildings erected after the street widening here – No. 14 of 1879 and No. 9 of 1889. The narrow-gabled stone fronts reflect the width of plots preserved from much earlier development. From here a few steps take us back to the Cathedral forecourt.

# Walk 3

# The Devonshire Quarter

The area covered by this walk was the focus of the first westward expansion of the town from its pre-industrial core and developed from the mid C18 on land owned by the Church Burgesses, who sought to impose a degree of architectural uniformity by requiring houses to conform to elevations drawn by their surveyor *William Fairbank*. Concentrating on Division Street and its continuation, Devonshire Street, developers included *Joseph Badger* and *William Flockton* but many plots were leased to small craftsmen who built houses with workshops for themselves and erected smaller houses nearby to provide income. The district was thus of mixed character from the start and manufacturers soon began to escape the smoke by moving further w to the exclusively residential

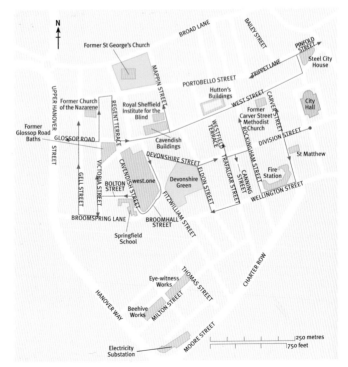

67. Walk 3

areas around Glossop Road and Wilkinson Street as they were developed. Building extended as far as Rockingham Street by 1820 and to Hanover Street by the 1830s. Widening of West Street in 1907–10 injected much Edwardian commercial architecture. By the late C20 the area was rundown and re-branded as the Devonshire Quarter (*see* Introduction, p. 42), which has led to major regeneration, much of it aimed at the city's student population. A number of small works still persist in this area.* The walk is divided into three parts but can be followed sequentially.

## Division Street to Devonshire Green

The walk begins w of the City Hall (*see* Major Buildings, p. 67) on the N side of **Division Street** with the handsome former **Sheffield Waterworks Co.** offices [68] by *Flockton & Abbott,* 1867 (now a bar). Palazzo style, a rarity in Sheffield, of seven bays. Ashlar façade, the remainder in brick. On the ground floor, round-headed windows are set back between attached columns, each arch with a carved keystone of a water god. Smaller first-floor windows in plain surrounds. Large cornice with a balustraded parapet above topped by urns. Substantial three-storey addition facing Holly Street, *c.* 1983, by *Malcolm Lister* for the National Union of Mineworkers. Top heavy, in brown glass and Darley Dale ashlar to match the City Hall, with aggressive triangular central projection.

*The account of the development of the Quarter is based on that in David Postles, 'The Residential Development of the Church Burgesses Estate in Sheffield' in *Transactions of the Hunter Archaeological Society* 10, 1979, pp. 360–4

68. Sheffield Waterworks Co., Division Street, by Flockton & Abbott, 1867

**Carver Street** crosses N–S. Northwards, on the E side, the **National School** dated 1812 on a large plaque with a four-bay gabled centre with one-bay wings on each side. Two doorways with half columns. Then, No. 23 **Kendal Works**, which has a pedimented front range of *c.* 1830 and workshop ranges of the usual Sheffield type (*see* topic box, p. 126) with a blank rear wall on to Carver Lane and large windows facing the yard. The rear range was probably a grinding hull. In the courtyard is an early C20 scissor forge, single storey with a hipped roof, large casement windows and two hearths. Part restored in 2004. Opposite, the lengthy and utilitarian façade of **Alpha Works** by *Holmes & Watson*, 1900. Four storeys in brick with extensive stone dressings to the projecting centre which has a pediment enclosing a circular window and an elaborate doorcase incorporating a trademark. Two large chamfered semi-circular openings with giant keystones at first-floor level. At the N end on the left, **Carver Street Methodist Chapel** (now a pub), 1804, by *W. Jenkins*. Large, of five by six bays with a three-bay pediment below a five-bay gable. Arched upper windows set in blank surrounds, the central one Venetian. Doorway with attached Tuscan columns and open pediment. The spacious interior has a wooden single-span roof, impressively wide for its date. Round-ended continuous gallery. Early C19 Sunday School at the rear in Rockingham Lane, six bays with round-headed windows.

Southwards now, to **St Matthew** [69], Carver Street, 1854–5, by *Flockton & Son*, the centre of High Church worship in the C19 city centre and the scene of much ritualist controversy during the long incumbency of Canon Ommanney (1850–1936). A simple building with an octagonal W tower and spire rising from the W wall with the entrance below. It is lit by clerestory windows and by those at the E and W ends of the church, there being no aisle windows. The E end was altered by *J.D. Sedding* who designed a new chancel and E window in 1886. Calvary above the W door of 1918 gives rise to the present odd arrangement of a Perp arch with a half-obscured, more sharply pointed arch behind. Perp style W windows. Of most interest are the rich **furnishings**, many designed by *Henry Wilson*, who took over Sedding's practice following his death in 1891, and executed by *Henry Longden & Co.* of Sheffield. The two collaborated on the Chapel at Welbeck Abbey, Nottinghamshire, completed in 1896. Magnificent **altar** and **reredos** by *Sedding*, 1886–92. Alabaster base and upper part of timber, the carving by *F. Tory & Son*, its centrepiece a painting of the Adoration by *Nathaniel Westlake*, 1890, flanked by gilded figures in canopied niches and roundels depicting angels below. Also by *Sedding*, the altar cross in the Lady Chapel. **Choir stalls** of 1897 inlaid with copper panels by *Wilson*, executed by *Longden*. **sanctuary walls** in alabaster and iron **gates** to the chancel and chapel with copper panels (executed by *Longden*) lettered in Arts and Crafts style. Wrought-iron grilles, based on those in Pisa Cathedral, separating the S chapel from the chancel, the gift of *Henry Longden*. In 1898, Wilson painted decorative bands on the chancel piers but these are

69. St Matthew's, Carver Street, furnishings by Henry Wilson 1897–8

now obliterated. **Pulpit** and **font**, both of 1903, by *H.I. Potter* in oak with brass panels similar to those on the sanctuary gates. Again, the carving by *Tory* and the metalwork by *Longden*. N chapel **altar** with gilded tracery and foliage decoration, 1958, by *George Pace*. **Organ case**, 1992, in mid-C17 style. **Stained glass**: E window by *Sedding*, 1884, the Incarnation with figures of St Matthew and other saints, W windows, N aisle given 1902, S aisle of similar date, both by *Lavers & Westlake*. Next door, the **Clergy House** and Sunday School of 1896 by *J.D. Webster* in red brick Tudor Gothic with a large oriel window.

## Cutlery Workshops

The design of Sheffield's cutlery workshops is unique to the city. The pattern of their development was set down in the late C18 when private dwellings in the town centre were adapted as works, the house serving as office and showrooms and even sometimes as workshops. It was more usual, especially after c. 1800, for workshops to be built at the rear, either in a single range or as several ranges forming a courtyard. This pattern set the standard for much of the C19 and could be carried out on a large or small scale; many of the larger works were nothing more than an aggregation of individual workshops. These were simple, roughly built of coarse brick, usually three storeys and narrow in width. The ground floor, often used for the storage of valuable materials, was commonly windowless but the first- and second-storey workshops had strips of small-paned casements to light the craftsmen's long benches or 'sides'. Where processes required more light, much larger windows, still made up of small panes, known as 'low shop' windows were employed. The internal planning depended on how the buildings were used. On a tenement basis, multi-occupied by 'little mesters' (*see* topic box, p. 6), each craftsman sometimes had a separate entrance. In the integrated works, i.e. where each stage of the cutlery manufacturing process was carried out under the control of one firm, they were planned as a series of interconnected workrooms, together with offices and large packing rooms. Although they began to disappear after the 1875 Public Health Act, which set down minimum standards for industrial buildings, the workshops were ubiquitous in the city centre until the 1960s.

Opposite the church are two office buildings that epitomize the different decades in which they were built. First, **Star House** by *Jefferson Sheard & Partners, c.* 1970, of five storeys, with a mansard roof and dark red brick cladding, chamfered below the window frames. Submitted for an RIBA regional award, the jury called it 'a Yorkshire pudding. Good, solid, honest – and dull'. This is contrasted, to great effect, by the simplicity and lightness of No. 38 of 1989–90 by the *Building Design Partnership*, partly for their own occupation. Unassuming yet satisfying with an all-glass façade to a central atrium and cladding of light-coloured brick to the side.

Turning w into **Wellington Street**, the corner is entirely taken up by the enormous **South Yorkshire Fire Service HQ** of 1983 by *Rotherham B.C. Architects Department*. Brick, of four storeys descending in steps with each part set forward under small tiled roofs, slightly Neo-vernacular. Splayed to the corner with the engine house in the centre, flanked by squat towers and with similar towers to the wings. On the left, **Telephone House** of 1972 by *Oxley & Bussey*: a curtain-walled slab over a multi-storey car park. On the right, No. 44 [72], the well-detailed Edwardian edge tool works of Robert Sorby & Sons, with brackets with fasces decoration and the firm's kangaroo trademark over the cart entrance.

Now up Rockingham Street to rejoin **Division Street**. On the N side, the former **Fire Station** of 1928 by the City Architect, *W.G. Davies* (now a bar). Municipal Neo-Georgian with Art Deco detail. Three storeys with an attic in a pinkish brick and ashlar cladding to the ground floor. Engine doors recessed between two wings. Nearly opposite, the former **YWCA** of 1939 by *J. Mansell Jenkinson*, Neo-Georgian with rounded corners.

**Devonshire Street**, is the W continuation of Division Street. S, in **Canning Street**, Nos. 4–14 [70], a group of six former blind–back houses, *c.* 1830 with simple three-storey façades, some retaining sash windows. N in **Westfield Terrace**, fronting offices of the 1990s, the façade of the handsome **Mount Zion Congregational Chapel**, 1834, probably by *William Flockton*. Stone, of three bays with two giant Ionic columns *in antis*. To the S, in **Trafalgar Street** is the **Aberdeen Works**, occupied since construction in 1883 by Francis Howard, silversmiths. Incised lettering along the façade. One office has a big tripartite window in an ashlar surround, otherwise casement windows. **Trafalgar Works** is later, *c.* 1900. Very plain fourteen-bay façade with central carriage entrance, two-storey workshops with casements around the courtyard behind. Four hand forges at the E end of the S workshop range, each with independent access from the yard. Threatened with demolition in 2004. In **Devonshire Street** Nos. 105–125, are a complete block of ten houses of *c.* 1840. Three storeys in painted brick with rounded corners to the ends and a higher central range slightly projecting with panelled brick pilasters and twin cornices. The shop windows in this central range have pilastered surrounds and there is a further pedimented window on the first floor. Then Nos. 140–146, the former warehouse and showroom of

70. Nos. 4–14, Canning Street, *c.* 1830

John Armitage & Sons' **Wharncliffe Fireclay Works**. Dated 1888 and liberally decorated as an advertisement for the firm's speciality of architectural terracotta and figures. Armitage's works were based at Deepcar: the only evidence of his work in Sheffield is his own house in Crookes Road, Broomhill (*see* p. 253) and Spartan Works, Attercliffe (*see* p. 197).

**Devonshire Green**, an open space created from a bomb site, forms the centre of the revitalized Devonshire Quarter, surrounded by recent developments. Its w side has **west.one**, a lively but overpowering group of apartments, bars and shops by *Carey Jones* 2000–4 in brick, glass, coloured renders and dark blue glazed tiles. The N part has three slab blocks with lower blocks between, topped by roof gardens. An opening five storeys high leads to a public space delineated by shops and restaurants with serpentine glass walls and an oval glass café. To the s, more slabs around a central courtyard.

w of Fitzwilliam Street is a residential area around **Cavendish Street**, mostly terraces of houses and small blocks of flats by the North British Housing Association. In Broomspring Lane, the **Springfield Board School** [15] by *Innocent & Brown,* 1875, a particularly impressive three-storey example, enlarged in 1891–2 to include a roof playground and again in 1897. Further N in Cavendish Street, the **Wilson Carlile College of Evangelism**, of 1989–91 by *APEC Architects,* in a low-key but attractive Neo-vernacular style in grey brick, mainly single storey but with a rendered upper-storey wing, projecting gabled bays and prominent roof ventilators. The building is planned around a landscaped central courtyard and has openwork roof trusses in the public areas, especially effective in the chapel which has a lantern. w of here in **Victoria Street**, a good pub, the refurbished **Bath Hotel**, built as a corner shop *c.* 1870 in a terrace of three-storey houses of similar date. The interior, remodelled by Ind Coope in 1931, with a brown-tiled counter front and slightly jazzy patterned obscured glass, retains all the ambience of a back-street local. There are two bars, the smaller lounge served through a hatch from the public bar with a further hatch by the door for off-sales. **Gell Street** gives an indication of how this area must have looked when it was laid out from the 1820s. Nos. 100 and 102, are a pair of three-bay houses, No. 98 a detached house of greater architectural pretension with a parapet and heavily chamfered stucco door surround and further along a row of small cottages of late Georgian proportions.

The walk can end here with bus or tram to the city centre from Glossop Road or continue on foot via West Street.

## Glossop Road and West Street to the City Centre

w of Gell Street on the s side of **Glossop Road**, a stylish block of shops (Nos. 243–253) *c.* 1910. It has a pair of canted bays with gables above and a range of dormer windows, some of which are circular. Then, at Nos. 255–259, two early C19 shops flank an early C20 infill, set back with a hipped roof, bow window to the first floor and iron balustrade above the shop front.

Opposite, the 1907 **Somme Barracks** (1st West Yorkshire Royal Engineers Volunteers) by *Alfred Ernest Turnell*, the Volunteers' Quartermaster. L-shaped Free Renaissance main block, canted on the corner with Gell Street with a large gatehouse as the focal point. Tower with a coat of arms and a large window above a Baroque arch with heavy rustication and banded columns. Wings of two storeys and basement, broad segmental-headed windows to the ground floor, segmental pediments to some first-floor windows, all with mullions and transoms.

N of Glossop Road in **Gell Street**, the **Victoria Works** of 1868 with six narrow bays, then on the corner, No. 34, the rare survival of a large plain brick villa *c.* 1830. Parallel to the E in **Victoria Street** is the former **Church of the Nazarene**, built in 1850–1 as the Catholic Apostolic Church. Gritstone, rather fussy w façade with a miniature sw broach spire, a plain NW tower in three stages, the top one curiously stunted, and three lancets grouped together. All other windows lancets, the nave of five bays and an apsidal chancel. In **Portobello**, the **Innovation Centre**, 1998, by *HLM Architects*. Wilfully asymmetrical elevations of set back lower two-storeys behind exposed steel beams. Prominent fire escape but the entrance is tucked away at the corner. Central atrium. Down **Regent Terrace**, workshops *c.* 1850 used for many years as a steeplejack's yard.

Back on Glossop Road, on the s side, the former **Glossop Road Baths** (now flats). The first public baths in Sheffield were built here in the aftermath of the cholera epidemic of 1832 and associated with the Public Dispensary (later Royal Hospital), West Street. Rebuilt in 1877–9 by *E.M. Gibbs* for the Sheffield Turkish and Public Bath Co. Ltd. A ladies bath was added 1898 with entrance on Victoria Street. The busy façade to Glossop Road is of 1908–10 by *Arthur Nunweek* (*see* also Heeley Baths, p. 230). Baroque Wrenaissance, well handled, with the entrances distinguished by rusticated giant pilasters with segmental open pediments above. In the centre, a pedimented window and lunette with keystones and Gibbs mouldings; Hampton Court-type circular windows with swags at each end. Roof garden and a timber-clad attic floor added 2002, above the balustrade, ill at ease with the complex façade below. Of the interior, only the sumptuous 1870s Turkish bath (restored 2003) has survived residential conversion. Octagonal cooling room with a mezzanine balcony and a hot room with deep arched recesses, both tiled and with mosaic floors.

Next **Barclays Bank**, on a difficult triangular site. Free classical work of 1906–7 by *Gibbs & Flockton* for the Birmingham District & Counties Banking Co. The building is divided into two halves with the bank on the left: a formal composition comprising a two-storey centre with single-storey wings topped with balustrades and urns. To the right, three shops in similar style with three canted bay windows.

**West Street** continues E. This was the principal NW exit from Sheffield, following the opening of the turnpike in 1821, and today has the greatest concentration of Edwardian commercial architecture in the city, the result of street widening in 1907–10. Decorative faience was extensively employed and the result has a satisfying urbanity. On the N side, Nos. 252–4 [71] of 1906 for Boots by *A.N. Bromley*. A riotously decorated Free Renaissance façade entirely clad with light brown faience, with big Flemish gables, an open parapet and a cupola on the corner with a dome (cf. the store in Attercliffe, p. 198). Next, No. 246, a former Post Office with much terracotta work and leaded lights in the mullioned and transomed windows. Attached, the former **Beehive** pub of *c.* 1913. Brick with stone dressings, of two storeys in a Free Tudor style with fleurons in the mouldings over the ground-floor windows and a carved beehive over the door. A very long faience block follows: **Cavendish Buildings** by *Hemsoll & Chapman*, 1907, extended 1910 and 1919. Built as garage and showrooms for the Sheffield Motor Co. Ltd with billiard saloons on the upper floors. Three oversized broken segmental pediments on the front elevation, each with a large swagged plaque bearing the dates of building and extension. Mullioned and transomed windows and an egg and dart cornice. In **Mappin Street** to

71. Boots store, 252–4 West Street, by A.N. Bromley, 1906

the N is the **Royal Sheffield Institution for the Blind**. Refined Neo-Georgian of 1938 by *Hadfield & Cawkwell* with moderne sculpture on the doorcase by *Philip Lindsay Clark* showing the liberating work of the Institution: on the left, a blindfolded figure with prison bars behind; on the right, a hand reading a book in braille with the sun behind.

Back on **West Street**, **The Hallamshire Hotel** of 1903 has an exuberant rich brown glazed faience façade to the ground floor with a lettered fascia. Round-headed windows to ground floor, detailing generally classical. Next **Hutton's Buildings** of 1885 for William Hutton & Sons, electroplaters. Established in Birmingham in 1800, they opened a Sheffield branch *c.* 1832. Plain red brick three-storey block on West Street with ground-floor shops and a very large works built around a courtyard behind. Further on, **Tiger Works** (Nos. 136–138) [74]. Dated 1884, the name incised on a narrow but ornate façade. Three storeys, five bays with segmental-headed windows on the top floor, round-headed on the first, paired on the right-hand side. Rendered ground floor with much carving in the spandrels and in the pilasters of the office and cart

entrances. Embellished with two carved tigers. Then in succession: an incongruous half-timbered 1930s pub built as the West Street Hotel, the Employment Exchange (*H.M. Office of Works*, 1934) in a weak, thin Neo-Georgian and at Nos. 98–104, **The Mortons Building**, a development by *Axis Architecture*, 2003–4, incorporating the façade of **Central Works**, occupied for many years by Mortons, knife makers. The two w bays are of *c.* 1830, three storeys with a later C19 shopfront. These are dwarfed by the flats built on the site of the workshop ranges behind of *c.* 1850.

West Street's s side was dominated from the 1830s until 1981 by the Royal Hospital, which grew out of the Public Dispensary. On its site, **Royal Plaza** of 2000–2 by *HLM Architects*, a massive apartment block, six storeys with set-back penthouse floors, in red brick with much tubular steel. It is followed by the seemingly interminable utilitarian interwar Revenue Buildings by *Arthur Nunweek*, and *W.J. Hale's* extensions to the **Methodist Sunday School** in a tired Neo-Georgian of 1927–9. The earlier part by *H.W. Lockwood*, 1898, is massive and of three storeys with a tall gable to Rockingham Street. It has a lecture hall and twenty-four classrooms. For the chapel in Carver Street *see* above.

E of Carver Street, the former **Sheffield Institute for the Blind** (now a bar) of 1905 by *Edmund Winder*. Well-proportioned in red brick with stone dressings. Dormer windows in the attic and a plaque with 'SIB' at parapet level. The Institute had workshops for the making of brushes, mats and baskets with meeting rooms on the upper floors and a shop on the ground floor. No. 49 (also a bar) was formerly the premises of J.W. Northend Ltd, printers. An expressive piece of Edwardian classicism of 1912–14 by *Chapman & Jenkinson* with some original detailing but the scale a little overpowering. Damaged in the Second World War but rebuilt to the original design. Red brick with light stone dressings, it has massive fluted pilasters surmounted by oversize triglyphs and a lunette in the top storey.

On the N side, **West Point** of 2002–3 by the *Bond Bryan Partnership*, eight-storey flats in brick with exposed steel balconies. It overshadows **Mayfield Court**, a bombastic Postmodern design by *David Lyons & Associates*, 1990. All the usual spurious references to classical precedent with a massive broken pediment and rock-faced rusticated bands.

## Trippet Lane and Neighbourhood

Now N down Holly Street to **Trippet Lane**. On the corner, **Anglo Works**, early C19, occupied for over a century by Walter Trickett. Three storeys with an L-shaped plan incorporating a showroom. The usual closely spaced casements but with sashes on the ground floor denoting its superior status. Opposite, another works of late C19 date, Nos. 28–32 with an attractive rounded corner, prominent sillbands and a pointed porch. **Walsh Court** is the most striking building in the street. Built in 1906 as a furniture depository and workshops by *Gibbs & Flockton* for John Walsh Ltd, Sheffield's leading department store. Confident Edwardian Neo-Baroque in red brick and stone dressings with banded pilasters and outsized keystones. Symmetrical façade with two gables, each with an open pediment with a 'w' and scrolls, all in cut brick. Also two relatively unspoiled pubs: the **Dog and Partridge**, rendered early–mid C19, once a Gilmour's house with their characteristic faience tiles on the ground floor, good lettering on the fascia and etched glass; and the **Grapes**, Edwardian, in brick with contrasting stone bands which run into the arches over the segmental ground-floor windows. Carved grapes in the keystone over the door and Art Nouveau tiles and partitions with coloured glass inside. Returning E, Trippet Lane becomes Pinfold Street and the walk concludes with **Steel City House** (the former telephone exchange), 1927, by *H.T. Rees* of H.M. Office of Works. Triangular plan, clad in Portland stone with rounded corners lending panache. Massive fluted Doric columns support a semi-circular portico to the main entrance. The upper-floor bays are divided by giant Doric pilasters with the end bays brought forward slightly and given emphasis by pediments.

This group forms a sub-walk for those with a special interest in industrial buildings.

Perhaps the best place to gain an impression of how the larger-scale Sheffield cutlery industry appeared is in **Milton Street**, SE of Devonshire Green: **Beehive Works**. At the w end, Nos. 98–100, a group of four three-storey back-to-back houses built between 1850 and 1864, quite substantial with late Georgian proportions and simple wooden doorcases. They adjoin the works in one continuous façade. The works are eighteen bays long and generally similar in style to the houses. A three-storey workshop range to the rear and a much taller four-storey shop, plain brick at the rear. Large casement windows for the ground and first floors on the courtyard elevation. **Eye-Witness Works** is the only traditional integrated works still in operation. Front range of several phases: the left hand part of five bays is *c.* 1852 with round-headed windows, a Venetian window over the cart entrance. Top floor added *c.* 1875, contemporary with the nine bays to the right. The final five bays are earlier and were also heightened *c.* 1875. Workshop ranges to the rear were used for grinding and an octagonal chimney provides evidence of steam power. At the back of Eye-Witness Works in **Thomas Street**, **Taylor's Ceylon Works**, a specialized horn-cutter's works (*see* p. 100). L-shaped, one three-storey range housing the offices, *c.* 1875, rather like a pair of semi-detached houses with paired doorways and sash windows. At the rear a workshop block of *c.* 1850 with casement windows and a single- (formerly two-) storey warehouse. Windowless, except for a skylight, owing to the high value of horn.

To the s in **Moore Street**, a little known but outstanding expression of the Brutalist ethos, the **Electricity Substation** [75] by *Jefferson Sheard & Partners*, 1965–8, for the CEGB. A massive and totally uncompromising design well-suited to its position on the ring road. It has been loathed by several generations of Sheffielders but firmly expresses its purpose – the

75. Electricity substation, Moore Street, by Jefferson Sheard & Partners, 1965–8

delivery of raw power – and is in all senses, an extraordinarily powerful building. In three stages, with a lower storey of thin concrete mullions, and two storeys of horizontal cladding divided by exposed vertical beams topped by a cornice of angled concrete panels. Detached glazed staircases at the E end. In complete contrast, almost opposite, part of the façade to **J. Pickering & Sons'** cardboard box factory of 1908 by *C. & C.M.E. Hadfield*, retained in a 1990s office development. Fireproof construction of steel frame and concrete, clad in flamboyant Renaissance-style terracotta. Spectacular splayed entrance with a great variety of different mouldings over the doorway, elaborate cornices, decorated spandrels and upper windows deeply inset behind arcading.

Walk 4

# The Cultural Industries Quarter

In the C18, the SE district of the town centre was open land on the Norfolk estate known as Alsop Fields. At the edge of this, the Sheaf provided power for a small number of cutler's wheels, lead mills and, in the area known as the Ponds, corn mills established in the C16. Development first took place in the 1730s on the edge of the town but only in the 1770s did the 9th Duke decide to exploit the estate for the creation of a select residential district for the town's increasingly prosperous manufacturers. Plans were prepared *c.* 1775 by *James Paine* (who had designed Worksop Manor and made alterations at Norfolk House, London, for the Duke in the 1760s) for a grid with the principal streets

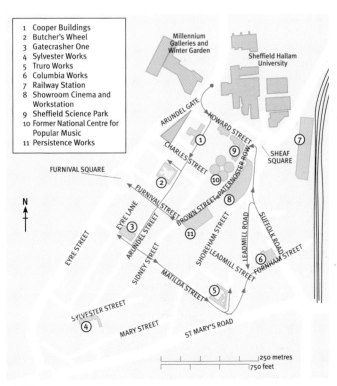

1 Cooper Buildings
2 Butcher's Wheel
3 Gatecrasher One
4 Sylvester Works
5 Truro Works
6 Columbia Works
7 Railway Station
8 Showroom Cinema and Workstation
9 Sheffield Science Park
10 Former National Centre for Popular Music
11 Persistence Works

76. Walk 4

and mews (aligned N–S) crossed by minor streets for tradesmen's dwellings. Paine drew up elevations for imposing but plain three-storey terraces but neither these nor designs for houses by *Thomas Atkinson* in 1776 were realized. The scheme foundered quickly and only part of the grid was laid out, with the major streets given names associated with the Duke: Howard; Eyre (from Vincent Eyre, his agent); Surrey and Arundel. From 1788 building leases were granted, mainly to cutlers, for modest dwellings. By 1800 restrictions on offensive trades had been removed. Building of workshops at the rear of the houses soon began but development of new streets was slow. By the 1820s, the first of the large cutlery works had begun to appear which, with the advent of steam, no longer required riverside sites for their power. The area was designated as the Cultural Industries Quarter (*see* Introduction, p. 42) in an attempt to regenerate the declining industrial district with a mixture of creative enterprises and residential use. This process, familiar elsewhere in post-industrial cities, began in the early 1980s with colonization by artists for cheap studios and has since been followed by formal regeneration initiatives by local government. The contrast here is that Sheffield has successfully sought to preserve and capitalize on the established creative industries rather than see their diminution through speculative development. Since the 1990s, the conservation of its historic fabric has been accompanied by imaginative new build.

The walk begins at the Millennium Galleries (*see* Major Buildings, p. 74) in Arundel Gate. From here we cross SE to **Howard Street**. On the right are some of the last surviving houses of the C18 development: Nos. 42–46 of 1788, are typical. Simple, of three storeys with incised lintels and dentil eaves. No. 44 retains a plain timber doorcase and beaded fanlight. The first tenants included a cutler, a grinder and a button maker. **Arundel Street** to the right was one of the major streets on Paine's plan and the survivals are more substantial: Nos. 105, 111 and 113, of 1791, are large and ornate with modillion eaves and the entrances emphasized by pilastered doorcases. No. 113 is plain brick, its neighbours were stuccoed later. No. 105 (Venture Works) [77] has a rear courtyard with a workshop added *c.* 1840, showing clearly the industrialization of a domestic building. On the other side of the street, the domestic scale of Venture Works is vividly contrasted with **Cooper Buildings**, the former Don Plate Works, a three-storey range (now Sheffield Hallam University Science Park), which occupies the entire block between Howard Lane and Charles Lane. Only the right part is the original of *c.* 1880; that to the left rebuilt in replica. A chimney has been retained and the rear ranges sympathetically rebuilt but much of its character has been robbed. In the courtyard, a wonderfully eccentric **sculpture**: Heavy Plant by *David Kemp,* 1988, symbolizing Alchemy, with a fountain exploding out of a Philosopher's Egg which is forced out of a brick furnace or Athanor surrounded by old tools, saws and scrap machinery. The weeds growing around the base refer to the decay of traditional industry and are an integral part of the work. On the corner with Charles Street, the former

77. Venture Works, Arundel Street, 1791

**St Paul's National School**, by *Joseph Mitchell*. Neo-Tudor of 1844. Opposite, further reminders of the area's late c18 domestic origins, at Nos. 137 and 137a, a pair of much altered two-storey, three-bay houses. Also three storeys, No. 126 Arundel Street and No. 158 Charles Street, similar to those seen in Howard Street.

Arundel Street's w side is dominated by the colossal brick flank of **Butcher's Wheel** [78]. One of the city's finest remaining integrated (*see* topic box, p. 126) cutlery, edge tool and file-making works and powerfully evocative of the working conditions once prevalent in the cutlery industry. Built up by William and Samuel Butcher from *c.* 1855–60 but incorporating their earlier works, which face **Eyre Lane**. The earliest part is of 1819–20, brick built of three storeys with sash windows and two cart entrances (now blocked) into the yard; NE extension (originally a house) in matching style probably built soon after. The third part is of the 1850s, four storeys with some very large segmental-headed casements. The austerity of the 130 ft four-storey façade to Arundel Street was atypical for its date, eschewing the 'polite' style of Cornish Place Works (*see* Walk 6, p. 170) or Eye-Witness Works (*see* Walk 3, p. 133) in favour of casements of the type associated with the lowlier Sheffield workshop. Treatment of the buildings around the inner yard is uniform with rows of closely spaced casements, round-headed on the s side (the larger ones on the first and second floors illuminate the grinding hulls), segmental and straight-headed on the e and n sides. The ground and first floors of the s range have fireproof brick vaults and a c19 grinding hull on the second floor. In the centre of the flagged yard stands a chimney, surrounded at the base by privies enclosed behind a curved screen wall: a most unusual arrangement. The 1820s w range has a wing extended into the centre of the yard and is irregular with low openings leading to

78. Butcher's Wheel, Arundel Street, courtyard, mainly 1820s

steep steps up to workshops on upper floors. Hand forges have the characteristic split stable-type door and window under a common lintel.

Next in Arundel Street, **Sterling Works** of *c.* 1870, again enclosing
a large courtyard, has a slightly more pronounced architectural treatment with sash windows, round-headed on the first floor. Opposite,
another integrated works, **Sellers Wheel** (Nos. 151–167), has two L-
shaped three-storey ranges, plain externally, possibly of 1855. On the
ground floor, three grinding hulls with ventilation grilles, with separate
access by an external stair to further hulls on the first floor, which were

designed for renting out. Front range with sash windows and a pilastered surround to the cart entrance, emphasized by tripartite windows above. On the w side is the earlier (*c.* 1840) and much smaller **Lion Works** (No. 92), part of a works which extended back to Eyre Lane. Its hipped-roof workshop range, at right angles to the road (cf. Walter Trickett, Walk 3, p. 132), was built in the garden of the surviving brick, hipped-roof, three-bay house of 1804. Also little altered but much more imposing is **Challenge Works** (No. 94), its name incised on the upper fascia, with an especially large segmental-arched doorway and an eaves cornice. Sash windows paired above and to the right of the entrance and grouped in threes to the left. Built *c.* 1883 for Louis Osbaldiston & Co., makers of steel, saws, files, etc. Narrow yard behind for the single-storey tool forges. On the corner with Matilda Street, **Gatecrasher One** nightclub (formerly The Republic) of 1995 by *Mills Beaumont Leavey* and in a fragmented style of Gehry-esque fractured geometry with a mono-pitch roof. Varnished timber cladding, not quite vertical with tiny square windows, to Eyre Lane flushboarding with a big irregular opening. It incorporates No. 112, the *c.* 1904 former premises of Roper & Wreaks.

Turning left into **Matilda Street,** we leave the C18 grid behind. On the sw side, the early C19 **Matilda Tavern**, stone behind a stucco front. Beyond Shoreham Street to the E, **Truro Works** for Joseph Cutts, manufacturers of silver plate and Britannia metal. By 1856, it was occupied by Atkin Brothers, cutlery manufacturers, who remained there until the 1950s. The earliest buildings, of the late 1840s, are the three ranges to the SE surrounding a triangular yard. Well-proportioned office block, with large sashes and a classical doorcase to its main entrance on the splay of Matilda and Mortimer Streets. Cart entrance on Matilda Street. Long, three-storey workshop range with small casements to Mortimer Street. Both have stone sillbands at first floor. Steam power was generated in a building to the N which retains a shortened chimney. The works expanded to the N *c.* 1850–80 with a four-storey block along Matilda Lane and further buildings within a courtyard to the NW. A four-storey thirteen-bay addition of *c.* 1900 to the N of the original offices forms a third phase. Converted to student flats, 1995, by *Capital Design Studio*. Behind in **Mortimer Street**, as part of the same development is **Truro Court** of 1994. Built around a courtyard with unusual jettied timber-clad upper floors, deep eaves and prominent eaves brackets. Attractively splayed corner to Leadmill Road and Leadmill Street. On the N side of **Matilda Lane**, the former **Leadmill Mission Hall** and **St Mary's Sunday School**, mid C19 in late C13 Gothic style, surrounded by **Leadmill Court**, a 2002 development of flats.

Down Fornham Street to **Suffolk Road**. **Columbia Works** has an ambitious stuccoed three-bay façade which with its first-floor paired pilasters and pediment, resembles a major public building. Built *c.* 1836, the large royal coat of arms over the entrance dates from its time as the premises of William Wigfall & Sons, brush manufacturers, 1868–71.

There is an L-shaped workshop range to the rear. Extended and converted to flats 2002–4. On the E side of the street, Nos. 35–37 (W.W. Laycock & Sons), also mid-C19, stucco-fronted with vestigial pilasters and cornice, and of the same period on the w side, **Scotia Works**, with its name recently incised on the lintel keystones at first floor. Suffolk Road joins Leadmill Road and Shoreham Street beyond this.

**Leadmill Road** contained lead mills in 1759, built on the site of a 1730s cutlers' grinding wheel close to the River Sheaf. Demolished in 1910 for the **Tram Depot**, whose twin octagonal towers have been retained as a frontispiece to a development of student flats by *Bond Bryan Partnership* in the angle of the junction with Shoreham Street. The relationship between old and new is unsuccessful, with some windows obscured by the retained walls of the depot. More re-use a little further s on the E side at the former Norfolk Corn Mills, now **The Leadmill Club**. Late C19 with a two-storey stone range end on to four storeys in brick with small segmental-headed windows and a clerestory, the sides fully glazed with sliding sashes. Cheerful sculpture of musicians, 1990, by *Mike Disley* over the door.

The walk now returns N to **Sheaf Square**. To the E is the **Railway Station**, opened in 1870 for the Midland Railway but extensively rebuilt in 1905 by *Charles Trubshaw*, the company's architect. A one-off design, quite unlike much of his work of this period which is characterized by the use of red brick and terracotta decoration. Here the style is broadly classical, faced in fine ashlar from quarries at Peasenhurst, Derbyshire, with a large cast-iron porte cochère behind an arcaded and gabled stone screen. The principal elevation has large round-arched openings, infilled with panelled windows or doors. The former refreshment rooms are notable, their decoration still largely preserved. The first class room has Minton tiled walls and an elaborate timber bar counter, inset with large mirrors. Ornate coved and glazed roof. Parts of the 1870 station remain on platform 2, used as offices. Rock-faced stone in the Italianate style. The original glass roof spanning the tracks was subsequently replaced by individual steel-framed canopies over the platforms.

On Sheaf Square's w side, the **Howard Hotel**: early C19 with C20 half timbering but with cutlery workshops, one (facing Surrey Lane) pre-1850, the taller one behind slightly later. Opposite, filling the space between Leadmill Road and Paternoster Row, the **Showroom Cinema** and the **Workstation**, built as Kennings' garage and showroom in 1936. Imaginatively converted in 1993–8 by *Allen Tod* and *Tatlow Stancer* for four cinemas, café and office space. Steel-framed with two floors of big windows and jazzy Art Deco cream faience cladding with black trim. The detail is echoed in the black faience piers of the new entrance foyer from Sheaf Square which leads to an atrium created from the original vehicle lift to the first-floor repair shop.

Facing, across **Paternoster Row**, the **Sheffield Hallam University Science Park** of 1996 by *Hadfield Cawkwell Davidson*, red brick with pitched roofs in an unadventurous style. The same could hardly be

79. Former National Centre for Popular Music, by Branson Coates, 1997–8

said of the next building, the ill-fated former **National Centre for Popular Music** [79] built in 1997–8 by *Branson Coates* and one of the few permanent structures designed by this firm. Truly a piece of 'pop' architecture with four drums of stainless-steel cladding over steel ribs (thirty for each drum), each tilting outwards from the centre and surmounted by revolving ventilation cowls (apparently modelled on the nozzles of shaving foam cans). Approaching the entrance are a series of canted steps with tubular 'pinball' flippers, stone balls and a red pathway. Inside, there are two floors and a basement. A tubular steel cross links the four drums and the foyer spaces are lit by a glass roof supported by a second central steel cross. The cruciform plan, which Coates called 'a device for amplifying the flux between concentric and eccentric space' and which he said was inspired by Palladio's Villa Capra, was central to the design, allowing visitors to select the order in which they visited the exhibits on the first floor. Closed soon after opening, it was acquired in 2003 by Sheffield Hallam University for use as a students' union.

**Brown Street** has a run of new building: No. 60 by *Escafield Design*, 1999, has a roof of sweeping curves, which makes a good foil to the Centre, then the **Site Gallery** by *Derek Trowell Architects* of 1997. It retains the gabled brick façade of a 1916 building for J.J. Saville, steel manufacturers, with a steel frame inserted behind and a third storey added. Extensively glazed ground floor. A minimalist interior of top-lit gallery space on the ground floor with darkrooms, teaching rooms, etc. on the upper floors.

**Persistence Works** [24, 80], 1998–2001 by *Feilden Clegg Bradley* is the first purpose-built (as opposed to converted) fine art and crafts studios erected in Britain for many years. Built for the Yorkshire ArtSpace Society, a co-operative which first took over redundant industrial buildings in this area for studios in 1982. Constructed of *in situ* fair-faced concrete, industrial in scale (fifty-one studios) and austerely dignified in design with minimal surface decoration, a welcome contrast to the

80. Persistence Works, Brown Street, by Feilden Clegg Bradley Architects, 1998–2001

Postmodern gimmickry so prevalent elsewhere in the city. Two elements: a long low block facing Brown Street, with cantilevered first floor above a glazed podium, and a parallel six-storey block behind, linked by an impressive glazed atrium [24] through which large art-works can be removed. Angularity is only relaxed in the reception area which has a curved outer wall, bowed like a ship's prow. Large and noisy activities are restricted to the double-height studios on the ground and first floors, quieter ones such as painting to the upper floors of the rear block. The rear elevation is punctuated by large set-backs at ground and first-floor level to provide balconies to the studios. Artworks integral to the building's design include a screen of rippling glass panels along the façade by *Jeff Bell*, the perforated steel gates by *Jennie Gill*, blue circular lights with steel 'hairs' protruding from the façade by *Jo Fairfax* and the reception area floor by *Jasia Szerszynska*.

Brown Street turns NW with the **Rutland Arms** of 1936. Probably the best surviving example of Duncan Gilmour's house style of applied faience decoration with bold lettering. To the SW in **Sidney Street**, Nos. 16–20, a mid-C19 electroplate works with a front range entirely domestic in scale, contrasting with its neighbour, one of the apartment blocks bringing a new scale to the area in the early C21. From here it is a short walk up Furnival Street to Arundel Gate and beyond it, the city centre.

**Sylvester Street. Sylvester Works.** Occupied in the C19 by Thomas Ellin & Co., steel and cutlery manufacturers and merchants. A substantial three-storey office range of 1875 by *H. Matthews* with a vaguely Egyptian doorway. Polychromatic effect of stone lintels in horizontal bands against the bright red brickwork. Recessed window bays with dentil sills on the first floor. Splayed corner and cart entrance on the return. There is a rear workshop range of typical Sheffield type of *c.* 1840.

**Mary Street**. An industrial backwater, evocative of the former character of the area. The street retains its stone setts but few of the plain late C19 works merit individual attention. Only No. 104 displays a hierarchy of architectural treatment by having sash windows for the offices on the lower floors and casements for the workshops on the top floor. The former **Mary Street Steel Works** is on the N side, *c.* 1878, with a mono-pitch roof crucible shop and a stack above it serving four of its twenty crucible furnaces.

Walk 5

# The Castle and Wicker

The earliest part of Sheffield to be settled was the area around the medieval castle (*see* topic box, p. 148) which overlooked the main crossing of the Don near its junction with the Sheaf. Markets grew up around the castle walls. A market charter was granted in 1296 and they subsequently spread down the hill towards the Sheaf. A new Town Hall was built in Waingate in 1807–8 but the completion of the present Town Hall in 1897 drew the civic focus away, a process followed in the late c20 with the decline of its commercial activity. The area retains its medieval street layout and some early buildings although wartime bombing and

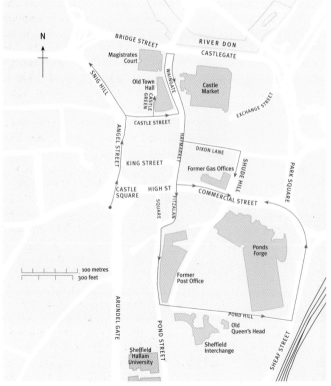

81. Walk 5

redevelopment of the markets destroyed much of the fabric. In 2004, it has lost much of its vitality, the major stores have moved out and it awaits the refurbishment or replacement of the Castle Market.

A stone bridge across the Don was first made in 1486, replacing an earlier wooden structure. By the C19 the riverside was dominated by industry, in particular steelworks, foremost among them those of Samuel Osborn. These packed tightly along the river banks and sometimes extended on iron columns over the river. Alongside were a brewery, cattle market and slaughterhouses – the Killing Shambles (dem. 1928) on the s side of the river giving visitors arriving from Victoria Station (1851, dem.) an appalling first impression of the city.

The opening of the Sheffield and Tinsley Canal in 1819 promoted increased waterborne traffic for the city centre but by the later C20 the story for the whole area around the Don is one of decline, following the closure of Victoria Station and the canal basin in 1970 and the steelworks thereafter. Regeneration has begun with the de-industrialized canal but extension of the inner ring road could deliver a terminal blow to Wicker and its neighbourhood.

## a) Castle Square to Pond Street

Start at the **Castle Square Tram Station** which has tubular stainless-steel **railings** of Gothic appearance by *Brett Payne,* 1999, and **sculpture** Fighting Rams, by *Jonathan Cox,* 1995. Castle Square was the site of the extraordinary 'hole in the road', a public space open to the sky with shops located below a roundabout, serving as a nodal point for subways to most of the main shopping streets. Opened in 1968, it was filled in barely two decades later for tramway construction. The square's buildings are mostly postwar, a reminder of the extent to which this part of Sheffield's commercial area had to be rebuilt postwar. The most striking is **T.J. Hughes**, built as Walsh's department store by *J.W. Beaumont & Son* in 1953, rebuilt with a splayed corner in the 1960s. Close-set mullions give the building a pronounced vertical emphasis, a treatment deliberately intended to be in keeping with the façades of older buildings. On the N side is the **Bankers Draft**, formerly the York City and County Bank, of 1904 by *Walter Brierley.* Edwardian Baroque, carried off with panache. Channelled rusticated ground floor, the central four bays above are set back behind attached composite columns. Big scrolls above the cornice and Gibbsian surrounds to the attic windows. From here walk down **Angel Street** which falls sharply to the N. **Argos** was built as Cockayne's (who started out as drapers) department store by *J.W. Beaumont & Son,* 1955–6, with emphasized verticals like the Hughes store. Then the **Travel Inn**, 2002–3, in modish bright colours and displaying the early C21 liking for jarring angles. On the E side at the junction with **Castle Street** is **Castle House** (the **SCS Department Store**) [23], built 1959–64 by *G.S. Hay.* Originally for the Brightside and Carbrook Co-operative Society as their headquarters and principal store and replacing premises destroyed by bombing. An impressive granite front with a massively splayed corner. This front is unbroken by windows, except in the upper floor, deeply set back above it in a band under very broad eaves. Some nice contemporary touches include a zig-zag edge to the concrete canopy, and inside, a stylish cantilevered spiral staircase with stainless-steel balusters under a dome lit by circular glass bricks. At the top of this, mounted on the wall, a metallic sculpture of a bird. To the rear, facing King Street, a 1962 block by *Hadfield Cawkwell & Davidson* with a rather emaciated glass fibre Vulcan (1960) by *Boris Tietze*.

On the N side of Castle Street, at the foot of a steeply descending grass bank are the **South Yorkshire Police Headquarters** (actually located in Snig Hill) and the **Magistrates Court**, intended to harmonize with one another by employing a combination of red brick cladding and rounded corners in rough-textured ribbed concrete. The Police Headquarters, 1970, by *B. Warren*, City Planning Officer and Architect, is of five storeys, the top and ground floors set back, and has a prominent stair-turret. The Magistrates Court (opened 1978) is taller and is entered at first-floor level from Castle Street across a footbridge. Otherwise clad entirely in ribbed concrete with slit-like windows, the s elevation has a smooth-faced projecting concrete screen which encloses a grid of glazing. Individual courtrooms project from the Bridge Street façade. Coherent in design if not particularly lovable. In **Snig Hill** to the w, **Corporation Buildings** by *Gibbs & Flockton*, early public housing *c.* 1904. Flats and maisonettes are accessed from the rear, with shops on the ground floor. Big gables and plenty of terracotta decoration. Half the block was destroyed by bombing.

Returning to **Castle Street**, Nos. 9–11, 1868, by *Charles Unwin*. Filling the end wall, a brick mural of 1986 by *Paul Waplington* depicting a steel-worker. The shop façade has paired round-headed windows linked by granite columns set within rounded arches on both the first and second floors. Carved heads within the spandrels of the first-floor windows, carved foliage on the second. Opposite, **The Cannon** (originally the Cannon Spirit Vaults), 1902–3, by *J.R. Wigfull*, for William Stones's brewery. Tudor Renaissance, with three big dormers, the windows flanked by tapered pilasters and topped by segmental pediments. Ornate stone panels including one of the brewery's cannon emblem and the company's initials.

Down **Castle Green**, now a short cul-de-sac. On the left, the **Hen and Chickens**, a classical pub of 1851 with paired sashes divided by Corinthian columns. Porch with double consoles. Decorative heads attached to the drainpipes including a lion. Next, the **Police Offices** of 1866 by *Flockton & Abbott*; contemporary with their remodelling and extension of the Town Hall (*see* below). Three storeys with attic and basement. Ashlar façade with a recessed centre, projecting bays at each end and a heavily rusticated ground floor. On the ground floor round-headed windows with chamfered surrounds; on the first, windows divided by shafts with Gothic acanthus capitals and a moulded foliage band continuing the

82. Old Town Hall, Waingate, by Charles Watson, 1807–8; as extended by Flockton & Abbott, 1866 and Flockton, Gibbs & Flockton, 1896–7. Photograph *c.* 1905

Gothic theme. Curious scrolls at the base of the projecting bays. The offices were linked by underground passages to the courtrooms in the old **Town Hall** [82] which stands at the corner of Castle Street and **Waingate**. Classical, built in three stages, the earliest by *Charles Watson* in 1807–8, to provide the Town Trustees with accommodation for themselves and the Petty and Quarter Sessions. Extension and remodelling by *Flockton & Abbott,* 1866, and further substantial additions, including a Police Court, made by *Flockton, Gibbs & Flockton* in 1896–7 when the new Town Hall was built on Pinstone Street (*see* Major Buildings, p. 61). Ashlar throughout except for the rear elevations of the 1897 additions, the greatest care taken to ensure the additions matched the original work.

Facing Waingate, Watson's building is symmetrical, of five bays. The ground floor is rusticated and has segmental-headed windows. The central three bays are brought forward slightly and emphasized by Ionic pilasters above which the 1866 **clock tower**, with a rounded top and large openings covered with metal grilles, is perched rather uncomfortably. The entrance was originally in Castle Street in the centre of what was a three-bay façade with a pediment. All this was altered in 1866 when the parapet was rebuilt with a balustrade and three bays extended on Waingate. This has the Judge's Entrance with an enriched pedimented doorcase with Ionic columns *in antis*. The remainder of the building is of 1896–7. The interior has a semicircular lobby with Doric columns and entablature, leading to three courts. Currently awaiting re-use.

On the E side of Waingate, **Castle Market** of 1960–5 by *J.L. Womersley* (project architect: *Andrew Darbyshire*), is one of the city's 1960s showpieces. Externally straightforward and not especially notable, as a piece of planning it was highly interesting and ingenious for its date. Designed not only to continue the old tradition of the market hall with stalls for traders but also as a covered shopping centre. The site slopes downhill so ground-floor access could be obtained on three levels, thus the difficulty of making people shop on the upper tiers, which faced C19 shopping arcades, was to be overcome. To the NE, the pre-war fish and vegetable market was incorporated. On the sides facing Exchange Street and Waingate office blocks were added. Shops were built into the street elevations with a recessed gallery at first-floor level connected by covered bridges to adjoining shops on the s side of Exchange Street by *Thomas & Peter H. Braddock* and eventually extended along Waingate to Haymarket. It is little changed today, even retaining much of its original signage, but, although still popular, is showing its age and numerous schemes for its replacement have been proposed. The first-floor walkways, like most such schemes of the period to separate pedestrians and traffic, have proved unsuccessful.

Waingate, s of Castle Street, becomes **Haymarket**. The w side exhibits a variety of commercial styles. On the corner is No. 32 Castle Street, 1904 by *Gibbs & Flockton*, built as a shop, café and restaurant for Arthur Davy & Sons Ltd. (*see* also Fargate, p. 120). Effective Free Style with two large gables linked by a circular tower, all in red brick with stone bands. The original door surround is just visible above the present shop front. Next, No. 25, plain early C19 houses with elaborate applied half timbering, a bay window with leaded lights and a rustic bellcote added in the C20. By way of contrast, No. 21, 1930s moderne for Arthur Davy with a staircase tower, then the early C19 stucco façade of Nos. 17 and 13–15, the former **Brunswick** pub, late Georgian with pillars and entablature to the first-floor windows.

Down **Dixon Lane** to the E, one gains an impression of what the streets in the markets area must once have looked like with small-scale three-storey C19 houses with shops. Nos. 22–24 is apparently early C18 with a steeply pitched roof and, at the end, the **Norfolk Arms**, an early

## Sheffield Castle

In *c.* 1100 William de Lovetot built a substantial timber castle with a motte-and-bailey. This was destroyed in 1266 and following the end of the Barons' War, in 1270 Thomas de Furnival constructed a massive crenellated stone castle. It had an inner and outer courtyard, the inner on the site of Castle Market, the outer extended to the s. The inner courtyard was in effect the castle, surrounded by a moat and stone wall. The castle was roughly rectangular, bounded on the N side by the Don and by the moat on the three remaining sides. Excavations in 1927–9 revealed that its entrance was in the SE corner, flanked by two towers. Numerous buildings were built up against the castle wall, including a great tower, great hall and chapel. The castle was demolished by Parliament after the Civil War, in 1648–9. Further excavations in 2001 revealed evidence of considerable remains beneath the Castle Market and proposals for its redevelopment envisage uncovering at least part of the site.

C19 corner pub. Round the corner in **Shude Hill**, the Hotel Ibis, a plain brick hotel of the late 1990s has an artwork, the **Silver Service Gates** (1999) by *Michael Johnson*, stainless steel embedded with knives, forks and spoons. The area to the E as far as Exchange Street was the site of Sheffield's open markets until 1973. Beyond, in what is now **Park Square**, stood *M.E. Hadfield & Son*'s handsome Neo-Tudor **Corn Exchange** of 1881. Demolished 1964, one of the city's greatest postwar losses.

Returning along Haymarket, one turns left into **Commercial Street**. On the corner with Haymarket and providing a strong accent on the corner of Fitzalan Square, is the **Yorkshire Bank**, built as the Post Office in 1871. Two storeys with an attic, in a classical style of such purity that it looks more like work of the 1850s with heavily rusticated pilasters dividing each window, two storeys with an attic and dentil cornice. Richly decorated with Greek key pattern and balusters at first-floor. Facing Commercial Street, Nos. 5–7 (used as a Stock Exchange 1911–67) built at the same time and continuing the same rhythm, one storey with basement, the frieze with a guilloche band and a pierced balustrade above the cornice.

Next is one of the finest C19 buildings in the city and one that compares favourably with the commercial palaces of Manchester, the former **Gas Offices** (Panache House) [83] of 1874 by *M.E. Hadfield & Son* for the Sheffield United Gas Light Co. which had their works nearby.

83. Gas Offices, Commercial Street, by M.E. Hadfield & Son, detail of Atlantes by Thomas Earp, 1874

Symmetrical two-storey palazzo style, derived from Early Renaissance, (particularly Venetian), models but with an unorthodox central attic surmounted by an enriched pediment and a mansard roof, clad with ornamental fish-scale tiles, broken by dormers and corner turrets with niches and spires. The Hollington stone **façade**, however, shows what a Sheffield architect could produce given the opportunity. It displays a riot of decoration yet none of it appears excessive or vulgar. The entrance is off-centre with an open segmental pediment supported by Atlantes [83], carved by *Thomas Earp*, and a pulvinated frieze with bay leaf decoration. Very ornate Corinthian capitals. Unduly prominent Portland stone addition of 1938 by *Hadfield & Cawkwell*. The style is somewhere between stripped classical and moderne e.g. a Greek key band and flutes representing pilasters combining with sculpture by *Philip Lindsay Clark* of a flying female figure with a sunbeam behind her and a male figure backed by flames. The ground floor contained a general office, showrooms and a manager's room, and the first the engineers, board and committee rooms.

The **interior** is as rich as the exterior. *J.F. Bentley*, friend and co-religionist of the Catholic Hadfield was commissioned to decorate the general office. Glazed 25 ft diameter dome, pilasters with exuberant capitals, a deeply coved panelled ceiling and an ashlar doorcase with rounded pediment and delicately carved panels. One of the grandest c19 rooms in the city, now a restaurant. The boardroom ceiling was the work of *Hugh Stannus*.

The walk returns to **Fitzalan Square**. In the centre of the square, is a bronze **Statue of King Edward VII**, 1913, by *Alfred Drury*, bronze, larger than life-size in robes on a corniced square pedestal with a moulded plinth. On the sides of the pedestal, bronze reliefs of allegorical scenes depicting, on the left, Philanthropy with figures holding a model of the King Edward VII Hospital (Rivelin Valley), on the right Peacemaker with women holding olive branches, and to the rear, Unity with figures including an African, a Native American, etc.

On the w side of the square, Nos. 6–12 **The White Building** [84], c. 1908, by *Gibbs & Flockton*, one of the most original buildings of its date in Sheffield with a faience façade enlivened by ten figures in relief by *Alfred and William Tory* depicting Sheffield trades [84] (*see* topic box, p. 110). Four storeys with a raised attic storey in the centre. French windows with balconies on the first floor with medallions above. Further balconies on the third floor which has unusual ogee-shaped hoods above the windows incorporating a scallop or fanlight design. Similar but segmental hoods over the first-floor windows. Adam-style frieze at the top of the building. Arcaded ground floor, the entrance with its original name plaque is recessed behind one of the plain elliptical arches.

The s side of the Square is taken up by the exuberant Baroque former **Post Office** of 1910 by *Walter Pott* of H.M. Office of Works. Ashlar, with two long façades along the square and its continuation, Flat Street. The corner between the two is marked by a tower with a dome supported by

84. The White Building, Fitzalan Square, by Gibbs & Flockton, figures of a grinder and hand forger by Alfred & William Tory, *c.* 1908

consoles, banded lower stages and stepped stair windows. Heavily rusticated entrance bays with giant pilasters and dentil cornices with half-round pediments. Giant order of engaged Ionic columns with a pulvinated frieze. Ground-floor windows have alternating segmental and triangular pediments, those on the first floor in the entrance bays divided by paired Doric columns. Big scrolled keystone over a coved round-arched entrance and portico with blocked granite columns. The Flat Street elevation is a little quieter, continued in the red brick Queen Anne of the earlier Post Office block of 1897 by *J. Williams.*

Down **Flat Street**, on the right, the former Odeon Cinema, now **Mecca Bingo** by *Roger Bullivant*, 1956. Unusual single-storey wedge-shape glass foyer projecting in front of the brick-clad auditorium. Next, the **Epic Development** of 1968–9 by *Jefferson Sheard & Partners*. Like Castle Market (*see* above), a massive project very much of its time and exploiting the steeply sloping ground. With the city's newly constructed inner ring road, Arundel Gate, on the boundary of the site at the higher level, the scheme was to provide an entertainment complex with shops and car parking below, linking the Pond Street Bus Station with the city centre by means of walkways, escalators and subways. Two large rectangular windowless blocks, clad entirely in panels of white tiles, one, the **Odeon Cinema** with a gable-roofed foyer, 1992, built as a nightclub with twin cinemas under, the other as a dance hall with conference suite (disused). Below the dance hall are the car parks and the shopping concourse, their parapet walls giving a powerful horizontal emphasis. The cinema perches above an open concrete framework, lightening what might otherwise have been an overpowering mass.

In **Pond Street**, the **Sheffield Transport Interchange** by the *John Brunton Partnership*, 1990, replaced an earlier bus station. Pleasant pitched-roof, yellow brick-clad main building with shops leading to bus stands and shelters, situated on a curve. Adjoining on the N side in **Pond Hill** and almost looking like an incongruous addition, is the oldest domestic building in Sheffield, the **Old Queen's Head** [5]. Small and timber-framed, it was once a house of some importance, considerably larger than it is today. Traditionally known as the Hall-in-the-Ponds, the name derived from the mill ponds (and possibly fish ponds) adjacent to the River Sheaf. Probably built in the C15 although the first documentary evidence is in an inventory for the Earl of Shrewsbury in 1582. It had ceased to be an adjunct of the Castle by 1637 and was let to tenants. Gosling's plan of Sheffield of 1736 shows a hall with a cross-wing parallel to Pond Hill. The wing is not shown in an engraving in Hunter's *Hallamshire* (1819) and the rest was further reduced in the C19 by road widening when the N wall was replaced in brick and stone. The hall has closely set studs and the first floor oversailing on a coved jetty. On the W façade, a bressumer with tracery and two figured brackets, one a queen's head, the other a male demi-figure. The windows with traceried wooden frames and curved jetties are restorations of 1993. Inside, on the first floor, two tiny mullioned windows of plaster set in a partition wall facing the foot of the attic stairs. Three carved heads in the bar. The adjoining early C19 brick building became the Old Queen's Head beerhouse *c.* 1840 and later incorporated the remains of the hall. Plain rendered addition of 1993. Further down Pond Hill is the former **gateway** (*c.* 1900) to the forge of George Senior, moved here from its original site in Sheaf Street when the works were demolished for the building of Ponds Forge. An anvil block may be seen around the corner in Sheaf Street.

Facing **Sheaf Street**, the **Ponds Forge International Leisure Centre** [85] designed by *FaulknerBrowns* in 1989 (project architect: *Jon Ignatowiez*) for the World Student Games. It comprises Olympic-sized competition swimming and diving pools, a leisure pool and a sports hall. The exterior combines classical order with deconstructive chaos: along Sheaf Street, the main body (enclosing the Olympic pool and the sports hall) is elegant and restrained with a rough plinth, silver-grey powder-coated aluminium panels and a shallow arched roof with broad eaves. But at

85. Ponds Forge, the competition pool, by FaulknerBrowns, 1989

the point where the leisure pool joins the main building, the architecture goes into free fall with projections at odd angles and a curving glass wall exposing the anarchic activity of the pool to the outside world. At the entrance on Commercial Street, a classical form is used with paired columns and entablature represented in tubular steel and an encircling masonry drum cut open to reveal a glass wall.

Inside, the Olympic pool is covered by a breathtaking shallow vault with a diagrid structure of tubular-steel trusses in a diagonal layout, the four primary trusses meeting at a joint at its apex with secondary purlins following a similar arrangement to create a criss-cross pattern. Clerestory lighting and bands of obscured glazing.

Opposite, the elegant **Supertram Bridge** of 1993 vaults over Park Square. From here one may return up Commercial Street to where this walk began.

## b) Wicker and Victoria Quays

The walk begins at **Bridge Street** by the River Don, where the former **Exchange Brewery** occupies a prominent site, but one so compact that part of the brewery is carried over the river on iron columns. Tennant Brothers Ltd moved here in 1852. The five-storey brewing tower is probably of that date but the brewery offices and ornamental gates with reliefs of wheatsheaves are of 1867 by *Flockton & Abbott*. They also designed the former brewery tap, the **Lady's Bridge Hotel** which fills the corner of the site with a curved stucco front with an elaborate

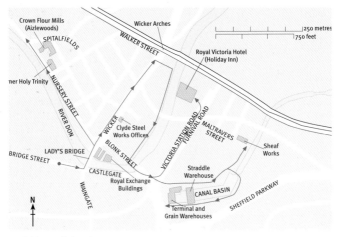

86. Wicker and Victoria Quays

cornice and banding. The brewery closed in 1993, part of the site has been cleared and the remainder clinically restored as offices with inappropriate plastic windows.

**Lady's Bridge** was built in 1486; its early masonry obscured by successive widenings, on the NW side in 1761 and on the SE in 1864 and 1909. Four arches with iron columns supporting the extensions on either side. It originally had a chapel dedicated to Our Lady Mary on the town side, demolished in 1767. Flanking the street also named Lady's Bridge is a development of 1899–1900, by *Flockton, Gibbs & Flockton* for John Henry Bryars, an animal breeder and vet. Both buildings are covered in light brown glazed bricks with dark brown bands, and have crow-stepped gables and finials. The ranges along Lady's Bridge are of four storeys. On the left **Royal Victoria Buildings**, triangular in plan with a mansard roof, had a bar, billiard and card rooms on the first floor. On the right, **Royal Exchange Buildings** [87] comprised twenty two-bed-roomed flats, houses for the veterinary surgeon and groom, shops, veterinary surgery and dogs' home. Access balconies at the rear of the dwellings have bridges to a staircase tower. Over the surgery doorway is a snake and sword, symbols of Asclepius, the Greek god of medicine. At the rear was accommodation for sick horses and the entrance to the dogs' home and hospital, the dogs being housed in kennels under the walkway. At right angles to this facing the river is a further range, **Castle House**, a multi-storey stables with iron frame and internal ramps for access. In 1931 the stables were converted to a pioneering pea-canning factory by *Chapman & Jenkinson* for Batchelors. Now a furniture store.

On the w, at the junction of **Wicker** with Nursery Street, backing on to the river, **City Wharf** of 2003–4, apartments by *Axis Architecture* in a tough warehouse aesthetic with small square segmental-headed windows, larger openings simulating hoist doors and short concrete columns on the ground floor. Continuing up **Nursery Street**, on the

87. Royal Exchange Buildings, Lady's Bridge, by Flockton, Gibbs & Flockton, 1899–1900

corner with Wicker Lane, the former **Coroner's Court**, 1913, by *F.E.P. Edwards*, City Architect, red brick with twin gables enclosing a five-bay central portion and scrolls on both gables. On the corner of Johnson Street, **Holy Trinity Church**, 1848, by *Flockton, Lee & Flockton*, built at the expense of Anne and Elizabeth Harrison, the daughters of Thomas Harrison of Weston House (*see* p. 286). The Misses Harrison insisted that it be an exact copy of Christ Church, Attercliffe, of 1826 (dem.). Hence it is old fashioned for its date, with thin spiky buttresses which project above a crenellated parapet, tall lancets, short chancel and gallery on iron columns, a church to incite Pugin's ire. Strong vertical emphasis throughout. The tower, which has lost its pinnacles, has three pointed openings on each side of its top stage with arcading below. Simple brick schools to the rear of 1848, enlarged in 1855. Beyond the church, the **Crown Flour Mills** built in the 1870s for John Aizlewood Ltd, now converted to offices and workshops. Tall six-storey L-shaped mill, once linked at high level to the Bridgehouses goods yard, with a mixture of segmental and round-arched windows and a tall rectangular chimney. Return along Nursery Street to Lady's Bridge (a small diversion to avoid the heavy traffic can be made by crossing the footbridge over the Don and walking along the riverside path).

By the junction of **Wicker** with Nursery Street, the **Riverside Court Hotel** (formerly the Lion Hotel) of 1879. Four storeys on a curve, quite plain, with a classical doorway. Most of the remainder of the w side of Wicker is mid C19. The E side was dominated by the **Clyde Steel Works** of Samuel Osborn & Co. from 1868 to 1970. Only the street elevation and one shop at the rear is left. The office block, built for Osborn's predecessors on the site, Shortridge & Howell, in 1853, has a richly decorated front. Tall, though of only three storeys, of brick with an ashlar façade in the classical style. Massive moulded wood cornice. Three arched recesses on the ground floor with voussoirs and prominent keystones, the central one was formerly a cart entrance. Then a balcony with an iron balustrade supported by chunky corbels, the outer two decorated with fish and the town's arms, the inner pair with elephants' heads. The first floor has Venetian windows set in coved arches with prominent voussoirs and deep keystones with carved heads. Channelled rustication to the two lower floors. The remainder of the frontage to the Wicker was built in the early C20 in plain red brick as shops with offices over.

Returning to the w side, at Nos. 87–91, the former **Sheffield and Hallamshire Bank** of 1893 by *Flockton & Gibbs*, in impressive French Second Empire style. In the centre, the banking hall with a flat for the manager over. Then the former **Station Hotel**, Edwardian, of brick with stone dressings. Vaguely Arts and Crafts including some fine naturalistic carving in the porch. Opposite, Nos. 122–126, formerly a branch of the Sheffield Banking Co. 1893 by *M.E. Hadfield, Son & Garland*. Italianate, built of thin red bricks. Parapet with ball finials and a cartouche with a foliage surround.

Wicker is closed by the 1848 viaduct of the Manchester Sheffield & Lincolnshire Railway and its bridge over the street, known as the **Wicker Arches** [88]. The viaduct has forty arches and is 660 yards long: the arch is 72 ft wide and was built of stone from Lord Wharncliffe's quarry at Wharncliffe Crags, by *John Fowler*, engineer, with architects *Weightman & Hadfield* who were also responsible for Victoria Station (1851) and many other stations on the MS&LR. The broad principal arch is flanked by two narrow arches for pedestrians. Above these, four crests are inset: the MS&LR, the Duke of Norfolk, the Earl of Yarborough and the Sheffield Town Trustees. On the SE side, the ashlar side entrance to the demolished **Victoria Station**. Five bays, the fifth projecting with an archway.

Take the path between the former station façade and Nos. 122–6 Wicker to the striking **Cobweb Bridge** of 2003 by *Paul Mallinder* and *Richard Coe* of Sheffield City Council. It is suspended from the arch of the railway viaduct above the Don on a forest of steel cables. From here, return s to **Blonk Street** along the **riverside path** on the w side of the

88. Wicker Arches, by John Fowler and Weightman & Hadfield, 1848

89. Straddle warehouse, Victoria Quays, 1895–8

Don. On the opposite bank a crucible stack of four flues may be seen above a remaining part of Samuel Osborn's premises (*see* above). **Blonk Bridge** is by *Woodhead & Hurst*, 1827–8 and altered *c.* 1913, with three elliptical rusticated arches and cast-iron balustrades, built to link Wicker directly with the canal basin. Across the river on the left, a lengthy ramp built in 1851 to serve Victoria Station now leads only to the **Royal Victoria Station Hotel** (Holiday Inn), 1862, by *M.E. Hadfield* large but simple Italianate, its design was stated by Hadfield (with no apparent justification) to have owed much to Inigo Jones. Pevsner thought it 'gloomy' and together with Victoria Station 'a singularly unpromising entry to Sheffield'. Dreadful roundel of Queen Victoria on the front. Enlarged in 1898 and extended to the rear over the former station site in the 1980s. Beside the hotel is the **Great Central Railway War Memorial** of 1922, nine columns of names set in three copper plaques. Formerly at Victoria Station, the original setting was within a Doric colonnade by *T.E. Collcutt*.

Across Furnival Road is the entrance to **Victoria Quays**, the former Sheffield Canal Basin of 1816–19, restored and redeveloped since 1992. The Sheffield Canal Company was promoted to construct a link with the Don Navigation (completed in 1751) at Tinsley Wharf, thus providing direct access from the coastal ports to the town centre. Sheffield basin was replaced as the head of commercial navigation by a new facility at Rotherham in 1968 and received its last cargo in 1970. Part of the site takes in the former coal yard of the MS&LR and close to the entrance is a handsome group of restored **Coal Merchants' Offices**. Stone with steeply pitched roofs, they curve gently along the ramp to the yard and are of one storey to the ramp but two to the rear. The coal yard was built on a viaduct which crosses the N side of the basin quay. His arches are infilled for shops and restaurants. **Sculpture**: on the bleak raised part of the N quay a life-size recumbent **Sacred Cow** by *Ronald Rae*, 1992, and **Heron and Fish**, carved out of a single block of stone by *Vega Bermejo*, 1995. The earliest building associated with the basin is the **Terminal Warehouse** of 1819 (restored 1994). It is of brick with large stone-dressed arched openings at ground floor, one forming a boat hole enabling goods to be hoisted from keels directly to the upper floors. The hoist survives on the top floor. Four storeys with a large gable incorporating a further storey, wide seven-bay pediments to the E and W elevations. Interior of wooden construction but the middle two floors had a steel framework fitted later. The roof is supported by a composite queenpost and kingpost with a truss span of over 66 ft. A two-storey brick extension provided the original offices for the basin. At right angles to the Terminal Warehouse a block built *c.* 1853 as the head office for the Tinsley Park Coal Co. To the N, a **warehouse** added in 1889 by the MS&LR, four storeys, brick with segmental-headed cast-iron casements and weatherboarded sack-hoist towers. Converted into a grain silo in 1925. The **Straddle Warehouse** [89] of 1895–8 was a thoroughly up-to-date design. Steel frame with concrete infill supported on blue brick arches, red brick end walls and five docking bays. Restored by *Robin Hedger*.

New construction around the quay is a mixed bag. On the S side, two long office blocks by *Hadfield Cawkwell Davidson* of 1994, both in a style fashionable at this date, in red brick with light powder-coated metal cladding and horizontal windows. The **Nabarro Nathanson Building** is slightly fussy with somewhat incongruous coped gables, kneelers and short columns. The **Parexcel Building** has a much cleaner appearance. In front of this, the Basin Manager's house and office, 1994–5, a simple but neat structure in the functional tradition, with a canted front providing good visibility.

A short walk N along the quayside leads to **Sheaf Quay** in **Maltravers Street**, the site of Sheaf Works, one of the earliest integrated steelworks. The works were built between 1822 and 1826 for William Greaves who produced cutlery, steel and edge tools. Taken over in 1839 by Thomas Turton who also made springs. All that remains is the handsome office building, resembling a country house built of ashlar and coursed stone. Four storeys and nine bays, with a five-bay central pediment. Converted by *Carey Jones Seifert Ltd* in 1989, with a Postmodern addition to the W with a semi-circular entablature supported by thin columns without capitals. It encloses a rounded single-storey addition with a clumsy rectangular block above.

From here, walk back along the Quays to Exchange Street and the city centre.

## Walk 6

# Scotland Street
# to Neepsend

The area bounded by Broad Lane, Tenter Street and West Bar was the
first expansion of the C18 town to the N beyond its medieval limits. The
streets were laid out following the boundaries of the open field strips
and Hollis Croft, White Croft, Lambert Street, Pea Croft (Solly Street)
and Lambert Croft (Scotland Street) had appeared by 1736 [6]. The
extreme narrowness of some of the streets still gives the area much of
its character today. By the mid C19, this was one of the city's most tightly
built-up areas with densely packed courts of houses and cutlery workshops, inhabited by a substantial Irish population for whom St
Vincent's Church was built. Clearance started in the 1890s but was not
completed until the late 1930s when the Edward Street flats were built
to house the remaining inhabitants. Small factories were built on the
sites of the demolished houses but the original street layout was
retained. Although much of it is now derelict land, the impact of
Sheffield University is beginning to be felt through renovations for student accommodation. One still obtains an excellent impression of the
small-scale industry once ubiquitous throughout the city centre.

The area on the E side of Gibraltar Street was developed at the beginning of the C19 on what had been Colson Crofts. Again a tightly packed
mass of courts and small factories evolved, those in the Acorn Street

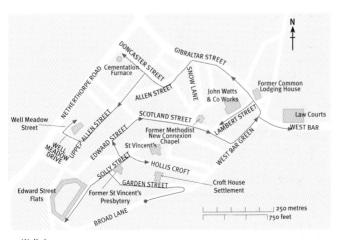

area becoming known as especially unwholesome. A number of much larger factories spread out along the Don engulfing Bridgehouses, a fashionable suburb in the early C18. Principal C19 developments were the building of the Sheffield, Ashton-under-Lyne & Manchester Railway's first Sheffield station at Bridgehouses in 1845 and the cutting through of Corporation Street in 1856. This provides access to Bridgehouses, which had become one of the city's principal goods depots following the opening of Victoria Station in 1851. Road-widening and the new Crown Court have altered the area beyond recognition. In the C19 this was the centre for Sheffield's popular entertainment. Regeneration is set to change the area still further as the fashion for loft apartments encourages the conversion of disused factories and building of new apartment blocks. Construction of a planned continuation of the ring road through the area is due to commence in 2005.

## a) Scotland Street and the Crofts

The walk begins in **Broad Lane**, opposite Newcastle Street, at the **James Montgomery Memorial Drinking Fountain** of *c.* 1875. Behind it, the sole remaining early house on this side of the road, No. 114, early C19, of three storeys with a simple fanlight and prominent steps. Across **Townhead Street** one of the earliest council housing schemes, 178 flats completed 1903 on a triangular site with inner courtyard. Three storeys, brick, very plain, but palatial compared with the Crofts slums they replaced. Then into **Garden Street**. Amidst a mixture of 1930s and later factories, there are numerous reminders of the area's past as a tightly packed mass of small houses and cutlery premises. On the right, the **Croft House Settlement** which began as a Congregational Chapel in 1866–7, an early work by *Innocent & Brown*, the architects of Sheffield's Board Schools. Inspired by the work of East London's Toynbee Hall, the building was converted to minister to the needs of the inhabitants of this poor district in 1902. Stone, the façade crudely rendered and with a large rose window with plate tracery as its centre. The 1902 alterations include the insertion of a floor at gallery level to form a second storey and enlargement at the E end to provide a top-lit room. Its Warden, Rev. William Blackshaw, lived in the Dingle, Bradway, a large house designed for him in 1904 in the leafy southern suburbs by *Edgar Wood*. On the left, the former **St Luke's National Schools** (now used for the cutlery trades), a classical building by *H.D. Lomas* of 1873. Brick with stone dressings on the ground floor and an open pediment over the central four bays. The name is carved in stone across the façade. Opposite is No. 38, the first of a number of cutlery workshops of the usual Sheffield type (*see* p. 126) comprising an early C19 house of three storeys in brick but disguised in recent years by thick textured render. Behind is a range of later brick workshops. At No. 48 is another similar works with an archway to a yard behind. The best example of these workshops is at Nos. 52–56 where there is a pre-1850 three-storey house adjoined at the rear by a slightly later blind-back house and workshop

91. Robens Building, by PSA Projects, 1993

range. A further workshop range alongside has the characteristic closely spaced casements. As the top of Garden Street is reached, we see the **Robens Building** [91] of the Health and Safety Executive, an occupational medicine and hygiene laboratory, 1993 by *PSA Projects* (project architect: *Gordon Wilson)*. The laboratory services are exposed around the outside, following the example of Louis Kahn's Richards Medical Research Building, Philadelphia. A concrete structure contains the laboratories within a near-square plan and wide external balconies partly mask the exposed air exhaust ducts. Brick offices are domestic in style, stepping up to the laboratories but clearly separated from them. The culmination of the building is the phalanx of sixteen plastic flues (popularly known as 'the organ pipes'), the tallest in the centre, a distinctive contribution to the skyline.

Turning to the left along **Solly Street**, at the end the **Edward Street flats** loom up. Designed by *W.G. Davies,* and built in 1939–43, this was the largest development of tenement flats in the city centre. Although the style is broadly Neo-Georgian, the influence of Dudok is evident in the pronounced horizontal emphasis given by the access balconies (since rebuilt in tubular steel), the streamlined staircase-turrets and the large arched principal entrance. The flats encircle a green and their location on a slope ensured adequate lighting. Retracing our steps, on the left is No. 216, **Cambridge Works**, formerly the works of James Lodge, cutlery and electroplate manufacturers. The front block is pre-1850, of three storeys and retains its small-paned windows. Doorway with unusual shouldered architrave. Restored as student accommodation. On the right, the **St Vincent's Presbytery** (now Provincial House), 1878, by *M.E. Hadfield & Son* must have dominated what was a poor, largely Irish neighbourhood. Italianate, of considerable refinement in cut and gauged brick, it was paid for by the 15th Duke of Norfolk. Four storeys with a porch of red Hollington stone, a plaque and a niche formerly containing a statue of St Vincent. Apsed chapel at the rear.

Up **Hollis Croft** on the right is **Industry Place**, a three-storey brick terrace bearing a plaque 'Erected by W. & M. Howe 1833' with a rear range. Then **St Vincent's R.C. Church** of 1856 (closed 1998), positioned near the top of a ridge and of great townscape value. Of coursed sandstone, it was the work of *Weightman, Hadfield & Goldie*, but *George Goldie* was probably the architect. It was the first of his many churches to show French influence, e.g. in the design of the shallow Continental-type apse. The s aisle and sacristy were not part of the original design and were added during the erection of the church. *M.E. Hadfield* added the pretty Perp-style polygonal chapel on the s side of the s aisle in 1861. The entrance porch and the lower part of the conspicuous sw tower was also by *M.E. Hadfield*, 1870. The N aisle, N porch and entrance followed in 1898–9 and the upper part of the tower in 1910–11, all by *Charles Hadfield*. The N aisle windows, which are accompanied by the parapet rising to form gables above them are broad in comparison to those of the s aisle. The somewhat stark ashlar top stage of the tower again displays French influence in the paired tall thin belfry openings in each face. The delicate canted corners flanked by equally thin buttresses contrast oddly with the massive clasping forms of those at the base. The SE Chapel of the Holy Souls, of 1964, by *Hadfield Cawkwell Davidson & Partners* is in an angular style making few concessions to the past. The lofty interior, now stripped of its furniture and stained glass, reveals no division between apse and nave. The six-bay nave has narrow arcading with octagonal piers and carved angels as label stops. The s chapel, separated from the aisle by a Perp-style stone screen has a vaulted ceiling and arcaded stone altar. The N aisle is quite different in character with arcading on round piers superimposed behind each window. NE of the church, on **Solly Street**, the former **Ragged School and Orphanage**, 1873, by *Flockton & Abbott,* and **St Vincent's Schools** of 1863. Gothic with an addition of 1892–7 with crowstepped gables.

From Solly Street, **Scotland Street** is reached via Brocco Street and Edward Street; by Furnace Hill the former **Methodist New Connexion Chapel** (now flats) dated 1828. Classical, brick of five bays with a broad pediment. There was a chapel here from 1765, and from 1797, the minister was Alexander Kilham, the principal figure in the founding of the New Connexion. Adjoining, the **Littlewood Memorial Hall**, 1897, by *Flockton, Gibbs & Flockton* has round-headed windows to match. Continue E along Scotland Street and turn left into **West Bar Green** to the **Central Division Police Station**, of 1962–4, by *J.L. Womersley*. Well-composed group in engineering brick and curtain-walling. Low range for vehicles and workshops and high slab for the offices. Next is the former **Police, Fire and Ambulance Station** of 1897 by *Joseph Norton*. A somewhat confused façade of red brick with Venetian windows and rounded gables. Short tower, topped by cupola and ball.

The **Law Courts** by *PSA Project Management* dominate this part of **West Bar**. A large and forbidding complex built 1993–6, they display a disconcerting mixture of Postmodern elements as though the archi-

92. Former Common Lodging House, by J.R. Truelove, 1912

tects were hedging their bets. The disparate elements simply do not add up and the result is a building that is as pompous as it is graceless. Alongside, the **Family Court** of 2003 by *Aedas AHR* is slightly self-effacing and all the better for it. Red brick with a hipped roof and a strong horizontal emphasis achieved through a continuous band of glazing on the top (third) floor.

Returning NW along **West Bar**, beyond the roundabout, there is a pair of houses (Nos. 117 and 119) dated 1794. Three storeys, brick with ashlar dressings and typical of much of the building of this area as it developed at the end of the C18. More late C18–C19 houses in **Lambert Street** as part of the premises of **John Watts**, a medium-sized cutlery works that has survived in largely C19 condition. The houses have been rendered and have raised plaster lettering bearing the firm's name. Behind are five courts taken into the works, which include some blind-back houses of the poorest type and workshops, some with northlight roofs (rare in Sheffield), including one toplit with an internal gallery. On the N side of West Bar, the former **Common Lodging House** [92] (now Mayfair Court), 1912, by *John Reginald Truelove*, whose father Alderman Truelove paid for the building. It provided hostel accommodation superior to the often insanitary lodgings of private landlords, together with public rooms and social facilities. One of the most interesting buildings of its period in the city. Tall and thin with a strikingly broad cornice, central balcony and accomplished detailing with rusticated brick quoins and contrasting red and yellow brick. The public rooms on the lower floors were lit by broad segmental-arched windows. Slit-like openings to the four floors of bedrooms above which were divided by a corridor into two rows of cubicles. At **Bower Spring** are the remains of two cementation furnaces, built *c.* 1828 for Thomas Turton's Franklin Works (*see* topic box, p. 165).

93. Former back-to-backs forming part of Sheffield Metal Co. Works, Snow Lane, *c.* 1800

In **Snow Lane** to the left, the **Sheffield Metal Co.'s** works [93]. Brick with round-headed windows built in several phases. In the 1890s, the works took in six adjoining back-to-back houses of *c.* 1800. They are almost unique survivals of what was the most common form of the Sheffield working man's house in the early C19. Built of small irregular bricks and with their original small sill-less casement windows, only two are still recognizable while the third was refronted to match the round-headed windows of the remainder of the works.

By way of Allen Street to **Doncaster Street** where in HSBC Bank's car park is preserved the only complete cementation furnace left in Sheffield, dating from 1848 and originally part of the steelworks of Daniel Doncaster. Bottle-shaped like a pottery kiln. Last heated in 1951, it now stands in isolation. Opposite, in deplorable condition, are the 1850s **Don Cutlery Works** of Southern & Richardson Ltd.

# Steelmaking: The Cementation Process

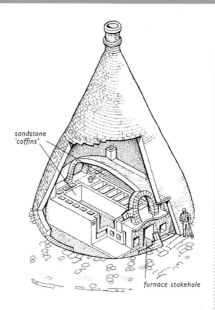

94. Cementation
Furnace

*sandstone 'coffins'*

*furnace stokehole*

The first positive record of steelmaking in Sheffield is in 1692, but the process remained on a very small scale for some time. Only two steel furnaces are shown in Thomas Oughtibridge's 1737 prospect of Sheffield. Both are of the cementation type for converting iron to blister steel, so called because of the blistered appearance of its surface. The key feature of the furnaces is the large conical chimney, 35 ft to 60 ft high, similar to a bottle kiln used in pottery manufacture. These furnaces were generally located at the end of a low workshop. The chimneys had two chests, usually made of sandstone, placed either side of a central flue. Further flues and chimneys sent a draught to the firegrate below. The chests would be packed with layers of charcoal and rows of Swedish iron bars until full. The top was sealed with clay and sweepings from the grinders' troughs. Preparatory to firing, the charging holes would be bricked up and sealed with clay. The coal fire below would be lit, reaching a temperature of about 1100°C and firing would take from seven to nine days. After another week had elapsed, the furnace would have cooled sufficiently for a man to enter the furnace and pass out the bars which had carbonized and converted to blister steel. They were then re-heated and forged or rolled into bars of shear steel suitable for edge tools. The covering of the chests, baked to a lava-like substance known as crozzle, was broken up and often used for wall coping.

Only three cementation furnaces remain in the Sheffield area; the Doncaster site (*see* p. 164), the partial fragments at Bower Spring (*see* p. 163) and the early site excavated at Millsands (*see* p. 174).

## Steelmaking: The Crucible Process

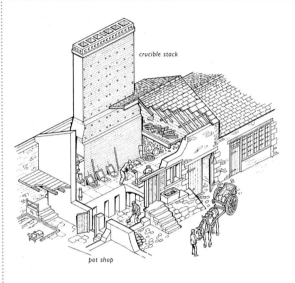

crucible stack

pot shop

Blister steel (*see* p. 165) was unsatisfactory for many purposes due to the many impurities that weakened it. By 1751 Benjamin Huntsman had developed to the stage of commercial production an improved method of steel manufacture by re-melting blister steel in small clay crucibles, which made it possible to remove the slag. This process remained the dominant method of steel production in Sheffield throughout the c19, and because blister steel was still required for it, both cementation and crucible furnaces would be found within integrated steelworks; smaller works would buy in blister steel from elsewhere.

The steel was broken into small pieces, placed in a preheated crucible and melted by burning coke around the covered vessel. A temperature of around 1600°c was achieved by introducing plenty of air through a large cellar below the furnace, and securing a powerful draught through a tall chimney: the distinguishing feature of a crucible furnace. Often 30–40 ft (9–12 metres) high, they were set in groups of three to six flues in each stack. Firing and repeated recharging of the coke surrounding the crucible was conducted until the metal was fully molten. The crucible would be taken from the furnace and its contents poured into an ingot mould. The ingots could then be hammered or rolled as required. The crucible process was still used for some specialized applications, such as turning tools, until after the Second World War.

Examples: Abbeydale Industrial Hamlet; Baltic Works, Effingham Street; Pluto Works, Princess Street; Sanderson's Works, Darnall; Peace's Works, Well Meadow Street, and Lion Works, Mowbray Street.

Returning to **Upper Allen Street**, on the left: three-storey houses *c.* 1840, No. 187 blind-back, No. 189 a pair of back-to-backs with a pilastered doorcase. Next there are the works of **Stephenson Blake Ltd**, the last traditional printers' typefounder in Britain, although production of type at the works has now ceased. C19, of three visually distinct periods, the earliest is in the centre with curious flattened arches including a Venetian window above the cart entrance to the right. Down Well Meadow Drive and hidden by later development, **Well Meadow Street** has an important example of a mid-C19 integrated steelworks of the type common in the city centre until well into the C20. At No. 35 [96] a complex built by the steel and file-cutting firm of Samuel Peace. The front range retains a manager's or owner's house (the only part in existence in 1851), a three-storey workshop and a furnace with a crucible stack comprising six flues with a brick-vaulted cellar below. In the yard behind, three-storey workshops of *c.* 1853, probably used for file cutting. Steelmaking ended in 1926. The buildings are in appalling condition but the complete nature of the site, representing two major aspects of Sheffield manufacturing – the production of crucible steel and the manufacture of steel files – renders it one of the most significant of the city's C19 industrial monuments. On the left side at No. 54, the **Well Meadow Steel Works** (originally Well Meadow Place), incorporates one through-house, two blind-back houses and three pairs of back-to-back houses. All pre-1820, with workshops and an early C19 crucible stack behind.

From here, trams run back to the city centre.

96. **No. 35 Well Meadow Street, crucible stack, works and owner's house, mid-C19**

## b) Green Lane and Neepsend

This walk starts on **Kelham Island**, created by the mill race for the medieval town mill and dominated by the former **Tramway Generating Station**, built for the electrification of Sheffield Corporation Tramways in 1899. Converted in 1982 to an Industrial Museum which provides a useful overview of many of the trades once carried on in the buildings to be seen on this walk. Across the mill race from the Museum are the **Globe Steel Works**. The part adjoining the Don comprises a long range of mid-C19 brick buildings on a stone base, the largest of four storeys with broad windows on the upper three. The part of the works on the s side of **Alma Street** has a carved globe as a motif and a long rendered range, built as part of a cotton mill in 1805, and subsequently converted in 1828–9 to form the workhouse for Sheffield township (the principal building was demolished in 1946–7 following bomb damage). Ibbotson Brothers took over the site in 1882 following the opening of the Fir Vale workhouse. Across Alma Street, the **Fat Cat**, a typical mid-C19 three-storey pub and hotel.

Off the s side of Alma Street in **South Parade**, the former **Ebenezer Wesleyan Chapel**, 1823, by *Joseph Botham*, curiously in the Gothick style, castellated with a s projection formerly rising to a tower, and octagonal buttresses which rose to short turrets. Window tracery of two lights, mildly flowing. **School** opposite with Gothick windows, now burnt out. Further school buildings of 1883 behind the chapel. On **Shalesmoor** (reached via Ebenezer Street opposite the chapel), the **Ship Inn**, rebuilt

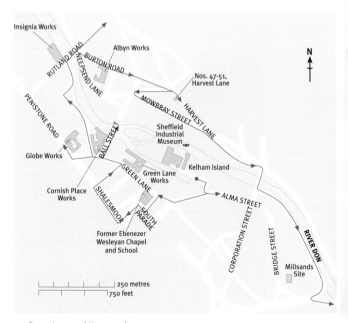

97. Green Lane and Neepsend

98. Green Lane Works, gateway, 1860

for Tomlinsons in the 1920s. Neo-Tudor, with a particularly fine brown faience ground floor and a tiled picture of a galleon on the fascia with raised lettering on the 'Dram Shop'. Turning left down Dun Street, we come to **Green Lane**, where the most coherent stretch of industrial landscape in inner Sheffield begins. Firstly, on the right, what Pevsner considered to be the most spectacular survival of factory architecture in the city, the gatehouse of **Green Lane Works** [98]. Built in 1860 by Henry Hoole, a manufacturer of firegrates, although it looks at first a full generation earlier. It takes the form of a tripartite triumphal arch, constructed to commemorate Hoole becoming Mayor of Sheffield in 1860. Female keystone head over the central entrance. Over the pedestrian entrances are relief panels of Hephaestus [14], the Greek god of fire and patron of metal craftsmen, and Athene, probably by the eminent sculptor *Alfred Stevens*, who designed for Hoole's between 1850 and 1852. Tall cupola on top. Principal workshop range to the rear along the Don, three storeys, twenty-six bays with very broad windows.

Next is **Brooklyn Works**, late C19, the site occupied by Alfred Beckett from 1865 to the 1960s. Two- and three-storey buildings restored as offices and apartments in the 1990s, much of the remainder demolished. Forge shop in Ball Street with five hand forges on the ground floor. Good raised lettering on the front and the gable by Ball Street Bridge. In **Ball Street** to the right, a three-span iron bridge with pierced Gothic parapets of 1865. Widened in 1900. It was cast by the Milton Ironworks, Elsecar.

Across **Ball Street** are the **Cornish Place Works** [100] of James Dixon & Sons, perhaps the only Sheffield works to rival the mills of Lancashire or the West Riding in terms of scale and architectural quality. James Dixon, who made Britannia metal, silver plate and cutlery, set up here in 1822. The only parts of the works to survive from that time are: the office and workshop range (1), second floor added *c.* 1903, what were probably casting shops (2) and the adjoining block (3). The next phase (4, 5) was built between 1835 and 1850. The dominant part of the works is an L-shaped block (6–8) put up in 1851–4 at the time of conversion to steam power, followed in 1857–9 by a block in matching style to the s containing a showroom and warehouse. Fireproof ground floor with central row of cast-iron columns supporting cast-iron beams carrying transverse brick arches across each bay. Tall circular chimney. The showroom block has an imposing staircase intended to impress potential customers. Because it was prominently located on Green Lane, a workshop block of the late 1850s (9) was given more elaborate treatment with the works' name carved in stone on the parapet. The plating shop (10) is of a type particular to an electroplating works and has a tall single storey over a basement lit by large round-headed windows and a clerestory. The works were sympathetically converted into loft apartments by *Axis Architecture* for Gleesons in 1998. Attached to the works is the former **Ball Inn**, a small early C19 pub. **Wharncliffe Works** (Nos. 86–88 Green Lane) is three storeys over a basement, built *c.* 1861 for Steel & Garland, manufacturers of stoves, grates and fenders. Three ranges

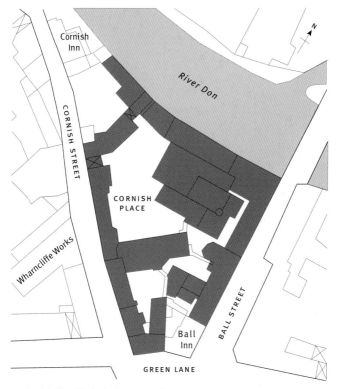

99. Cornish Place Works, before conversion

round a triangular yard, one subsequently demolished. Segmental arch over the cart entrance with a prominent decorative ashlar surround bearing the works name.

Beyond, in **Penistone Road**, is the **Globe Works** [101] of 1825 for Ibbotson & Roebank, edge tool manufacturers. Remarkably noble stone façade of nine bays, as if for a public building, the architectural treatment possibly explained by the incorporation of the owner's house at the s end. Two storeys, except for the three-bay centre which has another half-storey and a pediment. The first and last bays also pedimented. The ground-floor windows arched, those on the first floor flanked by short Ionic pilasters carrying shallow segmental arches – a personal and successful rhythm. To preserve the symmetry of the façade, the doorway to the owner's house is in the side elevation under a fine semi-circular porch while the cart entrance is also hidden. At the rear, the lower two floors are deeply recessed in the central three bays, the top storey oversailing, carried on another shallow segmental arch. External stone cantilevered dog-leg steps lead to a doorway on the first floor. Behind the grand front block are much humbler three-storey workshop blocks planned around the usual courtyard, but in contrast to most Sheffield workshops, they have coursed stone façades, the other

100. Cornish Place Works from Ball Street bridge, 1851–4

elevations mainly of brick. Large windows throughout, their sills forming a band at first-floor level, under broad lintels. The E block appears
to have four hand forges.

Right into **Dixon Street**, left into Cornish Street, then right along
Waterloo Walk running alongside the River Don brings one to **Rutland
Road**. **Insignia Works** was built in 1919–20 as the spring shop for
Samuel Osborn & Co.'s Rutland Works (since dem.). It was given its
name, following conversion to offices, from the Heart and Hand trade-
marks prominently displayed on its walls. The only known industrial
building by *W.J. Hale* (*see* topic box, p. 277), it is a clean piece of work
with large segmental-headed windows. On the corner of Rutland Road
and Hicks Street, **Rutland Hall**, 1906, now a printing works but built for
the Neighbourhood Guilds Association as an early community centre.
Founded in 1897, the Association operated in a similar manner to other

settlements. Brick-built and utilitarian, the central bay taller with a shaped parapet, a rounded cornice below enclosing the Hall's name in raised letters.

Returning along Rutland Road, on the s side of **Burton Road** at No. 81, **The Maltings** (now offices), *c.* 1870, formerly part of William Stones' brewery. Three storeys with gable-end to the road, segmental arches to doors and windows and a circular window in the gable. Next, the **Albyn Works** of 1875 by *T.E. Watson*, built as a works for cleaning powders and knife pastes. Blanco, which was invented *c.* 1880 by John Pickering, was made here. Opposite, surrounded by later buildings forming part of the works of Turton Brothers & Matthews, stands the inconspicuous **Brewery Tower** of Strout's Brewery. There had been a brewery here since 1835, taken over by Strout's in 1868. At the corner of **Neepsend Lane**, the three-storey office block of the **Neepsend Rolling Mills**, *c.* 1870, can be seen on the right. The central three bays are slightly raised with a parapet and ornamental surrounds to the windows. Rusticated ground floor. The remainder of the works were demolished in 2003.

In **Mowbray Street** there is a substantial pocket of surviving small steel and edge tool works whose backs are visible from Kelham Island. Firstly, the **Lion Works** with a crucible shop on Ball Street with the stack facing the street. Then a group comprising Nos. 41–51, all mid to late C19. Opposite, at No. 30, a blind-back house of the 1850s with a second blind-back behind. Further back-to-back houses at Nos. 47–51 Harvest Lane to the rear. Dated *c.* 1860, they are built to more generous dimensions than those seen in Snow Lane (*see* Walk 6, p. 164). At the end of Mowbray Street on the left, massive stone retaining walls of the 1860s are all that is left of the Manchester Sheffield & Lincolnshire Railway's Bridgehouses goods depot. On the right, **Borough Bridge**, 1853, by *Samuel Holmes* and *Samuel Worth* built as part of the improvements associated with the opening of Corporation Street in 1856 for access to the depot. s of the bridge, take the **Upper Don Walk**, opened 2003.

101. Globe Works, 1825

On the right, **Riverside Exchange**, a group of high-rise apartments and lower office blocks by *Hadfield Cawkwell Davidson,* 1999–2001, mark a considerable change in style for Sheffield. The four blocks of flats are up to eight storeys in height with varied elevations in brick, cream and blue cladding and enlivened by angled roof slabs forming a cornice; the offices are more conventional with pitched roofs and red brick. To the E is the site of **Millsands Works**, once Marshalls Steelworks, established by 1774 and one of the group of large works that heralded Sheffield's domination of the world's steel trade. Millsands was also one of the first commercial steelworks to contain both cementation and crucible furnaces and three cementation furnaces were excavated in 1999 (*see* topic boxes, pp. 165 and 166). Two are of the usual C19 type but the third, which is to be displayed under glass, is an early type. Over 4½ ft (1.4 metres) of the rough-hewn sandstone base remains. It may be either the central flue and one chest of a two-chest furnace or a rare single-chest design. Possibly the furnace drawn by G. Jars in *Voyages Métallurgiques* (1774) and noted in 1796 by the British traveller, Charles Hatchett, it provides the earliest known physical evidence of steel production in Sheffield.

At the end of the Upper Don Walk, turn left on to Bridge Street for Lady's Bridge and the city centre.

# Outer Sheffield

# North

## a) Crabtree, Pitsmoor, Shirecliffe and Burngreave

In 1758, the turnpike road to Barnsley passed the small hamlet at Pitsmoor and smaller settlements at Shirecliffe, around Shirecliffe Hall, and at Crabtree. Suburban development began in earnest in the early C19 with working-class housing on the lower s slopes of the Woodside area and at Burngreave (now largely replaced by the Burngreave-Woodside estate). A new turnpike with a gentler gradient, now Burngreave Road, was opened in 1835–6 and encouraged the building of middle-class housing along it and to the w along the upper slopes of the valley around Andover Street. A final phase of development was concluded in the early C20 in the NE part of the district.

The hamlet of Crabtree lay NE of Barnsley Road. At its heart stands **The Ivies** in **Crabtree Drive**, now surrounded by later housing. Late C17 vernacular, extended, as indicated by three datestones inscribed H.F. 1676, J.F. 1841(s wing) and M. 1948 (rendered N wing). J.F. was John Frith, a traveller and writer who acquired the estate in 1839.

At the N end of **Barnsley Road**, at the corner of Firshill Avenue, **Norbury** a large Italianate villa of 1848 (now a TAVR Centre), built for Thomas Blake of the typefounders Stephenson Blake. Further s along Barnsley Road, a brief detour up **Scott Road** for **St James Presbyterian Church Hall** of 1911 by *H.L. Paterson* in the mild Perp style much favoured for small Nonconformist chapels at the time. In **Barnsley Road**, on the w side, **Firs Hill Junior School**, a Board School of 1893 by *J.B. Mitchell-Withers*. Jacobean as opposed to the Gothic of Innocent & Brown's schools. On the E side, in grounds which became Abbeyfield Park on purchase by the Corporation in 1909, is **Abbeyfield**, built in the late C18 for William Pass. It originally faced Barnsley Road but following sale to Bernard Wake *c.* 1852, was reorientated to face enlarged grounds with a new N wing, followed by further extensions to the s, probably in 1883, the date of a prominent sundial. Ashlar-faced, asymmetrical with several canted bay windows, one on the principal façade and two more on the return. Striking **gateway** into the Park from Abbeyfield Road designed in 2000 by students from Fir Vale School with assistance from local sculptors *Johnny White* and *Amanda Wray*. A tubular arch in stainless steel depicting a vine; hands hold a ceramic centrepiece festooned with fruit.

Barnsley Road becomes **Burngreave Road**. At the junction with Pitsmoor Road, **Toll Bar Cottage** by *Woodhead & Hurst* for the

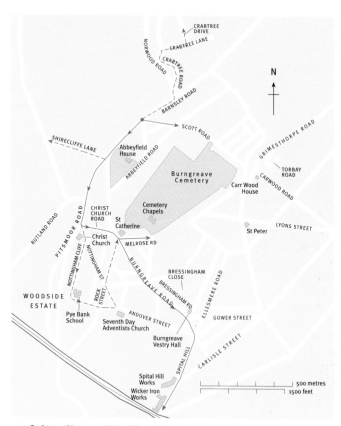

102. Crabtree, Pitsmoor, Shirecliffe and Burngreave

Sheffield and Wakefield Turnpike Trust, 1834–6. Classical with round-headed windows, mostly paired and a canted end. The tollgates were taken down in 1876. Beyond on the w side of Burngreave Road, Nos. 161–183 and 1–4 **Burngreave Place**, three blocks of houses built between 1845 and 1855 in a simple Regency survival style, of brick with string courses and pilastered doorcases (cf. Hanover, p. 256).

At this point, a detour may be taken up **Shirecliffe Lane** to the w where there are some houses that provide a reminder of the high status that this area enjoyed from the late C18. Of that date, firstly, **Shirecliffe Grove** (No. 27), a hipped-roof villa, now much altered. Only the early C19 Lodge of **Shirecliffe Hall** survives, one storey, with ornate barge-boards and plain mullioned windows. Opposite and bargeboarded also, No. 92, **Shirecliffe Cottage**, a little-altered C19 stone villa in the Tudor style with a rampant dog carving on the porch. The classical style reappears next door at **Shirecliffe House**, a villa of c. 1840.

Rejoin the walk at **Pitsmoor Road**, which still has the sense of a village street with a much-altered modest C18 pub, the Bay Horse Inn, a former National School of 1836 (also much altered) and a few old cottages. As the road runs downhill towards the city centre, there is a series of substantial early C19 villas, all with hipped roofs and of two storeys. Nos. 255–259 are of brick; the first of these of three bays with an open-pedimented doorcase. The remainder are smoothly faced in ashlar. No. 253 is the most ambitious with its roof hidden behind a parapet, twin bands across the façade and a fine Doric porch. Nos. 249–251 are a pair of double-fronted villas of five bays each, the central one projecting slightly with a timber Doric porch. Deep ground-floor windows. On the left, **Christ Church** by *Flockton & Son* of 1849–50. Large and handsome in the Dec style, built to cater for an affluent congregation. The w tower has tall pinnacles and set-back buttresses. Large transepts. The interior is simple but spacious and still retains its galleries at the w end and in the transepts, that in the N now contains the organ. Carved Gothic reredos, choir stalls, clergy desks, font and pulpit all date from 1913, as does the mosaic floor in the chancel and baptistery. **Stained glass** – four-light E window of the Crucifixion and the Ascension, St Wilfrid and St Helena, 1903. N aisle: Works of Charity by *Kayll & Reed*, 1915, and a further window of 1915, Christ Blessing Little Children. **Church Hall** by *Ken Murta* and *Austin Peter Fawcett* added to s wall of nave in the early 1980s, simple with small square windows, forms and materials well matched to the church.

Steeply uphill, a further detour may be taken by way of Nottingham Street and Nottingham Cliff to **Andover Street** and the impressively sited **Pye Bank School** [103] by *Innocent & Brown*, 1874–5. Extended in 1884, it makes a most effective counterpoint to the Seventh Day Adventist Church (*see* below) seen on the high part of the ridge to the E. Between here and Pitsmoor Road, the **Woodside Estate** of 1960–2 by *J.L. Womersley* replaced much of the C19 housing in the area. It was

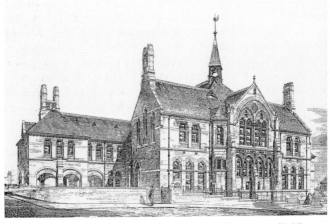

103. Pye Bank School, by Innocent & Brown, 1874–5. From *Illustrations of Public Elementary Schools* (1874)

perhaps the most sculptural of Womersley's hilltop compositions. The estate consisted of stepped terraces of reversed two-storey houses with barrel-vaulted roofs, maisonette blocks along and down the slopes and, originally crowning the top of the hill, four point blocks, the demolition of which has greatly diminished the impact of Womersley's conception. Both houses and some maisonette blocks are being demolished, despite revamping with pitched roofs. The oldest house in the immediate area is No. 108 **Andover Street**, a very small cottage, *c.* 1830, of one storey with an attic lit by windows in the gables. Stone, roughly rendered with hoodmoulds over the windows. The **Church of the Seventh Day Adventists** (the former Methodist New Connexion Church) of 1865 by *William Hill* of Leeds is a prominent landmark from the city centre. sw tower with an octagonal broach spire. Straightforward Gothic with rose windows in the transepts and trefoil-headed nave windows but some lively carving of angels as label stops. Largely original interior with a gallery on three sides on cast-iron columns. **School** of 1862 behind. Return via Nottingham Street and Rock Street, past 1860s–70s middle-class housing, to Burngreave Road.

The main walk continues to the e side of **Burngreave Road** and to **St Catherine's R.C. Church** of 1925–6 by *Charles Edward Fox & Son*. Red brick in the Early Christian style much favoured for Catholic churches of the period. Tall Romanesque campanile with a pyramidal roof. The w front has a rose window and mosaic roundels of St Teresa and St Catherine. Light and spacious interior lit by a clerestory with a coffered nave ceiling and narrow-vaulted aisles behind arcading of round-headed arches on Carrara columns with decorated block capitals. A rounded chancel apse has inlays of marble and a mosaic frieze. The dominant motif is the enormous **baldacchino** on marble columns whose canopy bears a gilded figure of Christ the King. Full width **communion rail** of marble, the balusters of red sandstone and capped with Connemara marble. Opposite is the **Methodist Church** by *Peter F. Smith*, 1972, unassuming, of brick with adjoining blocks of flats, a development of his United Reformed Church, Manor Road, Stoke Newington, London.

**Melrose Road** at the side of St Catherine's leads to **Burngreave Cemetery** [104]. Built as the Brightside Bierlow Cemetery, it was opened in 1860. The buildings, by *Flockton & Son*, 1860–1, include lodges, railings and the Church of England and Nonconformist mortuary chapels which are linked by an arch surmounted by a spire, the favoured solution of cemetery architects. War Memorial: standard *Blomfield* designed Cross of Sacrifice with a low surrounding wall at the ne end. s down **Burngreave Road**, the area's former standing is apparent from the substantial 1890s semi-detached houses, extensively renovated in 2001–2.

**Burngreave**'s centre is the green at the top of **Spital Hill**. On the corner of Burngreave and Grimesthorpe Roads, the Tudor style **Burngreave Vestry Offices** of 1864. Symmetrical, two storeys with the city coat of arms carved on the porch and paired, banded pilasters

104. Burngreave Cemetery Chapels, by Flockton & Son, 1860–1

providing a strong accent. Mullioned and transomed windows, a parapet with urns. To the s in **Gower Street**, the former **Library** of 1872 by *James Hall*, the first to be built in the suburbs. Classical and chapel-like with a pediment and round-headed windows. To the N, council housing in **Bressingham Close** and **Ditchingham Walk** of *c.* 1977 by *J. Winter*, Director of Planning and Design (project architect: *John Guy*), representing the move away from monolithic developments such as Park Hill and Kelvin to an approach that respects local scale and style. An adventurous and attractive urban village concept of houses on winding pedestrian alleys that follow the line of the old streets. W of Spital Hill, the **Burngreave Estate** of 1962–4 by *J. Mansell Jenkinson & Son*, maisonettes and flats of traditional brick construction, contiguous with the Woodside Estate (q.v.).

Spital Hill leads down to the Wicker Arches (*see* p. 156) which mark the boundary of the city centre. On the right, **Spital Hill Works**, occupied by the edge tool manufacturers John Sorby from 1823 and then Lockwood Brothers by 1849. The present buildings comprise two long ranges. The two-storey range which has lunettes with ornamental grilles is of 1864–5 by *M.E. Hadfield & Son*. They were also responsible for the front office block of 1878, three storeys with ornamental stone dressings. The taller range of 1891 by *M.E. Hadfield, Son & Garland* is of four storeys, part with vaulted brick ceilings, and set into the hillside. Immediately before the arch, the **Wicker Iron Works** with a long late C19 brick range to the street, its first-floor windows set in pairs in panels and with big segmental-headed windows on the ground floor. Probably by *Holmes & Watson* who are recorded as carrying out alterations in 1899. The roof-line is broken by five gables. To the s, a large rusticated archway and to the N, a wing at right angles. It is currently under threat from plans for a new ring road.

In Ellesmere Road, **St Peter**, 1980, by the *G.D. Frankish Partnership*. Built on the site of *Flockton & Abbott*'s All Saints Church of 1868–9 which had been paid for by the steel manufacturer, John Brown. Circular, brown brick piers surmounted by a steel ring-beam, low pitched conical roof with lantern and skeleton spire.

**Carr Wood House**, Grimesthorpe Road, E of the cemetery. Simple but handsome classical three-bay house of *c.* 1835. Ashlar, pediment to the central bay. Used for many years as All Saints Vicarage. Stables and a late C19 former Church Institute attached. In **Torbay Road**, No. 19, timber-framed house by *Pat Borer,* using the Walter Segal self-build method.

## b) Fir Vale, Firth Park and Wincobank

Fir Vale has as its centre the steep-sided valley of the Bagley Dyke. A handful of large houses, mostly still extant, stood in isolation until the area was developed late in the C19 with a mass of closely packed terraced houses. Dominating the vale are the two churches of St Cuthbert and Trinity Methodist, both of which are in **Firth Park Road**.

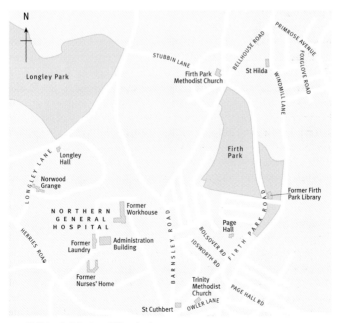

105. Fir Vale, Firth Park and Wincobank

106. St Cuthbert, E window by Archibald Davies, *c.* 1920

**St Cuthbert** of 1901–5 by *J.D. Webster & Son* is a large work by this prolific local architect. Set on a hill, its most dominant feature is its roof, a vast expanse of bright red tiles. E.E. style with transepts. Plain NW tower of 1959. The interior is well lit by closely spaced paired lancets in the clerestory. Round piers with nailhead decoration on the capitals. **Choir stalls** have carved ends depicting St Mark, St Matthew and scenes from the life of St Cuthbert. Fine octagonal **font** with carved baptismal symbols of a Gate, a Lily, the Ark, etc. Excellent **stained glass** [106] by *Archibald Davies* of the Bromsgrove Guild. Davies worked occasionally for Morris & Co. between 1909 and 1928 and Morris's influence is evident in the foliage and rich colouring, especially in the fine five-light War Memorial E window of the Resurrection and the Ascension. War widows in purple mourning fill the foreground with the Risen Christ above. Two baptistery windows by *Davies* of 1938 and N aisle 1920, s aisle Good Samaritan, 1936. s aisle window, 1917, by *Kayll & Reed*, brighter colours and more conventional than the Davies work.

**Trinity Methodist Church**, 1899, by *John Wills*, is a conventional large Gothic chapel in rock-faced stone with a tall thin spire with pinnacles at the corners, clerestory of timber-framed windows with trefoil heads forming a continuous row. Paired lancets in the aisles. The nave has been split for meeting rooms but the E part is unaltered. Thin iron columns support an elaborate trussed roof. Large and handsome arcaded alabaster **pulpit**. The accompanying **school** of 1907 is now an Islamic centre.

w of Barnsley Road, the **Northern General Hospital** was built as the Sheffield Union Workhouse and Infirmary in 1876–80. The Workhouse's architect, *James Hall*, had in 1874 drawn up plans to incorporate administration, accommodation, infirmary and dining room under one roof. Although advised of the benefits of separate blocks by the Poor Law Inspectors in London, Hall only applied these principles to part of his revised design. The main building was planned as two three-storey wings linked by a 645 ft (195 metre) central corridor to an administration block with canted end bays and clock tower projecting slightly forward. Only the N wing and the central block survive, with some French Second Empire detailing in the mansard roof and circular dormers above the bays. Lavatory towers linked to the accommodation block. To the w of the main block, H-shaped pavilion blocks were constructed for the workhouse infirmary, most of which remain, albeit much altered.

A decision to separate the infirmary from the workhouse was taken in 1899 (finally achieved in 1906) and it was necessary to build a separate administration block, nurses' home and laundry. The chosen architect was *E. W. Mountford* who may have received this commission as a result of the impression created by his Town Hall but who also had experience of hospital design at Stratford-upon-Avon (1883–4) and Shipston-upon-Stour (1897). The **administration building** of 1901–4 is rather like an enormous country house, its canted bays reminiscent of Ernest Newton's Red Court, Haslemere, Surrey. Segmental-headed windows, two storeys with attic dormers. The large **Nurses' Home** of 1899–1902 is of three storeys in similar style. Three large canted bays with the principal doorway located under the central bay, the bay supported by Doric columns. Steeply-pitched roof punctuated by plain but massive chimneys and dormers. Two projecting wings to the rear extended in 1913–14 by *Potter & Sandford*. The Arts and Crafts style **laundry** (1900) [107] has Mountford's trademark large semicircular windows (cf. Booths Distilleries, Cowcross Street, London) set in rendered panels, flanked by battered buttresses in red brick. L-shaped **stable block** in the same style. Within the grounds is **Goddard Hall**, an early C19 brick house with an ashlar front and a doorcase with Greek Doric columns and cornice. Currently derelict. On the s edge of the site by Herries Road, the **Cottage Homes for Children**, 1894, by *C. J. Innocent* were early examples in Sheffield of a more humane approach to the treatment of orphan children. Only the Receiving House remains, plain red brick with little decoration. The three blocks of cottages have been demolished in recent years.

107. Northern General Hospital, former Laundry by E.W. Mountford, 1900

Great expansion of the hospital has taken place over the last twenty years. Among the newer buildings are the **Osborn Building** by the *George Trew Dunn Partnership* of *c.* 1995 and the **Brearley Wing** by *HLM Architects, c.* 1989, on a sloping site with a cascading roofscape of hipped roofs. The **Medical Education Centre** (Sheffield University) of 1979 has a fully glazed oversailing second floor, broad cornice and domed stair-turret projecting. The lower floors are clad in brown and red brick. More coherent is **Samuel Fox House**, a library, 1995–6, by *Trent Regional Hospital Board Architects*. Two wings, supported on columns over a recessed ground floor, and linked by a glass-fronted stair hall. Roofs gently curve up to the centre. Steel columns run the full height of the building, linked by branch-like trusses to the roof.

Only a few other buildings in Fir Vale deserve mention: these include the former **Page Hall Cinema**, Idsworth Road, by *Ernest Shepherd*, 1920. Long brick frontage with pilasters and circular windows. It contained a café and billiard hall; ballroom added in 1929. In Page Hall Road, E of Firth Park Road, the former **Brightside & Carbrook Co-operative Society Shop** (Nos. 18–22), *c.* 1910, with a most elaborate faience façade of three bays flanked by panelled pilasters and large round-arched windows under swags. Small aedicules with segmental pediments. A few of Fir Vale's superior houses survive: **Norwood Grange**, Longley Lane is a Jacobean style early C19 house, much altered, with delightful carved stags' heads in the centre of the gables and sheeps' heads under the kneelers. Good range of stables and groom's house. Further along Longley Lane to the N, **Longley Hall**, late Georgian, red brick, quite plain with a large central bay window and attached outbuildings. E in Cammell Road is **Page Hall** of 1773, by *John Platt* for Thomas Broadbent, banker. One of the first houses to be built in the suburbs by a man who had made his money from commerce rather than industry (*see* also Walk 2, p. 111). Coursed sandstone of two and a half storeys with a three-bay ashlar front. Two canted bay windows flank the main doorway with pediment on attached Adamesque columns. Late C20 additions to the left incorporate the arcaded front of the stables.

**Firth Park** was created from 35 acres of the Page Hall estate and given by Mark Firth in 1875 for the city's second public park. In Firth Park Road, the **Refreshment Room** by *Flockton & Abbott*, 1875. Rock-faced stone with a fanciful Italianate clock tower linked to a single-storey pavilion which has had its roof extended at the front to form a loggia. A little s in a smaller piece of park on the E side of Firth Park Road, is the former **Public Library** of 1937 by the City Architect, *W.G. Davies*, superior Neoclassical with the central bays projecting, the doorway recessed behind Doric columns and the city coat of arms above, surmounted by a swag. The library served the burgeoning suburb of Firth Park which expanded greatly after the tramway reached it in 1909. Middle-class semi-detached houses were built all the way up Firth Park Road and a substantial new shopping parade was provided *c.* 1910. Terraced housing was built around the lower part of Bellhouse Road and new council estates in the 1920s saw the area fully built up around **Stubbin Lane**. At the heart of the new suburb, **Firth Park United Methodist Church** of 1911 by *Chapman & Jenkinson*. Attractive Neo-Perp in red brick with a broad w window above a porch flanked by two short octagonal towers with spirelets. A flèche in the centre of the roof.

NE along **Bellhouse Road** brings us to **High Wincobank** and the **Flower Estate**. The land was acquired in 1900 by Sheffield Corporation which held a national competition for the design of workmen's houses on garden suburb principles. It was won by *Percy Houfton* of Chesterfield. The designs were influenced by Raymond Unwin whom Houfton had met while working on housing at Cresswell Model Village in Derbyshire. But the rents for Houfton's houses proved too high for Sheffield and *H.L. Paterson* won the competition to design further houses on the estate in 1906. Before then, the National Housing Reform Committee proposed an exhibition of model housing similar to that held at Letchworth in 1905 with prizes to be awarded for different classes of housing and for the layout of the estate. The Committee for the **Yorkshire and North Midland Cottage Exhibition** of 1907

## Wincobank Camp and the Roman Rig

High Wincobank provides the earliest evidence of human settlement in Sheffield with the Iron Age fort, **Wincobank Camp**, on Wincobank Hill. The fort has a single rampart constructed from earth and rubble, laced with timber and clad with vitrified stone, an external ditch and a counterscarp bank, enclosing 2½ acres, with probable entrances to the NE and sw. It has been dated to the first century BC. To the N is the line of the **Roman Rig** or ridge, an earthwork extending from Wincobank ten miles NE to Kimberworth where it splits into two broadly parallel routes ending at Mexborough and Kilnhurst. It is a bank often with a ditch to the s and an overall width up to 30 ft. Despite its name, there is no evidence of its date and its purpose remains unclear.

included W.H. Lever (of Port Sunlight) and Sir John Tudor Walters (M.P. for Sheffield Brightside – later involved in Garden Suburb promotion at Gidea Park, Romford) who gave his name to the influential 1918 report on working-class housing.

The winning entry for the estate **layout** [108] was by *W. Alexander Harvey & A. McKewan*, the architects of Bournville. It displayed some advance on the Bournville plan, most notably in the employment of an irregular building line and the offset of buildings at junctions, planning ideas espoused by Raymond Unwin. In addition, it introduced the formality of a central axis (Primrose Avenue) with a semicircular open space in front of a church (not built, its place later taken by Hinde House Junior School) and therefore represents both the opposing elements that were to be used extensively in interwar municipal suburban development throughout Britain, the axial plan and the informality of gently curving estate roads.

The picturesque planning of the estate is not matched by the appearance of many of the cottages, which were much criticized at the time in *The Builder* for their poor façades and lack of originality in interior planning, including a reluctance to do away with the parlour. However, as some were to be constructed for between £135 and £175, a degree of meanness was almost inevitable. In 1907, the houses were acquired by the Corporation but further development was delayed until 1912 and not completed until 1923. In spite of unsympathetic modifications, all the early cottages may still be seen. Starting in **Wincobank Avenue** and **Heather Road**, forty-one houses to *Houfton*'s design were built in 1903–4, laid out in long rows in an unimaginative grid. They are of two types, Classes A and B, both being broad-fronted and with no rooms projecting at the rear. Class A, a double-fronted design, improved on Parker & Unwin's New Earswick cottages in having a separate upstairs

108. Cottage Exhibition, official plan by W. Alexander Harvey & A. McKewan, 1907

bathroom and a toilet accessible from inside. Class B had the same features but was single-fronted with the scullery behind the living room. *Paterson*'s twenty houses of 1906 in **Heather Road**, were built more cheaply and to a notably lower standard with a narrow frontage, smaller living room and no bathroom. Quite attractive elevations with decorative brickwork.

The Cottage Exhibition houses begin at the N end of **Primrose Avenue** with Nos. 102–104 by *F.W. Chapman*, followed by Nos. 78–84 (Myrtle Cottages) by *H.L. Paterson* with rounded tops to the gables. On the opposite side, Nos. 73–75 by *H. Stanley-Barrett & Driver* of London, who also designed for the 1905 Letchworth exhibition, look like a detached house with one gable facing the road. Then Nos. 69–71, a plain hipped-roof semi by *Henry Webster* and at Nos. 65–67, also by *Webster*, a double-gabled design, which, modified, was used extensively by the Corporation in the 1930s on the Parson Cross estate. Opposite on the junction with Jessamine Road, one of the best designs, Nos. 59–63 by *W. Alexander Harvey & A. McKewan*, red brick with cogging below the eaves and tile-hung full-height bay windows. Next, a distinctive pair, Nos. 39–41 by *Claude Batley* of London, with a 'Noah's Ark' roof and dormers. On the N side, Nos. 50–52 with a gambrel roof by *C.J. Innocent*. Similar styles of house were built in Letchworth in 1905. **Acacia Avenue** runs off to the N with two groups, Nos. 1–3 by *H.L. Paterson* with a big central gable and Nos. 5–7 by *F.W. Chapman*. Returning to Primrose Avenue, Nos. 17–19 [109] by *Pepler & Allen* of Croydon are the closest to one's expectation of an attractively composed model cottage with segmental-headed ground-floor windows, prominent brick arches above them and a roughcast upper storey. Next a terrace of four houses, Nos. 9–15 by *J.C. Brameld & Son* with the centre pair slightly taller. Back on **Foxglove Road** to the s, Nos. 161–163 with half-timbered gables are by

109. 17–19 Primrose Avenue, by Pepler & Allen, 1907

110. St Hilda, Windmill Lane, interior of nave, by Leslie Moore, 1935

*Benton & Roberts*. The last of the 1907 houses are somewhat non-descript, Nos. 140–146 by *F.W. Chapman* and Nos. 136–138 by *J. Smith* of Leeds. Surrounding and interspersed with the 1907 houses are plain council houses of 1912–23 in terraces of red brick and roughcast.

To serve all this housing, although located on the edge of the estate and having no visual relationship with it, there is **St Hilda** [110], Windmill Lane, by *Leslie Moore*, one of his best designs. Drawings were produced in 1922–3 for a church with a crenellated tower and windows with Gothic curvilinear tracery, a design which mirrored Temple Moore's conception at St Mary, Nunthorpe. By the time funds were raised in 1935, the design was modified. On sharply sloping land, the church appears long and low from the road but towers above the valley on the N side. Temple Moore's influence is still evident in such details as the lancets and the individually designed capitals of the piers. The extensive glazing represents Leslie Moore's first attempt at flooding an interior with natural light and the effect is enhanced by the open scissor-braced roof of unstained pine. A very effective oak chancel screen (well classicized by *George Pace* in 1952) provides the only decoration. C18 organ case from St James' Church, St James' Street (dem.).

# The Don Valley

The Don Valley has been the centre for Sheffield's heavy industry since the 1840s. Until then it was mainly farmland, with water-powered works along the river and some small-scale coal mining the only industrial activity outside the settlements at Attercliffe and Darnall. Sheffield's only flat land is here, where the Don turns towards the Humber and the North Sea and the valley broadens out into a wide corridor. For centuries this provided the best route for communication with the outside world. The South Yorkshire Navigation finally reached the town in 1819 (*see* p. 157) and in 1838 the first railway line, the Sheffield & Rotherham, was completed, its terminus at the Wicker a link to the national network. This was the impetus for the development of the valley on an unprecedented scale, providing fast, efficient access for incoming raw materials and fuel and outgoing manufactured products. In 1837 Spear & Jackson, sawmakers, were the first to build new works on open land leased from the Duke of Norfolk. From 1845 first Cammell's and then firms like Firth's and John Brown followed suit, moving their works from the town centre. By 1902 the biggest firms, Cammell's, Brown's and Vickers', each with over 5,000 employees, were world leaders in armour plate production and had their own shipyards at Birkenhead, Clydeside, Belfast and Barrow. After the unprecedented expansion and profits that the armaments trade brought before 1918 the industry survived fluctuating fortunes in the c20 by specializing in alloy and special steels and engineering. Today little survives of either the older fabric of the industry or the communities which served it. Most of the valley's housing was swept away in the 1970s by planning policies and much of the industry's infrastructure demolished in the next decade, although black steel-clad sheds and ranges of gabled brick workshops continue to make a distinctive contribution to the landscape. Regeneration began in the 1980s with new industries, offices, retail parks and sport and leisure facilities, which include some of the most impressive new buildings outside the city centre, as well as the creation of a linear park along the riverbanks.

## a) Savile Street to Brightside Lane

This is a linear tour, best done by car, which starts at the edge of the city centre, close to the Wicker Arches (*see* Walk 5, p. 156) and follows the line of the former railway to Brightside and the River Don Works.

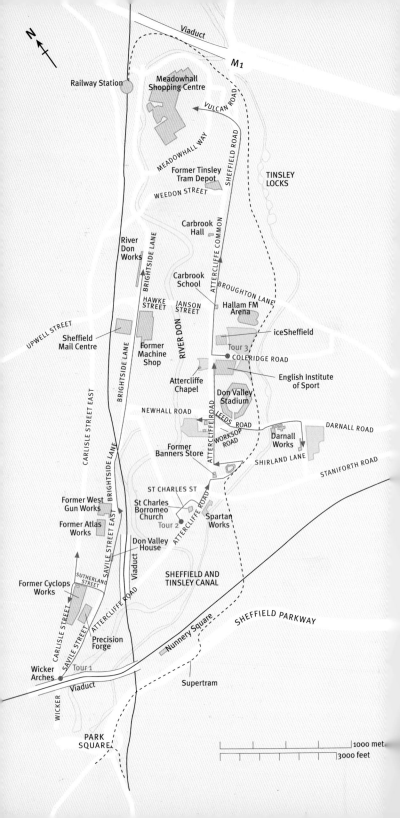

N

Viaduct

M1

Railway Station

Meadowhall
Shopping Centre

VULCAN ROAD

SHEFFIELD ROAD

MEADOWHALL WAY

Former Tinsley
Tram Depot

WEEDON STREET

TINSLEY
LOCKS

River
Don
Works

BRIGHTSIDE LANE

Carbrook
Hall

ATTERCLIFFE COMMON

Carbrook
School

BROUGHTON LANE

HAWKE
STREET

JANSON
STREET

Hallam FM
Arena

UPWELL STREET

Sheffield
Mail Centre

BRIGHTSIDE LANE

Former
Machine Shop

RIVER DON

iceSheffield

Tour 3

COLERIDGE ROAD

Attercliffe
Chapel

English Institute
of Sport

Don Valley
Stadium

NEWHALL ROAD

LEEDS   ROAD

CARLISLE STREET EAST

ATTERCLIFFE ROAD

WORKSOP
ROAD

Former
Banners Store

Darnall
Works

DARNALL ROAD

SHIRLAND LANE

BRIGHTSIDE LANE

STANIFORTH ROAD

ST CHARLES ST

St Charles
Borromeo
Church

Tour 2

ATTERCLIFFE ROAD

Spartan
Works

Former West
Gun Works

Former Atlas
Works

SAVILE STREET EAST

Don Valley
House

SHEFFIELD AND
TINSLEY CANAL

Former Cyclops
Works

SUTHERLAND
STREET

Viaduct

Nunnery Square

SHEFFIELD PARKWAY

CARLISLE STREET

SAVILE STREET

ATTERCLIFFE ROAD

Precision
Forge

Wicker
Arches

Tour 1

WICKER

Viaduct

Supertram

PARK
SQUARE

1000 met

3000 feet

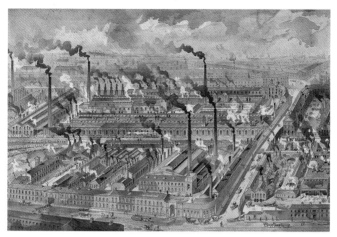

112. Cyclops Works, Savile Street. Engraving (1887)

We begin at the w end of **Savile Street** at the site of **Wicker Station**, opened in 1838, for the Sheffield and Rotherham railway. Two gatepiers on Savile Street's N side and a massive battered retaining wall along Spital Hill and Carlisle Street. Blocked opening in the wall for the tunnel linking the line to the Manchester and Sheffield railway after 1847. Closed for passenger traffic in 1870, the station remained in use for goods until 1965 and the track continued to serve the steelworks thereafter. Now its line has been obscured by new development. On Savile Street's s side is the former **Ye Olde Hole in the Wall** pub, a curiously asymmetrical ashlar front with Tuscan pilasters and heavy cornice. Beyond, the gabled front of the **Don Steel Works** with decorative pilasters and spiky finials, stylishly converted to a car showroom in 2002 by *Ward McHugh Associates*. Then, curving into Attercliffe Road, **Albion House**, 1902, with later additions, formerly the head office of T.W. Ward, who supplied the steel industry with coal, metal and machinery. Long plain façade of brick with stone dressings. Stone-faced pedimented main entrance and square tower with hipped roof. The principal offices were once lined with panelling salvaged from the luxury liners that the firm broke up for scrap.

The N side of the street is dominated by the colossal, but surprisingly elegant, grey steel-clad shed of Firth Brown's precision forge. Built 1980 by *Husband & Co.*, 433 ft long by 51 ft high (132 by 15.5 metres), it was designed to house an innovative forging press with four hammers over 184 ft (56 metres) long and weighing 1,228 tonnes, processing ingots up to 8 tonnes. The forge partly occupies the site of Cammell's **Cyclops Works** [112], a vast steel complex that straddled the railway between Savile Street and Carlisle Street to the N. Designed by *Weightman, Hadfield & Goldie, c.* 1845–52. Only an original, heavily rusticated

111. The Don Valley

Tuscan-style stone gateway (now blocked) survives on **Carlisle Street** (reached by turning left up Sutherland Street), where early C20 gabled sheds rise behind dramatic sheer walls of steel framing infilled with brick and stretching half the length of the street. Towering higher in the centre, a rectangular generating station, of five bays by three, with tall round-headed openings in the upper stage.

Along **Carlisle Street East** all the older works have gone. On the N side, **Bessemer House** by *Holmes & Watson,* 1901. The former offices of Henry Bessemer, facing the site where in 1859 he began the first commercial production of cheap bulk steel from pig iron (*see* topic box, p. 193). Hard, smooth, soot-resistant red brick with stone dressings, five storeys dignified by a large central porch with polished granite pilasters and three-storey canted bays on either side.

Running parallel to the s is **Savile Street East**, the space between filled since the 1980s with undistinguished industrial units on the site of the railway line, but with a few older survivals. **Don Valley House**, on the s side, was built in 1968 by *Hadfield Cawkwell Davidson & Partners* as Firth Brown's headquarters and computer centre. Slate, engineering brick and tiny white-glazed tiles for dressings and facings demonstrate the continuing need to withstand the valley's sooty and sulphurous pollution. (Nearby to the s, on Attercliffe Road, the company's laboratory building, of the same date and architects. Granite facings between the window bands and stainless-steel-clad columns. Curved canopy to the ground floor.) On the N side of Savile Street East the former **Gateway** of the Norfolk Works' Siemens melting shop of 1918 by *W.S. Purchon*, preserved (and repositioned) when the works were demolished in the 1980s. Of triumphal arch form, faced in rusticated ashlar and inscribed 'Thos Firth & Sons Ltd Siemens Dept' above the arch. Beyond are two ranges of offices which typify the frontages of the mid-C19 steelworks – modest but solid, two storeys in a simple brick Italianate style with long sequences

113. Former President Works offices, Savile Street East, *c.* 1852

## Steelmaking: The Bessemer, Open-Hearth and Electric Arc Processes

The **Bessemer process** for creating steel entailed blowing air through the perforated bottom of a container (the Bessemer Converter) of molten pig iron to oxidize the carbon, silicon and manganese. In Sheffield it was of limited use as only crucible steel (*see* p. 166) could produce the quality required for edge tools and cutlery. However, it found widespread application elsewhere in England by the 1870s and fostered the great expansion of heavy steel production in the Don Valley. By 1900, the Siemens **open-hearth process** had taken over most forms of steelmaking, other than tool steel. Pig and scrap iron is melted on an open hearth under slag to which iron ore is added to oxidize the carbon and other impurities. This process is associated with the great steel-framed and corrugated iron-clad sheds still seen e.g. at the River Don Works. Since the 1960s, the fuel-less and cleaner **electric arc process**, which involves heating the metal in a refractory vessel surrounded by electrical wire, has become universal. This method ensures the requisite purity for the alloy steels produced in Sheffield and has completely superseded both the open-hearth and crucible processes.

of arched or segmental-headed windows. First, the twenty-bay, former **Queen's Works** of 1853 for Armitage, Frankish & Barker. A pedimented entrance bay at the s end was demolished during refurbishment in the 1990s. The works became John Brown's Atlas Works from 1856, later absorbing the slightly grander **President Works** [113] of Moses Eadon and Sons, *c.* 1852. Almost symmetrical either side of a three-bay gatehouse. Rusticated stone quoins and voussoirs to the carriage arch and doorway and a third storey with paired windows either side of a blank stone roundel under a pyramidal roof. Brown's workforce rose from 200 to 4,000 in ten years, as the company exploited the Bessemer process for production of steel rails.

The once continuous street frontage up to **Carwood Road** was broken by demolition in the late 1980s, separating these buildings from the last range, built as the gun shop of Firth's **West Gun Works**, 1863–4, for the manufacture of heavy artillery barrels. Long brick frontage with a curved corner, the offices at the s end have been partly altered with an oriel window while the workshops are lit by fifteen tall round-headed windows below five blank lunettes, all with stone sillbands. Inside, the barrels were forged using two 25-ton steam hammers (among the most powerful then in use), bored, fitted with wiring and mountings and finished. Imaginatively converted in 1994 by *Maynards Chartered Surveyors* for Gripple Ltd, whose clips for linking wire have been used to ingenious effect in a spider's web sculpture by *Johnny White* 1995, on the s wall of the range.

114. River Don Works, Brightside Lane, offices, by Holmes & Watson, 1906

**Brightside Lane** begins beyond Carwood Road. On the E side is the goit or channel that leaves the Don just above Brightside Weir and carried the water which powered Attercliffe forge from the C16. The wall beside the goit has an exceptionally long stretch of 'crozzle' coping, rough black lumps of a hard, lava-like substance produced during the cementation process of steelmaking (*see* topic box, p. 165). About half a mile further on, at the northern end of Brightside Lane, is a group of three buildings representing the new and old faces of the valley. First, on the left, **Sheffield Mail Centre**, 1997, by *Race Cottam Associates*, is quietly stylish with the three-storey main offices in pale grey cladding within a broad dark blue frame with slender columns supporting sun shades and walkways. Wing to the right with freely curving glass front. In the **Machine Shop** across the road, 1956, by *English Steel Corporation Architects' Department*, the industry embraced the new style of architecture in the postwar boom with a gigantic rectangular block of fifteen bays, 600 ft long and 168 ft wide. Steel-framed, faced in brick with panels of yellow tiles and glass block infill on the w side. The three main bays inside could accommodate 40-ton cranes with a span of 50 ft.

The once characteristic canyon effect of the valley's streets created by the works is best preserved at the **River Don Works** in the last stretch of Brightside Lane. Naylor Vickers (Vickers Sons & Maxims from 1911) moved here from Millsands in 1863, gradually extending over more than 100 acres on both sides of the road. From the 1890s, as armament production soared, the company invested over £1 million in the redevelopment of the works with modern plant. It manufactured not only steel, armour plate and armaments but was also involved in shipbuilding, motor cars and aircraft. The chairman boasted that it could, uniquely, 'build and equip a complete warship'. On the w side of the road the impressive four-storey classical revival **offices** [114] (currently empty) by *Holmes & Watson*, 1906, when Vickers was one of the top six industrial concerns in Britain with subsidiary companies in Europe, Japan, Russia and Turkey. Steel-framed, with dirt-resistant, hard red brick walls and almost symmetrical façade of twenty-eight bays. The fittingly intimidating exterior is relieved by the columns and pediments at the fourth storey and the canted stone oriels, which helped to catch whatever natural light was available in the gloom that existed under the valley's permanent pall of smoke. Narrow cantilevered concrete balconies along the upper floors for window cleaning. The interior has a number of innovative features, including a ventilation system with 'vacuum steam' heating, a lift, well-appointed caretaker's flat and a sumptuous marble-lined staircase and boardroom [115], reputedly the result of payment in kind for guns supplied to Italy. A nineteen-bay extension to the left, built 1911, has been demolished, leaving the ground-floor wall as a screen. Window openings with embossed cast-steel keystones. The site, still used by Corus for special steels and heavy forgings and castings, retains the best range of black steel-clad sheds in the valley. They have typical large openings for easy movement of large items from one processing area to another, and gabled vents along the ridge to release the intense heat inside. The group to the s includes the high, four-gabled gun heat-treatment tower of 1913 by *Sir William Arrol*.

115. River Don Works, interior, c. 1906

## b) Attercliffe

Attercliffe was always the most independent and self-sufficient of Sheffield's suburban communities and was separate enough for its leading inhabitants to build a chapel-of-ease in the C17. Its religious and political traditions were strongly radical and produced the Dissenters' Attercliffe Academy in the 1690s and Sheffield's first Labour M.P. in 1909. In the second half of the C19, as fields and gardens disappeared under rows of terraced houses and vast steelworks, it was transformed from a rural village with a mixed agricultural and small-scale metalworking economy to a heavily industrialized working-class suburb which flourished until the 1960s. Then industrial pollution and housing clearance saw the mass exodus of its residents, followed by its industry in the 1980s. Just enough survives among the new media and sports buildings to give a sense of continuity, which will be invaluable if the revival of the area with new housing, proposed since 1993, is realized.

**Attercliffe** is centred on Attercliffe Road, beyond Washford Bridge. We begin in **Birch Road**, to its N, where the **manager's house** for Attercliffe Corn Mill survives (now a club), elegantly refronted in the early C19 with fine sandstone ashlar and double-height canted bays at each end, disguising the fifth bay added on the left. It has been used as a club for many years and was home to the first African-Caribbean social club in Sheffield in the 1970s. Turn into Stevenson Road and then right into **St Charles Street**, to **St Charles Borromeo**, now the only church in Attercliffe still in use. Plain Gothic style in coursed rubble-faced stone. Aisleless nave of five bays and presbytery, both by *Innocent & Brown*, completed 1868. E and w extensions, including chancel and baptistery, by *Innocent*, 1887. Oak pulpit, screen and stalls by *Harry Hems*.

Returning to Attercliffe Road up **Heppenstall Lane** we face **Spartan Works**, a typical small Victorian crucible steel- and wire-making complex of *c.* 1880 with a courtyard and workshops behind the long front range. Its window heads and other details display a rare and here slightly incongruous use of flowery terracotta decoration from the Wharncliffe Fireclay Works (*see* p. 128). Turning left we come to two former banks. First the small but nicely composed **Trustee Savings Bank** of 1899–1900 with three tall arched windows, fluted pilasters and balustrade with urns, in keeping with the house style of the Norfolk Street and Heeley branches. Then on the s side at the corner of Staniforth Road, the **Yorkshire Penny Bank**, 1905, also in stone with oriel windows and decorative sculpture with children's heads. Turn up **Staniforth Road** to the bridge over the canal. On the left is the Supertram **bridge** by *Sir Owen Williams,* 1993, with steel skew arches, and beyond that the elegant arch of a **footbridge** by *Sheffield Design and Building Services,* 1991.

Returning to **Attercliffe Road**, the shop on the corner was the first of two branches of Burton's the Tailors to open in the township, this one from 1931 and built in their usual white faience, here with a hint of Art Deco detailing. The billiard hall on the upper floor offered an additional attraction to customers. A Jewish immigrant from Lithuania, Montague Burton established his tailoring business in Sheffield before moving to Leeds, and revolutionized working men's clothing by mass-producing affordable suits. Further along on the right the prominent four-storey classical-style block decorated with urns along the parapet was **Banners Store**, 1926–8, by *Chapman & Jenkinson* with extensions 1933–4, the only suburban department store in Sheffield and the first shop in the city to have escalators. The self-cleaning properties of its white faience were severely tested by the hundreds of tons of soot that fell annually on each square mile of the valley and blackened other buildings. It dwarfs the former Post Office next door in **Shortridge Street**, also in white faience and boldly decorated with big brackets and festoons.

Walk up to the **Science and Technology Park** on **Shirland Lane**, created to help revive the area with new employment opportunities after the massive job losses in the steel industry. Its focus is the group of two-storey angular blocks by *Sheffield Design and Building Services,* 1987, forming an irregular octagon around a courtyard. Their brightly coloured blue, red and green cladding and glazing bars contrast with the flashier black glass and gold finishes of the **Yorkshire Cable / Telewest** offices, by *William Walker Partnership,* 1994, behind them on **Chippingham Street**. Two storeys, on a butterfly plan, the main block sits low under overhanging hipped roofs and has a gigantic gabled porch supported on square gold columns set diagonally.

Return to Attercliffe Road down Shirland Lane and continue to the right, passing the former Wesleyan Reform Chapel of 1890 on the right in **Bodmin Street** (now a Muslim Community Centre). Bulky, red brick, with memorial stones laid by the great and the good, including

Sir Frederick Thorpe Mappin, along the front. The buildings grouped around the junction with **Worksop Road** still convey something of the character of Attercliffe in its heyday, in particular the handsome Renaissance Revival **Bank** on the left by *Gibbs & Flockton,* 1902. The arched windows have vigorously modelled heads as keystones and the entrance is flanked by polished pink granite Doric columns. Inside, a richly appointed and well-preserved banking hall with a panelled mahogany counter decorated with extraordinary and expressive grotesques. In the churchyard behind, the former **National School** by *Thomas Taylor,* 1824. Plain stone Gothic with lancet windows and open octagonal bellcote. Taylor also designed the parish church of 1826, demolished after bombing in 1940.

On the corner opposite the bank is the **Zeenat Restaurant**, designed in 1904 by *A.N. Bromley* as a branch of Boots (cf. Boots, West Street, p. 130). Three storeys, in a Renaissance Revival style, clad in caramel-coloured faience with a jolly mixture of decorative details around the two large windows on the corner and on the large gable above the balustraded parapet. A few steps up **Worksop Road** is the **Britannia Pub**, with the date 1772 in steel figures on its gable. It incorporates one of the area's oldest surviving houses, by tradition the home of Benjamin Huntsman whose original works were nearby.

Continue down **Attercliffe Road** to **Vicarage Road** on the N side, turning left past a second **Burton's** shop, 1932, by *Harry Wilson*, again in white faience. Next the former **Adelphi Cinema**, designed by *William C. Fenton* and opened in 1920. Red brick front with decorative brick details and lattice windows, the three central bays emphasized by a giant arch and projecting pilasters in bold Baroque Revival faience. The little dome on the squat square tower above has four oddly large projections with oval windows.

Attercliffe Road continues NE as Attercliffe Common. Over on the left in **Maltby Street** is **Dr John Worrall School** by *F.E.P. Edwards,* 1915, a large block in brick with classrooms on three floors. Main front, of eighteen bays, enlivened by gables above the six principal windows and an octagonal-domed bellcote. Set back on the left a little further on, the **Yemeni Community Centre** was built as Attercliffe Vestry Hall in 1865, with offices in front added 1875, all in brick with plain Gothic doorways and window heads. The first family planning clinic in the city, the Women's Welfare Clinic, was set up here in 1933. The older Overseer's House on the left, refronted to match the offices, was the birthplace of the eminent metallurgist Sir Robert Abbott Hadfield in 1858. At the brow of the hill which gave it its former name of Hill Top Chapel, **Attercliffe Chapel** is a solitary landmark in the burial ground on the left. The second oldest building in the valley, it has survived a succession of alterations and several long periods of neglect since it opened in 1630, being restored to its present form by *J.D. Webster* in 1909 and *Martin Purdy* in 1993. Simple rectangular stone building with a late C18 kingpost roof under stone slates. Coped gables with kneelers at E

116. Don Valley Stadium, Leeds Road, Sheffield Design and Building Services and YRM Anthony Hunt Associates, 1989–91

and w ends, four-light E window with trefoil heads and transom. Side windows square-headed. Simple slate pediments on carved brackets to the N and s doorways, the N one has a datestone of 1629. Memorials on the walls and in the chapelyard, including an inscription to Benjamin Huntsman (d. 1776).

s of Attercliffe Common now to **Leeds Road**. First the prominent curved corner of the **Public Baths** of 1879. Classical style, in stone, with pedimented upper windows and dentil cornice. The return range plainer Italianate in brick with stone dressings. Next to it the Neo-Jacobean **Public Library** of 1894 by *Charles Wike* in red brick with stone mullions and transoms and three big coped gables. Both buildings now converted to offices. Across the road, on the site of Brown Bayley's steel-works, is the **Don Valley Stadium** by *Sheffield City Council's Design & Building Services* and *YRM Anthony Hunt Associates*. Built for the 1991 World Student Games' athletic events: the first, and largest, of the sports facilities in the valley and a vehicle for the area's regeneration. Grandstand constructed with twinned **A**-frames, which support the raked seating on one side and provide space below for a range of facilities for both spectators and athletes, including an indoor running track. The stand's white tent-like canopy, supported by a prominent structure of twelve bright yellow Vierendeel ladder masts with cantilevered horizontal ladder trusses, is a distinctive landmark in the city.

Beyond the Stadium the road dips down under the tramway and the adjacent three-arched stone **aqueduct** of 1819 for the Sheffield & Tinsley Canal, emerging as **Darnall Road**. We end the walk a short distance on the right, at one of the most important steelmaking sites in the country, containing a unique group of late C19 crucible shops. The western part of the works, currently derelict, was developed from 1912 by Kayser Ellison. Behind the offices, which face the road, two large steel-framed and glazed workshops of 1913 in a state of shattered fragility. One is two storeys, with brick infill in the gables and in the panels below the continuous glazing. Concrete sills and lintels. The second has pedimented gable, cornice, sills and floor bands in concrete, and fully-glazed first and second storeys. The site to the E was Sanderson Bros. & Co.'s **Darnall Works**, redeveloped in 1871–2 for bulk crucible steel production with 180 melting holes. The entrance further up Darnall Road has a brick lodge and weighbridge cabin flanked by high boundary walls. Within the site detached villa-like offices with hipped roof and two corniced Venetian windows on the ground floor. The surviving brick crucible shops form an L-shaped range, with five small interconnected shops stepping up the hill along Wilfrid Road, their massive transverse stacks containing the flues for forty-eight melting holes. The large gabled shop set at a right angle in the top corner of the site had a group of twenty-four holes on each side of its impressively cavernous interior. The stacks are set longitudinally between the outer walls and the melting floor, creating narrow side aisles which were lined with shelves for storing crucible pots. Last used during the Second World War, the group is now the only surviving example of a crucible furnace with the capacity to produce large amounts of cast steel by the process that dominated the industry until the end of the C19.

From here we can retrace our steps along Worksop Road to Attercliffe Road for buses to the start of the walk or the city centre, or turn left after the aqueduct for the Chippingham Street tramstop. An alternative route back to the city is the two-mile walk along the canal towpath, reached up the steps on the left beside the aqueduct, which passes a variety of industrial sites and ends at the historic canal basin (*see* p. 157).

## c) Carbrook and Meadowhall

The north-eastern end of the Don Valley has seen the most dramatic transformation, as swathes of land cleared of C19 industry and housing have been developed for shopping, leisure and sport on a grand scale. Some older industrial buildings and the odd school and pub cling tenaciously among them, including the most extraordinary survival of all at Carbrook Hall. The buildings are located along or close to Attercliffe Common and Sheffield Road, but mostly sit in isolation, so are listed in order going NE from Coleridge Road, near the Arena/Don Valley Stadium tramstop.

117. English Institute of Sport, Coleridge Road, FaulknerBrowns, 1999–2003

The **English Institute of Sport**, Coleridge Road, 1999–2003 by *FaulknerBrowns* (engineers, *Anthony Hunt Associates*) at a cost of nearly £28 million. One of several national training centres for world-class athletes, covering five acres and including a 200-metre oval running track and six 132-metre straight running lanes. Spirited and graceful in spite of its size. Seven parallel bays, each spanned by an asymmetrical shallow-curved roof, the trusses suspended from eight 50-metre-high needle-like masts with fine rigging. Fully glazed entrance, with a mix of glass and timber cladding either side and on the returns. The rest finished in pale grey cladding.

A similarly ambitious effort is made at **iceSheffield**, Coleridge Road, by *Building Design Partnership*, opened in 2003. Clad in cool silvery grey, with green-tinted glazing, the building sits low under the sweeping double curves of its roof. On three sides the ground is banked up around it, so one enters at the upper level with views from the foyer down onto the recreational rink. Inside, two Olympic-standard rinks each 60 by 30 metres. One is for recreational and community use, the other for training and competitive ice sports at international level, with seating for 1,500 spectators. On the E side continuous glazing overlooks the **East End Park**, allowing views across the Don Valley Bowl, a grassed amphitheatre created in 1987–91 on a former steelworks site. Near the entrance an elegant 10-metre-high blade-like **sculpture** in stainless steel by *Michael Johnson* 2003.

**Carbrook School** on Attercliffe Common is almost the sole survivor of C19 Carbrook, 1873–4, by *Innocent & Brown*, in their usual Gothic. Symmetrical two storeys with a striking tall gabled front and a small stone spire above the central bell-turret. The open arcaded play areas

118. Carbrook Hall, Attercliffe Common, *c.* 1620

on the ground floor of the rear cross-wing were later enclosed to provide additional classrooms. Caretaker's house of 1877 and *Innocent's* additional block of 1889 have been demolished.

In **Broughton Lane**, the style and panache of the earlier sports venues is entirely absent at the **Hallam FM Arena**, a hulking rectangular block by *HOK Sport* and *Lister, Drew, Haines, Barrow*, opened in 1991 for the World Student Games and now Sheffield's largest multi-purpose indoor venue for entertainment, sport, events and exhibitions. Its dreary concrete, off-white cladding and aggregate panels are, frankly, dull. The impressively vast interior has 8,000 seats in raked blocks on three sides allowing flexible use of the central area as an ice rink, sports arena, or for additional seating for 3,000. On the opposite side of Broughton Lane, **Valley Centertainment** complex of 1999–2000 including a twenty-screen cinema, restaurants, nightclubs and bowling alley. Large, almost windowless blocks but with a coherent identity. Further NE, on Attercliffe Common, **Meadowhall Retail Park**, by *David Lyons Associates* 1993. At the front, Marbles Players, a charming little sculpture by *Vega Bermejo*.

**Carbrook Hall** (now a pub), on the w side of Attercliffe Common, is the surviving stone wing added *c.* 1620 to an older house (demolished in the C19), which was the seat of the Bright family. Unpromising and much-altered exterior, with some mullioned and transomed windows but, inside, the parlour represents the pre-classical C17 better than any other in Sheffield. Sumptuously decorated with oak panelling, a carved overmantel and plaster ceiling for Stephen Bright, who was appointed

Bailiff of Hallamshire in 1622. The geometric panelling is divided by pilasters carved with stylized sunflowers and foliage, below a frieze. Above this a moulded plaster frieze with foliage trails. The richly decorated ceiling is divided by deep plastered beams into six compartments, with sprigs of flowers and bold curled-up strapwork in curious frames. Carved oak overmantel, almost identical to the one from Norton House, now in the Cutlers' Hall, which is dated 1623. Its central panel has a relief of a person in long garments stepping on a monstrous corpse with blown-up belly and a tail. A chamber above has stencilled wainscot panelling, an impressive Renaissance overmantel and some surviving plasterwork. Features of the work at Carbrook indicate that it is probably by the same craftsmen who worked at Bolsover Castle, Derbyshire.

Nearby in Carbrook Hall Road, **Carbrook House**, offices of 1992 by *Building Design Partnership*. Three storeys, in glass and white cladding. With its white metal verandas around the upper floors and big glazed atrium it has a refreshingly jaunty, seaside sort of character. Additional offices next door, 1998, by *Alan J. Smith Partnership* and opposite, five linked office blocks, by *Andrew Sebire Architects*, 1990.

On Sheffield Road the former **Tinsley Tram Depot**, part now Sheffield Bus Museum. Gabled brick sheds built 1874 for horse trams, extended 1899 for the new electric service.

**Meadowhall Shopping Centre**, Meadowhall Way, by *Chapman Taylor Partners*, 1990, extended 1999. The first and largest of the post-industrial developments in the valley, on the site of the East Hecla Steelworks, its green-clad roofs and glazed domes are a prominent landmark beside the M1 viaduct. Radiating from the central dome are three top-lit galleried malls with over 270 shops on two levels, each mall separately themed. The attached 2,000-seat circular food court, The Oasis, originally masqueraded as a village square in Spain, the 'buildings' around it copied from the Plaza de los Naranjas in Marbella.

# East

The SE side of Sheffield formed the hunting park of the lords of Hallamshire from at least the C13; a charter of 1296 confirming the right of Thomas de Furnival to hunt in his park. A survey of 1637 stated it to be 2,461 acres in size. The ruins of the Earl of Shrewsbury's hunting lodge and some portions of the boundary wall and ditch survive in the Manor area (*see* below). The district known as Park was developed

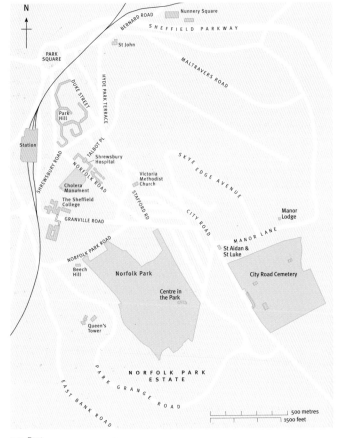

119. East

120. Manor Lodge, Turret House, interior of second floor room, *c.* 1574

from the late C18, followed by Norfolk Park which was built up with high-quality villas. Ribbon development of terraced houses grew out along City Road, but otherwise the SE side of the city remained undeveloped until the sprawling Wybourn, Manor, Arbourthorne and Woodthorpe council estates were built in the 1920s and 1930s. Further public housing followed post-1945 with extensions to some of the earlier estates but most significantly with the creation of the Park Hill flats.

**Manor Lodge**, Manor Lane. The earliest documentary reference to a hunting lodge in the Park was in 1479–80, but its remains are few. Excavation of the ruins of the lodge, carried out 1969–79, revealed something of its development. It is known to have comprised a rectangular structure in an outer courtyard with corner towers at the N end, demolished in the second half of the C16. The lower stonework of the N half of the W front, known as the Long Gallery, is also late medieval. The upper part has the blocked remains of two four-light traceried windows.

During his visit in 1529, Thomas Wolsey lodged in a new tower, believed to be the block at the N end of the Long Gallery and now known as Wolsey's Tower. The rebuilding of the upper story of the Long Gallery took place at the same time. A double courtyard layout emerged during the C16 with a smaller service court to the E. Much of the standing stonework in the S wing dates from the last half of the C16 and is likely to overlie and incorporate earlier structures. A cross-wing, dividing the two courtyards, underwent several stages of rebuilding and alteration in the C16. These works were undertaken as the Lodge was developed into the principal residence of the Lord of the Manor when Sheffield Castle fell out of favour.

The S half of the W wing represents a complete rebuild in the last half of the C16. This resulted in an imposing new entrance, flanked by brick-faced octagonal towers, a new courtyard and revised garden lay-out. It is possible that Bess of Hardwick, who was married to the 6th Earl of Shrewsbury, may have had some hand in this and that the work was carried out to accommodate Mary, Queen of Scots, who was kept in Sheffield under his custodianship, 1570–84. References are made in 1582 to 'the queens gallery there' and to 'the Quenes kitchen at the lodge'. Following its inheritance by the Howards, the house was allowed to decay and it was largely demolished in 1708. Some surviving fragments (a piece of wall and mullioned window) were removed by Samuel Roberts about 1839 and re-erected in the grounds of Queen's Tower (see p. 216).

Architecturally more interesting than the scanty fragments of the main house is the Elizabethan summer house or standing, called **Turret House** [120], to the s of the main building, possibly begun in 1574 – there is a reference that may relate to it in a building account of William Dickinson. It had fallen into disrepair by the mid c19 and in 1873 the 15th Duke of Norfolk commissioned M.E. Hadfield to survey and restore the building. It is to him that the building owes its present appearance. Hadfield reopened blocked windows and doors and removed others. Three-storeyed, of stone, with a higher circular angle turret of brick, it has diagonally set chimney stacks and cross-windows. There are two rooms on each floor. The far room on the first floor retains a plaster ceiling with simple ribbed geometrical patterns. On the second floor, the most important room is distinguished by a fine fireplace and elaborate plaster ceiling. The fireplace has an over-mantel with two fat columns flanking the arms of George Talbot modelled in deep relief, the ceiling fashionably decorated in a pattern of eight-pointed stars with heads, leaves, flowers, etc., all of the highest quality. David Bostwick* suggests that the design, which incorporates a hand grasping a spray of flowers by the stems – a motif derived from Claude Paradin's Devises Héroïques (1557) – represents Mary Stuart's loss of freedom, reinforced by the depiction of Talbot dogs standing guard. It is possible that the decoration was carried out at the behest of Bess of Hardwick. She is symbolized in the choice of white briar roses or eglantine (the flowers on the Hardwick arms). It may be one of several examples of plasterwork with hidden meanings in buildings associated with her. Decorated frieze. The **stained glass** added during the 1873 restoration is by J.F. Bentley and made by Lavers, Barraud & Westlake.

The ruin of a cruck-framed building to the e of Manor Lodge has walls of late c18 origin, probably of material from the Lodge, possibly an enlargement of an earlier two-bay structure.[†]

---

*D Bostwick, 'Plaster to puzzle over', Country Life 184, 12 July 1990, pp. 90–3.
[†]The above account is partly based on Pauline Beswick 'Sheffield Manor', Archaeological Journal 137, 1980, pp. 468–9.

## a) Park Hill and Hyde Park

**Park Hill** [121] is the one building in Sheffield to have achieved international fame; it is also the most controversial. One of only a handful of high-rise developments to be granted statutory protection (listed Grade II* in 1998), it has had more written about it than any other post-war British public housing scheme and has been described as a 'Modernist icon'. There can be no easy interpretation. Pevsner in 1967 was unsure about the soundness of the concept itself, admiring the cleverness of it all but declaring that 'there can alas be no doubt that such a vast scheme of closely-set high blocks of flats will be a slum in half a century or less', though in mitigation, 'a cosy slum'.

One's first sight of Park Hill is unforgettable. It lines the eastern hillside above the railway station, providing a powerful horizontal accent that is visible from much of the city centre. Its appearance is Janus-like; from a distance, sunlit or at night, it is like a multi-coloured chequer board, its continuous roof-line emphasizing the relationship created with the land on which it stands; close up from the shopping centre, it is brutal in conception, sublime in its scale and materials.

Topography is the key to Park Hill; it has much to do with why it was built and to the form of access that led to its fame. Sheffield had wanted to extend its boundaries in 1951 and was unable to do so. To carry out its slum clearance programme therefore, it had to move away from the spreading suburban estates it had hitherto built in favour of flats on the restricted sites near the city centre. Park Hill was selected as it included the oldest outstanding slum clearance order in Sheffield, some of the land already having been cleared in the 1930s. Its proximity to the centre and Don Valley industry, though situated on the unpolluted windward side, together with the topography of the land-made it suitable for high-density housing at 193 persons per acre (net). The initial idea

121. Park Hill from the city centre, by J.L. Womersley, 1955–61

evolved in 1953 when *J.L. Womersley* recruited two young architects *Jack Lynn* and *Ivor Smith* to design a scheme for Norfolk Park. When that was deferred, he gave them Park Hill and Hyde Park to work on, assisted by *Frederick Nicklin*. The original unbuilt scheme was to have had blocks set at right angles to each other on Park Hill with angled blocks for the development at Hyde Park, higher up. Hyde Park has always been in the shadow of its more famous neighbour, but the two schemes were conceived as one and should be considered as such (for buildings of the old Park area *see* below).

The go-ahead for the Park Hill **scheme** was given in 1955, work commenced in 1957 and it was completed in 1961. As built, it comprises four blocks varying in height from four storeys at the s end to fourteen at the N, the sloping ground allowing the roof-line to remain level throughout

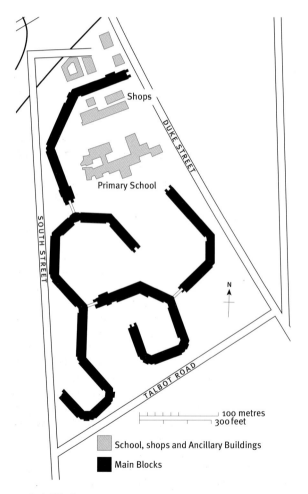

122. Park Hill, plan

and all but the top deck to reach ground level. The blocks, which in plan resemble fragmentary polygons, were linked by bridges at angles of 135 and 112 degrees to enable the 10 ft (3 metre) wide access decks, provided on every third floor, to shift from one side to the other so as to ensure each got as much sun as possible. The decks, each taking the name of an existing street (*see* topic box, p. 211), were wide enough for small electric trolleys to deliver milk, something that perhaps caught the public imagination more than any other detail. The decks were served by thirteen eight-person lifts located at the ends of the blocks, together with three goods lifts, a total that proved inadequate. On the ground floor was a shopping centre, a laundry, a police station and four pubs. The blocks were so arranged as to create courts within which a primary and a nursery school were eventually built, together with playgrounds. In

## Brutalism

'Brutalism', declared the critic Reyner Banham in *The New Brutalism* (1966), is 'an ethic, not an aesthetic'. It describes not so much a style as an expression of a set of values and beliefs. Its meaning, however, is ill-defined and altered over time.

The expression was coined in Sweden in 1950 by Hans Asplund, son of the architect Gunnar Asplund, and the following year some young English visitors brought it back to England where it was taken up enthusiastically by a generation of architects and critics, the most vociferous of whom were Peter and Alison Smithson and Banham himself. They rejected not only the rationalist approach of the International Style but also the romanticism implicit in the architecture associated with the Festival of Britain and identified by Pevsner in his explorations of informal English picturesque landscape. 'New Brutalism' was expounded by Banham in 1955 in response to what the *Architectural Review* termed 'The New Humanism', a style whose hallmarks of low-pitched roofs and timber boarding owed much to Swedish architecture. Instead it drew on the harsh, Corbusian-inspired forms of Continental Modernism.

The essence of Brutalism is 'truth to materials' with expressive articulation of structural elements. Concrete framing expressed on the exterior, exposed roof trusses and bare brick interior walls are all characteristic. In this, it adopts an industrial aesthetic, seen as a living tradition in the 1950s when discussed in J.M. Richards's series of articles in the *Architectural Review*. The Smithsons' school at Hunstanton (1950–4) is the classic example of this with its legible plan, structure and services. Honesty is all important: there should be no sham based on nostalgia for the past but 'a direct expression of a way of life', a response to the needs of the present based on a sense of place.

Banham concluded that 'the moral crusade of Brutalism for a better habitat through built environment probably reaches its culmination at Park Hill'.

this, with an unbroken front range and largely open rear to the estate, they resembled Quarry Hill, Leeds, of 1935–41 where the Viennese-inspired perimeter wall (which in contrast to Park Hill failed to make such creative use of the contours) and individual blocks also framed the playgrounds, a day nursery and a community hall. The Park Hill playgrounds were provided with furniture (since removed) designed by the abstract sculptor, *John Forrester*, who also advised on the modelling and colouring of the façades of the blocks, street lighting and footpaths.

There were 994 dwellings for 3,448 persons in a mixture of one and two-bedroom flats and two to four-bedroom maisonettes. The design was built around a three-bay, three-storey unit [123] with maisonettes at and above deck level and flats below, all dovetailed together with the front doors paired. To ensure quiet for the living rooms and bedrooms within each unit, internal back-to-back and interlocking staircases and halls were the only parts that abutted on to the decks. These staircases formed a rigid H-section unit that added much strength to the structure. Within the grid of the elevations [20], the dominant motif is the concrete balustrades with closely-spaced uprights that mark the decks and the balconies of the flats. Walls are of brick, differently coloured for each three-storey unit, which Pevsner found fussy. Non-structural exterior and party walls could be varied as required, enabling the complex internal arrangements of the flats to be expressed in the external grid. This expression of the structure fits the tough Brutalist (*see* topic box, p. 209) ethos as much as the use of *béton brut* (rough concrete, showing the impression of the timber shuttering used in its construction), praised by Reyner Banham for its 'gutsy finish', and the rejection of any attempt to hide function, most notably in the hammer-headed lift towers and exposed bridges.

Dwellings were originally provided with Garchey waste disposal, whose units were placed below sinks. Still a novelty in Britain (it had previously been employed at Quarry Hill and Spa Green, Clerkenwell,

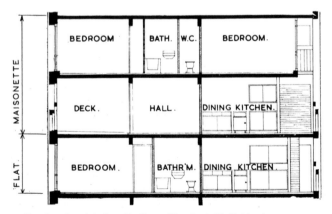

123. Elevation of module. From *Ten Years of Housing in Sheffield*, 1962

London), the units were connected to double-sided vertical service ducts placed either side of the internal staircases within each three-bay unit. The ducts connected at their base with a horizontal duct leading to the Garchey Refuse Disposal Station and a boiler house supplying hot water and central heating, all now abandoned.

## Streets in the Sky

Park Hill's most celebrated feature is its access decks or 'streets in the sky'. There are several precedents for deck access in *avant-garde* c20 housing, e.g. Moscow. The most famous is Le Corbusier's Unité d'Habitation, Marseilles which had an internal 'street' with a single entrance from the ground.

The idea was taken up with enthusiasm by the younger generation of British postwar architects because it appeared to offer new forms of planning that sought the right relationship between old urban fabric and new function. *Jack Lynn*, with *Gordon Ryder*, had submitted an entry in the competition for the City of London's Golden Lane estate (1951–2) which featured access decks, as did the Smithsons' more famous (and published) entry. Decks also featured in the Smithsons' 1953 Sheffield University competition entry (q.v.) but Park Hill is the first built expression of such an idea. Significantly, both Lynn, who expressed his debt to the Unité, and Ivor Smith had been students at the Architectural Association of Peter Smithson. The Smithsons were influential members of Team X whose manifesto, issued after their emergence at the 10th Congrès Internationaux d'Architecture Moderne in 1956, laid down the need for architecture and planning that emphasized human association and community.

Such ideals were expressed by architects in a variety of ways but common to all was the desire to reproduce the richness of traditional working-class street life, perceived as being undermined by consumerism in the writings of the literary critic, Richard Hoggart and the sociologists, Willmott and Young. An important part of this was the need for individual front doors to the street. Lynn saw this as essentially English, unlike the communal approach of the French concierge system, even if the expression of individuality was limited to the doors 'being painted in individual colours'. Its Englishness did not preclude contemporary use of the access deck abroad; the Quartiere Forte Quezzi in Genoa built in 1956–7 by *L.C. Daneri* has a deck running along five long connected blocks. The importance of the Sheffield design was that it was the first to combine social facilities with decks that could be accessed from ground level and continued through several linked blocks, moving away from the older ideal of stand-alone blocks to create a true street. Ironically, Park Hill's 'streets in the sky' did not actually reflect the pre-war street life of Sheffield, which was based on the court rather than the street. The houses had in any case largely been cleared so that there was little opportunity to decant an existing community into the new flats.

**Hyde Park**, which had 1,313 dwellings and was completed in 1966, has been described as a step too far. The central block, demolished 1992, rose to eighteen storeys with no opportunity to walk up from the level but it made a fine vertical counterpoint to Park Hill (compared by many in Sheffield to a castle keep). What remains, now isolated from each other, are the two lower blocks, Castle Court and St John's Court, both re-clad, the decks glazed in and the entrances controlled by concierges. Immensely long blocks of three-storey maisonettes on Hyde Park Terrace and Hyde Park Walk are equally unrecognizable today. Tellingly, a photograph of these blocks entitled 'Raising the Standard' was published in the *Architects Journal* in 1961 to celebrate the project 'forging ahead'; by 1967, a similar photograph was used to show the soul-destroying monotony of a 1,000-ft-long wall relieved only by plain front doors. In 1990–1, the terraces were taken back to the bare concrete framework and clad in yellow and red brick, given pitched pantiled roofs and timber balconies, the decks enclosed and gardens provided in an attempt to secure defensible space.

Hyde Park is modified beyond recognition; Park Hill awaits its own fate. Repairs to its spalling concrete and its draughty windows, together with updating security, insulation and services, are urgently needed. Reconciling the aspirations of the residents for improvements to the environment in which they live with the wish to pay homage to the ideals of what is regarded by many as a heroic age in British architecture is the central dilemma at Park Hill. The recognition by listing of the estate's significance as an exemplar of mid-C20 views of housing (with a show flat furnished in 1950s style at No. 56 Gilbert Row) may be seen as a way forward for its eventual regeneration, through the injection of private capital and mixed use.

## b) Park

Of the old Park, once notorious for its tightly packed early C19 houses, there is little left. Its clearance was a postwar priority for Sheffield Corporation, followed by the building of the Park Hill and Hyde Park flats. Dividing the flats are Duke Street and Bernard Street which retain a few relics of the pre-war district.

In **Duke Street**, the **Christian Centre** (formerly Wesleyan Chapel), 1830, and 'designed by an amateur' according to the local historian R.E. Leader. Classical, round-headed windows, rendered and much altered. Up Duke Street to the s, the **Baths and Library** of 1902. A rather incoherent piece of work in a watered-down Arts and Crafts style in red brick with shaped parapets and a tower to the rear. The side elevation, which gives entry to the baths, is more elaborate than the front. Tall circular chimney at the rear. Walk-up tenement flats of the mid-1930s slum clearance scheme were built in **Bard Street**. Mostly demolished and the remainder re-clad to provide flats for sale in 1989–90. The transformation is such that they appear to be new build. As part of the same project, maisonette blocks of 1958–9 were halved in height to provide two-storey houses.

124. Nunnery Square Phase 1, by Allies & Morrison, 1993

In **Bernard Street**, surrounded by the re-clad Hyde Park flats, **St John**, 1836–8, by *M.E. Hadfield*. Re-roofed and restored by *E.M. Gibbs* in 1889–91. It was reordered *c.* 1971 by *K.H. Murta* and *J.B. Hall* who added a church hall on the N side. In many respects a typical preaching box of the period with no aisles, a very short chancel and thin detailing, Hadfield's first church accords with contemporary taste in having Norman-style doorways at the W end (that in the tower having well-executed chevron mouldings), Norman windows in the lower stages of the W tower and a broad rounded chancel arch. The remaining windows are all lancets. The tower has a tall broach spire. Inside, a gallery on iron columns and a vast open nave, the impression of space made even greater by the removal of pews during the reordering. The sanctuary is almost a niche behind the chancel arch. The octagonal, blockwork church hall has a projecting angled skylight, similar to Casson and Conder's Elephant and Rhino Pavilion at London Zoo.

N of here in **Bernard Road** are the remaining buildings of the London & North Western Railway's **Nunnery Goods Depot**. Opened in 1895, these comprise stables with a sick bay, manager's house and goods office, built to standard company designs of the period in blue and red brick with cogging. The stables are single storey with iron segmental-headed windows and some bays retain hayracks and baskets. The goods branch of the railway was extended in 1903 to a large facility s of the Canal Wharf (*see* Walk 5, p. 157), demolished in the late 1960s.

Further out on this side, accessible by tram, a business park, **Nunnery Square** [124]. Built as a speculative development. Three buildings were intended, facing a central oblong lawn, but only two completed. The first phase of 1993 by *Allies & Morrison* is one of the first buildings to be seen in Sheffield as one drives in along the Parkway and, fortunately, one of the best. It is essentially a box with floor-to-ceiling glazing and white panels. A steel framework supports horizontal walkways for window cleaning and sun shades wrap around it. This thin framework is proportioned so as to create what equates to a classical structure of base and *piano nobile*, the latter being the frame of the upper two floors, exactly twice the size of the ground floor. An attic is provided by the raised service pod. The larger second block of 1999 by *HLM Architects* lacks the exposed frame and is less striking but still far superior to most other late C20 office developments in the city.

## c) Norfolk Park

The district of **Norfolk Park** lies SE of Park Hill and the passage from the tough aesthetic of the estate is both striking and effective in showing the thoughtful relationship between the scale of the flats and the older terraced houses. In **Talbot Place**, **Talbot Crescent** and **Talbot Gardens** to the NE, terraced houses *c.* 1850 with pilastered doorcases, some with unusual scalloped faux-incised lintels.

In contrast, **Norfolk Road** is lined with substantial villas of the 1830s to 1880s. Starting at the N end, on the E side is the **Shrewsbury Hospital**, 1825, by *Woodhead & Hurst*. A handsome group of almshouses in fine ashlar, Tudor, three ranges round a spacious court, single storey with a taller central chapel. Ten more added to the E, again in Tudor style, in 1930 and between these and the road, two groups of pentagonal almshouses and a meeting hall by *Mansell Jenkinson & Partners*, 1976. The latter is entirely in a modern idiom but blending in well with walls of local gritstone and Westmorland slate roofs. Opposite, the **Cholera Monument**, 1834–5, by *M.E. Hadfield*, stands in a small burial ground within which 402 victims of the 1832 epidemic were buried. An earthbound Gothic pinnacle or spire, which Pevsner in 1967 suggested was the Gothicist's equivalent of an obelisk. It has somewhat unfairly been compared to a space rocket.

Of the houses, the following may be singled out, all classical, on the E side: Nos. 9–11, 13–15, *c.* 1830, ashlar semi-detached, with doorcases with engaged Tuscan columns on side elevations, Nos. 43–45, 47, 49, similar but with pilastered doorcases, *c.* 1856. The villas on the W side tend to be larger and in the Tudor style or variations of it; typical are Nos. 38–42 (Belmont), both with Dutch gables and drip-moulds to the windows but built twenty years apart, *c.* 1841 and *c.* 1860 respectively. Then Nos. 72–74, *c.* 1842, by *Weightman & Hadfield* for their own occupation, with bay windows on the ground floor and No. 82, a Tudor-style villa with coped gables and an ornate timber porch. In the grounds, a timber-framed coach house with diagonal pattern boarding, a similar but smaller outbuilding. Then No. 82a, a bargeboarded cottage *c.* 1870. *Charles Hadfield* built No. 84 Park Cottage for himself in 1875, the house much altered in the early C20. At No. 90, the Sale Memorial Vicarage, 1880, a Gothic villa with an especially fine tall staircase window with wooden quatrefoils probably by *Flockton & Gibbs*, the architects of the Sale Memorial Church (dem.).

125. Norfolk Park, lodge, 1851, and screen wall, 1876, by M.E. Hadfield & Son

**Norfolk Park** lies at the s end of the road. Bernard Edward, the 12th Duke of Norfolk, laid out the remains of his manorial park between 1841 and 1848, when it was opened to the public, one of the first such benefactions. He had hopes of residential leases being taken on his land surrounding the new park. The layout of the park with its simple planting reflected a c18 pastoral style. Henry, the 15th Duke, presented it to the city in 1912.

Two **lodges** survive on Norfolk Park Road and Granville Road, both pretty in the Tudor style with elaborate fretted bargeboards and tall chimneys. The lodge in Norfolk Park Road dates from 1841, that in Granville Road is of 1851 and is adjacent to the screen wall [125] of 1876 by *M.E. Hadfield & Son*, in c15 style with big octagonal stone piers and a long pierced stone balustrade incorporating quatrefoils. In front of this, an impressive Gothic iron gas lamp with five ogee lanterns supported on brackets with cusping. Within the park, the **Centre in the Park** of 1998–2000 by *DBS Architects*, single storey, successfully blending with the contours of the landscape, in a continuous gentle curve which becomes sharper at one end. The other end is taken up with a drum, lit by glass bricks and clad in smooth stone. The rest is rockfaced. The roof is covered in lead sheeting whose joints combine with the curve of the structure to create a satisfying rhythm. Nearby a restored Ionic stone arch is carved with an image of the 15th Duke of Norfolk, 1912. It was originally the porch of a half-timbered pavilion, destroyed by fire and forms the entrance to a viewing platform.

To the NW in **Granville Road**, the **Sheffield College** (formerly Granville College of Further Education), 1958–61, by *J.L. Womersley*. An intricate grouping of mainly three-storey blocks all up a bank above the street, each connected with glazed links. The principal teaching block is cantilevered towards the street. A little to the N in **Shrewsbury Road**, No. 19, a former workshop, 1843, stone, two storeys built into the hill, used as a studio by the local sculptor Charles Green, 1910–16.

**Norfolk Park Road** has one house of significance, **Beech Hill**. Described in 1831 as 'recently built', by *Woodhead & Hurst*. Tudor style with crowstepped gables and the Duke of Norfolk's coat of arms on the chimney. Extended in 1859. Matthew Ellison, the Duke's agent, lived there from 1858 and following the death of Ellison's son in 1898, the 15th Duke retained it as his Sheffield home. The Farm, his home prior to 1898 and another Tudor fantasy, was demolished in 1967.

Further SW **East Bank Road** was originally a cul-de-sac of large houses built in the early C19 with leases from the Duke of Norfolk. Only three are left: **Knowle House**, occupied 1856–85 by M.E. Hadfield who built the entrance lodge, inscribed 'M&SH 1858'; **Mid Hill House**, classical with an ashlar façade; and **Queen's Tower** [126], 1839, by *Woodhead & Hurst*. The last is a remarkably romantic gesture by Samuel Roberts, a silver-plate manufacturer and antiquary who was an enthusiast for Mary, Queen of Scots and who saw in the house a way of honouring her. The house, which was a wedding present for his son, also named Samuel, is inevitably a mixture of Tudor motifs with embattled walls, towers and turrets and has a crenellated lodge. It was enlarged in the 1860s. Large stable court and an archway in matching style. In the grounds, laid out by *Robert Marnock*, were fragments of old wall and a mullioned window (through which Mary is traditionally said to have looked) from Manor Lodge (q.v.) which have now disappeared. Conversion to flats in 2003–4.

126. Queen's Tower, by Woodhead & Hurst, 1839. C19 photograph

Running around the edge of the public park on steeply sloping ground is the **Norfolk Park Estate**, built 1962–7 on the last open space near the city centre. Much of it could not be built on, due to early coal mining on the site. It has an interesting layout with a curving spine road and total segregation of traffic and pedestrians. Rivalling the Gleadless Valley (*see* p. 243) in its setting, it is unfortunate that finances did not permit building of the housing types originally intended, which included patio houses and stylish point blocks. What was built is conventional, a mixture of clusters of towers, four-storey maisonettes and Vic Hallam houses, largely being redeveloped in 2004 with housing association and private housing by *Axis Architecture* and *HTA Architects*.

NW of the park, in **Stafford Road**, **Victoria Methodist Church**, 1899–1901, by *John Wills*. The most impressive of Wills's four Sheffield churches, it cost £10,000, much of it contributed by Joseph Bassett, brother of the sweet manufacturer. NW tower with a tall broach spire. Flamboyant Dec tracery in the E window, Geometrical in the w, lancets elsewhere. Enriched tympanum over the w door. The interior has a plain wagon roof and was converted in 2003 with a two-storey space for meeting rooms, etc. by *Bramall & Blenkharn*. **Stained glass**: E window by *Abbott & Co.* of Lancaster, windows of 1909 in N and S aisles removed from Talbot Street Chapel. Tucked in close by is **Stafford Mews** (known as the **Gin Stables**), built to accommodate the horses that powered the gins at the Duke of Norfolk's Park collieries. The original portion (Nos. 1–4), comprising a range of rendered two-storey buildings, are probably pre-1750. Nos. 5–8, a large barn with quatrefoils and a doorway with a pointed arch is *c.* 1851. Converted in 1985–6 into flats and houses.

In **City Road**, close to Manor Lane, are a few buildings of note, from N–S. **Manor Lodge School**, 1877 by *Innocent & Brown* is a single-storey example of the first batch of Board Schools in the Gothic style. Additions by *Wightman & Wightman* of 1889 and, in the Renaissance style by *Charles Hadfield*, 1907.

On the opposite side, **St Aidan**, 1932–3, by *Flockton & Son*. A cruciform church in the Perp style with a tower with a squat spire. Very traditional for its date but some hints of modernity in the concrete window frames and stylized carved timber corbels of a lamb, eagle, etc. in the nave. The chancel is a side-lit broad low recess under a Tudor arch with blind tracery panels and Perp windows above and to the side of it. A pioneering social and educational centre for the local community was created in 1999 by *Roger Barnes* of *Niall Phillips Architects* who added a glazed timber cloister on the N side and turned part of the nave into a hall separated from the worship space by a movable partition. Fine **furnishings** of 1999 in limed oak, some built around a steel core, by *Andrew Skelton*, including an altar table, side altar, lectern and font. A cross has copper waves as a background echoing the crinkle-crankle form that unifies the design of the other fittings. **Stained glass**: St Aidan preaching to the heathen, s transept, 1956, and others by *Alfred*

*Wilkinson*. The **Vicarage** is adjacent, originally Manor Grange. Early C19, plain three-bay classical.

**City Road Cemetery**: the cemetery was opened by the Sheffield Burial Board in 1881. *M.E. Hadfield & Son* created an imposing landmark in the tall Tudor-style gateway which included a lodge, and bell-turret with an octagonal finial and was flanked by offices with full-height bay windows. Massive stone boundary walls. Inside were Anglican (now demolished) and Nonconformist chapels of equal size but slightly different in design. A crematorium was added in 1905 to the designs of *C. & C.M. Hadfield*, based quite closely on the Abbot's Kitchen at Glastonbury Abbey, which had the undeniable advantage of enabling them to disguise the metal crematorium chimney with an ornamental stone flue (since replaced in brick). When it was designed, there were less than ten crematoria in the country. The Duke of Norfolk paid for a Catholic chapel, also by *C. & C.M. Hadfield* 1899–1900. Free Gothic, with a hexagonal chancel and a lantern almost Early Christian in character. The vaulting was in lath and plaster with moulded wooden ribs and tie-beams. Near ruinous in 2004. The **Belgian War Memorial** of 1921, a tapered octagonal cross-shaft with panelled sides and fleurons based on a French example of the C15, commemorates the wounded Belgian servicemen and refugees of the First World War who died in Sheffield. Second World War blitz grave of *c.* 1941, a low wall enclosing a kidney-shaped enclosure and the 1914–18 War Memorial, *c.* 1920; the standard *Sir Reginald Blomfield* design of a Portland stone cross, with a bronze sword, and octagonal pedestal.

Off **Manor Lane**, housing in **Skye Edge Avenue**. Long low 1970s terraces of striking design by *Ivor Smith & Hutton*, crown the ridge and here spectacular views over the city.

# South

## a) Highfield, Lowfield and Sharrow

Highfield, Lowfield and Sharrow blend almost imperceptibly into one another and are best considered as a whole. The original hamlet of Little Sheffield located at the N end of London Road was the centre of ribbon development that extended along that road and a short distance either side of it by the early C19. By 1860, development had extended E from London Road towards St Mary's Church and SW up Cemetery Road but much of the area remained rural until the 1870s with scattered larger houses standing in extensive grounds. A major phase of house building began in the 1860s–70s spreading outwards along the main roads. Industry was concentrated in Highfield and between Abbeydale Road and the Chesterfield–Sheffield railway (opened 1870). By 1914 the area was almost entirely built up with small bylaw terraced houses, the only part remaining undeveloped was the W end of Sharrow Lane.

The streets of earlier back-to-back houses in Little Sheffield and in Cemetery Road were replaced in the mid 1960s by the Lansdowne Estate. Since the 1970s many of the later bylaw houses have either been demolished and replaced by low-rise council housing or included in

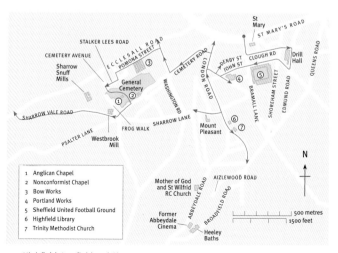

127. Highfield, Lowfield and Sharrow

enveloping schemes. Today, it is a typical inner-city area retaining a substantial amount of its C19 character but with its shopping centre, which ran along the whole length of London Road, having lost much of its vitality. Moves to regenerate it, led by Sheffield's Chinese community, are beginning to take effect.

Bramall Lane and London Road

The walk commences by the ring road at its junction with **Bramall Lane**. **St Mary** [128], 1826–30 by *Joseph & Robert Potter*, is a large and handsome Perp-style Commissioners' church with 140-ft (42.5 metre) high w tower with tall pinnacles. Substantial buttresses also with large crocketed pinnacles. Tall Perp three-light windows divided by a deep transom with tracery below. Grotesque headstops. Very short chancel. Damaged by bombing, the w part was a pioneer conversion of 1950 by *Stephen Welsh* into a community centre. In 1999–2000, the rigid division of the church was softened by *APEC Architects*. They removed the 1950 work and created a new community centre of two floors and a mezzanine, filling all but the chancel and the two E bays of the nave which

128. St Mary, Bramall Lane, by Joseph and Robert Potter, 1826–30

are still used for worship. The work is in a light neutral style with few associations with the past history of the building. A new pointed porch gives access to a central narthex, extensively glazed to allow views from the one part to the other. A Gothic organ case survives.

Turn left into **Clough Road**. On the right, on the corner with Countess Road, is **Chaucer Yard**, the former Wardonia Works of Thomas W. Ward Ltd who made razor blades. It shows the domestic scale of much of Sheffield's cutlery trade, with mid-C19 houses and a small cutlery works of c. 1879 (India Works) on Clough Road. Now small workshops. At the junction with **Edmund Road**, the red brick Tudor tower of the former **Drill Hall** of 1878–80 by *M.E. Hadfield & Son* for the 4th West York Artillery Volunteers, now used as a car workshop. Mullioned façade with a carved shield by *W.S. Gillman* bearing the arms of the Duke of Norfolk. The 180 ft by 90 ft (55 by 27.5 metres) hall has shallow cast-iron lattice trusses by *Andrew Handyside*. The arch ribs spring from the floor in the manner of St Pancras Station, bearing on brick buttresses. Between each buttress is a shallow pointed arch. These are deeply recessed on the E side. There is a balcony for reviewing the troops at the N end and a further shed to the S for gun drill. On the W side, stables and a riding school added by 1889. On the E side of Edmund Road, the **Edmund Road Estate** of terraced Corporation houses built in 1905. With segmental-headed windows and doors, and dormers lighting attic rooms, they show little advance on earlier house designs.

Retrace one's steps back to Shoreham Street and then right at **John Street** which runs alongside the **Bramall Lane Football Ground** of Sheffield United. The site, arguably the oldest major football ground in the world, is more interesting than its buildings. The earliest surviving stand, along Bramall Lane, was erected in 1966, the S stand by *Husband and Co.* from 1975 and the John Street stand for 6,842 in 1996. E stand of 1982.

On the W side of Bramall Lane is an important enclave of C19 industrial buildings. Four of them are in John Street. **Stag Works**, a large courtyard works built in 1877 by *J.H. Jenkinson* for Lee & Wigfull, makers of silver and electroplated goods. Thirteen bays of three storeys with a mansard roof. Large rear yard, workshops with mono-pitch roofs, all in similar style. Then **Harland Works** and **Clifton Works**, with adjacent gateways and a shared yard with three-storey front ranges of c. 1900, the former with continuous glazing on the upper floors. Opposite, the **Freedom Works**, late C19 with a vestigial pediment. To the N in **Denby Street**, **Kenilworth Works** of the late 1860s–70s, occupied in the C19 and early C20 by George Tandy, manufacturer of horn and tortoiseshell combs. Its front range follows the curve of the road, behind is a yard and rear range. Windows are the usual Sheffield workshop casements. To the S in **Randall Street**, at the corner of Hill Street, No. 79, **Portland Works** of 1877 by *J.H. Jenkinson*: built in one phase for R.F. Mosley, cutlery manufacturer. On a corner site, the corner of the works is rounded with a two-storey entrance gateway with rusticated pilasters. Elaborate frontage, the works name flanked by panelled pedestals with ball finials. Round-headed sash windows to the first floor and sill and lintel bands, that on the first floor cogged and in contrasting cream bricks. Ornamental panels of diagonal brickwork and an octagonal chimney. A three-storey rear range used for grinding has a room with four transverse fireproof bays, suggesting the presence of a central engine house with the position of hearths indicated by ridge stacks. On the ground floor of the w workshop range are the best preserved examples of hand forges in the city. These may have been let separately and retain combined stable-type doors and a window under a rolled-steel lintel.

Back up Hill Street to **London Road**, turn s, on the e side, to the **Old Crown Inn**, late C19 with blue and yellow moulded glazed terracotta on the ground floor and good etched glass. Opposite, on the w side, No. 136, the former **Highfield Cocoa & Coffee House**, 1877, by *M.E. Hadfield & Son* for Frederick T. Mappin. Large, two storeys in brick, quite plain with round-headed windows. It contained reading rooms, billiard room and a skittle alley at the back. Further along the w side, at the corner of Sharrow Lane, the **Natwest Bank**, part of a terrace of shops *c.* 1890 with ornate brickwork. Ground floor rebuilt in stone in 1909 with the Sheffield arms over the door and pilasters with capitals in the form of carved heads at intervals along the fascia.

Returning to the e side, just off to the left in **St Barnabas Road**, some late C18 fragments. Nos. 11–17 are terraced three-storey houses with C19 façades and Nos. 25–27 of two storeys with hipped stone-slated roofs. Back in London Road, **Highfield Library** [129] of 1876 by *E.M. Gibbs*.

129. Highfield Library, London Road, by E.M. Gibbs, 1876

Florentine Renaissance style similar to the Upperthorpe Library (*see* p. 284) but with an oriel window at the N end and a house for the librarian attached to the rear. Figure sculpture representing Medical Science and Literature by *J.W. Cooper* flank a quotation from Carlyle above the entrance. Behind it, **St Barnabas**, 1874–6, by *Flockton & Abbott*. Early English with plate tracery, very tall aisles, an apsidal chancel and a SW tower with large openings on each face. Now converted to housing. The congregation now shares the **Trinity Methodist Church** [130], opposite, of 1877–9 by *J.D. Webster*. An impressive early work by this prolific local architect, most of whose work was for the Anglicans, and designed to challenge them architecturally. Geometric tracery in the W window, the

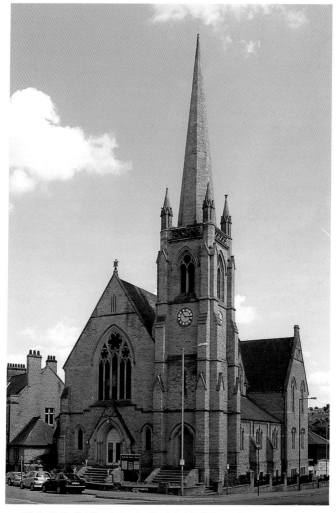

130. Trinity Methodist Church, London Road, by J.D. Webster, 1877–9

remainder lancets. A range of large clerestory windows breaks through the eaves, the resulting gables giving some vigour to the side elevations. Tower with prominent angle buttresses extending to form pinnacles and tall spire. Interior rebuilt in the 1970s. Next door in **Highfield Place**, the **Wesley Institute** of 1905–6 in an elegant Tudor style by *C. & C.M. Hadfield* which in the detailing of the porch doorway, the railings and the vestigial tower flanking the gable is reminiscent of the Crookes churches (*see* p. 276–7) of another local architect, W.J. Hale.

Slightly further s at the junction of London Road with Queens Road, **Lowfield Primary School**, 1874, by *Innocent & Brown* with two well-detailed Gothic single-storey buildings, one with a short tower and turret, squeezed into a restricted site. Nearby, on the SE side of **Queens Road**, No. 635, a standard design for the Sheffield Savings Bank, dated 1900, with a busy façade in stone with tall round-arched windows, a balustrade, a clock on the rounded corner and fluted pilasters with carving in the spandrels. The interior has a glazed office, counter and Art Nouveau tiling to the walls.

### w of London Road

In **Sharrow Lane**, No. 1, the former **Sheffield & Hallamshire Bank** of *c.* 1890, has a semi-circular corner porch with giant granite columns and a pediment incorporating a clock above. Red brick embellished with stone pilasters, enriched window surrounds, base and dentil band. Beyond it is one of the best C18 houses in Sheffield, **Mount Pleasant** [131] (The Sheffield College), built in 1777 by *John Platt* for Francis Hurt. Brick-built, three storeys of five bays on the principal (E) façade, the central three brought forward and given a pediment. A Venetian window on the first floor is set in an arch with a balustrade below. Pedimented doorcase with Adamesque swags in the frieze and attached Corinthian columns. The s elevation has a full-height canted bay

131. Mount Pleasant (The Sheffield College), Sharrow Lane, by John Platt, 1777

window. The arcaded stable block also has a Venetian window. Little of the interior survives. The principal ground-floor room on the s side is an unequal octagon with scalloped niches in the two shortest walls and Adamesque ceiling. Similar plasterwork ceiling to the principal stair. Opposite No. 10 Sharrow Lane, the **Charnwood Hotel**, a three-bay house of *c.*1780 with a coach house. Much restored in the 1990s. On the s side, the plain former **Special School & Handicraft and Cookery Centre** of 1907 by *Holmes & Watson*, the first provision in Sheffield to enable special needs children to gain practical skills. Finally on this side of the road, **St John's Methodist Church** (Methodist New Connexion), Free Gothic, built in two stages in a virulent red brick. The earliest part is the **school** to the left, of 1889 by *Denton & Haigh* with a prominent inscription, then the **church** of 1905–6 by *J.C. Brameld.*

Retracing one's steps along **London Road**, beyond Hill Street on the e side, Nos. 75–85, modest housing (with later shopfronts) typical of the area's development in the late c18 and early c19. No. 85 is a well-preserved example of a blind-back working-class house. Three storeys, stone lintel with prominent keystone. Further along on this side, the former **Lansdowne Cinema** of 1914 by *Walter G. Buck*, is Moorish with suitably oriental arches in the windows and a splendid pagoda tower on the corner. Originally green and white faience, now painted black. On the w side, at the junction with St Mary's Gate, the former **Sheffield Union Bank** of 1894 by *J.B. Mitchell-Withers & Son*. Impressive corner building with ashlar façades. Lively Baroque with giant pilasters superimposed one upon another, tightly modelled with narrow window bays and heavily rusticated banding. Rounded corner porch with big brackets, segmental pediments to the windows.

Boston Street leads to **Cemetery Road** which begins with the 1960s **Lansdowne Estate**, three sixteen-storey point blocks and four-storey deck-access maisonette blocks, lacking the imaginative planning found at Netherthorpe (*see* p. 285). On the n side, the **Vestry Hall** of 1857. Gothic with an oriel above the main entrance. Single storey with a large hall behind. Then the **Baptist Church**, 1859, by *Flockton & Son*. Strange Romanesque design with gable facing the road, inset with a large rose window flanked by two octagonal turrets. Steps and doorways unsympathetically modernized in the 1960s. The interior has a deep moulded cornice and a panelled ceiling. Galleries on all four sides with rounded corners to the front and round cast-iron columns. Next to it, the Plymouth Brethren's **Lansdowne Chapel** of *c.* 1900, red brick and quite plain with a simple pediment. The back-to-back houses formerly lining the road have given way to views over modern offices. Beyond Washington Road on the s side, terraced houses of *c.* 1850, some stuccoed.

Turn n along Summerfield Street to reach **Ecclesall Road** and the former **Sheaf Brewery**. Brewing on the site began in 1837 as Bradley's Soho Brewery. It was taken over in 1876 by Kirby & Ward (later Ward's) who had occupied the Sheaf Island Brewery, Effingham Street, from which the brewery derives its present name. Some stone buildings from the 1850s, a three-storey brick block converted from back-to-backs and the plain brick brewery tower of 1874 have been submerged within residential development of 2001–2 by *Finnegan Design and Build*. Relocated entrance gateway with sheaves of corn and the brewery name in raised letters.

In **Pomona Street**, immediately behind Ecclesall Road, stands **Bow Works**. Steel measuring tape was invented by James Chesterman whose firm moved here in 1864 and remained as Rabone Chesterman until 1989. The works were restored and extended in an unexciting manner by *Hadfield Cawkwell Davidson* in 1993 for Norwich Union. The façades of the long street front are of 1891 onwards. Long narrow blocks behind for the manufacture of the tapes (akin to those employed in rope works) of 1871 by *W.J. Hemsoll*. Impressive **gates**, 1993, by *Michael Johnson* with bronze detailing resembling horseshoes within a formal steel structure. **Portercroft School (C. of E.)**, 1900, *Holmes & Watson* with strange elaborately Mannerist-shaped parapets to the gables and buttresses that turn into pilasters above the ground floor.

At the end of Pomona Street, turn left into Stalker Lees Road and left again into Cemetery Avenue which leads to the **General Cemetery**. This was built by the joint stock Sheffield General Cemetery Co. (formed 1834) and opened in 1836 as one of the first group of provincial cemeteries. It retains its original buildings, making it possibly the best of its date outside London. Acquired by the City Council in 1977. *Samuel Worth* initially laid out the cemetery and its buildings for Nonconformists. The design, like all early British cemeteries, was influenced by Père Lachaise in Paris in its picturesque layout of sweeping drives amongst evergreens. Worth's use of an Egypto-Greek style is possibly one of the first examples in England, followed shortly after by Bartholomew Street Cemetery, Exeter, in 1837, and Highgate Cemetery, London, 1839–42. It has been suggested that its popularity was due to it being associated neither with popery nor dissent, although this would hardly have been an advantage here. The mixture of Doric and Egyptian styles was criticised in the *Sheffield Mercury* for lack of harmony but the writer argued that on reflection, Worth could be defended for 'If the architect of the present day is to be fettered, and manacled, and bound down by the arbitrary rules and requirements of more than two thousand years ago, what defence can be set up for the liberties so freely taken by the celebrated Mr Nash, to whose admirers I leave the vindication of the designer of the Sheffield Cemetery. . . .'

The principal entrance to the cemetery was from Cemetery Avenue, at the end of which is a **gateway** with Greek Doric columns *in antis* which forms a bridge over the River Porter. The driveway then sweeps up the hillside in a gentle curve so as to draw the eye to the climax of the cemetery, the **Nonconformist chapel** [132], which has a Greek Doric tetrastyle portico with a triglyph frieze, Egyptian-style windows (originally iron-framed) and doorway, and bases for acroteria along the

132. Nonconformist Chapel, General Cemetery, by Samuel Worth, 1836

eaves. A sculpted relief of a dove is placed above the door. The processional route from the gateway to the chapel was designed to offer views across the Porter Valley. It has been suggested that the chapel, The Mount, the Wesley (now King Edward VII) School and the glasshouses of the Botanical Gardens on the N side of the valley (*see* Broomhill and Broomhall), all built within three years of each other were intended to form elements in a classical landscape, carefully designed to relate visually to one another*. That Thomas Asline Ward was the principal backer of both the cemetery and Botanical Gardens lends some credence to the idea. To the N of the road, two curved tiers of **catacombs**

*Helen Bishop, '"Mansions of the Dead": The Place of Sheffield General Cemetery in the Historical Landscape'. BA Dissertation, University of Sheffield, 1999.

were built with massive battered retaining walls, punctuated by plain oblong openings, intended to be closed by iron gates. They were not a success, only ten were sold in the first ten years. The upper tier has a concrete balustrade added by *Hodkin & Jones* in 1936. The **cemetery offices** in Cemetery Road have an austere ashlar façade with Doric pilasters, a pedimented gable on the road elevation and Egyptian windows on single-storey wings. The **entrance** to Cemetery Road nearby is again Egyptian with a behudet (winged sun motif) on the cornice.

By the late 1840s the cemetery was filling up and the Cemetery Company commissioned *Robert Marnock* to lay out a new Anglican cemetery to the E. The **chapel** by *William Flockton,* 1848–50, is Dec with a tall broach spire on a tower whose lower stage is open as a porch. The gravestones were partly cleared in 1980.

Among the **monuments** may be mentioned those to William Parker of 1837, based on the Choragic Monument of Lysicrates; John Fowler, father of the engineer Sir John Fowler, of 1845, by *Edwin Smith* with a relief of a dying tree in a niche below a rounded arch; George Bennet, a missionary, d. 1850, also with a relief by *Smith* showing him leaning on a globe with a palm tree behind; Thomas Burch, 1870, a 15-ft (4.5 metre) column topped by an urn; the Nicholson family, *c.* 1872, a chest tomb with a statue of a woman praying on the top and Mark Firth of 1869–76, a pedestal, topped by a draped urn and with railings made in his Norfolk Works.

Opposite the cemetery and hidden behind later building is No. 311 Cemetery Road, **Sharrow Head House** believed to be by *John Platt* in 1763 for William Battie, an attorney. Brick, two storeys with an attic, the roof hipped and with a modillion eaves cornice. Diocletian window set within a pediment. It adjoined at right angles to the w a house of 1664 (dem. *c.* 1900).

At the end of Cemetery Road at the top of the hill on **Sharrow Vale Road** is the former steam-powered **Westbrook Mill** of J. and H. Wilson (now offices). Built in 1831 as a result of a family dispute at the Sharrow Snuff Mills (*see* below). Plain, stone, three storeys with a pediment on the N façade, surrounded by many later additions. It was converted after 1989 and still retains an oven room on the first floor with a round brick vault. Below the mill and built for the Wilson family, on Sharrow Vale Road is **Westbrook** of 1794–5 with late C19 additions. Brick of five bays, doorcase with attached Doric columns. The entrance hall has a moulded span beam carried on Ionic columns and pilasters.

The manufacture of snuff became an important industry in the area in the C18 and continues to the present along the River Porter. The **Sharrow Snuff Mills** [133] of Wilsons & Co. can be seen from further down Sharrow Vale Road, opposite Bagshot Street. A grinding wheel existed on the site by 1604 and Joseph Wilson introduced snuff grinding *c.* 1740. The mill today is a remarkably well-preserved example of water-powered industry. Although steam was introduced in 1796, the 19 ft wheel is still in working order. The head goit and the dam can be

133. Sharrow Snuff Mills, the manager's house, late C18; and mill, c. 1740 with later additions

clearly seen. The mill of c. 1740 is of stone with strutted kingpost roofs, still domestic in scale. Inside, the wheel drives sixteen weighted iron pestles around a post by means of bevel gearing. The late C18 brick **manager's house** has an open pedimented doorcase and modillion eaves. Adjoining is an early C19 **counting house**, also brick completing a picturesque and well-maintained group. Behind these, a complex of buildings built around a courtyard. These include an early C19 warehouse and stable, the red brick New Mill of c. 1885 by *Wightman & Wightman* (doubled in width in matching style in the early C20) and a large L-shaped stable block built between 1819 and 1825 with pitching eyes, stone walled to the N elevation, the remainder of brick.

Further down Sharrow Vale Road, the simple classical red brick **Wesleyan Reform Chapel** of 1902 and at the bottom **Hunters Bar Infant and Junior Schools** by *A.F. Watson* of 1893 with a squat pyramidal tower, coped gables and C17 vernacular detailing. A second block of 1907 by the same architect is larger but plainer.

From Hunters Bar, buses run back to the city centre down Ecclesall Road.

The area around Abbeydale Road contains some scattered outliers.

The **Sufi Centre**, **Vincent Road**, was built as Abbeydale Primitive Methodist Church in 1891–3 by *Joseph Smith*. Red brick Gothic with a prominent rounded corner turret on a triangular site. In **Abbeydale Road**, at the junction with St Ronan's Road, **Mother of God and St Wilfrid R.C. Church**. Formerly a Congregational Chapel and school by *Hemsoll & Paterson*. Schoolrooms built 1883–4, chapel 1899–1901. Both are large, of rock-faced stone, in Free E.E. style. The chapel is more simply detailed, omitting the shafts and capitals employed in the school windows. The chapel has sloping buttresses flanking the w front, enormous transepts and windows of three lights. Vast open space within. Very large Gothic arch at E end now blocked off to form chapel behind.

N of Broadfield Road, the former **Abbeydale Cinema**, 1920, by *Dixon & Stienlet* of North Shields. The most impressive of Sheffield's surviving suburban cinemas. Built with a flytower enabling its use as a theatre and now being refurbished for that purpose. It also had a ballroom and billiard hall. Steel-framed with a façade in white faience, splendid if coarse decoration of swags and with a row of circular windows and a domed turret over the entrance. The disused interior retains much of its classical decoration.

E of Abbeydale Road is an industrial area. In **Aizlewood Road**, **Finbat Works** conceals one of the few surviving Hoffman brick kilns. Built 1878–9 for the Sheffield Patent Brick Co. Oval in shape with a vaulted tunnel inside and a central service tunnel. Uniquely, it was converted for car production when it became the the paint shop for the Richardson light car, 1919–22. **Loxley Brothers Printing Works** was built as the Empire Roller Skating Rink. Loxley Brothers moved here in 1921. Classical façade with a raised centre, rebuilt in 1923 after a fire. Paired Doric columns with a projecting entablature and a deeply chamfered doorway with prominent rustication.

**Broadfield Road** has the former **Express Dairy**, 1939. One of the city's few Modern Movement-style buildings. Well-mannered and restrained brick and rendered design with a glazed semi-circular stair-turret. Nearby, **Public Baths**, 1909, by *Arthur Nunweek*. Red brick and stone Neo-Baroque with a Gibbs surround to the entrance and a tall chimney.

## b) Nether Edge and Brincliffe

Prior to the second half of the C19, Nether Edge and Brincliffe were mostly farmland (the farms commemorated in names such as Cherry Tree Hill and Nether Edge itself) but included the hamlet of Machon Bank and a scattering of country residences. The district is hilly, forming a ridge between the Porter and Sheaf Valleys and rises to the s to Brincliffe Edge along which winds what is still a narrow lane with extensive views. Its relative isolation may have encouraged the building of the workhouse near Machon Bank in 1842. The ancient Psalter Lane

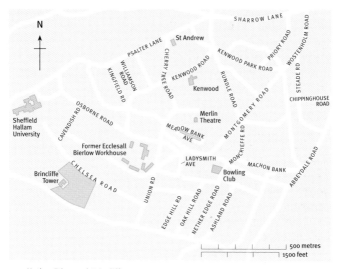

N

SHARROW LANE
PRIORY ROAD
WOSTENHOLM ROAD
PSALTER LANE
St Andrew
CHERRY TREE ROAD
KENWOOD ROAD
KENWOOD PARK ROAD
STEADE RD
WILLIAMSON ROAD
KINGFIELD RD
Kenwood
RUNDLE ROAD
CHIPPINGHOUSE ROAD
OSBORNE ROAD
CAVENDISH RD
Sheffield Hallam University
Merlin Theatre
MEADOW BANK AVE
MONTGOMERY RD
Former Ecclesall Bierlow Workhouse
LADYSMITH AVE
MONCRIEFFE RD
MACHON BANK
ABBEYDALE ROAD
CHELSEA ROAD
Brincliffe Tower
UNION RD
Bowling Club
EDGE HILL RD
OAK HILL ROAD
NETHER EDGE ROAD
ASHLAND ROAD

500 metres
1500 feet

134. Nether Edge and Brincliffe

linking Sheffield to the village of Ecclesall was the only through road of consequence. Major developments including Kenwood Park and those of Thomas Steade and the Newboulds took place from the early 1840s with large houses to the w and more modest properties for the middle classes on the lower ground to the E. Further building took place in the interwar years so that the area was fully built up but it retains a spacious look with large gardens and tree-lined roads. The complicated pre-suburban land ownership is reflected in a confusing road pattern with few through roads. The only shops are along Machon Bank Road which was a tram terminus and is the closest thing to a centre for the area.

Our tour of Nether Edge and Brincliffe begins in **Kenwood Park Road** at the gates of **Kenwood** (now the Marriott Hotel), built in 1844 by *William Flockton*, for George Wostenholm, one of the city's largest cutlery manufacturers. Relatively modest in size, the house is in the favoured Tudor-Gothic style in limestone quarried at Stanton, Derbyshire. The grounds were laid out by *Robert Marnock* and those parts nearest the hotel, which include a lake, survive. Enlarged 1882–3 with a large canted bay window by *Flockton & Gibbs* and many subsequent additions by *J. Mansell Jenkinson* following conversion to a temperance hotel in 1924. Imposing **gatehouse** of *c.* 1868 at the junction of Kenwood and Kenwood Park Roads with a Gothic archway and lodge to the side. A coat of arms over the arch is by *Harry Hems*, Wostenholm's nephew. Wostenholm named the house after a town near Oneida Lake in upstate New York, which had particularly impressed him. Inspired by this and other American suburban developments, he decided to emulate them on land around Cherry Tree Hill. *Marnock* was employed in 1851–61 to lay out picturesquely curving roads, radiating from a rond-point outside the principal gate to Kenwood.

Although many of the houses on the estate are smaller than Wostenholm had originally envisaged and are unspectacular, the layout is noteworthy as an example of a planned middle-class development. The largest houses were built over a thirty-year period on Kenwood Park Road, Kenwood Road and Priory Road and are generally Gothic, of two storeys with big attic gables and ornate bargeboards, e.g. No. 19 Kenwood Park Road dated 1861 with a frieze of ballflowers. There is an especially good grouping of villas in the roads around the rond-point, most of them Gothic but with a sprinkling of pleasant if slightly dour Italianate houses. Around 1900 a new style, less heavy with plenty of applied half-timbering, is apparent, e.g. No. 50 Kenwood Road for Thomas Roberts of the department store family. In **Kenwood Park Road**, unique in Sheffield and rare elsewhere, the private **Lantern Theatre**, built 1893 by William Webster, a cutlery manufacturer who lived in the adjacent house. Cottage-like with a stone ground floor, tile-hung above and a pyramidal roof with a prominent ventilator topped by a glazed lantern. Still in use, the interior largely unchanged, with a proscenium arch, coved ceiling and a small gallery. In **Rundle Road**, No. 10 **Stoneygate** of 1925, by *J. Mansell Jenkinson* for himself, the finest of his houses but submerged in extensions of 2003–4. Firmly in the Arts and Crafts tradition with leaded light casements, stone-tiled steep-pitched roofs and uncoursed stone walling, it borrows freely from vernacular sources though from the Cotswolds rather than Yorkshire. The name reflects Jenkinson's marriage into the Gimson family: Stoneygate is the Leicester suburb where Ernest Gimson built a number of houses, including his own. **Kenwood Croft**, in Kenwood Road also by *Mansell Jenkinson*, 1925 displays many of the same features on a larger scale. Back in Rundle Road, No. 16 **Spring Leigh** is a little-altered classical villa of 1868 for Henry Booth, cutlery manufacturer. Fine door-case with attached Corinthian columns, tripartite windows in Gibbs surrounds on the first floor and a hipped roof with a lantern. Extensive gardens laid out by *Robert Marnock*.

To the E of **Montgomery Road**, there are several roads laid out in 1863–83 by the speculative builder *Thomas Steade* who had worked closely with Wostenholm. Steade, who had set up an iron foundry in the late 1850s, used many cast-iron details: lintels in the shape of a pediment are the most distinctive. His houses are broadly Gothic with bargeboarded gables on narrow plots. To the s of this, in **Moncrieffe Road**, No. 16 of 1879 is an entertaining showpiece for the architectural joinery sold by its builder and owner *John Johnson*. Good timber Gothic porch.

To the NW on **Psalter Lane, St Andrew** of 1928–30 by *J.A. Teather*. Built as a United Methodist Church but used ecumenically since 1998 following the unfortunate demolition of *J.B. Mitchell-Withers*'s fine St Andrew's Church of 1867. Very traditional in Perp style with bulky towers flanking a broad w window. Transepts and short chancel. Well-executed carving of the emblems of the Passion on the corbels supporting the roof trusses. Reordered in 2002 by *Barlow, Wright & Phelps* to provide a narthex and a bright, spacious interior. **Stained glass**: nave and w windows by *Robertson & Russell*. E window of 2002 by *Rona Moody*, representing the Creation with light pouring from a golden source into a rich blue darkness. Nearby, the workmanlike **Salvation Army Citadel**, 1998, by the *Salvation Army Chief Architect*. Linked stone pavilions with hipped roofs. **Clifford School**, dated 1832, became a church school in 1869. Symmetrical Tudor style with an oriel window over a Gothic door. Extended 1896.

s of Psalter Lane, most of the roads were laid out from the mid C19 on the estate of the Newbould family who owned virtually all the land known as Cherry Tree Hill. On the corner of **Cherry Tree Road** and St Andrews Road, **Shirle Hill** (now hospital and school) of 1809 owned by John Brown while Endcliffe Hall (*see* p. 265) was being completed. His managing director, William Bragge, then occupied the house which, in 1865, he extended with a large Italianate wing by *Frith Brothers & Jenkinson* and refronted the older house to match. An odd mixture of rendered elevations, enriched stone lintels and rusticated giant pilasters which terminate in elaborate finials on the older part. A tall Italianate tower to the rear. Further sw, **Williamson Road** has some attractive villas. Nos. 3, 5 and 7, each with a variety of Tudor motifs: bargeboards and an angled porch on No. 3; No. 7 with a squat pyramidal tower over the door. Built by *John Law*, curator of the Botanical Gardens, who was forced to resign in 1857 because of the time he was spending on his speculative ventures. No. 11 **Argyle House** has a tall tower of Italianate style to enliven an otherwise plain house.

Due s, **Prior Bank**, Cherry Tree Road, is an early C19 house of some size, brick with a hipped roof and two canted bay windows, the home of John Cole of Cole Brothers from 1863 to 1899. Then in **Meadow Bank Road**, the Expressionist **Merlin Theatre** [135], 1965–9 by *Black Bayes & Gibbs*, as part of a Rudolf Steiner centre in the grounds of **Tintagel House**, a Tudor villa by *Joseph Mitchell* of *c.* 1855. It is built in accordance with the principles of Steiner architecture, the subject of a book by *Kenneth Bayes*. The entrance screen is derived directly from that of Steiner's Goetheanum in Dornach, Switzerland, and other doors and windows, together with the proscenium arch of the theatre, employ the distinctive organic forms favoured by Steiner. The ten-sided theatre is concrete-framed, stone-clad externally and brick within. Flytower to the s. Its most distinctive feature externally is the long range of large eyebrow-like windows which light a meeting room occupying the entire top floor, and the complex tiled roof, which again echoes on a small scale the Goetheanum. The theatre has steeply raked seating for 201 and dressing rooms on a lower floor. The meeting room is reached by an external staircase. Its ceiling had its exposed rafters plastered so that it now consists of an extraordinary range of curved and angled planes emanating from a central boss and metamorphosing into each other.

135. Merlin Theatre, Meadow Bank Road, by Black Bayes & Gibbs, 1965–9

**Meadow Bank Avenue** was laid out *c.* 1896 with a rectangular central lawn and gated entry but the houses are mostly unremarkable. Further s, in **Ladysmith Avenue**, **The Edge** is a rarity: a late c18 house probably by *Joseph Badger*, with an austere five-bay brick front, the rest in coursed stone. Canted two-storey bay at the rear with a full-height window. The house incorporated part of a c17 building including a mullioned window, since removed. On Nether Edge Road, the **Nether Edge Proprietary Bowling Clubhouse** was originally single storey by *George Kinder*, 1867, upper storey added in 1874. A large bow window on the ground floor and big, lively bargeboards.

The sw part of Nether Edge is characterized by a grid laid out from 1853 on land rising steeply to Brincliffe Edge to the s by *Samuel Holmes*, initially for the Reform Freehold Building Society (*see* topic box, p. 282). No requirements concerning the treatment of elevations were set out and the resulting houses show a pleasant if unremarkable profusion of styles. Small and quite plain three-bay detached houses, mostly of stone, many the work of *Scargill & Clark*. Amongst the larger houses the following stand out: No. 40 Edge Hill Road of 1875, with deep eaves and ornate bargeboards by *E.M. Gibbs*, No. 40 Ashland Road, *c.* 1878, with finely carved dressings to its Gothic bay windows and No. 71 Grange Court of similar date for Louis Osbaldiston, file manufacturer. A tall house, picturesquely sited on a hilltop, its height exaggerated by large chimney stacks. Ostentatious entrance gateway with a rounded pediment.

**Byron Road** was developed with villas from 1862 onwards for the Montgomery Land Society and displays how a Georgian tradition was maintained with simple timber doorcases; Nos. 15, 23 and 25 are good examples. At its w end, **Fountside** of 1965 by *Peter Lee & Associates*, small blocks of flats in blue brick, around a well-landscaped courtyard, one of the best of the many such developments on the w side. s of Byron Road, the **Brincliffe Oaks Hotel**, in Oakhill Road, incorporates Nether Edge, the c17 farmhouse with mullioned windows that gave its name to the area.

Nether Edge and Brincliffe are separated by **Union Road** which is dominated on the w side by the former **Ecclesall Bierlow Workhouse** [136]. An **E**-shaped block was built 1842–3 by *William Flockton* with male and female wings either side of a central block containing hall, kitchen, chapel and administrative offices. Elizabethan style, of three storeys with gables, canted bay windows and a large clock above the entrance. To the rear, a screen, formerly part of a roofed arcade, of four-centred arches and with a battlemented parapet runs the length of the building. Enlarged with flat-roofed wings either side of the central block in 1894 and an infirmary block to the rear in 1895, both by *J.D. Webster*. Cruciform lodges, single-storey with attics, on Union Road. The institution became Nether Edge Hospital in 1929 and was converted to housing by *Gleesons* in 2000–3. Besides the original Flockton building (the Kingswood block), the surviving buildings include the Alexandra Imbeciles block of 1859, the Workhouse Infirmary (Peveril block) dated 1864, the male ward block (Cliff block, 1891) of pavilion plan with sanitary towers at each end topped by pyramidal roofs, the Victoria Diamond Jubilee Maternity Hospital (1897), its sanitary turrets topped with castellated parapets, the administration block (Sharrow) of 1898–9 by *J.D. Webster*, the men's sanatorium (Edward block) dated 1904 by *W.H. Lancashire & Son*. All are built of rock-faced coursed masonry and have long, sparsely fenestrated elevations punctuated by dormers and chimney stacks.

136. Former Ecclesall Bierlow Workhouse, Union Road, by William Flockton, 1842–3. Perspective drawing (*c.* 1842)

On Union Road, opposite the Workhouse, the former **Ecclesall Bierlow Poor Law Union Offices** by *Holmes & Watson* of 1902. Neo-Georgian with a central open pediment and deeply-moulded main entrance. Then a nicely contrasting pair of chapels both *c*. 1865: the former **United Methodist Free Chapel**, classical, twin doorways with Ionic pilasters and a heavily modelled pediment; and the tall Gothic **Montgomery Chapel** (now the Kings Centre) by *Wilson & Crosland* with a steeply pitched roof.

### Brincliffe

The suburb of **Brincliffe**, situated on high ground w of Union Road is grander than Nether Edge, characterized by very large villas set in extensive grounds and rivalling Ranmoor (*see* p. 267) in their scale. The earliest was **Brincliffe Tower**, Chelsea Road, of 1852 for James Wilson, solicitor and clerk to the Cutlers' Company. Highly picturesque Tudor house on a raised terrace with two gabled wings linked by a three-storey crenellated tower with a traceried oriel window. N of this and near the top of the ridge, **Cavendish** and **Osborne Roads** have large houses of the 1860s and later with all the trappings of later c19 suburbia, laurels, monkey puzzle trees and pines. No. 6, **The Towers** (formerly Brincliffe Grove) in **Brincliffe Crescent**, of 1874 for an accountant, Alfred Allott, is arguably the finest of the city's many late c19 Gothic houses. Almost certainly by *Innocent & Brown*, who are recorded as being responsible for the substantial stables, it shares the skilled handling of Gothic detail, massing and picturesque skyline of the firm's Board Schools. The garden front is divided into two parts, that on the right of twin gables clasping a rounded three-storey tower in the French manner with a high conical roof balanced by that on the left which has a lower tower. Extensive and finely executed carved decoration throughout; blind tracery above the windows, inset panels between storeys on the towers and gargoyles. Oriel window to the left return and carved crest. The entrance façade has a big columned porch with birds carved on the capitals. The interior retains much of its Gothic character.

s along **Psalter Lane**, the former **Boys Charity (Bluecoat) School** (now part of the campus of Sheffield Hallam University). Founded in 1706 in East Parade but moved here in 1911 with new buildings by *Gibbs & Flockton*. Neo-Georgian, H-shaped, two storeys with the seven-bay N front relieved by the central three bays brought forward with an open pediment over the centre. A round-headed window has a large Diocletian window below it which collides uncomfortably with a Doric porch. Semicircular pediments on the E and w fronts. Following occupation by the **College of Art**, additions of 1970 by *Bradshaw, Rouse & Harker* were in the tough sculptural manner of the time, one four-storey block with groups of deeply inset window bays in chamfered pre-cast concrete surrounds which erupt from the brick-clad façade. Prominent glazed stair-towers. Single-storey link to a three-storey block clad entirely in concrete panels.

## c) Heeley and Meersbrook

At the beginning of the c19, Heeley comprised hamlets located on the ancient Chesterfield Road and on the steep slopes just above it, together with water-powered industry along the River Sheaf. Development N of the Meers Brook, which formed the boundary with Derbyshire until 1901, took place from the mid c19. Albert, Shirebrook and Kent Roads were laid out *c.* 1860 by the Meersbrook Land Society with quite large middle-class red brick villas. The Artisan View Land Society developed Artisan View in a similar manner to the Walkley societies (*see* p. 282) with houses set irregularly in their plots. To the s of the Meers Brook, Meersbrook Park and the neighbouring c16 Bishops' House enjoyed a fine prospect across the Sheaf valley. Housing development followed between 1870 and 1900. Much of lower Heeley was demolished following a bypass proposal first

137. Heeley and Meersbrook

mooted in 1963 but abandoned in 1978. Gleadless Road was the heart of Heeley but now has only scattered public buildings with some low-density council housing built from 1978 onwards. Other parts of the area retain their c19 character with factories mixed in with terraced housing.

## Heeley

We start in London Road (well served by bus routes from the centre) close to the former **Heeley Station** of 1901 by the Midland Railway's architect *Charles Trubshaw* in his characteristic style. Red brick with plenty of terracotta dressings (now overpainted). Almost opposite is **Gleadless Road**. On the left side, a former **Primitive Methodist Chapel** of 1858, classical with two round-headed windows flanking the porch. Then the **Chinese Christian Church and Bethany School**, formerly St Andrew's Primitive Methodist Church, 1895–7, by *J. Taylor*. A central gable, flanked by two wings marks the w end of this large Free Gothic chapel in rock-faced stone on the elevations facing the street and brick elsewhere. Two large windows each of two lights with plate tracery, four lancets below, the doors in the wings each surmounted by a pointed hoodmould. The chapel and schools are all expressed as one building. The school entrance on Anns Road is marked by a gable. Closely spaced windows, straight-headed on the ground floor and pointed on the first, each pair forming a bay. Forming a good group with the chapel, **Anns Grove School**, built as Heeley Board School, on the corner of Gleadless Road and Hartley Street, a large and complete example of 1890–2 in free Renaissance style by *C.J. Innocent*. Girls' department with cookery school added in 1899. A little way N is **Heeley City Farm** in Richards Road. **Visitor Centre** of 2001 by *Andrew Yeats* of *Eco Arch*. L-shaped energy-efficient design with rendered blockwork walls, overhanging eaves, super-insulated sedum roof and solar panels. A curved stable block has an arcade of rough timber posts in a consciously primitive manner. s off Gleadless Road in **Wilson Place** is a survival of Heeley's rural past: No. 10, a simple cruck barn of *c.* 1600, used as a foundry for much of the c20.

Continuing uphill along Gleadless Road, the **Church Institute** is the former Wesleyan Methodist Chapel of 1826, the oldest religious building in Heeley. Simple structure with three round-arched windows and coped gables, restored and extended in 2001 as a community centre. Above it is **Christ Church** of 1846–8 by *Joseph Mitchell*. A large and well-proportioned cruciform church with the tower unusually over the N transept rather than the crossing. Dec style with reticulated tracery in the E and transept windows, ambitious flowing tracery similar to that at Holbeach, Lincolnshire, in the w window. In 1890 the nave was lengthened by one bay and N aisle and vestry added in 1890 by *J.D. Webster*. A s aisle was added in 1897. Large heads of kings, queens and angels decorate corbels. Arch-braced principal rafter roof with king-posts in the nave, traceried spandrels in the chancel braces and a

138. Derby Terrace, by Sheffield City Council, Planning & Design, 1978–9

timber vault in the crossing. The two w bays have been enclosed for community use. Octagonal **font** with crocketed ogee tracery and more heads carved at the bottom on a base of eight shafts and carved font cover. Oak **pulpit** of 1890. Elaborate carved dark oak double **sedilia.** **Stained glass**: E window of 1913 depicting Christ and the four Evangelists and E window of s transept by *Mayer & Co.* of Munich. Large **obelisk** in the churchyard to John Shortridge, d.1869. Beyond a small shopping centre, No. 302, **Heeley Green Surgery**, *c.* 1987 by *Brenda and Robert Vale*, an energy-efficient design. L-shaped, buff brick with red bands. Opposite, the former **Heeley National School** of 1801 with additions of 1833, 1868 and 1898. Twin gables, coped, facing the road. School House of 1868 behind and off to the right, in Fitzroy Road, the **Church of the Nazarene**, formerly St Peter's Mission Church 1895–7, a humble brick church with weatherboarded clerestory.

Off to the left up Jeffrey Street in **Denmark Road**, **Derby Place** and **Derby Terrace** [138] is the most innovative public housing built in Sheffield since the 1960s. This group of four stepped-back **terraces of flats** of 1978–9 by *Sheffield City Council, Planning & Design,* (project architects: *John Taylor* and *Peter Jackson*) on a steep s-facing hillside look as though they have been transplanted from California's Marin County or Laurel Canyon. Elderly people live on the top two floors, families on the ground floor, the latter enjoying private gardens. The flats are deck access and have extensively glazed façades articulated by projecting greenhouse porches and rain waterspouts carried forward on slim timber brackets. The organic feel of the buildings is enhanced by the massive baulks of timber used to support the ends of the decks, by the planters of rough creosoted timber used to line them and by the low-pitched roofs. They are a development of the prototypes put up at Netherthorpe (q.v.) in 1976 but differ from them in having bridges to the flats to ensure that each level has its own access, giving the impression that the residents are living not in a block of flats but in bungalows that happen to be on top of one another. At the time they were built, council policy was to build only conventional semi-detached houses and bungalows. However, the difficulties posed by the site gave the architects the opportunity to produce a design that so successfully balanced private and public space that in these, some of the last deck-access flats to be constructed in Britain, they at last achieved the humane approach to housing that the Smithsons and others believed such planning would provide. Similar terraces were built at Stannington and in the Gleadless Valley (q.v.). Just to the E, in **Edwin Road**, Nos. 22–28, four detached houses using the Segal self-build method, quite conventional in form with gabled front elevations.

From here, return to Gleadless Road, for buses back to the city centre.

**Heeley Bank Community Centre** (formerly Heeley Bank School), Myrtle Road, by *E.R. Robson* of 1880, blends the Sheffield idiom with the style of his London schools in the use of Renaissance gables crowned with miniature pediments common to both. A pair of chimneys are each linked by a balustraded arch and enlivened by a pediment halfway up.

### Southern Heeley and Meersbrook

The **White Lion**, No. 615 London Road, was built as a beerhouse, the present ground-floor façade and much of the interior dating from the 1920s. The back portion may date from 1781 but was extended towards the road between 1877 and 1884. It still retains snugs and a private smoke room. Green tiles and elaborate 1920s coloured glass. To the S, Nos. 9, 11, 11A Thirlwell Road are the former **Midland Confectionery Works** built *c.* 1879 for William Pike. Three storey and gabled like a warehouse with a projecting canopy and a rounded chimney. In Albert Road, a former **Horse Tram Depot** and **Stables** of 1878 inscribed Sheffield Tramways Company. A gable-end with a Gothic arch with an L-shaped range along Albert Road and two similar ranges in the yard. Brick and quite modest. Further E, in Shirebrook Road, **Meersbrook Bowling Club** of 1875 by *H. Matthews*. Extensive clubrooms in a heavy Italianate style, quite unlike anything else in the city. Single storey with a two-storey caretaker's house at the N end. White brick with terracotta string courses giving a vivid polychromatic effect, rare in

139. Meersbrook Vestry Hall, Meersbrook Park Road, by Joseph Norton, 1903–4

Sheffield. Round-headed windows, all the eaves with decorative bargeboards and a porch with iron columns and decorative brackets like
those of a railway station awning.

s of the Meers Brook is an industrial enclave. Nos. 41–65 Chesterfield
Road was **Meersbrook Tannery**, built *c.* 1870 for Francis Colley & Sons,
manufacturers of machinery belts. Extensive front range, three storeys
with a central stone pediment, segmental arcading and pilasters. In
Valley Road are Nos. 19–21, **Meersbrook Saw Works** (now Meersbrook
Enterprise Centre) of Joseph Tyzack & Co., built *c.* 1880. A long three-
storey range of twenty-one bays. The central pediment has the firm's
three-legged trademark. On the s side, the **Victoria Park Works** is
elaborate with a campanile chimney on a square base and heavy decorative corbelling. Probably by *Flockton, Gibbs & Flockton* who built a
warehouse here in 1896. s in Meersbrook Park Road is **Meersbrook
Vestry Hall** [139] (now flats), 1903–4 by *Joseph Norton*. Excellent Free
Baroque in brick with ashlar dressings. Three-bay N façade with a
bowed oriel. Small corner tower topped with a square timber cupola
with a lead dome. At the rear is a hall with each bay divided by battered
buttresses.

**Meersbrook Park**, Brook Road, was formed in 1886. The late C18
house was used as the Ruskin Museum 1890–1950 (*see* topic box, p. 74).
Two storeys, brick, the N front of five bays with a canted bay window.
The s front has pedimented wings and a recessed centre with a Venetian
stair window. Modillion eaves. The house was extended to the w in the

140. Bishops' House, Norton Lees Lane, *c.* 1500, cross-wing of *c.* 1550

late C19 in similar style but treated more elaborately with stone bands and a triple-arched loggia forming a new entrance. Adjoining mid-C19 stone offices.

At the SE corner of the park in Norton Lees Lane is **Bishops' House** [140], the most outstanding timber-framed house in the city. The name is recent and there is no documentary evidence that bishops lived here. Post and truss construction, L-shaped and picturesque in appearance with closely spaced posts and much diagonal studding above a later stone ground floor. The hall block is believed to be *c.* 1500, the W cross-wing a rebuild of *c.* 1550 (one post of its predecessor survives). The hall and wing are of two bays each with kingpost roofs. In the early C17, a floor was inserted in one of the hall bays and a new chimneystack built to serve the parlour and chamber over it at the S end of the cross-wing. A stone extension was built on to the N end of the wing *c.* 1650, housing a wide dog-leg oak staircase and the 'New Chamber' (so called in an inventory of 1665). The rebuilding of the ground floor in stone dates from the same time. In the parlour, early C17 plaster ceiling with rose motifs and in the hall, wooden panelling carved with strapwork, inscribed 'WB [William Blythe] 1627'. A carved C17 overmantel from Greenhill Hall (dem.) has been installed in the chamber over the hall in recent years. In the chamber above the parlour, arcaded plaster frieze over the fireplace, decorated with grapes, vine leaves and figs. Further simple plaster decoration of two dogs' heads and paired tapered pilasters above the fireplace in the N wing's New Chamber.

## d) Gleadless Valley

Gleadless Valley vies with Park Hill (*see* p. 207) as Sheffield's greatest contribution to the postwar development of public housing in Britain. A mixed development designed to house 17,000 people, it was planned as a whole, commenced in 1955 under *J.L. Womersley*, the City Architect, and completed by 1962. Described at the time by the Council as being Mediterranean in appearance, perhaps because of the way the buildings caught the sun as it moved across the valley, it is a highly successful fusion of two, apparently opposing, ideals: high-density housing types on small plots and the garden city.

The Gleadless Valley, which remained entirely rural until the building of the estate, is triangular in shape and rises to the s. The slopes of the valley are steep, averaging 1 in 8 and up to 1 in 4 in places and it is this that really sets the development apart. There are views not only within the valley, across it and up it, but also outside it, to the moors on the w of the city and NE to the city centre. So both enclosure and prospect co-exist. A wedge of woodland (which provides the estate's open space) divides it into three neighbourhoods, **Hemsworth** to the w, **Herdings** to the s and **Rollestone** to the E, their names taken from the area's farms and hamlets for continuity. Each is provided with its

141. Gleadless Valley

own primary school and local shops, with a main shopping centre at Newfield Green on the NE fringe. A footpath system independent of the roads links the neighbourhoods, shops and schools.

The character of each neighbourhood differs accordingly in response to topography. Much of Hemsworth and Herdings resembles a new town with conventional terraces of houses, some in plain brick, others clad in timber on the first floor. What became known in the 1950s as 'people's detailing' is much in evidence in the low-pitched roofs and square windows. The layout is carefully designed with traffic-free squares such as Raeburn Way. Rollestone [142], however, which lies on the steep E slope, is highly impressive with chalet-like houses clustered on the hillside in a scene that is the antithesis of conventional estate planning and can only be matched in landscaping terms by contemporary Span developments for a very different market. Some of the houses use similar elements to those employed by Span, warm red brick, tile-hanging and weatherboarding along the fascias of flat roofs.

A focal point for the entire estate was provided by three (now two) thirteen-storey point blocks off Raeburn Road in the centre of Herdings, now re-clad. A further group of six towers are at the extreme N edge at Callow Road, Newfield Green. Development took three forms: both along and across the valley's contours, and on land with 'irregular contours' necessitating a variety of house-types to fit specific locations. Along the contours housing types include a reversed plan design for steep slopes with a living room on the first floor, e.g. in **Raeburn Road**, and six-storey maisonettes with bridge access which can be entered at various levels. Other designs include flat-roofed houses with pedestrian entrances at first-floor level and garages underneath accessed from the rear. Examples are in **Fleury Place**.

Across the contours designs include narrow-fronted terraces with mono-pitch roofs, accessed by footpaths with the houses staggered to enable the paths to be diagonal with the contours (some can be seen on the E side of **Blackstock Road** by the shopping centre). Irregular contour designs are for sites where levels make terraced housing difficult and include cluster blocks of three-bedroomed houses with floor levels that can be varied to suit the slope, found throughout the area. These have flat roofs and back onto each other, initiating almost a revival of the back-to-back at the time when the Council was ruthlessly eliminating the last examples of the type elsewhere in the city. Striking two-storey patio houses in **Spotswood Mount** [143], on a 1 in 5 slope with an enclosed patio between each house and first-floor living rooms giving unobstructed views across the valley over the house below. These contrast to patio house designs elsewhere which are generally single storey, e.g. Bishopsfield, Harlow. Research collected by the MHLG in the early years of the estate revealed high levels of satisfaction but the biggest

142. View from Hemsworth of Rollestone with Holy Cross Church, by Braddock & Martin-Smith, 1964–5, and patio houses in Spotswood Mount below

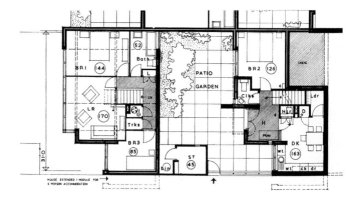

143. Patio houses, plan. From *Ten Years of Housing in Sheffield*, 1962

criticism today is that the houses are small with inadequate sound-proofing. As a whole, the estate retains its freshness, although the shopping centres are sadly neglected. Some selective demolition of small blocks of flats and maisonettes is taking place.

A private development at Rollestone is **Paxton Court**, a group of ten energy-efficient houses of 1984 by *Cedric Green* for the Solar Buildings Co-operative. Brick-clad with pitched roofs, they incorporate much timber framing and have very large s-facing conservatories to collect and store solar heat.

Of the other buildings on the estate, the following may be mentioned. **Holy Cross Church**, Spotswood Mount, 1964–5, by *Braddock & Martin-Smith*, dramatically sited on the Rollestone hillside. Canted E front, broadly triangular with a concrete centre column rising to form a cross. Plain white interior rising towards the altar and dominated by the very striking full-height **stained glass** window by *John Baker*, made at Whitefriars Studio, with immensely tall figures of the Virgin Mary and St John with their traditional symbols and a Crown of Thorns above them. Other glazing by roof-lights. Chunky rough-hewn **font** on one side of altar balanced by wood **pulpit** on the other. Silver **cross** by *David Mellor*. **Gleadless Valley Methodist Church**, Blackstock Road, 1960, by *J. Mansell Jenkinson & Son*. Boxy, roof pitching down to the centre, separate tower of four brick piers topped by a cross. Of the three **primary schools, Hemsworth** (now closed), Constable Road, 1955, was built in the Derwent system. It has an informal layout of low, mostly single-storey blocks. At Herdings, retained as a youth centre and together with the point blocks and the shops intended to act as a focus for the area is **Herdings Farmhouse**. C17, probably built around three remaining trusses of a larger cruck building. A fireplace in the E bay is dated 1675, perhaps the date of reconstruction.

# West

## a) Broomhill

The boundaries of Broomhill are ill-defined but it possesses its own distinct and agreeable character, appreciated by John Betjeman, who, argued against its demolition, saying of it 'Broomhill is to Sheffield, what Regent's Park Terraces are to London, or the layout of Edgbaston is to Birmingham'. It is the city's West End and its first middle-class suburb. Glossop Road (opened in 1821) and the streets immediately N and S were developed from the 1820s with substantial brick-built houses on land owned by members of the Newbould family and their relatives. The leases of this property all forbade trade. Subsequent development to the W along Glossop Road and its continuation (what is now the shopping centre on Fulwood Road) was piecemeal and less subject to restrictions, due to the fragmentation of land ownership. Five landowners were responsible for much of the development from the mid C19: John Hobson who developed Taptonville; the Vicar of Sheffield (N of Fulwood Road); William Fowler (Victoria Park); and John Shepherd and the Cadman family who were responsible for more modest housing. To the N, since 1945, the area has been transformed by the University and the Royal Hallamshire Hospital which demolished many large villas, although pockets of earlier housing remain. To the S

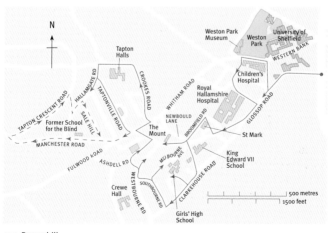

144. Broomhill

and w the leafy streets of houses remain largely intact. Broomhill's villas are widely scattered; what follows is only a selection of the best.*

The walk is long; however, as it broadly follows Glossop Road, with frequent buses back to the city centre, it can conveniently be split into smaller sections. We begin in **Glossop Road** at the junction with Upper Hanover Street, where the beginnings of the late Georgian suburb can be seen, e.g. Nos. 267–285, a group of large but plain three-storey detached villas of the 1830s on the s side, red brick but each slightly different, the last of them with stone dressings, pilastered and a rusticated door surround with a coved opening and a semicircular fanlight. Opposite them Nos. 338–356, similar in size and style but later (1850s) and terraced, before, on the s, a succession of handsome early C19 houses, notably **Brunswick House**. Regency stucco with recessed window bays. No. 305 is of *c.* 1835 by *William Flockton* and occupied by him from *c.* 1845, ashlar with incised decoration to the pilasters and recessed panels beneath the windows. Ground-floor windows with shouldered architraves splayed in the Egyptian manner. Nos. 329–335 are a terrace of well-preserved artisans' cottages.

On the N side, the buildings of the University (*see* p. 78) dominate. It has co-opted many of the buildings in the vicinity, e.g. the former **Glossop Road Baptist Church** of 1871 by *Innocent & Brown*, and the schools to the rear along Shearwood Road extended by the same architects in 1886. Large and impressive Gothic chapel with gabled aisles and a slim sw tower and spire. Tripartite chancel arch with big piers, the spandrels above pierced by large openings. Converted in 1970 by *Alec Daykin* for the University's Drama Studio.

In **Clarkson Street**, at the corner with Western Bank are buildings of the **Children's Hospital** which moved here in 1881. The earliest surviving building is on the corner. By *J.D. Webster* (one of the hospital's founders and chairman of its management committee), 1902. Red brick Tudor with a tower with lantern over the main entrance; carved spandrels show a child receiving help. Extended in matching style in 1931. Stephenson Teaching and Research Unit (1968), the surgical block of 1976 and a massive extension to the rear of 1998 by *James Totty Partnership* are the principal subsequent additions. **Sculpture**, Double Somersault: twisted interlocking stainless-steel tubes by *William Pye*, 1976.

Continue along Western Bank, turn down Northumberland Road, right into Palmerston Road and return via Claremont Place to Glossop Road. In these and neighbouring streets, many more small villas of the 1840s and 1850s, mainly classical, others asymmetrical in the Tudor style. The impact of the **Royal Hallamshire Hospital** has been particularly detrimental to what was once a pleasant residential district. *Adams, Holden & Pearson* won the competition in 1940 but only the concept of

---

*This account owes much to Dr Nyra M. Wilson's unpublished Ph.D. thesis, 'The development of middle-class housing in western Sheffield during the nineteenth century' (University of Sheffield. 1998) and to Eva Wilkinson's researches into the building dates and architects of the houses in the area.

a tall slab with a low front block survived its long gestation period. The hospital as built comprises two main parts, a three-storey outpatients department commenced in 1958 (completed 1971) and a massive eighteen-storey block for inpatients completed in 1978 (concrete, weathered to a dingy grey) with canted two-piece bay windows. Behind it, off Tree Root Walk, the **Jessop Wing**, 1993–2001, by *George Trew Dunn Partnership* in a rather incoherent, vastly enlarged domestic style, steeply pitched roofs with great overhangs and oddly truncated gables. The **Charles Clifford Dental Hospital** of 1951–3 by *Adams, Holden & Pearson* in Wellesley Road is in the firm's familiar utilitarian red brick, extended with the **University School of Dentistry** by the *James Totty Partnership* in 1989–91.

s of the hospitals, we return to the suburban housing in **Glossop Road**. Beyond Broomspring Lane, Nos. 361–373, a pair of *c.* 1840 terraces with the doorways of the end houses placed on the return. Fluted attached half-columns on Nos. 361–365 and panelled pilasters and wreaths on the entablature of the porches on Nos. 367–373. On the N side, beyond Beech Hill Road, Nos. 440 and 442, both Neoclassical of 1853. No. 440 is very pure with fluted Greek Doric columns and a pedimented porch; No. 442 'Broomfield House', for George Walker of the electroplaters Walker and Hall, is less so with Soanian detailing to the cornice. Five bays with fluted Ionic columns to the porch.

**St Mark's Church** [145] is the key building, set back behind the green of **St Marks Crescent**, around which stand good mid-C19 houses. The church was built for a wealthy congregation in 1868–71 by *W.H. Crossland*. It was bombed in 1940 and only the handsome Gothic tower with spire (shorn of its crockets) and s porch were left. To this *George Pace* added a new church in 1958–63 that brilliantly succeeds in balancing a sympathy for Gothic form with the smooth, hard, mechanical forms of Modernism, drawing a logical progression from the work of Lethaby, Randall Wells and Prior. The church is of concrete, partly rubble-faced and with ashlar dressings, harmonizing with the remains of Crossland's church, the tower of which is closely integrated with the new building. The new building's shape is an irregular hexagon, with a nave of even width, but aisle or passage spurs left and right and a broad area for the choir to the NE which produces the irregularity of outline. Massive cantilevered concrete trusses supporting the roof. Slit windows in two to three tiers, the tiers jumping about, i.e. not all starting or ending at the same levels, showing the influences of Le Corbusier's Ronchamp. Pevsner thought the tracery of the E and W windows 'wild' but its organic tree-like form has a clear logic of its own. The interior was designed with the precepts of the Liturgical Movement in mind, with a free-standing altar and unrestricted views of the liturgical area and incorporated social facilities such as meeting rooms (subsequently extended and with an additional staircase added in 2002) within the body of the church. The view from the narthex is one of serene beauty, the light shining onto smooth walls, partly blocked by a plain beam

145. St Mark, the nave looking E, by George Pace, 1958–63; window by H.J. Stammers

similar to Pace's use of the pulpitum in Llandaff Cathedral to break the vista from the w door. A complete set of **furnishings** by Pace includes the pews, choir stalls, font and a stone lectern and pulpit. In the NE corner, a fine **organ case** whose pronounced vertical bars act as a counterpoint to the adjacent E window. **Stained glass**: w window, abstract by *John Piper* and *Patrick Reyntiens*, the E *Te Deum* window with good Expressionist figures by *H.J. Stammers*, both providing brilliant colour to offset the predominantly white interior.

From the main entrance of the church, turn left into **Broomfield Road** where No. 11 is ornate Neo-Gothic, built in 1875 by the speculative builder *Francis Dickinson*, having a big canted bay, a tower and some especially elaborate bargeboards. No. 5 (and No. 2 Newbould Lane) are a pair of severe ashlar-fronted villas of 1840 by *William Flockton*, perfectly symmetrical, with only the thinnest of Tudor veneers overlaying a classical plan.

To our right in **Glossop Road**, stands **The Mount** by *William Flockton, c.* 1830–2. Designed, like the Wesley School (*see* below), to be seen across the Porter Valley. Together with the General Cemetery (*see* p. 226), they form the one monumental Neoclassical composition in Sheffield. Flockton described The Mount as 'a handsome Ionic edifice . . . substantially built and in design and taste far exceeding any of the present erections in the neighbourhood of Sheffield'. It is a s-facing terrace of houses seventeen bays long, with an Ionic giant portico of six columns carrying a pediment and end pavilions with giant columns *in antis*. Converted to offices with extensive additions to the rear of 1961 by *J. Mansell Jenkinson & Son* and marred by a remarkably insensitive car park built into the rising ground in front of it. To the w of it is No. 463 of *c.* 1836, a specially fine Grecian villa of three bays, the central one brought forward and with two giant fluted Ionic columns and corner pilasters. Its first occupant, *Samuel Worth*, was probably the designer.

We return E on Glossop Road where on the right **Mount View**, No. 1 Melbourne Avenue, was built *c.* 1840 for David Ward but altered and extended probably in the 1860s. A handsome classical s-facing villa. Three bays, the central one brought forward slightly and given a pediment. An Italianate tower-like wing was added to the N, more ornate with Corinthian capitals to panelled pilasters. Turn s down **Newbould Lane** where the s-facing principal front of **King Edward VII School** [146] is on the E side. Built in 1837–40 by *William Flockton* as the Wesley Proprietary Grammar School (later Wesley College), and a quite exceptionally ambitious piece of school design for its date. Twenty-five bays wide, with a pedimented centre of seven bays with eight giant Corinthian columns on a ground floor treated as a pedestal. The s entrance on the first floor is reached by a big outer staircase. End pavilions of three bays, also with giant Corinthian columns. Low-aisled

146. King Edward VII School, by William Flockton, 1837–40

entrance hall divided by eight timber Corinthian columns. Chapel behind, with semi-octagonal galleries. The interior was gutted in 1905–6 by *Gibbs & Flockton* to provide additional height for classrooms in place of dormitories. A **teaching block** of 1996 by *DBS Architects* (project architect: *Sue Williams*) slopes downhill on a curve with colonnaded front and walls of powder-coated panels.

Opposite the school entrance in **Newbould Lane** but best seen from Ash Grove, off Clarkehouse Road, is the former **Broompark Congregational Church**. 1864, by *Innocent & Brown*, enlarged with transepts, apse and vestries in 1870. A w porch and spire were intended but not built. Low NE tower with pyramidal roof. The nave windows have plate tracery, the transepts rose windows and the apse, large quatrefoils. Also visible from Ash Grove, an extraordinary **chimney** built in 1868 as part of a greenhouse for William Stones, the brewer. It has a square base surmounted by a circular shaft with three deep, heavily moulded bands which appears to be modelled on a column of the SE gate to the Great Court at Bolsover Castle. Why it took this form remains a mystery. To the w in **Rutland Park**, the imposing **Sheffield High School for Girls**, of 1884 by *Tanner & Smith*, for the Girls Public Day School Trust. Eclectic Free Tudor with Arts and Crafts detailing, its dominant motif is three big half-timbered gables with four chimneys flanking them. External covered staircase at the w end, central corridor with a spacious hall off it to the N and a semi-basement that originally contained a gymnasium. Adjacent is No. 8 (formerly **Moor Lodge**), a very large house of *c.* 1870 now incorporated into the school. Conventionally Neo-Tudor except for a massive machicolated tower and a third-floor room with an open ceiling, expressed externally by a loggia and lit by a large triangular window above it. Fine plaster ceilings in C17 style.

To the sw, **Victoria Park** was developed by William Fowler from 1854 with a great variety of substantial middle-class villas along the curving Southbourne and Westbourne Roads. It includes work by many prominent local architects, e.g. *Flockton & Abbott* at Nos. 28–30 Southbourne Road, which has an ingenious interlocking party wall plan (used widely in Sheffield in the C19) to give the impression of a single house, and by William Hill's partner *S.L. Swann* at Nos. 21 and 23. To the e in **Melbourne Avenue**, the enormous **Melbourne House** (formerly St Mark's Vicarage) was first occupied in 1885. The architect is not recorded but was probably *W.H. Crossland* who built the church; certainly the use of French motifs is characteristic of his work at this time. It has a tower-like wing with a steep-pitched roof in the French manner topped by ornate iron cresting and a massive Gothic staircase window. Carvings of the symbols of St Mark and diocesan badges above the entrance.

Opposite the end of Southbourne Road, in **Westbourne Road**, a large Gothic house, No. 60 **Ashdell Grove** of 1857, which had a ballroom topped by a turret with an oriel and a castellated top, added in 1870 by

*Flockton & Abbott* for Thomas Moore in preparation for entertaining in his mayoral year. Turn N into Westbourne Road; here and in Ashdell and Ashgate Roads, the houses are more closely packed. More Gothic and Italianate villas in the upper part of Westbourne Road, those on the SE side have their principal façades and gardens facing away from the road. No. 21, *c.* 1854 by *T.J. Flockton* for himself, is a picturesque Italianate with a diminutive tower, reminiscent of the cottages at Edensor, Derbyshire. On **Ashdell Road** at the corner of Westbourne Road, **Ashdell** (now part of Westbourne School), a large villa with an Ionic porch flanked by one slightly projecting bay on each side, designed by *Samuel Worth* but completed by *William Flockton* in 1840 following Worth's disagreements with the client, John Shepherd. Follow Ashdell Road round to the NE where on the N side is **Summerfield**, a formal arrangement of communal gardens with two large terraces of 1869–70 by *James Hall*, both with open pediments and big canted bay windows; then **Ash Mount**, Nos. 6–20, Ashgate Road is a handsome terrace of eight brick-built houses of *c.* 1860, still classical with small-paned sash windows and prominent window surrounds, some pedimented and with a rhythm set up by projecting the entrance bay of each house. At the end of Ashdell Road, turn left up Glossop Road to the busy shopping centre, developed in the mid 1870s, where Fulwood and Glossop Roads meet. At the corner, the **HSBC Bank**, built for the London City & Midland Bank, 1911 by *A.F. Watson* has a most original façade with Neo-Mannerist detailing.

**Crookes Road** goes up the hill to the N from Glossop Road, No. 91, **Etruria House** (now a hotel), of 1876 is by *E.M. Gibbs* for John Armitage of the Wharncliffe Fireclay company (*see* also Walk 3, p. 128) and incorporates much of his patented decoration. Despite appearances, it was built as a single house but retains a pair of modest *c.* 1830 houses as a rear wing. These were part of a group whose front gardens have subsequently been built over. Matching lodge and stables. Immediately to its s, **Pisgah House**, No. 17 Pisgah House Road. Three bays, *c.* 1830. Higher up the hill, Sheffield University's **Tapton Halls** by *Tom Mellor & Partners*, 1967–9, a four-storey L-shaped block with angled window bays similar to Earnshaw Hall, Endcliffe, and dining hall block all clad in dark red brick. Then to the left down **Hallamgate Road**. No. 20 of *c.* 1905 is in the Domestic Revival style. Stone ground floor, tile-hung above. Near flush casements with leaded lights throughout, symmetrical with late C17 style brackets over the front door and a hall window. Very accomplished, one wonders as to the identity of the architect. No. 26 is by *Roger Thorpe* of 1971, flat roof and tile-hung, in the style of Eric Lyons' Span houses but with a first-floor living room cantilevered out over the ground floor.

Running s, **Taptonville Road** prompted Sir John Betjeman's oft-quoted description of Broomhill as the prettiest suburb in England. On the left is a pretty **Lodge**, No. 46, dated 1852. Below, its house, No. 38 **Hadow House**, formerly Tapton Elms, built *c.* 1850 for John Hobson,

147. 13–15 Taptonville Road, c. 1851

who developed the road. Neo-Tudor, the principal room with a fine plaster ceiling and a black marble fireplace. Nos. 9–19 [147] are six plain but particularly handsome semi-detached villas *c.* 1851 with deep ground-floor windows. Still entirely Georgian in design with no trace of Victorian heaviness. On the E side, **Taptonville Crescent**, large houses grouped around a small private garden in a glorious mixture of Tudor, classical and Gothic styles. At the bottom of Taptonville Road on **Fulwood Road**, **Broomhill Methodist Church**, completed in 1997, by *David Lyons & Associates*. A complicated and curious combination of motifs. A tower to the left with a Rhenish lantern sits unhappily in proximity to industrial metal cladding, red brick and stone dressings.

From here there are frequent buses back to the city centre.

A number of Broomhill's outliers can be seen in an extension walk of about one mile, half of which is W up the busy **Manchester Road**. On the N side *Flockton & Gibbs*'s former **School for the Blind** of 1879. It accommodated thirty-five boys and thirty-five girls. Gothic, two-storey and symmetrical with a pair of gabled wings, the central part of the building brought forward with an oriel to provide a focal point. On the S side, **Kersal Mount Nursing Home** (formerly Castle Mount), 1869, by *Hill & Swann* for Joseph B. Jackson, of Spear and Jackson, saw manufacturer, which has an oriel with a conical roof over the entrance, delightfully lively carving below the oriel of cherubs and a bird and animals along the elaborate cornice. Then **West Royd**, Tudor with a Gothic porch, is of similar date. At the summit, on the N side, **Tapton Hill Congregational Church**, 1913, by *Chapman & Jenkinson*, modest with a Perp window over the porch. Up **Tapton Crescent Road** to the right, the **Ryegate Centre**, 1978, by *Design Research Unit*, which was intended as a model in caring for people with learning difficulties in small units as an alternative to large institutions. *Kenneth Bayes*, the partner in charge, was responsible for the Merlin Theatre (*see* p. 233). The day care unit quite dramatic with exposed beams, a first-floor balcony and three heating flues employed as a visual motif, very high-tech for its date. No. 92, **Hallam House**, is in the usual C19 gabled Tudor style but with a billiard room extension of 1908 by *Edgar Wood*. It has a flat roof and a broad, rounded two-storey bay window with narrow mullions and transoms. The treatment is characteristic of Wood's work with slim buttresses projecting above a parapet and simple dentil decoration between them. No. 26 is an attractive Arts and Crafts house of 1920 by *A.E. Turnell* with big gabled dormers, a hipped roof and tile-hung bay windows. Return via Tapton House Road and Sale Hill to Manchester Road for buses back to the city centre.

## b) Broomhall

The Broomhall estate lies s of Clarkehouse Road and was laid out from *c.* 1830. In 1809 John Watson acquired most of the estate which he farmed for some years. His first impulse was to develop the E fringe with lower-middle-class housing to separate his land from the industrial development underway on the neighbouring Fitzwilliam lands to the E of Upper Hanover Street. Hanover Place, Hanover Buildings and part of William Street were complete by 1832. The proposal to establish

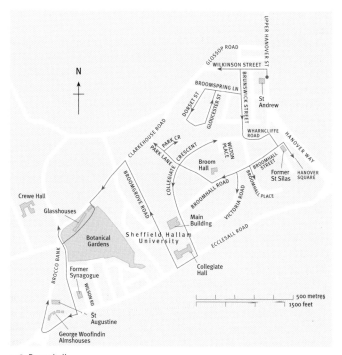

148. Broomhall

the Collegiate School (opened in 1836) provided the motivation for development of the rest of the estate as Broomhall Park. This was intended for a wealthier class of resident, its gated entrances on Broomhall Road were not removed until 1916. The plots are larger, the houses set further back and roads curved in a picturesque manner replace the near grid pattern of the earlier developments. Some houses even have narrow drives running off the main streets. The architecture is the usual mixture of classical and Tudor designs although iron was used for some of their detailing. Collegiate Crescent was laid out by the publication of White's map of 1841 and the first lease issued the following year. Twenty-two houses had been built by 1851 and, other than Victoria Road, building was virtually completed in the next two years. George Hague and George Travis were the principal builders of the houses which were let on 800-year leases. The w part of Broomhall has been greatly altered by the development of the Sheffield Hallam University campus since the 1960s but, aided by designation as one of Sheffield's first conservation areas in 1970, it retains much of its original character: only two of the original villas have been demolished.

The area of earlier development is known as **Hanover**. We start in **Upper Hanover Street** which marks both the boundary between the Broomhall estate and the Fitzwilliam lands, the historical and present-day division between the suburbs and the city centre. **St Andrew's Scottish Presbyterian Church**, 1855–6, by *Flockton & Son* has a tall spire rising out of a short sw tower. The straight-headed side windows make much use of trefoils in the tracery. Dec style w window. The interior was gutted in 1940. Its replacement is by *Teather & Hadfield*. **Stained glass**, 1963 by *Donald Robertson*. Turn left into **Wilkinson Street** which retains almost all the (mainly detached) villas mostly built between 1830 and 1840 on the Church Burgesses' land. They are all of two storeys and, in the main, very plain but with small variations of detail to keep the interest. No. 22 is the largest with five bays, Nos. 33 and 35 are later (*c.* 1855) and semi-detached with paired Italianate windows on the ground floor and big door surrounds with attached columns. Nos. 36 and 38 make more of a show with pilasters continued up above the eaves. **Peel Terrace** off the N side is a formal terrace of six houses of *c.* 1855, the central pair brought forward slightly for emphasis and with prominent quoins.

From Wilkinson Street, s down **Brunswick Street** whose modest terraced houses belong to the 1850s and 1860s but still largely in the Georgian tradition. To the right in **Broomspring Lane** at No. 120a, completely hidden from the road and inaccessible, is an extraordinary survival, a one-storey cutlery forge and assembly shop. Together with a grinding hull, all of *c.* 1864. It retains a blade forge and back boiler. s off Broomspring Lane in **Gloucester Street** [149] and Dorset Street, a group of forty-three experimental houses designed by the *MHLG Research and Development Group* in collaboration with *Sheffield City Council's Architect's Department*. Built between 1962–3, at a time when

149. 5M houses, Gloucester Street, by MHLG Research and Development Group and Sheffield City Council, 1962–3

few industrialized techniques for low-rise housing were available. Structural timber and steel frames on a concrete slab, flat roofs, with concrete, timber or tile cladding. There are four types including single-storey patio houses and five- and six-person houses with integral garages, a rarity for their date.

We return along Broomspring Lane to **Brunswick Street**. Turn left at Clarke Street and right along **Upper Hanover Street** to the **Wright Memorial Church Room** with an elaborate red brick and terracotta façade dated 1903. On the corner with Broomhall Street is No. 200, formerly the Broomhall Mews and carriage manufactory, built c. 1890 for Joseph Tomlinson & Sons Ltd, an imposing three-storey works with elaborate brickwork and intricately detailed proprietary leaf-form capitals to its pilasters.

Facing us in **Broomhall Street, St Silas' Church** (now redundant) by *J.B. Mitchell-Withers*, 1867–9, has a five-bay nave with a sw tower, generally E.E. with plate tracery but with a four-light Dec style E window. Immediately to the E of the church is **Hanover Square**, not really a square at all but a wide cul-de-sac. Four double-fronted semi-detacheds of the late 1840s, red brick with hipped roofs in a simple late Georgian style, face a terrace of seven houses of identical style. Nicely restored with all glazing bars reinstated. To the s of this are the rather depressing maisonette blocks and tower of the Council's late 1960s **Broomhall Estate**.

Continue w along Broomhall Street. To the s in **Broomhall Place** stood a stately ashlar-fronted terrace of c. 1830 that had a pediment and slender Doric porches. After years of neglect, it was demolished in the early 1980s and replaced by a Neo-Georgian council development. Although the centre is pedimented with the name in raised lettering, the thinness of the mouldings and poor proportions of the replacement

150. Broom Hall, Broomhall Road, *c.* 1498, extended *c.* 1614; E wing, by Joseph Badger, *c.* 1784

fail to convince. In **Wharncliffe Road** to the N, small Neo-Jacobean houses, by *George Hague*, in short terraces as if to mark the boundary between the affluence of Broomhall Park and the merely respectable streets to the NE. The division is emphasized by the two- and three-storey brick-built 1840s terraces on the E side of the road and by the lodges at the junctions with Broomhall Road and Collegiate Crescent that once controlled the gates to the **Broomhall Park Estate**.

Back on **Broomhall Road**, as we enter the Park, we move away from the formal grid plan of the earlier parts to gently curving roads where we are immediately surrounded by an eclectic mix of large villas in generous plots. Unusually for Sheffield, there are no grand vistas because the estate is mainly on level ground with only a gentle rise to the N which becomes more pronounced at its W end. **Victoria Road** is to the left, laid out by 1855 and made up mainly of Tudor and Gothic villas and semi-detached houses; the finest are Nos. 1–3 and 5–7. Nos. 22–26 are classical three-bay villas with good doorcases.

The most important house in the area is **Broom Hall** [150] on the N side of Broomhall Road. The medieval home of the de Wickersleys, it was gradually extended and passed through several families, most notably the Jessops. It was sold in 1826 to James Watson who wished to remain at his family home Shirecliffe Hall and therefore let it out as three separate tenancies. The house remained divided and in a deteriorating state until it was restored in 1974–5 by *Mansell Jenkinson & Partners* for occupation as a workshop and home by the designer and silversmith David Mellor. The E wing is of *c.* 1784 by *Joseph Badger* for the Rev. James Wilkinson, Vicar of Sheffield. Hipped roof, and a seven-bay ashlar façade, the central window given emphasis by an enriched surround and blind balustrade below. Broad and most handsome Adam-style fanlight

151. 1 Park Lane, by Patric Guest, 1961

above a door with sidelights. To the rear, however, is a significant survival; a timber-framed house, the earliest part tree-ring dated to *c.* 1498, and extended *c.* 1614. It was built to a half-H plan of central hall and wings projecting s. Much of the timber framing of the w wing survives. The N front has a projecting close-studded gable over a stone ground floor. Pretty carving with patterns, also of tracery. Attractive oriel and coving below the gable (cf. Bishops' House, Meersbrook, p. 242). The roof, which has no ridge beam, falls between the two major roof types found in South Yorkshire: principal rafter truss and common rafter types. The hall and E wing were rebuilt in stone in the C17 and the s front given an ashlar façade with a sun dial and sash windows, probably at the time of construction of the late C18 wing.

Beyond Broom Hall, **Park Lane** diverges to the NW. First, on the w (No. 14 Broomhall Road), **Park House**, is an especially handsome three-bay house with pediment and Greek Doric porch. Then, completely hidden, the best modern house in Sheffield, No. 1 [151], 1961, by *Patric Guest* for David Mellor. A combined house and workshop, the design brief looked to Scandinavia but the influences of US examples, notably the Eames House and Mies van der Rohe's Farnsworth House are evident. Long façade almost completely glazed, flat roof with a fine interior making extensive use of natural timber. Much care was taken with the detailing including full-height internal doors that pivot with no hinges. Large studio at the w end, with extra height gained by a lower floor level on the sloping site. The house is little altered other than the replacement of the original galley kitchen with its folding bed (which attracted much attention in contemporary journals) by a more conventional kitchen and two additional bedrooms at the E end. Park Lane continues N of Collegiate Crescent. Off its E side in **Park Crescent** are Nos. 1–2 Hyde

Villas, brick with stuccoed ends *c.* 1860, and Nos. 3–4 Hyde Place dated 1868. They are like nothing else in the city. Picturesque with Italianate gables, large eaves brackets and ornamental stucco work, they look as though they have escaped from Nash's Park Village East. Further up Park Lane to the w, **Southbourne**, converted from a large stucco villa of 1819. This has unusual extensions of the early 1900s in a quite convincing Neo-Regency with broad eaves and bowed bays.

Back on the N side of **Broomhall Road**, No. 20 Oakburn is similar to No. 14 but with Gothick glazing bars and porch. For Woodville Hall opposite on the s side, *see* below. Beyond here Broomhall Road joins the sweeping **Collegiate Crescent** where there are many more Tudor villas, some with tracery in the mullioned ground-floor windows. Two short cul-de-sacs near the E end, Wilton Place and Mackenzie Crescent, have groups of smaller villas, symmetrical with Jacobean gables, the trademark of their builder *George Hague*. The earliest houses in the road, Nos. 2–4 and 6–8, are classical, semi-detached and double fronted.

The w end of Collegiate Crescent is almost entirely taken up with the campus of **Sheffield Hallam University**, which spreads between here and Broomgrove Road. Much new building has been undertaken since the 1960s although many of the larger villas in the area have been retained by the University. The finest are set out picturesquely along Collegiate Crescent including Nos. 32–40, mostly Gothic with bargeboards and bay windows with tracery; the campus is linked by footpaths through the former gardens of the villas. Its heart is the former Anglican Sheffield Collegiate School built in 1835 by *J.G. Weightman*. **Collegiate Hall**, facing **Ecclesall Road**, is the former headmaster's house. Probably by *Weightman*, in a very convincing Tudor of 1837. Flanking it are substantial stone blocks, originally halls of residence built by *Gibbs & Flockton* in 1906 (when the college became a training college for teachers) to which additions were made by the City Architect *F.E.P. Edwards* in 1911. Behind Collegiate Hall, the **Saunders Building**, refurbished in 2001 by *Michael Self Partnership*. Then the large, flat-roofed **Collegiate Learning Centre** with a sweeping glass wall added in 2002 by *Jefferson Sheard* and the adjoining **Mary Badland Lecture Theatre**, 1976, by *Hadfield Cawkwell Davidson & Partners*, built as a library. The **main building** is the original Collegiate School of 1835–6. Perp style. It had a central hall with a large window and two flanking blocks, each having two bays brought forward. In 1911 *F.E.P. Edwards* raised the central hall by inserting a new ground floor, at the same time adding a first floor and extensions to the wings. The exterior retains the general proportions and details of the earlier school. Canopied niches flank a large window in the central hall. Three large halls of residence were put up in the 1960s. **Marshall Hall** (stylishly extended 2002–3 by *Bond Bryan Partnership*) and **Broomgrove Hall** (six storeys, L-shaped) are tall slabs by *Hadfield Cawkwell & Davidson*. **Woodville Hall** is a little off the campus on the s side of Broomhall Road. All have reinforced concrete grid-like frames with brick infill.

152. Botanical Gardens, glasshouses by Benjamin Broomhead Taylor, 1836, colonnades reinstated 2001–3

### Broomgrove Road to Brocco Bank

The final part of the walk starts at the w edge of the University campus in **Broomgrove Road**, developed from the 1830s with big villas on the w side, some stone-faced, some brick such as the Italianate Nos. 8–10. There is one outstanding house, No. 13, a Neoclassical villa of *c.* 1830 with a three-bay ashlar façade and Greek Doric porch. Low-pitch hipped roof topped by a platform with a timber balustrade. On the right at the top of Broomgrove Road, No. 59 Clarkehouse Road, **Broomgrove House**, is stuccoed, of *c.* 1836. Main s façade of five bays, broad eaves with small brackets and paired square columns to the porch.

Numerous pleasant mid-C19 houses on the s side of **Clarkehouse Road**. Further w, Nos. 61–67 **Broomgrove Terrace** are a group of four Italianate houses *c.* 1844 with shared doorcases. In **Clarke Drive**, to the s, **Clarke House**, a large three-bay brick villa of *c.* 1833 with a porch with fluted Greek Doric half-columns flanked by pilasters. At the top of Clarke Drive on the right, No. 99 **Belmayne House**, a big Gothic villa of 1873, has carved dragons crawling around its door and a medallion of a dragon on the chimney.

Beyond Clarke Drive are the **Botanical Gardens**. Eighteen acres were purchased by the Sheffield Botanical and Horticultural Society in 1833, for about £18,000 from the Wilson family, owners of Sharrow Snuff Mills (*see* p. 228). Opened in 1836 with free access granted only to share-holders and subscribers. *Robert Marnock* won the competition for the design of the gardens which were laid out on gardenesque principles, i.e. an informal layout with the emphasis on a variety of small-scale features such as rock gardens surrounded by mounds planted with trees. The land rises gently to the N and sinuous paths weave through small dells which are interspersed with lawns. Marnock had viewed botanical gardens in Manchester, Birmingham and London prior to the work being completed. The gardens are now administered by the Sheffield Botanical Gardens Trust.

*Benjamin Broomhead Taylor*, who had won the second prize in the competition, is believed to be responsible for the designs for the buildings. The main entrance on Clarkehouse Road has a fine Neo-classical **gateway** with a portico supported on paired Ionic columns and a rounded arch with a big keystone. It resembles a scaled-down version of Decimus Burton's Hyde Park screen of 1825. A lengthy curved screen wall concealed single-storey offices and a caretaker's house. Three pavilion **glasshouses** [152] (often but erroneously referred to as 'the Paxton pavilions') were also built by *Taylor*. Each originally had quadrangular-domed roofs of slender iron ribs and walls of Hathersage sandstone with glazed panels separated by Corinthian pilasters. The central one is seven bays wide, the end pavilions only three. They were linked by lower gabled colonnades, destroyed before 1939 but reinstated during restoration by *Sheffield Design & Property* in 2001–3. Restoration of the Gardens to their original appearance by the removal of later formal features is also under way. Within the Gardens is a **bear pit**. Centrally placed in the Gardens, the **Crimean monument** of Victory holding a sheathed sword in one hand and a laurel wreath in the other (the latter broken off) by *Henry Lane* of Birmingham, the base by *George Goldie* of *Weightman, Hadfield & Goldie*. First erected in 1863 following a competition, it was originally sited on a granite column at Moorhead in the city centre and placed here in 1957.

Leave the Botanical Gardens by its NW gate. Opposite on the N side of Clarkehouse Road, No. 65 Westbourne Road, **St Cecilia House** of 1865 is by *M.E. Hadfield & Son* for William Stacey, a piano dealer. Eclectic in style, a canted bay is embellished by a medallion (depicting St Cecilia playing a portative organ) designed by *J.F. Bentley* and carved by *Theodore Phyffers*. From here, a diversion can be made to the W, for two large houses converted as student accommodation for the University of Sheffield. Up a long drive is **Crewe Hall**, formerly Oakholme, a three-bay house of *c.* 1828 (the heavy porch added later in the C19). Restrained Neoclassical extension of 1936 by *John C. Procter*, who created three wings around an open court. Pretty mid-C19 Italianate stable. Behind it in Oakholme Road, **Stephenson Hall** is centred around Carrysbrook, an Italianate house of 1869 almost certainly by *Flockton & Abbott*. The hall itself by *J.W. Beaumont & Sons*, 1952, is large and clad in stone. A new wing added in 1989 by the *University Architectural Consultancy Unit (David Bannister)* has three linked blocks with a rusticated ground floor.

Back at the NW gate of the Botanical Gardens, go down Botanical Road. Turn left into **Wilson Road** for the **City Church**, formerly the Synagogue, 1929–30 by *J. Mansell Jenkinson*. Classical, brick-built with faience decoration including pilasters, swags and a semicircular portico on Doric columns. All rather heavy in appearance. Continue downhill to **Ecclesall Road** and **Endcliffe Methodist Church**, 1902–4, by *Joseph Smith*. Impressive with tall spire, clerestoried nave and apsed chancel. School of 1927. To the w on Ecclesall Road, the **George Woofindin Almshouses** by *W.R. Bryden* of Buxton, 1898–9. Eighteen red brick cottages in a crescent picturesquely sited by the River Porter. Woofindin was a cutlery manufacturer whose bequest also paid for the Woofindin Convalescent Home at Fulwood. To the n, up **Brocco Bank, St Augustine's Church**, by *J.D. Webster*. Built in memory of Archdeacon Favell in 1897–8, St Augustine's is unique among Webster's later churches in having had its tower completed to his designs; 95 ft tall with a stair-turret, pinnacles, a pierced parapet and a spirelet, it has three large openings on each side. The church is in his usual E.E. style with groups of triple lancets in the clerestory and single lancets in the aisles. The severe interior which has a broad lofty nave and narrow aisles was crudely divided in 1973 to create a hall from the rear three bays. Large arches for unbuilt transepts continue the nave arcading. War memorial carved oak **screen** of 1920, resited at the w end of the nave, by *Temple Moore*, executed by *F. Tory & Sons*. **Memorial**: s wall of chancel to Mary Eddershaw, painting of the Angel in the Marketplace by the *Bromsgrove Guild*. **Stained glass**: William Favell Memorial e window by *Kempe*, 1901; other windows by *Kempe & Tower* in n and s aisles.

Buses return to the city centre from Hunters Bar at the junction of Brocco Bank and Ecclesall Road.

## c) Endcliffe and Ranmoor

### Endcliffe

A tour of this area should begin in **Endcliffe Crescent**, an arcadian landscape of villas grouped informally around a large irregular green. It was developed by Thomas Asline Ward and eight others who in 1824 acquired part of the Endcliffe Hall estate and formed the Endcliffe

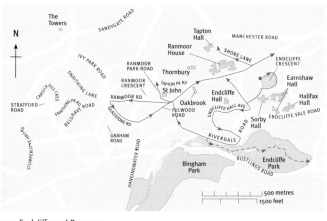

153. Endcliffe and Ranmoor

154. Earnshaw Hall, University of Sheffield, by Tom Mellor & Partners, 1960–5

Building Company. *William Fairbank* was commissioned to draw up plans for the development. Nos. 20–30 are the remains of four pairs of semi-detached houses of 1827–8. Plain with hipped roofs, the brickwork painted in accordance with early regulations requiring that they be either stuccoed or 'coloured like stone or of a light colour'. The other houses in the crescent were built only sporadically from 1856 to 1881. Mostly large ornate villas, several in the favoured mix of Tudor and Gothic styles: Nos. 1, 3 and 5 by *Flockton & Abbott* of 1869–71; No. 4 (Birkdale School) is *Francis Dickinson* at his most flamboyant with bargeboards and big canted bays; No. 7 (Birkdale School) is of 1880–1 in the fashionable French style with steep-pitched roofs and rounded corners to the window surrounds. No. 11 by *Hill & Swann* of 1878–9 has a small open pediment and a most eccentric porch with Corinthian capitals and gross detailing.

Endcliffe is now dominated by the buildings of Sheffield University with halls of residence set in a grassy landscape. Endcliffe House was acquired in 1923, renamed **Halifax Hall**, *c.* 1832, with a tower added in 1891 by *Flockton & Gibbs* with a deep prostyle Greek Doric porch as its base: a strange addition to an otherwise chaste building. Inside, a library containing panelling from the White Star liner, *Homeric* (sister to the *Titanic*) installed in 1936. An adjoining seven-storey slab of 1962 by *Hadfield Cawkwell & Davidson*. The surrounding campus was created from the grounds of Endcliffe Grange (1867, dem.). **Sorby Hall** was built first, 1960–1 by *Hadfield Cawkwell & Davidson*. Thirteen storeys, the male and female students originally separated by a single-storey dining block each side. Exposed concrete frame, the façade articulated by prominent mullions. Quite different in approach is **Earnshaw Hall** [154] of 1960–5 by *Tom Mellor & Partners* with a main hall and two separate four-storey residential blocks, each with lively façades, the window bays serrated like the blade of a saw providing the maximum amount of light to students' bedrooms. Conference hall added in 1992. A move away from communal halls to self-catering flats is seen with **Woodvale Flats** of 1979 by *David Roberts & Geoffrey Clarke*, four blocks in pale brick whose simple elevations are enhanced by a rhythm built up by alternating projecting bays. s of Earnshaw Hall, **Endcliffe Vale Flats**, 1992 by *HLM Architects,* are an attractive group of three blocks canted to each other with deep eaves and roofs that are extended to a sharp point as triangular porches.

**Endcliffe Vale Road** can be reached through the University campus or via Endcliffe Avenue. On the w side, Nos. 89–91, an austere pair of houses with Tudor detailing of *c.* 1840 by *William Flockton*. These adjoin the entrance to **Endcliffe Hall** [155] (a TA centre, since 1913), built in 1863–5 by *Flockton & Abbott* for Sir John Brown. It replaced an earlier house of *c.* 1818 that incorporated some c18 work. This is the largest and most sumptuous of all the steelmakers' mansions, estimated to have cost £100,000, it was hailed by the *Sheffield Telegraph* as 'the public advantage of personal munificence' with all its furniture and decorations designed and made in Sheffield. Italianate, square with the central bays brought forward on each side, those on the w extended to form a tower (originally mansarded), those on the s with a canted bay window. Some decoration that Pevsner considered 'dissolute' with much use of rusticated pilasters. Balusters line the pierced roof parapets. Stone carvings of figures representing the four seasons by *E.W. Wyon* above the porch. On the s front, two carved figures by *Papworth* representing Labour (who has lost his head) and Art. Structurally interesting, the house was of fireproof construction with iron joists and concrete floors. The windows were protected by retractable Belgian-made iron shutters (some of which survive) which in turn were hidden on the inside by large mirrors that slid into the walls.

The **interior** retains much of its profuse decoration. Inside, on entering, a conservatory is to the left and a vestibule leads to a grand **staircase hall** with glazed centre to the coved ceiling and a profusion of columns and pilasters with enriched Doric capitals. The richly decorated principal rooms include a 60-ft (18-metre) long **salon**, built to house Sir John's art collection. Decorated by *John & Joseph Rodgers*, with the case for a water-powered organ in classical style at the e end. The **dining room**, like the other principal rooms, has a fine ceiling by *Charles Green*, who carried out the plasterwork throughout. The chimneypieces are by *Joseph Hadfield* of the Norfolk Lane Marble Works; that in the **drawing room** was exhibited at the 1862 Exhibition and that

155. Endcliffe Hall, drawing room, by Flockton & Abbott, 1863–5

in the dining room is also outstanding. The drawing room has painted door panels and coving by the *Rodgers* and the ceiling has a central oval panel containing painted figures representing Music, Painting and Poetry attributed on stylistic grounds to *Godfrey Sykes* who is also said to have done the murals (now overpainted) on the grand staircase. Heavy gilded pelmets and ornate door surrounds, one of which incorporates Sir John Brown's coat of arms. The Grand Conservatory, 160 ft long with a domed tower, has been demolished save for part of the wall linking it to the house but the lodge and stables, converted to a drill hall in 1914, remain. They formed a fine composition in themselves, with a tower placed asymmetrically by the entrance gateway and the w front of three two-storey pavilions linked by lower bays. The gardens have been destroyed.

Part of the Endcliffe Hall estate was sold as early as the 1890s and a development of large Edwardian houses was begun in Endcliffe Grove Avenue. In **Endcliffe Hall Avenue**, some interesting postwar houses: Nos. 50 and 54–58, of 1968–9 by *Peter F. Smith*, are set on falling ground, several are entered at first-floor level with ground-floor bedrooms. Very low-pitched roofs, the façades mainly glazed. No. 52 by *James Hall* in the same style.

To the s, surrounded by large Victorian and Edwardian houses is **Endcliffe Park**, which was acquired in stages by the City Council which commissioned *William Goulding* in 1885 to adapt it for public use. It marks the start of a remarkable series of linear parks which enable one to walk up the valley of the River Porter, starting in suburbia, and almost imperceptibly to find oneself walking out into the green belt of the Mayfield Valley and beyond onto the moors of the Peak District. Good Arts and Crafts **Park Keeper's Lodge** of 1891 near the Hunters Bar entrance; also two memorials to **Queen Victoria** – a bronze **statue** of 1904 by *Alfred Turner*, originally in Fargate, now near the lodge. Life-size bronze figures of Industry (an artisan holding a sledgehammer by an anvil) and Motherhood (with two children) on the sides of the base, which is by *E.W. Mountford*. Near Rustlings Road, an **obelisk** by *Flockton & Gibbs*, originally also in Fargate to mark the Queen's Silver Jubilee in 1887 but replaced by the statue and removed to the park. NW of the park at No. 89 **Graham Road** is **Riverdale**, hemmed in by flats. Sumptuous Gothic of *c.* 1872, built for Charles Firth, the youngest brother of Mark Firth, and later the home of J.G. Graves, perhaps Sheffield's greatest benefactor. Fine **lodge.**

## Tapton and Ranmoor

The walk continues up Riverdale Road to the junction with **Fulwood Road**. Set imposingly on rising ground on the N side, **St John**, **Ranmoor** [16], the finest of Sheffield's C19 parish churches. The parish was created in 1877 and the first church, by *E.M. Gibbs*, opened in 1879. Only the tower and spire survived a disastrous fire in 1887, and these were incorporated into the new church, also by *Gibbs* (of *Flockton & Gibbs*), consecrated in 1888. Inspired by the High Victorian ideal of creating a treasure house for God, its prosperous parishioners were generous in their donations. Following its completion the building was enhanced by furnishings and stained glass, given in the spirit of Ruskin's essay 'The Lamp of Sacrifice' – 'the offering of precious things, merely because they are precious, not because they are useful or necessary'. Giving to God's house the beauty and luxury its congregation enjoyed in their own homes, they presented them 'for a memorial that our pleasure as well as our toil has been hallowed by the remembrance of Him who gave both the strength and the reward'.

Described by Pevsner as 'opulent outside and inside', the church has an apsidal chancel, transepts, nave with N and S aisles, narthex, baptistery and vestries. The SW tower, with its large gabled bell-openings and tall spire, forms a porch. The walls are built in rock-faced Ancaster stone with ashlar dressings and articulated with sturdy gabled buttresses and decorative corbel tables below the slate roofs. The style is E.E., with Geometrical tracery. The elegant proportions of the **interior** [156] are matched by the outstanding quality and richness of its detailing and fittings, the only jarring notes being some of the alterations made in the controversial reordering by *Ronald Sims* in 1991.

Amid the finely cut and decorated ashlar stonework, the mellow tones of the original woodwork and the jewel-like colours of the stained glass, the lifeless bleached oak of the choir stalls, pulpit and the new sanctuary furniture with its angular black ironwork seems incomprehensibly unsympathetic.

At the w end the intimate space of the little baptistery, with octagonal rib-vault, opens off the narthex. From this a triple-arched opening gives access to the impressively spacious **nave** of five bays, heightened by the introduction of a triforium, a most unusual feature in a parish church of this date and unique in Sheffield. It has two pairs of arches to each bay and continues across the w end below the big rose window in the gable. Plain round piers to the arcade and slender shafts to the upper stages, the exquisitely and densely carved capitals and corbels by *Frank Tory*. His decorative sculpture throughout the church is one of his finest achievements, matching the depth and finish of the medieval work that inspired it and displaying artistry and craftsmanship in every leaf, flower and figure.

Wooden roof with moulded rafters and purlins, the arched braces have traceried spandrels. Similar flat roofs in the aisles, these too have pretty stencilled decoration on the panelled plaster ceilings. The octagonal chancel has refined detailing. Blind arcades on each side, those to the n and s have sedilia under cusped arches. Slim wall-shafts with delicately carved capitals supporting the wooden ribs of the vault which has flowing vine scrolls painted in red and green.

**Furnishings:** stone and marble **reredos** by *Frank Tory,* 1888. The Last Supper carved in alabaster, flanked by St Peter and St Paul, under a canopy with crocketed gables and coloured marble shafts. Octagonal oak **pulpit,** 1888, on stone and marble columns. Elaborately carved arcades on each side with figures of the Evangelists under nodding canopies at the corners. Stone **font** on a fat marble column, its carved base has open trefoil arches on short marble shafts. Conical mahogany and oak cover of 1975 suspended on wrought-iron stand by *Ronald Sims,* 1991. Superb brass **lectern,** 1892, with lions and angels.

A fine collection of Victorian and Edwardian **stained glass** in rich reds, blues and gold. Mostly animated groups of figures in New Testament scenes, with architectural surrounds. The eastern windows in the chancel all 1890, the Crucifixion by *W.F. Dixon,* flanked by the Entombment and Resurrection by *Heaton, Butler & Bayne* and the Baptism of Christ and Christ Bearing the Cross by *Powell Bros.* In the s transept (Lady Chapel), the Good Shepherd, 1898, and the Good Samaritan, 1897, by *Clayton & Bell,* who also made the chancel s window and three in the s aisle. The other s aisle windows by *W.F. Dixon,* the Adoration of the Magi, 1893, and Christ Blessing the Children, 1894. The baptistery windows by *Shrigley & Hunt,* 1888, the rose window and two in the n aisle by *Victor Milner.*

156. St John, Ranmoor, Fulwood Road, interior, by E.M. Gibbs, 1887–8

Around St John's Church in **Ranmoor Park Road**, No. 5 **West Lea**, 1870, and **Ranfall**, 1871, both by *J.D. Webster* and both classical, showing how conservative Sheffield tastes could be. Both have pediments and large eaves brackets, West Lea has gained a big bay window and a billiard room. Off the N side of Fulwood Road, the much earlier and narrow lane, **Ranmoor Road**, climbs the hill. Although few of the buildings are of great individual architectural interest, they make a most harmonious assembly, varying in scale from vernacular cottages of the C17–C18, e.g. No. 34, to the Neoclassical **Ranmoor Grange**, 1877, by *Flockton & Abbott*, with its centre emphasized by a heavy door surround and outsize segmental pediment which breaks through the eaves. To the s in **Ranmoor Crescent**, No. 9 **White Gate**, *c.* 1908, Arts and Crafts with a half-hipped roof, tile-hung bay windows and No. 15 (and No. 55 Ranmoor Road) also Arts and Crafts of similar date, especially attractive large semi-detached houses with white timber balconies, snecked masonry walls and Westmorland slate roofs, the chimneys roughcast.

Back in Ranmoor Road, No. 83, a dignified Italianate **lodge** of 1874 by *J.D. Webster*. At the top of Ranmoor Road, to the right, No. 45 Ranmoor Cliffe Road, **Cliffe End** is by *E.R. Robson*, 1879, for John Moss, Clerk to the Sheffield School Board. Riotously patterned half-timbering to the first floor, coved eaves and a big four-light dormer. Opposite**, Hill Crest**, a large house in the Tudor style with a prominent stained glass staircase window built for Arthur Davy (provision merchant) *c.* 1886 on a corner site.

Return to Fulwood Road and bus services via **Gladstone Road** with more large houses. As the name suggests, No. 7 **Tylecote** of 1880 by *Herbert Wightman* for the cutler James Dixon is unusual in being tile-hung in the Surrey style. No. 408 **Fulwood Road, Storth Lodge** of *c.* 1860, Neo-Gothic, is by *Flockton & Abbott*. On the s side of Fulwood Road are Nos. 385, 389 and 389a, a group of three stone houses built *c.* 1939 by *J. Mansell Jenkinson* in his Arts and Crafts style. Then more large late C19 and Edwardian houses in their own grounds. No. 381 **Esholt House**, brick with half-timbered gables, built *c.* 1897 for A.J. Hobson, Master Cutler that year, has a garden alcove, steps and potting shed of 1905 by *Edwin Luytens*, carried out in stone, plain, almost astylar. Further E, the shops of Ranmoor with two early C19 inns, the **Bull's Head** and the **Ranmoor Inn**, make a pleasant group with particularly attractive double-fronted cottagey houses in **Deakins Walk** some of which look C18 but are of *c.* 1850.

Now E along **Fulwood Road**: on the s side, **Notre Dame High School** incorporates **Oakbrook** [157], *Flockton, Lee & Flockton*'s house of *c.* 1860 for another of Sheffield's leading steel manufacturers, Mark Firth of Norfolk Works, Savile Street East (*see* p. 192). Again Italianate, it has a s range incorporating a big bay window and a tall tower with the top stage open as a belvedere and given rusticated pilaster strips, a balustraded parapet and finials. The heavy porch and other additions were made in 1875 by *Flockton & Abbott* when the Prince and Princess of Wales stayed

157. Oakbrook, Fulwood Road, by Flockton, Lee & Flockton, *c.* 1860

here as Firth's guests on a visit to the city. The ground-floor **drawing room** has a painted ceiling bordered by delicate Rococo plasterwork repeated in the panelling. In the **library**, fine bookcases removed from Page Hall. Oakbrook became a convent in 1919. **Chapel** (now converted to a drama studio) by *Langtree Langdon,* in a stripped Romanesque, was added in 1955. Roof supported on quite florid brackets and arcading with round columns and Byzantine capitals. The **school** is of 1935 by *Henry C. Smart,* red brick, Neoclassical. **City Learning Centre** of 2003 by *Burnell Briercliffe Architects,* with a bulbous dormer and circular windows. **The Fulwood Inn** opposite (formerly Moordale) of 1868 probably by *Hill & Swann* for James Nicholson of the Mowbray Steel Works is Neo-Jacobean with a tower.

The same style is evident off the N of **Tapton Park Road** at **Tapton House** (formerly Tapton Park), Tapton Park Gardens, of 1866–8 and probably by *H.D. Lomas* for William Howson, cutlery manufacturer. Three gables and a big semi-circular bow window. Next, **Thornbury** (now a hospital), designed by *M.E. Hadfield & Son* for Frederick Thorpe Mappin of Thomas Turton & Sons Ltd, Sheaf Works (*see* p. 158) in 1864–5, in an ostensibly classical style, with two wings flanking a big two-storey bow and balustraded parapet, a steep-pitched roof, tall chimneys and gables. Two-storey porch and a large oriel with scalloped niches on the asymmetrical entrance front and large recent additions. The gardens were by *Robert Marnock* and the long sweeping drive and gardenesque clumps remain. **Ranmoor House**, 1964, by *Hadfield Cawkwell Davidson & Partners,* housing 630 students in groups of four-storey blocks of concrete slab cross walls with light coloured brick cladding. In the centre, a courtyard with attractive hard landscaping.

A little way up **Shore Lane** on the w side, **Tapton Edge** of 1864 by *Flockton & Abbott*, for Edward Firth, a younger brother of Mark Firth, Italianate with the entrance recessed behind a twin-arched loggia. A bowed oriel rises improbably from the centre of the loggia, the key-stones of the arches doubling up as brackets for the oriel. **Tapton Hall** (now the Masonic Hall), *c.* 1855, by *Flockton, Lee & Flockton* for Edward Vickers, one of the major figures in the development of Sheffield's steel industry. Also Italianate but a much more formal composition with a big rounded bay window, the roof concealed behind balustrades. Grand entrance hall with open-well stairs and arcading to the first floor. Large uncompromisingly modern extension with a meeting hall added in 1967 by *Hadfield Cawkwell Davidson & Partners*. A large concrete mural by *William Mitchell* symbolizes the turmoil and chaos of the outside world. On the e side, **Tapton Court**, 1868, Italianate, for J.H. Andrew, steel manufacturer. Symmetrical entrance front with a recessed centre and a porch with paired Corinthian columns between two gabled wings. Tower and terrace to the garden front.

Back on **Fulwood Road**, Neo-Tudor **Tapton Cliffe** of 1864, for John Cowlishaw, pearl manufacturer and nephew of John Newton Mappin. The walk finishes at the landmark tower of the former **Holiday Inn** of 1963–5 by *N. Foley* of *Trust Houses Architectural Department* with bands of white cladding. Strikingly set in sloping grounds on the site of Mappin's Birchlands. Two-storey podium and at right angles to this is the bedroom slab of eight storeys, projecting to form the entrance porch.

### NW Ranmoor and Carsick

This area has several substantial and interesting houses, mainly of the early C20. They are spread out over steeply climbing hills and could be toured by car.

On **Ivy Park Road**, No. 60 by *Russell Light*, 2000, is stone-clad and has two boxy, flat-roofed wings linked by a full-height entrance hall and a glass atrium.

No. 37 **Pembury** is a large roughcast house of 1924 by *Arthur Nunweek* taking its stylistic cues from Voysey, notably in the chimneys and ashlar window surrounds. Built for Albert 'Bertie' Bassett, the sweet manufacturer, for whom Nunweek built a new factory at Owlerton in the same period. Then No. 106 of 1966 by *Hadfield Cawkwell Davidson & Partners*, timber-framed and flat-roofed with brick cladding to the ground floor and vertical timber above. Big balcony and full glazing to the ground-floor.

At the northern edge of this area, **The Towers**, Sandygate Road, at the corner of Coldwell Lane. An extraordinary Scottish baronial fantasy by *Flockton & Gibbs*, 1895–6, for C.D. Leng, proprietor of the *Sheffield Telegraph*. Extended westwards in 1905. To the N, a U-shaped stable block and a lodge at No. 316 with a conical turret, also 1905. The house was built on the N side of what had been a public pleasure ground laid out in the early C19, probably by a miller, George Woollen. There were

158. Tainby, 55 Snaithing Lane, by W.J. Hale, 1909

two levels of castellated terraces, known as the Roundabout, from which fine views of the Rivelin Valley to the N were to be had. Some survives amongst later developments, including natural glens and artificial caverns, a stone grotto, dated 1812, and a sunken garden in the grounds of No. 384 Sandygate Road.

**Snaithing Lane** runs SE from near the top of Ivy Park Road. First, on the E side, **Bishopscroft** built as The Côte in 1912–13 by *Sydney L. Chipling* of Grindleford Bridge, an Arts and Crafts villa in random rubble with a turret and leaded lights, rather in the manner of Walter Brierley. Then Nos. 55–61, a group of large houses set back. No. 55 **Tainby** [158] of 1909 is by *W.J. Hale* for his own occupation. Restrained s-facing garden front with two big gables flanking a narrow central bay and unusual heavy moulding to the door. No. 57 **The Croft** (originally Snaithing Croft) was built 1909–10 by *Briggs, Wolstenholme & Thornely* with a big half-timbered porch set between stone wings. No. 59 **Springfield** and No. 61 **Snaithing Garth** are in similar vein. Then **Snaithing Grange** of 1904 for W.F. Osborn of the steel manufacturers, Samuel Osborn & Co. Tudor style with a large staircase window. The s front generally symmetrical with three big square bay windows topped by carved panels with recessed gables above. Panelled hall with deep decorated foliage frieze. Finally a rural survival, **Snaithing Farm** with a long combined house and barn range *c.* 1700.

Further s in **Belgrave Road**, **Ranmoor Hall** (formerly Snaithing Brook), 1880–1 for William Wheatcroft Harrison, cutlery and electroplate

159. The Croft, 5 Stratford Road, by Briggs, Wolstenholme & Thornely, 1909

manufacturer, in the usual Tudor style with a s-facing terrace. It was acquired in 1899 by Henry Andrew, steel manufacturer, who doubled the size of the house, building a new wing on the e side with a billiard room (elaborate plaster ceiling in the Tudor style) and a front porch which bears his initials.

Further w in **Snaithing Park Road**, the Lodge to **Carsick Grange**, Neo-Tudor of 1883 which is hidden up a long drive to the N (visible at No. 52 Carsick Hill Crescent). Then, **Rydal**, by *W.J. Hale*, built for his daughter on her marriage to Maurice Cole in 1921. Simple but well-proportioned roughcast exterior, battered chimneys and slate roof sloping low at the rear, not unlike Mackintosh's Windyhill, Kilmacolm.

In **Carsick Hill Way**, **Quarters**, built as Carsick Hill Court of 1914 by *Hickton & Farmer*, combines half-timbering and tiling with a most elaborate stone porch and a three-storey tower, much altered. **The Croft** [159], No. 5 Stratford Road of 1909 by *Briggs, Wolstenholme & Thornely* for the tool manufacturer James Neill, is one of the larger houses in the area. Built in an attractive Arts and Crafts style with a stone ground floor, rendered above. The road front is symmetrical with a two-storey porch and twin gables, the garden front asymmetrical with two bay windows and an oriel. Tall chimneys and attic dormers.

Finally, **Storth Oaks** (now a clinic) at No. 229 **Graham Road** was originally built as a pair by *J.D. Webster*, 1869, but remodelled by *S.L. Swann* in 1875 for Alderman W.H. Brittain. Double-fronted with a tower and offset entrance. The staircase ceiling is copied from a room at Clumber Park. Stained glass of foliage, flowers, fruit and birds by *Heaton, Butler & Bayne*. *Robert Marnock* undertook the landscaping of the garden. A little to the w, an 1870s cast-iron **bridge** with decorative traceried parapet and spandrels carrying Stumperlowe Crescent Road over Storth Lane.

# North-West

The NW suburbs differ substantially in character and history. Netherthorpe and Upperthorpe developed as predominantly working-class suburbs from the beginning of the C19. They were largely cleared in the 1950s–60s and rebuilt, at Netherthorpe with a mix of twelve-storey towers and maisonette blocks and at Upperthorpe with the Kelvin flats, similar in design to Park Hill and demolished in 1991. The higher areas in Walkley and Crookes were developed later and have survived as a closely-knit pattern of streets of late C19 and early C20 terraced artisan housing. Lower Walkley was redeveloped in the 1970s–80s with housing of similar scale. To the S, the Crookesmoor district was developed from the 1880s with larger houses for the middle classes. To the N, Hillsborough was focused on the Halifax turnpike while the River Loxley attracted water-powered cutlery and edge tool works from the C16, examples of which can still be seen w of Malin Bridge. By the end of the C18, Hillsborough Hall and Burrowlee House stood in isolation w of the turnpike and the only other settlements were the hamlets that grew up around the river junctions at Malin Bridge and Owlerton. By the late C19, these were linked by ribbon development and Hillsborough had become a major shopping centre. It was incorporated into the city in 1901 and, after the advent of the electric trams in 1903, Hillsborough became one

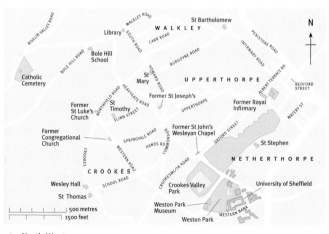

160. North-West

of the fastest-growing areas in Sheffield. Large numbers of terraced houses and small villas were built, most of which remain. Only Upperthorpe, Netherthorpe and Hillsborough provide a rewarding walk; the other districts are best viewed as a series of highlights.

## a) Crookes

**Crookes** developed as a suburb somewhat later than its neighbours to the E; the 1853 O.S. map shows a village with farmhouses and cottages end on to the eponymous main thoroughfare and only a few terraces with further scattered development along Commonside. From the 1880s, there was rapid expansion further encouraged by the extension of the electric tram route in 1901. Development took place following the boundaries of the strips of the common fields which are commemorated in some street names. Frequent buses travel to Crookes from the city centre.

The architectural highlights of Crookes are the three Nonconformist churches by the little-known but highly accomplished local architect, *W.J. Hale* (*see* topic box, p. 277). The first of these, **St Luke** [161], Northfield Road, of 1900 is conventional in form with four bays, an apsidal chancel and a segmental traceried window of five lights at the E end. The slender buttresses rise to form miniature towers. In the porch, excellent carved imposts depicting the four evangelists as angels, by *Frank Tory*. Also by him, a Tree of Life on the gable-end. The church is linked by an arch to a school in similar but simpler style. Both now converted to flats. Hale's other churches are octagonal. The earlier of the two, **Crookes Congregational Church**, in Springvale Road, of 1905, is particularly impressively sited on sharply rising land. Its height is accentuated by the prominent buttresses, some massive and battered, others slender, which lead the eye upwards from the rounded apse to the gables and thence to the lantern which is surmounted by a flèche. The slender buttresses extend through the tracery of the E window. Over the porch, carving of a Tree of Life with pomegranates, probably by

161. St Luke, Northfield Road, by W.J. Hale, 1900; detail of impost by Frank Tory

## W.J. Hale

William John Hale (1862–1929) produced Sheffield's most striking early C20 architecture. He was especially successful in taking elements of fashionable styles and tailoring them to conservative Sheffield tastes. He developed an eclectic personal style, initially blending Perp Gothic with Arts and Crafts at St Luke's in 1900 and the great octagonal chapels of Crookes Congregational, 1905, and Wesley Hall, 1907, adding further Art Nouveau motifs at Lydgate Lane School, 1907, and incorporating Baroque elements at Hammerton Street School, 1904, and the tower of Victoria Hall, 1908. By the 1920s, at Banner Cross Methodist Church, he was working in an angular Gothic with few period allusions. His work is testimony to his view that good architecture does not 'lie in pinning one's faith to any particular style to the exclusion of all else but rather in admitting that there is good in all'.

Hale was active from 1896 until his death although no works by him are traceable between 1909 and 1919, possibly due to ill-health or other business interests. He was well placed through family, religious and business connections to secure work. Brought up as a Wesleyan, he served his pupilage with *Innocent & Brown* which brought him contacts with local Congregationalists (Innocent was an active member). His marriage brought him further Wesleyan contacts in estate agency, property development and accountancy.

*Frank Tory,* with more carving below the caps of the buttresses. Converted after 1988 to offices for their own occupation by the *Bond Bryan Partnership.* The great open space is flooded with light, a quality emphasized by the white painted walls and gallery fascias, the galleries retained as work spaces. Like the Congregational Church, *Hale's* **Wesley Hall** [162], Crookes, of 1907 is octagonal in plan but with radial wings flanking the porch and a pyramidal roof topped by a lantern. The massive buttresses culminating in ashlar caps and the shaped parapet provide a great impression of movement while the broad seven-light windows spring directly from the buttresses rather in the manner of W.D. Caröe. The interior originally had shallow galleries on five sides of the octagon with a platform rostrum and choir on the other three sides. Hale's brief was to enable the congregation to concentrate on the sermon without being distracted by discomfort or straining to see or hear the preacher. The church was praised by contemporaries for its luxury: 'looks more like the Hippodrome than a place of worship' was meant as a compliment by the *Sheffield Daily Telegraph.* Converted in 1992 by *Byrom Clark Roberts* to form a worship space above and a hall below, together with other facilities, thereby losing much of its original character.

Crookes has four other churches of interest: **St Thomas**, Nairn Street, of 1839. A simple building with w tower and nave lit by lancets. The

162. Wesley Hall, Crookes, by W.J. Hale, 1907

church was drastically altered in 1979 when a long range by *Brandt Potter* incorporating meeting rooms was added across the end of the chancel and the E–W orientation of the church reversed. Although carried out in stone and intended to harmonize with the existing work, the addition and consequent alterations have submerged the character of the 1839 building. **Stained glass** in N wall by *Morris & Co.* of St Michael, 1900, and by *Ward & Hughes* of 1896 in the s aisle. **St Timothy**, Slinn Street, by *J.D. Webster & Son*, 1910, a large church broadly in the Perp style, externally plain, built to cater for the expanding suburb. The gable faces the road. A sw tower and spire were intended but not built. Spacious nave of four bays with broad chamfered arches, octagonal piers, no capitals, clerestory, transepts and narrow aisles. **St Vincent R.C.**, Pickmere Road, 2001, by *Jos Townend* of Manchester. Bright red brick with bands of buff brick and including meeting rooms and presbytery. Hipped roofs throughout and the church lit by a pyramidal lantern over the sanctuary. Font: c19 from St Vincent, Solly Street. **Wesleyan Chapel** (former), School Road. Built 1836 by *J. Ridal*, mason, a typical chapel of the period of three bays with round-headed windows and a hipped roof. School wing added to the rear in 1843.

**Rivelin Valley Catholic Cemetery**. The cemetery was opened in 1862 and *M.E. Hadfield & Son* provided a **chapel** in 1878 in E.E. style with an apsidal E end, w bellcote and sw porch. This has a niche above with sculpture of St Michael slaying the dragon. The fine masonry bears tooling in wave patterns, perhaps suggesting Celtic influence amongst the masons. Rich interior with altar of polished marble and veined alabaster with a figure beneath behind arcading of the dead Christ in white alabaster by *Boulton* of Cheltenham. In 1884, four **wall paintings**

of the Resurrection with painted decoration incorporating linked ogee arches above and below them were added by *Charles Hadfield* and *Nathaniel Westlake* to the E end of the chapel. **Stations of the Cross** in terracotta, mainly paired below Gothic canopies. **Stained glass**: three E windows by *J.F. Bentley*, executed by *Lavers, Barraud & Westlake*. W window of 1884 by *Hadfield* and *Westlake*. Two **monuments** in the cemetery to the W of the chapel deserve mention: the **Foster family vault** of *c*. 1894, ornate pinnacled Gothic with angels at the corners, crocketed canopies, red and grey granite shafts and finely carved capitals of a squirrel and oak leaves, an owl with thistles, etc., and the **Walsh family vault**, *c*. 1901 by *Edmund Sharp* of Dublin, Neoclassical.

The former **Crookes Endowed School** was founded here in 1791 and developed in stages. To the left is the earliest part, probably early C19, classical, of four bays with an open pediment enclosing a prominent plaque. Then a three-storey gabled addition dated 1880, a single-storey portion and the former master's house (Tudor) dated 1866.

## b) Walkley

Due to the influence of the Freehold Land Societies (*see* topic box, p. 282), **Walkley** gained the reputation of being a place to which the artisan could aspire: 'the workers' West End'. A pocket of more substantial housing lies between Upperthorpe and Walkley in the Birkendale district. As with Crookes, there are a few surviving vernacular houses, notably the Old Heavygate Inn, and Walkley has the first council houses to be built in the city, Nos. 8–46 Hands Road of 1903, identical in appearance to contemporary terraced houses.

**St Mary**, Howard Road. Two bays and a chancel of a mission church were erected in 1861. The nave was completed in 1869 when aisles, a NW tower and broach spire were added by *J.G. Weightman* in association with *T.A. Wilson*. The development is evident from the trefoil clerestory windows which change subtly in shape from the second bay. Simple Dec style. Elaborate stone pulpit of 1901 and the Perp carved oak reredos erected 1907. Classical font cover and light fittings by *George Pace*. **Stained glass**: E window of 1893 and S chancel window 1896 by *Kayll* of Leeds. **Schools** (now the Sheffield College, Walkley Centre) of 1871 by *T.A. Wilson*. Symmetrical with an E-shaped plan, a feature made of a chimney in the centre. Steeply pitched roofs with wings forming catslides.

**St Bartholomew**, Burgoyne Road, 1991, by *David Greenwood* of *Ashfields Architects*, incorporating some arches and shafts of the former church (1882) by *J.D. Webster*, and sited on the footprint of the former Sunday School. A complex multi-purpose building on sloping ground with the worship space and offices linked by a foyer on the upper level and community rooms below. The sacred and secular elements are distinguished by the worship space being faced with white artificial stone as opposed to the brick of the remainder. From the S the new church appears to rise amidst the ruins of the old, the continuity emphasised

163. Ebenezer Primitive
Methodist Church,
South Road, by W.J.
Taylor, 1890

by the flèche from the old church topping a slim, almost free-standing
drum that has an entrance at ground-floor level and an oratory above.
The principal entrance to the worship space is on the N side at the upper
level. Pitched roofs with a sharks-fin roof-light. Cheerful and light
worship space but all is revealed at first glance; there is little sense of
mystery. **Stained glass** by *Mark Angus* symbolizing the Four Gospels
and the Five Wounds of Christ and some glass from the former church
re-used.

Former **Ebenezer Primitive Methodist Chapel** [163], South Road, of
1890 (now student flats). Designed by *W.J. Taylor*, the epitome of the big
C19 chapel. Massive E façade with pediment topped by ball-in-cup
finials, giant pilasters rising up to dentil eaves. Executed in rock-faced
stone with heavy detailing. It is extraordinary that only ten years separate it from Hale's St Luke's, so different is it in feeling; mid-Victorian
as opposed to C20. The congregation has moved into the Sunday School
and Institute behind, a building of 1904 also by *Taylor*.

**St Joseph**, Heavygate Road, dramatically sited on rising ground, was
formerly a reformatory for Catholic girls managed by the Sisters of
Charity and founded in 1861. The surviving buildings comprise an early
C19 stone house used as a boarding school before being taken over as a
dwelling for the Sisters. Former chapel by *M.E. Hadfield & Son* 1871, following E.W. Pugin's favoured approach in its unified nave and chancel
with a steeply pitched roof, apsidal nave and bellcote at the E end.
Schoolrooms below took advantage of the sloping site. Below the
chapel on the other side of Howard Road is the former **St Joseph's
School**, 1889, by *Goldie, Child & Goldie*, E-shaped in coursed stone in

164. Walkley Reform Club, Fir Street, by H.L. Paterson, 1909

the Renaissance style with mullioned and transomed windows. Oval windows in segmental gables. The central bay has a pediment broken by a niche containing a statue of St Michael slaying Satan. An attractive composition. Restored and converted to offices 1990.

Walkley has three noteworthy **Board Schools**. Two are powerful Gothic compositions, typical of Sheffield's first group of Board Schools. The earliest is **Walkley Board School**, Greaves Street, one of the first batch of schools to be designed by *Innocent & Brown* in 1874 as architects to the Sheffield School Board. The main part is now in residential use but the infants' department of 1906 built in a Renaissance style by *Hemsoll & Paterson* remains as Walkley Primary School. **Burgoyne Road Board School** of 1881 by *Innocent & Brown* is a three-decker towering above the surrounding houses with additions of 1889 by *C.J. Innocent*. **Bole Hill School**, Bole Hill Road (now the Unity Centre), is by *W.J. Hale* of 1896, one of only three to be designed by him. It has the characteristic large windows, powerful massing and buttressing of the other Board Schools (*see* topic box, pp. 20–1) but lightened by the use of Hale's favoured shaped parapets and crowsteps on the gables. Attractive carved lettering on a naturalistic background.

**Carnegie Library**, Walkley Road (*Hemsoll & Paterson,* 1905), the only library built for the Sheffield Corporation to receive Carnegie funding. Skilfully making the most of its corner site, it consists of two wings in a gabled Tudor style linked by a rounded portico on paired columns with Ionic capitals, a combination that shows how well the Edwardian Free Style could combine such disparate elements. **Ruskin House**, Bole Hill Road, by *H.W. Lockwood,* designed as a girls training home preparing girls for domestic service, was put up in 1893. It incorporates to the N a small cottage in which Ruskin's St George's Museum was established in the N in 1875 (*see* topic box, p. 74). The museum moved to Meersbrook Hall (*see* p. 241) in 1890. **Walkley Reform Club** [164], Fir Street, 1909 by *H.L. Paterson*, is a small building in a minimal Art Nouveau with first-floor balconies provided for young men 'to act as a counter attraction to the public-house influence'. **The Old Heavygate Inn**, Matlock Road, is the oldest building in the area with a 1696 datestone, converted from a farmhouse, its appearance ruined by a remarkably insensitive addition of the 1970s.

## Freehold Land Societies

Freehold Land Societies played an important role in the growth of Sheffield's suburbs *c*. 1840–70. Big landowners were reluctant to sell off small parcels so the Societies acquired whole estates and divided them into plots, for their members, who paid a monthly contribution to the cost and charges for road-making. Once payment for the plots had been reimbursed, the Society would be wound up. Usually, the vendor or mortgagee of the land would impose restrictions prohibiting offensive trades. The movement was also political in its intention: the Sheffield Reform Benefit Building Society was sponsored by middle-class Liberals to enable deserving working men to acquire the vote as householders and to gain economic power by the accumulation of land.

The societies were most active in Nether Edge, Walkley (where there were a dozen societies with around 3,000 members holding 292 acres), Ranmoor (where membership was entirely middle class, *see* p. 267), Abbeydale and Meersbrook. One of the best examples of society development is in **Carr Road**, Walkley, developed by the Walkley Benefit Land and Building Society *c*. 1849–65, 'Formed by working men and for their own benefit solely'. Here the cultivation of allotments was as important as the housing. A 'garden house', a very simple two-room dwelling, was often built first, e.g. No. 109 Carr Road, in coarse rubble. A little-altered house with rough stonework ground floor and brick above survives behind No. 143 **Walkley Crescent Road**. The deep plots, with houses placed at the rear boundary, give a more open and leafy aspect than was the norm in the inner suburbs. Typical examples of the larger houses in Carr Road are No. 47 with coped gables and kneelers, and No. 140, **Laurel Grove**, ashlar with a hipped roof, built for Thomas Ibbotson of Globe Works. The **Birkendale** development of detached and semi-detached villas, largely complete by 1849, set back from the road in Birkendale, Birkendale View and Upperthorpe displays the continued use of quarter-acre plots for allotments.*

* This section is based on Martin Olive's researches into the Freehold Land Societies.

## c) Upperthorpe, Netherthorpe and Crookesmoor

Trams from the city centre stop in **Infirmary Road**, close to the former **Royal Infirmary** [165] (now Heritage Park), in Albert Terrace Road. This was the first hospital in Sheffield and located in the fields when opened in 1797. It closed in the 1980s and, stripped of many later additions, was converted to office use in 1990. The remainder of the site has been used for a supermarket and the presence of this with its 'Crystal Palace' atrium and attendant car park diminishes the appearance of the surviving buildings.

The original building of 1793–7 (now Heritage House) by *John Rawstorne* survives and with its central pediment and bows at each end resembles an enlarged country house. In that respect, it is typical of Georgian hospital design. The building is plainly detailed but of excellent proportions. Under the Doric porch, niches with statues of Hope and Charity, very early work of 1802 by *Francis Chantrey* (now replicas). Each floor had four wards extending the width of the building and stairs at each end. At the s end to the rear, *William Flockton* added the Recovery House (later known as the Norfolk Wing) in matching style in 1839, separated internally from the remainder of the hospital to form an isolation wing. Behind this is the former Outpatients' Department of 1884 by *J.D. Webster* (now the Roundhouse), an innovative octagonal structure whose design was perhaps influenced by advocates for the circular hospital ward, the first of which (at Greenwich) was opened the same year. The pyramidal roof is lit by a cupola and carried on wrought-iron lattice girders with monograms in the spandrels. Round-headed windows light what was a tiled waiting room with consulting rooms radiating from it (extensions by *Young & Hall* of London, 1900). The other remaining buildings are a lodge (presumed to be by *Rawstorne*) and the Nurses Home (Centenary House) of 1897 also by *Webster*, a large building with big bow-fronted end pavilions, still essentially domestic in appearance, whose elaboration forms an instructive contrast to Rawstorne's original building.

165. Royal Infirmary, by John Rawstorne, 1793–7. C19 photograph

166. Upperthorpe Library, by E.M. Gibbs, 1874; detail of carved figures of a workman and factory girl, by J.W. Cooper

The **Upperthorpe Healthy Living Centre** is a conversion of 2003 by *Tatlow Stancer Architects* of the **Public Baths**, dated 1895, by the Improvement Surveyor *Charles Wike*, red brick Jacobean with a large central gable and two wings lit by clerestories. **Upperthorpe Public Library** [166] by *E.M. Gibbs*, 1874, is almost identical to his design at Highfield (*see* p. 222) [129] of the same year. Plain brick with Florentine windows and an elaborate doorcase; below the brackets, figures of a workman with an axe and a factory girl reading, by *J.W. Cooper*. In the tympanum, the Sheffield arms of arrows and wheatsheaves. Ornate ironwork along the roof ridge. In **Blake Grove Road**, No. 22 is a sole survivor of *c.* 1830, three bays, ashlar with a Doric porch. It owes its preservation to having been the home of Ebenezer Elliott, the Corn Law Rhymer and ironfounder. To the s, in **Watery Street**, the **Medico-legal Centre** of 1975 by *Hadfield Cawkwell Davidson & Partners*. Notable as one of the first buildings in the UK to combine a coroner's court, public mortuary and University department of forensic pathology. Box-like, concrete framed with good-quality brick cladding but few windows.

To the E in **Infirmary Road**, Nos. 136–144, former back-to-back houses with shops on the ground floor, brick of three storeys *c.* 1850 and two examples of early Corporation flats over shops dating from 1904 when the road was widened for the electric tramway. **Kelvin Buildings**, by *C. & C.M. Hadfield*, are quite imposing with a pediment enclosing a semi-circular window, pilasters and canted bay windows on the first floor; and **White House Buildings** by *H.I. Potter* are in a vaguely Arts and Crafts style with plenty of pebbledash. The contemporary **George IV** pub has an elaborate Art Nouveau door surround and lettering in the same style. Off Infirmary Road, **Bedford Street** has late C19 former stables, coach houses, workshops and stores for Joseph Tomlinson, horse cab and motor bus operator and funeral director. Two ranges survive, converted into loft apartments and a house, with an archway bearing the name Bedford Mews.

Beyond is the excessively busy **Penistone Road**, the principal northern exit from Sheffield. There is little left of the industrial area to its E known as Philadelphia, except **Bath Steel Works**, a small forge. Rendered buildings, one with a roof of stone slates. The two-storey forge building is lit by large unglazed windows with metal bars and wooden shutters for ventilation. Four steam hammers still in use. The works' offices are in part of the former Philadelphia steam corn mill (1843 datestone) while a former penknife works is incorporated at the rear. In contrast, the adjacent bulk of the four-storey former **Osborn Mushet Tool Works** (now Hydra Tools) of 1943 is in white concrete with modest Art Deco detailing.

s of the Royal Infirmary (*see* above) **Netherthorpe** was cleared of its back-to-back housing from 1956 as part of a comprehensive redevelopment scheme over 120 acres. The new housing of 1959–72 was a characteristic mixed development of eleven point blocks (re-clad in brightly coloured metal 2000–1) running down the hillside and three- and four-storey maisonette blocks arranged in interlocking squares with small flats on the ground floor for elderly people to live near their families. In recent years, many of these have been refurbished or demolished and replaced with two-storey houses. In Morpeth, Bonville and Dover Gardens, three blocks of flats of 1976, with flat roofs and access by tiers of steps, the prototype for a design fully developed at Heeley (q.v.) and Gleadless Valley.

The most striking feature was the replacement of packed C19 housing by linear parkland, made much of in contemporary publicity. Retained to serve the new housing is **St Stephen**, Fawcett Street, 1856, by *Flockton & Son*. An imposing town church of cruciform plan with a tower rising from the centre with gallery at the w end. Nave lengthened in 1865. Extensively altered internally to provide a worship space at the w end, the remainder converted for community use. Further reordering undertaken in 2004. Gothic Institute of 1886 and school of 1860. **Netherthorpe School**, Netherthorpe Street, of 1873 by *Innocent & Brown*, similar to their first Board School, Newhall School, Sanderson Street (dem.), is the only other C19 survivor in the area.

**Crookesmoor**, sw of Netherthorpe, is an area of late C19 housing, some of it quite large. Besides the churches, a few interesting earlier buildings remain; in particular, a good early Board School, **Crookesmoor School**, Oxford and Tay Streets, by *Innocent & Brown*, 1873. In **Crookesmoor Road**, the **Crookesmoor Vestry Hall** of 1853–4. Neo-Jacobean but with a Gothic gable. Also the former **St John's Wesleyan Chapel** of 1889 by *C.J. Innocent*, an exciting composition perched on the side of a steep hill with a lofty four-bay nave, aisles, transepts and an octagonal flèche with a spire and rooms below the church. Innocent's use of Gothic is highly original; the transepts each have rose windows set within pointed arches with the form of a cross created within the tracery and extended beneath the window as blind arcading. Being converted to flats in 2004. Attached, a three-storey school of 1880 at a lower level, possibly also by *Innocent*.

sw of Netherthorpe, **Weston Park** was the first Council-provided open space. It was formed out of the grounds of Weston House, formerly the home of the Misses Harrison. The house was converted to a museum in 1875 and replaced in 1937.

The **Mappin Art Gallery** [167] was set up under the will of John Newton Mappin, whose wealth derived from his ownership of the Masboro' Old Brewery, Rotherham. He left his collection of 153 narrative and historical pictures to the city on condition that an art gallery was to be provided to display them. The collection was expanded by his nephew, Sir Frederick Thorpe Mappin. The commission for the gallery was won in competition by *Flockton & Gibbs* in 1885 and it was completed in 1887 at a cost of £15,000. Pevsner thought it 'an amazingly pure Ionic building – amazing if one considers its date'. He considered, doubtless on the strength of the Ionic giant portico with pediment, that the pattern was Klenze's Glyptothek in Munich rather than the English Greek Revival. The Ionic giant colonnade in the recessed parts left and right also recalls Schinkel's Altes Museum in Berlin and the attic storey above the portico, von Hallerstein's rival design for the Glyptothek. Semi-circular apses at each end and very competent and elegant detailing throughout. Gibbs pointed to the internal planning (for which he was largely responsible) as innovative in the use of a cruciform central gallery, divided into bays or recesses each with its own ceiling light. Two further galleries were provided at the front. The central 'special' gallery, where J.N. Mappin's bequest was hung, was magnificent, the bays delineated by fluted Ionic columns, the central part of the ceilings barrel-vaulted and coffered. All but the façade and the two front galleries was destroyed by bombing in 1940. The annexe to the s, housing an extension to the Gallery and the **City Museum**, by *W.G. Davies*, City Architect, 1937, survived. Its stripped classicism blends well with the restrained 1887 work. **Sculpture** on the frieze above the entrance to the Museum by *F. Tory & Sons* depicts the Shrine of Knowledge carved with crustaceans, fishes, reptiles, mammals and birds in the order of their appearance. Another frieze on the E side shows men working in the Sheffield trades.

167. Mappin Art Gallery, by Flockton & Gibbs, 1885. Engraving (1890)

The Special Gallery, rebuilt in 1961–5 by *J.L. Womersley* in brick with a well-lit 90 ft by 40 ft open gallery space, has been demolished in a scheme by *Purcell Miller Tritton*, due for completion 2005, to turn the gallery into the Weston Park Museum. A new path and steps will strengthen the link between the existing Museum entrance and the Park.

The Park was laid out by *Robert Marnock* and opened in 1875. The s **gate** on Western Bank was designed by *E.M. Gibbs* and the terracotta piers incorporate extremely pretty panels decorated with putti (designed for panels flanking the windows of the main quadrangle of the South Kensington Museum) in the North Italian Renaissance style by *Godfrey Sykes*. Sykes was a student and a teacher at the Sheffield School of Design until he was called to London in 1859 to superintend the decoration of the South Kensington Museum. He died young in 1866 and the work was carried out by *Blanchard*, the piers being designed by *James Gamble*, Alfred Stevens's assistant. Sykes is commemorated in a terracotta **column**, to the NE of the Gallery made in 1871, but not erected until 1875. The column is a copy, made by students of the National Art Training School, of those originally made by Blanchard for the main façade of the South Kensington Museum of 1864–6. Ornamented with bands, modelled by Sykes, of figure friezes depicting the Three Ages of Man between fluted sections decorated by foliage. The base of the column and an urn surmounting it are by *James Gamble*. The portrait of Sykes is based on that by *Gamble* at the Victoria and Albert Museum and the railings around the column are *Stevens*'s design for the Museum. Other memorials include one to **Ebenezer Elliott**, the Sheffield poet, by *N.N. Burnard*, 1854, re-sited from High Street, and two **war memorials** to the York and Lancaster Regiment. The earlier, for the Boer War, 1903, by *J.D. Webster* is a bronze triptych with Gothic tracery, the central panel giving the names of the fallen, the outer ones depicting a soldier under a blazing sun. It was removed from the Cathedral graveyard, Church Street, in 1957. Accompanying this, the impressive 1914–18 War Memorial of 1923. Its design is based on a sketch by *Francis Jahn* who taught modelling at the Sheffield School of Art, translated into models by *G.N. Morewood* and *Roy Smith*, and made by members of the school under the supervision of *Holmes & Son*. An obelisk surmounted by a great winged figure of Victory with two life-like bronze soldiers on each side of the shaft, one an officer holding a revolver by *Morewood*, the other a private soldier by *Smith* who also modelled the regimental badges above the shaft's pedestal. Realistically rendered uniforms are piled up on the other sides of the stone base.

## d) Hillsborough, Owlerton and Malin Bridge

Hillsborough is easily reached by bus and tram from the city centre.

### Hillsborough and Owlerton

The natural centre of the district is Hillsborough Corner where **Langsett Road** crosses the Loxley. On the corner is a prominent local landmark, the former **Hillsborough Inn**, of *c.*1850, with a curved ashlar façade, now shops. Opposite on **Holme Lane**, Nos. 25 and 27 and Nos. 389 and 391 Walkley Lane. Shops with dwellings above of 1911 by *Chapman & Jenkinson*, of brick with faience dressings. On the N side, the **Tramway Medical Centre** incorporates the front wall, with two large openings, of the former tram depot as the screen. The Medical Centre was built in 1991; accomplished Neo-vernacular by *Clayton Rodgers*. Travelling s on **Langsett Road**, on the w side, the **HSBC Bank** built for the Sheffield Union Banking Co., 1895 by *J.B. Mitchell-Withers* and completed by his son of the same name. Italianate, red brick with stone dressings and pedimented windows. Adjoining this, the **Walkley**

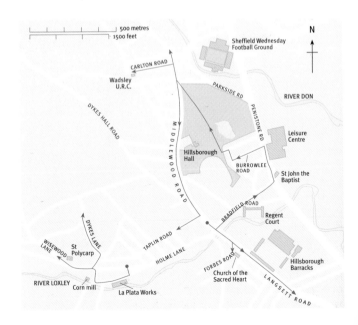

and **Hillsborough District Baths** of 1926 by the City Architect *F.E.P. Edwards,* with quite a sophisticated Neo-Baroque ashlar façade. Circular and segmental-headed windows and prominent quoins, tall chimney to the rear. Now, as so often in Sheffield, a bar. Superintendent's cottage, roughcast with a hipped roof.

Standing slightly above and much enhanced by its raised position in **Forbes Road** to the right, the **Church of the Sacred Heart** (R.C.) [169], 1936, by *C.M.E. Hadfield,* one of the best interwar churches in Sheffield. Hadfield adopted the modern style but allied it to an Arts and Crafts sensibility and it is to be regretted that this is his only essay in this vein. The building is simple by comparison with the work of the more *avant-garde* church architects of the 1930s such as Cachemaille-Day, which it superficially resembles, but the skilful massing combines with the excellence of the materials to great effect. The thin bricks were specially made. Tower, w gallery and vestibules, nave and aisles of five bays, transepts, apsidal chancel. Portland stone tympanum by *Philip Lindsay Clark* above N doorway. The essence of the interior is the contrast between the superb quality of the plain brickwork and the richness of the decoration at the E end of the church. The centre of the decorative treatment is the tall mosaic figure of the Sacred Heart with supporting angels in the apse by *Eric Newton* and his Ave Maria and Ave Joseph above the two chapels adjoining the chancel. All this work dates from 1936. Newton added the reredos mosaics in the chapels in 1961. Statues of Our Lady of Lourdes, St Joseph holding a model of the church, the Stations of the Cross, St Teresa and the font are by *Philip Lindsay Clark.* Organ case by *Albert Keates.* Opposite, the **Owlerton Church War**

168. Hillsborough, Owlerton and Malin Bridge

169. Church of the Sacred Heart, Forbes Road, by C.M.E. Hadfield, 1936

170. Hillsborough Barracks, Langsett Road, officers' quarters and mess, by H.M. Office of Works, 1850–4

**Memorial Hall**, 1925–6, by *Henry Webster*, pilastered with alternating bands of red brick and terracotta. Segmental pedimented porch, heavily detailed, and the clock tower offset to the right. Its base has a large dedication panel bearing the words 'Lest We Forget'.

On the opposite side of **Langsett Road**, the vast bulk of the **Hillsborough Barracks** [170], 1850–4 by *H.M. Office of Works*, converted in 1990 by the *John Brunton Partnership* for office and retail use. Built shortly after the Chartist demonstrations of 1848, the barracks were among the largest in the country and, as elsewhere, intended to provide a strong military presence in industrial towns. Troops were deliberately drawn from regiments from outside the county. The buildings are in a simple Tudor Gothic style of ashlar, generally symmetrical with crenellations and Gothick glazing bars. Facing Langsett Road is a three-storey block for officers' mess and quarters. Central Tudor gateway. At the N end, a Gothic chapel (later used as an institute). Behind this the infantry parade ground (now a car park) and quarters. Set below that to the E, the cavalry quarters with stables flanking at right angles to enclose a second parade ground, now covered by a large supermarket. A magazine, mobilization store, squash court and riding school were in separate buildings on the s side of the site at right angles to the barrack blocks. All are of ashlar and are in a simple Tudor Gothic style with Gothick glazing bars to some windows. Surrounding buildings on the N side have been converted to shops approached via a covered walkway from Langsett Road. Enclosing the barracks is a wall, partly crenellated with corner turrets.

By sad contrast on the N side on the corner of Hammerton Road is the shabby **Soldiers' Home**, 1907, by *George Malam Wilson*, Arts and

Crafts, brick on ground floor, roughcast above, formerly with a turret. Provided for the soldier to 'find amusement, comfort and friendship, without any temptation' (*Sheffield Red Book,* 1905). It included a reading room, photographic darkroom, a piano and a garden for croquet, tennis and bowls. Then at No 328, a former **toll house** in use between 1840 and 1857, stone with a prominent bargeboarded gable and originally with a canted bay. From here housing of the 1980s rises steeply up the valley side.

Retrace one's steps up Langsett Road to **Bradfield Road**. On the s side is the massive **Regent Court**, a block of nine-storey balcony-access flats by *Edgar Gardham,* 1936, a rare example of flats in a working-class area erected by private enterprise. They were built for private renting (the original rents of 18s to 25s per week were high by Sheffield standards) and were the only block on this scale to be built in Sheffield prior to Park Hill (*see* p. 207). Lip service was paid to the Modern Movement in the flat roofs, strong horizontals and white rendering, which contrasted with brick used for the entrance and the balcony walls but the overwhelming scale of the development represented precisely what postwar planners sought to avoid. The plan comprised a shallow frontage and two wings containing 202 flats, varying in size from one to three bedrooms and with three lifts to serve them. The advertised intention (never realized) was to provide a swimming pool and a bowling green although refrigerators, tennis courts and a communal lounge were supplied. Gardham built a similar but smaller block in Duke Street, Park (now dem.). On **Penistone Road** to the E, **St John the Baptist** of 1874 by *J.B. Mitchell-Withers.* More picturesque in outline than most Sheffield churches of this period by virtue of its slender sw tower which has a traceried wooden belfry capped by a pyramidal slate roof. Lofty interior with tall chancel arch and scissor-brace roof. Brick arches supported on stumpy piers, alternating round and octagonal. The 1994 reordering has left the chancel hidden behind the 1907 oak reredos. **Stained glass**: E window by *Kayll & Co. c.* 1900; further *Kayll* window of 1898 in the s aisle; s and N aisles, windows by *Jeffrey & Foster* of 1900; N aisle, Mothers Union window of Virgin Mary with angel and dove of 1960 by *Harry Harvey*, angular, with a distinct Festival of Britain feel to it.

To its N, the **Hillsborough Leisure Centre**, 1989 by *William Saunders & Partners*, erected for the 1991 Student Games. It comprises two parts, a sports hall and an Olympic-sized swimming pool, with an innovative moving floor enabling its use for leisure or competition. Impressive exterior, dominated by the exposed roof trusses of the pool hall which extend outside the walls and are supported on external columns. Extensive glazing above masonry cladding.

In **Burrowlee Road** to the w is **Burrowlee House** [171] built for Thomas Steade in 1711 but incorporating an earlier house. Ashlar of five bays with a balustrade over the central three. Quoins and a band below the first floor, door surround with segmental pediment and the keystone bearing the date. In 1779, the Steades built **Hillsborough Hall**

171. Burrowlee House, Burrowlee Road, 1711

(now public library) nearby. It stands in the public park, reached via
**Broughton Road**. Three storeys, ashlar, of seven bays, the central three
in a canted full-height bay window. The only decorative elements in an
otherwise austere building are the central first-floor window which has
moulded architraves and a balustraded apron, a Venetian window in
the w front and the dentil cornice. Attractive stabling behind, incorporating a pediment with a Diocletian window. Three lodges at the
entrances to the public park.

Then return to Penistone Road and up **Parkside Road** for the
**Hillsborough Schools** of 1884 by *Wilson & Masters* for the Ecclesfield
School Board. Rock-faced stone of one storey with diagonal nogging
over the windows. The area is dominated by the **Sheffield Wednesday
Football Ground**. Sheffield Wednesday F. C. was founded in 1867 and
moved to Hillsborough in 1899. Major works were carried out in 1913 but
there is little left of *Archibald Leitch*'s South Stand other than a decorative football on the roof ridge and a central gable retained after redevelopment in 1993. The North Stand by *Husband & Co.* of 1961 was the first
in Britain to have a cantilevered cover running the length of the pitch,
the aluminium sheet roof suspended from a steel frame supported by
pre-stressed concrete units. It was also the first to have entry on two levels, one entrance 12 ft higher than the other and accessed by spiral ramps.
The West or Leppings Lane stand was built for the 1966 World Cup by
*Husband & Co.* and the tragic loss of life here in April 1989 led to football grounds throughout the country becoming all seated. The East
Stand or Kop was roofed in 1986 by *Eastwood & Partners*. A little to the
N in **Middlewood Road**, the **Hillsborough Park Cinema** (now a super-
market), 1919–20, by *P.A. Hinchliffe* of Barnsley for Sheffield Suburban
Cinemas Ltd. A 1,900-seat cinema with a classical façade in red brick
with much use of faience dressings.

Returning down Middlewood Road, in **Carlton Road** to the w is
**Wadsley United Reformed Church**, 1910 by *Norman Doncaster* with an

Arts and Crafts feel to it, five bays, doorcase with broken pediment, stone facing to the front, the remainder of brick. Hall at the rear with a cupola.

In Middlewood Road on the right, **Hillsborough Trinity Methodist Church and Sunday School**, 1901 by *John W. Firth* of Oldham, completed by his son. Gothic with NW tower with octagonal lantern and short spire. Partly stone-clad, the rest in brick. The interior retains its pews and simple Art Nouveau glass. Middlewood Road N from Hillsborough Corner is the main shopping street and one of the few thriving C19 suburban shopping centres remaining in the city. To the W in **Taplin Road** is the **Hillsborough Baptist Church**, 1914 by *Chapman & Jenkinson*, brick in a minimal Perp with a hall behind. Opposite, a substantial former suburban branch of the **Brightside & Carbrook Co-operative Society** of 1900 by *Henry Webster* with extensive terracotta work on the first floor.

### Malin Bridge

An exploration of **Malin Bridge** should begin at the tram terminus. In **Holme Lane**, built on the site of a 1690s cutlery grinding wheel, the **La Plata Works** of Messrs Burgon and Ball (since 1873), now the only British manufacturers of hand sheep-shears. Rusticated ashlar façade to the offices, inscribed with the name of the works, with adjoining brick two-storey workshops. At the crossing of the River Loxley, **Malin Bridge Corn Mill**, possibly *c.* 1850, with an undershot wheel and an L-shaped low stone range, rendered at the rear. At the bottom of **Wisewood Lane**, **St Polycarp**, built in 1933–4 by *H.I. Potter* of *Fowler, Sandford & Potter*, in an Early Christian style. Of rustic brick with pantiled roof and apsidal E end. Windows grouped in threes with those in the clerestory set in panels. Tiling above the windows gives an Arts and Crafts feel to the building. Circular windows at E and W ends, no tower. Attractive light interior, four-bay nave with brick arcading of rounded arches and square piers. Broad chancel with tall chancel arch. Sympathetic reordering by *David Greenwood* in 1992. New W porch and rear bay of nave enclosed.

Opposite, a former **Methodist New Connexion Chapel** (now workshops) of 1834. Ashlar with roof gabled at E end and hipped at W. Its replacement, **St Mark's** of 1904 by *John Wills & Sons* (now a Pentecostal church), is a little to the N in the steep **Dykes Lane**. Gothic and workmanlike, the adjoining **Ward Memorial Sunday Schools** of 1930 are more striking: late Perp style with canted bay windows, mullioned and transomed with decorative glass in upper lights. Opposite, in a prominent position, the **Malin Bridge Schools** of 1905 (enlarged 1910) by *H.I. Potter*, four gables and a prominent ventilation tower. To the N and w of Dykes Lane is the Council's **Wisewood Estate**, well maintained and little altered since completion in 1932 and probably the best place to gain an impression of how Sheffield's interwar estates looked in their prime. Many of the houses have retained their Neo-Georgian glazing bars.

# Further Reading

There are no substantial general works on Sheffield's **architecture** although the period 1843–1993 is covered in R. Harman and R.H. Harper, 'The Architecture of Sheffield' in C. Binfield et al., *A History of the City of Sheffield 1843–1993*, 1993. For **local architects**, the late Stephen Welsh's unpublished lists of buildings by the principal c19 and early c20 practices are especially useful. J.W. Davidson continued the list for the Hadfields, later Hadfield Cawkwell Davidson & Partners, up to 1976 (lists available in Sheffield Local Studies Library). See also R.H. Harper, *The First Hundred Years of the Sheffield Society of Architects 1887–1987*, 1987, and R.E. Leader, *Surveyors and Architects of the Past in Sheffield*, 1903, for biographies. For individuals and firms: Hadfield Cawkwell Davidson & Partners, *150 Years of Architectural Drawings – Hadfield Cawkwell Davidson, Sheffield, 1834–1984*, 1984; P Howell (ed.), 'Letters from J.F. Bentley to Charles Hadfield', *Architectural History* 23, 1980 and 25, 1982; J.C.G. Binfield, '"A Climate for Art's Encouragement": A Provincial Architect and his Contacts: John Mansell Jenkinson (1883–1965)', *Sheffield Art Review*, 1992 and N.D. Wilson, '"Sane if Unheroic": the work of William John Hale (1862–1929) Wesleyan Methodist and Architect', *Miscellany 1 The Chapel Society*, 1998. For artists, see Janet Barnes, *Ruskin in Sheffield*, 1985 and Michael Diamond, *1850–1875 Art and Industry in Sheffield: Alfred Stevens and his school*, 1975 for the work of Stevens, Hugh Stannus and Godfrey Sykes.

For Anglican **churches**, William Odom, *Memorials of Sheffield: its Cathedral and parish churches*, 1924, is a reliable and detailed account and some individual church guides give much additional information. D. Evinson, *The Lord's House: A History of Sheffield's Roman Catholic Buildings 1570–1990*, 1991, provides an excellent modern account of Catholic churches, while Charles Hadfield's *History of St Marie's Mission and Church*, 1889 is still valuable. For the nonconformists, C. Stell, *An Inventory of Nonconformist Chapels and Meetinghouses in the North of England*, 1994.

For **early buildings**: A.L. Armstrong, Sheffield Castle in *Transactions of the Hunter Archaeological Society* 4, 1937; P.F. Ryder, *Timber Framed buildings of South Yorkshire* and David Bostwick, 'Decorative plasterwork of the Yorkshire region 1570–1670' PhD thesis, University of Sheffield, 1993 and *Sheffield in Tudor and Stuart Times* 1985; for Sheffield Manor, Charles Hadfield, *The restoration of the Lodge at Sheffield*

*Manor* in *Transactions of the RIBA*, 1875, Thomas Winder, *The Manor Lodge, Sheffield,* 1919; for the Bishops' House, Pauline Beswick, *The Bishops' House*, 1976.

Derek Bayliss (ed.), *A Guide to the Industrial History of South Yorkshire*, 1995, is a succinct introduction with a gazetteer to **industrial buildings**. Water-powered industry is covered in David Crossley (ed.), *Water Power on the Sheffield Rivers*, 1989. For the steel and cutlery industries, English Heritage's *'One Great Workshop': the buildings of the Sheffield metal trades*, 2001, is based on a detailed report of the same title by Nicola Wray, 2000 and indebted to Victoria Beauchamp, 'The Workshops of the Cutlery Industry in Hallamshire 1750–1900', PhD thesis, University of Sheffield, 1996. James Symonds (ed.), *The Historical Archaeology of the Sheffield Cutlery and Tableware Industry 1750–1900*, 2002, also covers cutlery buildings. K.C. Barraclough, *Sheffield Steel*, 1976 has especially valuable illustrations of buildings and processes. For the Don valley and the role of the Sheffield Development Corporation, D. Hey, M. Olive & M.Liddament, *Forging the Valley*, 1997. On transport, S. Ogden, *The Sheffield & Tinsley Canal*, 1997; C.C. Hall, *Sheffield Transport*, 1977; S.R. Batty, *Rail Centres: Sheffield*, 1984.

On **C19 and C20 buildings and institutions**, S. Johnson, *From Bailey to Bailey, a short history of military buildings in Sheffield*, 1998. Joan Flett, *The Story of the Workhouse and the Hospital at Nether Edge*, 2002 and P. Speck et al, *The Institution and Hospital at Fir Vale: A Century of the Northern General Hospital*, 1978. C. Binfield and D. Hey (eds.), *Mesters to Masters: a History of the Company of Cutlers in Hallamshire*, 1997, M. Tooby, *'In Perpetuity and without Charge': The Mappin Art Gallery 1887–1987*, 1987. Jan Carder, *The Sheffield Botanical Gardens: A Short History*, 1986 and Jane Horton, *Remote and Undisturbed: A Brief History of the Sheffield General Cemetery*, 2001. C. Shaw, *Sheffield Cinemas*, 2001.

On **housing**, Jon Fox, *Working Class Housing in Sheffield c. 1760–c. 1860* is an invaluable unpublished survey in Sheffield Local Studies Library. On the Norfolk estate, Donald J. Olsen, 'House upon house' in H.J. Dyos and Michael Wolff (ed.) *The Victorian City: Images and Realities*, 1973, and Dan Cruickshank, 'Secrets of Georgian City Planning', *Architects Journal*, 22 October 1998. Sidney Pollard, *A History of Labour in Sheffield*, 1958, describes working class housing and sanitary matters as does T.J. Caulton, 'The Tentacles of Slumdom: A case study of housing and urban structure in Sheffield c. 1870–1914', PhD thesis, University of Sheffield, 1980. R. Hebblethwaite, 'The Municipal Housing Programme in Sheffield before 1914', *Architectural History* 30, 1987, sets the Wincobank Cottage Exhibition in its national context. On the development of the w suburbs and Freehold Land Societies, J.H. Stainton, *The Making of Sheffield 1865–1914*, 1924 is valuable as is J.N. Tarn, 'Sheffield' in M.A. Simpson and T.H. Lloyd (ed.), *Middle Class Housing in Britain*, 1977. The **postwar period** is well covered by L. Esher, *A Broken Wave, The Rebuilding of England 1940–80*, 1981, the housing programme in V.M. Hughes, *History of the Growth and Location of the Corporation Housing Schemes*, 1959; Sheffield Corporation, *Ten Years of Housing in Sheffield, 1953–63*, 1963. For Park Hill, Andrew Saint, *Park Hill: What next?*, 1996, C. Bacon, *Park Hill in its Social Context*, 1985 and 'Streets in the Sky: The Rise and Fall of a Modern Architectural Utopia', PhD thesis, University of Sheffield, 1980. Ian Nairn, *Britain's Changing Towns*, 1967, provides an incisive view. C.R. Warman, *Sheffield, Emerging City*, 1969 conveys the optimism of the 1960s.

Some **suburbs** have received treatment in short monographs including those by Mary Walton on Sharrow and Nether Edge, also covered in Nether Edge Neighbourhood Group, *They Lived in Sharrow and Nether Edge*, 1988. Others include Eva Wilkinson, *Endcliffe Crescent*, 2001, Nyra Wilson, *'Houses of a respectable class': the development of Victoria Park in the Nineteenth Century*, 1994, Heeley History Workshop, *Heghlegh Then and Heeley Now: Work Play and People*, 2000, and Crookes Local History Group, *Crookes, the History of a Sheffield Village*, 1982 and *Crookes Revisited*, 1989.

The classic **general history** is Joseph Hunter's *Hallamshire: the history and topography of the parish of Sheffield*, revised edn. by Alfred Gatty, 1875. The most recent is David Hey, *A History of Sheffield*, 1998, but Mary Walton, *Sheffield: its story and its achievements*, 1948 (5th edn. 1984), and J. Edward Vickers, *A Popular History of Sheffield*, 1978, are still useful. C. Binfield et al, *The History of the City of Sheffield 1843–1993*, 1993 is more academic, with comprehensive bibliographies. For the geological background and much else, D.L. Linton (ed.), *Sheffield and its region: a scientific and historical survey*, 1956. Melvyn Jones (ed.) *Aspects of Sheffield 1 and 2*, 1997, 1999 is a valuable series of essays.

Local **guides and directories** include *Pawson & Brailsford's Illustrated Guide to Sheffield and Neighbourhood*, 1862, 1879, 1889 and 1899, and the various editions of *White's* and *Kelly's* Directories together with the *Sheffield Red Book*, the *Sheffield Annual Year Book and Record* and the *Sheffield Local Register* which indexes the principal local newspapers. A **bibliography**, Sylvia M Pybus (rev.), *Basic Books on Sheffield*, 1975 (Sheffield City Libraries) had a supplement in 1982.

**Websites:** www.lookingatbuildings.org.uk – the Pevsner Architectural Guide's website – has further information on Sheffield buildings and architects. www.picturesheffield.com has thousands of C19 and C20 photographs from the Local Studies Library's collection, while information from the Public Monuments and Sculpture Association's National Recording Project is at public-art.shu.ac.uk/pmsa

# Glossary

**Acanthus:** *see* [2D].

**Acroterion:** plinth for a statue on ornament on the apex or ends of a pediment.

**Aedicule:** architectural surround, usually a pediment on two columns or pilasters.

**Ambulatory:** aisle around the *sanctuary* of a church.

**Anthemion:** *see* [2D].

**Apse:** semicircular or polygonal end, especially in a church.

**Arcade:** series of arches supported by piers or columns (cf. *colonnade*).

**Architrave:** *see* [2A], also moulded surround to a window or door.

**Art Deco:** a self-consciously up-to-date interwar style of bold simplified patterns, often derived from non-European art.

**Ashlar:** large rectangular masonry blocks wrought to even faces.

**Atlantes:** male figures supporting an *entablature*.

**Atrium:** a toplit covered court rising through several storeys.

**Attic:** small top storey within a roof. Also the storey above the main entablature of a classical façade.

**Baldacchino:** solid canopy, usually free-standing and over an altar.

**Ballflower:** globular flower of three petals enclosing a small ball.

**Barrel vault:** one with a simple arched profile.

**Batter:** intentional inward inclination of a wall face.

**Bay:** division of an elevation by regular vertical features such as columns, windows, etc.

**Beaux-Arts:** a French-derived approach to classical design, at its peak in the later C19–early C20, marked by strong axial planning and the grandiose use of the *orders*.

**Billet:** ornament of small rectangular blocks.

**Bressumer:** big horizontal beam supporting the wall above, especially in a jettied building; *see* [4c].

**Broach spire:** *see* [1].

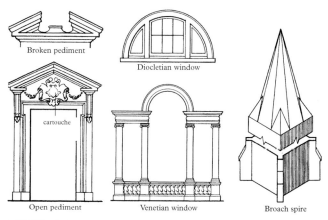

Broken pediment

Diocletian window

cartouche

Open pediment

Venetian window

Broach spire

1. Miscellaneous

## 2. Classical orders and enrichments

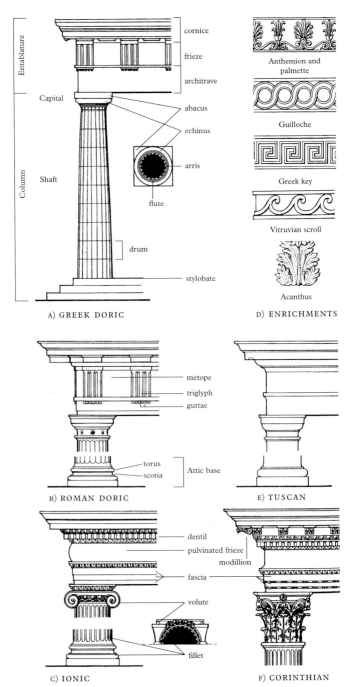

Entablature
- cornice
- frieze
- architrave

Column
- Capital
  - abacus
  - echinus
- Shaft
  - arris
  - flute
- drum
- stylobate

A) GREEK DORIC

D) ENRICHMENTS

Anthemion and palmette

Guilloche

Greek key

Vitruvian scroll

Acanthus

B) ROMAN DORIC
- metope
- triglyph
- guttae
- torus
- scotia

Attic base

E) TUSCAN

C) IONIC
- dentil
- pulvinated frieze
- modillion
- fascia
- volute
- fillet

F) CORINTHIAN

**Brutalist:** used for later 1950s–70s Modernist architecture displaying rough or unfinished concrete, large massive forms, and abrupt juxtapositions.

**Bush-hammered:** concrete with hammered impressions.

**Capital:** head feature of a column or pilaster; for classical types *see* [2].

**Cartouche:** *see* [1].

**Castellated:** with battlements.

**Chancel:** the E part or end of a church, where the altar is placed.

**Chapter house:** place of assembly for the members of a monastery or cathedral.

**Choir:** the part of a great church where services are sung.

**Clerestory:** uppermost storey of an interior, pierced by windows.

**Coade stone:** ceramic artificial stone, made 1769–*c.* 1840 by Eleanor Coade and associates.

**Coffering:** decorative arrangement of sunken panels.

**Cogging:** a decorative course of bricks laid diagonally.

**Colonnade:** range of columns supporting a flat *lintel* or *entablature* (cf. *arcade*).

**Coped gable:** gable with protective capping course of masonry.

**Corbel:** projecting block supporting something above.

**Composite:** classical order with capitals combining Corinthian features (acanthus, *see* [2D]) with Ionic (volutes, *see* [2C]).

**Corinthian; cornice:** *see* [2A; 2F].

**Cove:** a broad concave moulding.

**Crenellated:** with battlements.

**Crocket:** leafy hooks decorating the edges of Gothic features

**Crucks:** pairs of inclined timbers, usually curved, set at bay-lengths that support the roof timbers and in timber buildings, also support the walls; *see* [4B].

**Crypt:** underground or half-underground area, usually below the E end of a church.

**Cupola:** a small dome used as a crowning feature.

**Dado:** finishing of the lower part of an internal wall.

**Decorated (Dec):** English Gothic architecture, late C13 to late C14.

**Diocletian window:** *see* [1].

**Doric:** *see* [2A, 2B].

**Drum:** circular or polygonal stage supporting a dome.

**Dutch or Flemish gable:** *see* [3].

**Early English (E.E.):** English Gothic architecture, late C12 to late C13.

**Electrolier:** ornamental fitting for a number of electric lights.

**Embattled:** with battlements.

**Entablature:** *see* [2A].

**Enveloping:** substantial grant-aided refurbishment of C19 housing on an area basis that replaces all services, windows, roofs, etc.

**Faience:** moulded *terracotta* that is glazed white or coloured.

**Fleurons:** carved flower or leaf.

**Frieze:** middle member of a classical *entablature, see* [2A, 2C]. Also a horizontal band of ornament.

**Geometrical:** of *tracery,* a mid-C13–C14 type formed of circles and part-circles, *see* [6].

**Giant order:** a classical *order* that is two or more storeys high.

**Gibbs surround:** C18 treatment of an opening with blocked architraves, seen particularly in the work of James Gibbs (1682–1754).

**Gothic:** the style of the later Middle Ages, characterized by the pointed arch and rib-vault.

**Grinding hull:** room where grinding of cutlery and edge tools took place.

**Groin vault:** one composed of intersecting *barrel vaults.*

**Guilloche:** *see* [2D].

**Half-timbering:** non-structural decorative timberwork.

**Herm:** head or bust on a pedestal.

**Hipped roof:** *see* [3].

**Hoodmould:** projecting moulding above an arch or *lintel* to throw off water.

**In antis:** of columns, set in an opening (properly between simplified pilasters called *antae*).

**Ionic:** *see* [2C].

**Italianate:** a classical style derived from the palaces of Renaissance Italy.

**Jamb:** one of the vertical sides of an opening.

**Jettied:** with a projecting upper storey, usually timber-framed.

**Kingpost roof:** one with vertical timbers set centrally on the tie-beams, supporting the ridge.

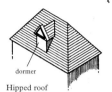
dormer

Hipped roof

Mansard roof

Flemish or
Dutch gable

3. Roofs and gables

**Kneeler**: horizontal projecting stone at the base of each side of a gable on which the inclined coping stones rest.

**Lancet**: slender, single-light pointed-arched window, *see* [6].

**Lantern**: a windowed turret crowning a roof, tower or dome.

**Light**: compartment of a window.

**Lintel**: horizontal beam or stone bridging an opening.

**Loggia**: open gallery with arches or columns.

**Louvre**: opening in a roof or wall to allow air to escape.

**Lunette**: semicircular window or panel.

**Machicolation**: openings between *corbels* that support a projecting parapet.

**Mannerist**: of classical architecture, with motifs used in deliberate disregard of original conventions or contexts.

**Mansard roof**: *see* [3].

**Mezzanine**: low storey between two higher ones.

**Millstone grit**: a coarse sandstone from the southern Pennines.

**Moulding**: shaped ornamental strip of continuous section.

**Mullion**: vertical member between window lights.

**Narthex**: enclosed vestibule or porch at the main entrance to a church.

**Newel**: central or corner post of a staircase.

**Norman**: the C11–C12 English version of the *Romanesque* style.

**Oculus**: circular opening.

**Ogee**: of an arch, dome, etc., with double-curved pointed profile.

**Orders (classical)**: for types *see* [2].

**Oriel**: window projecting above ground level.

**Palladian**: following the examples and classical principles of Andrea Palladio (1508–80).

**Parapet**: wall for protection of a sudden drop, e.g. on a bridge, or to conceal a roof.

**Paternoster lift**: lift with open platforms in continuous motion.

**Pavilion**: ornamental building for occasional use; or a projecting subdivision of a larger building.

**Pediment**: a formalized gable, derived from that of a classical temple; also used over doors, windows, etc. For types *see* [1].

**Pendentive**: part-hemispherical surface between arches that meet at an angle to support a drum, dome or vault.

**Penthouse**: a separately roofed structure on top of a multi-storey block of the C20 or later.

**Perpendicular (Perp)**: English Gothic architecture from the late C14 to early C16.

**Piano nobile** (Italian): principal floor of a classical building, above a ground floor or basement and with a lesser storey overhead.

**Pier**: a large masonry or brick support, often for an arch.

**Pilaster**: flat representation of a classical column in shallow relief.

**Pilotis**: C20 French term for pillars or stilts that support a building above an open ground floor.

**Piscina**: basin in a church or chapel for washing mass vessels, usually wall-set.

**Pitching eye**: circular or oval opening through which hay is pitched to the upper part of a stable or barn.

**Plinth**: projecting courses at the foot of a wall or column, generally chamfered or moulded at the top.

**Polychromy**: the use of contrasting coloured materials such as bricks as decoration, particularly associated with mid-C19 Gothic styles.

**Porte cochère** (French): porch large enough to admit wheeled vehicles.

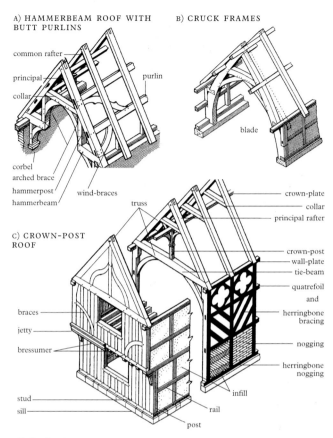

A) HAMMERBEAM ROOF WITH BUTT PURLINS

- common rafter
- principal
- collar
- purlin
- corbel
- arched brace
- hammerpost
- hammerbeam
- wind-braces

B) CRUCK FRAMES

- blade

C) CROWN-POST ROOF

- truss
- crown-plate
- collar
- principal rafter
- crown-post
- wall-plate
- tie-beam
- quatrefoil and herringbone bracing
- nogging
- herringbone nogging
- braces
- jetty
- bressumer
- infill
- stud
- sill
- rail
- post

4. Timber Framing

**Portico:** porch with roof and (frequently) *pediment* supported by a row of columns.

**Portland stone:** a hard, durable white limestone from the Isle of Portland in Dorset.

**Presbytery:** a priest's residence.

**Prostyle:** of a *portico*, with freestanding columns.

**Pulvinated:** of bulging profile; *see* [2C].

**Quatrefoil:** opening with four lobes or foils.

**Queen Anne:** the later Victorian revival of the mid-C17 domestic classical manner, usually in red brick or terracotta.

**Quoins:** dressed or otherwise emphasized stones at the angles of a building.

**Rainwater head:** container at a parapet into which rainwater runs from the gutters.

**Render:** a uniform covering for walls for protection from the weather, usually of cement or *stucco*.

**Reredos:** painted and/or sculpted screen behind and above an altar.

**Rock-faced:** masonry cleft to produce a natural, rugged appearance.

**Romanesque:** round-arched style of the C11 and C12.

**Rood:** crucifix flanked by the Virgin and St John, carved or painted.

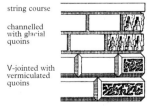

- string course
- channelled with glacial quoins
- V-jointed with vermiculated quoins

5. Rustication

lancet

transom

Geometric    Intersecting    Reticulated

Panel

6. Tracery

**Rubble:** of masonry, with stones wholly or partly rough and unsquared.

**Rustication:** exaggerated treatment of masonry to give the effect of strength. For types *see* [5].

**Sacristy:** room in a church used for sacred vessels and vestments.

**Saddleback roof:** a pitched roof used on a tower.

**Sanctuary:** in a church, the area around the main altar.

**Scagliola:** composition imitating marble.

**Sedilia:** seats for the priests in the chancel wall of a church or chapel.

**Spandrel:** space between an arch and its framing rectangle, or between adjacent arches.

**Stanchion:** upright structural member, of iron, steel or reinforced concrete.

**Stripped classicism:** buildings whose proportions conform to classical precedent but where the usual classical decoration is implied or removed altogether.

**Stucco:** durable lime plaster, shaped into ornamental features or used externally as a protective coating.

**System building:** system of manufac-tured units assembled on site.

**Terracotta:** moulded and fired clay ornament or cladding (cf. *faience*).

**Tie-beam:** main horizontal trans-verse timber in a roof structure.

**Tilt forge:** where steel was hammered or 'tilted' into bars, initially powered by water, later by steam.

**Tracery:** openwork pattern of masonry or timber in the upper part of an opening.

**Transept:** transverse portion of a church.

**Transom:** horizontal member between window lights.

**Trefoil:** with three lobes or foils.

**Triforium:** middle storey of a church interior treated as an arcaded wall passage or blind arcade.

**Truss:** braced framework, spanning between supports.

**Tunnel vault:** one with a simple elongated-arched profile.

**Tuscan:** *see* [2E].

**Tympanum:** the area enclosed by an arch or pediment.

**Undercroft:** room(s), usually vaulted, beneath the main space of a building.

**Vault:** arched stone roof, sometimes imitated in wood or plaster. *See* Barrel vault

**Venetian window:** *see* [1].

**Vermiculation:** *see* Rustication.

**Vierendeel girder:** truss without diagonal members between the vertical struts.

**Volutes:** spiral scrolls, especially on Ionic columns (*see* [2C]).

**Vomitory:** passage from a theatre auditorium to the stage.

**Voussoir:** wedge-shaped stones forming an arch.

**Wagon roof:** with the appearance of the inside of a wagon tilt.

**Weathering:** inclined, projecting surface to keep water away from the wall below.

**Wrenaissance:** early C20 work inspired by the architecture of Sir Christopher Wren (1632–1723), especially the E front of Hampton Court.

# Index
## of Artists, Architects and Other Persons Mentioned

Names of artists, architects etc. working in Sheffield are in *italic*; page references including relevant illustrations are in *italic*.

Turton, Thomas 158, 163, 271
Turton Brothers & Matthews 173
*Twigg, E.E. & Co.* 66
*Twiss, Christine* 90
Tyzack, Joseph & Co. 10, 241

*University Architectural Consultancy
Unit* 262
*University Estates Department* 80
*Unwin, Charles* 146

*Vale, Brenda & Robert* 239
Vic Hallam Ltd 37
Vickers (Vickers Sons & Maxims)
16, 29, 189, 195
    James 12
    Edward 272

*Waddington Son & Dunkerley* 27, 120
*Wailes (of Newcastle)* 59
Wake, Bernard 176
Walker, George (Walker & Hall) 249
*Walker, William see William Walker
Partnership*
Walsh, John Ltd 132
Walsh family 279
Walters, Sir John Tudor 186
*Waplington, Paul* 146
Ward, David 251
*Ward, Ronald & Partners* 118
Ward, Thomas Asline 227, 263
Ward, T.W. Ltd 191, 221
*Ward & Hughes* 278
*Ward McHugh Associates* 85, 191
*Warren, Bernard* 90, 146
Waterhouse, Alfred 24, 61
*Waterhouse & Son* 26, 96
*Watson, A.F.* 24, 28, 29, 229, 253
*Watson, Charles* 45, 50, *147*
Watson, James 258
Watson, John 255
*Watson, T.E.* 173
Watson, Thomas 56
*Watson, Pritchet & Watson* 15
Watts, John & Co. 14, 163
*Webb, Aston* 81
*Webb, Christopher* 54–6
*Webster, Henry* 187, 290, 293
*Webster, John Dodsley* 24, 25, 26, 27,
88, 96, *106*, 107, 117, 120, 125, 198,
223, 235, 238, 248, 263, 270, 274, 279,
283, 287
*Webster, John Dodsley & Son* 24, 182,
278
*Webster, John Douglas* 24
Webster, William 232
*Weightman, J.G.* 14, 15, 24, 260, 279
*Weightman & Hadfield* 22, 24, 57, *58*,
156, 214

*Weightman, Hadfield & Goldie* 24,
162, 191, 262
*Weintraub Associates* 96
*Welsh, Stephen* 85, 220
Wesley, John 114
*Westlake, Nathaniel* 23, 59, 124, 279;
  *see also Hadfield & Westlake;
  Lavers, Barraud &
    Westlake; Lavers & Westlake*
Wharncliffe, Lord 156
Wharncliffe Fire Clay Company
253
*White, Johnny* 176, 193
*White, Laura* 92
Whiteley, Seth 107
*Whitfield, William* 36, 84, 86
de Wickersley family 258
Wigfall, William & Sons 139
*Wigfull, J.R.* 86, 146
*Wightman, Herbert* 270
*Wightman & Wightman* 217, 229
Wike, Charles 199, 284
*Wilkinson, Alfred* 217–18
Wilkinson, Rev. James 56, 258
*William Saunders & Partners* 291
*William Walker Partnership* 197
*Williams, J.* 151
*Williams, Sir Owen* 197
*Williams, Sue* 252
*Wills, John & Sons* 27, 182, 217, 293
*Wilson, C.D. Carus* 98
*Wilson, George Malam* 290
*Wilson, Gordon* 161
*Wilson, Harry* 198
*Wilson, Henry* 27, 124, *125*
Wilson, James 236
Wilson, Joseph 228
*Wilson, T.A.* 279
*Wilson, T.H.* 107
*Wilson & Crosland* 236
*Wilson & Masters* 292
Wilsons & Co. 228, 261
*Winder, Edmund* 132
*Winter, J.* 90, 180
Wolsey, Thomas 205
*Womersley, J. Lewis* 32, *33*, 35, 36, 147,
162, 178–9, *207–8*, 215, 243, 287
*Wood, Edgar* 30, 160, 255
*Woodhead & Hurst* 15, 16, 86, 88, 111,
157, 176, 214, *216*
Woofinden, George 263
Woollen, George 272
*Worth, Samuel* 24, 70, *71*, 109, 173,
226, *227*, 251, 253
Wostenholm, George 12, 23, 231–2
*Wray, Amanda* 176
*Wright, Peter* 88
*Wynne, David* 98
*Wyon, E.W.* 265

# Index

## of Localities, Streets and Buildings

Principal references are in **bold** type; page references including relevant illustrations are in *italic*.

Polytechnic *see* Sheffield Hallam
  University
Pomona Street 28, **226**
Pond Hill 152
Pond Street 89–90, 152
Ponds Forge International Leisure
  Centre 40, **152**, *153*
Porter Croft School 28, **226**
Portland Works 221–2
Portobello 87, 129
Portobello Street 87
President Works *192*, 193
Primrose Avenue *187*
Prior Bank 233
Priory Road 232
Prudential Assurance Company
  Offices 26, **96–7**
Psalter Lane 230–1, **232–3**, **236**
Public Dispensary (Royal Hospital)
  129, **132**
Pupil Teachers Centre, Holly Street
  118
Pye Bank School 20, *178*

Quaker Meeting House, St James'
  Street 115
Quarters 274
Queens Road 224
Queen's Tower *216*
Queen's Works 193

Raeburn Road 245
Ragged School and Orphanage 162
Randall Street 221–2
Ranfall 270
Ranmoor 23, *263*, **267–74**, 282
Ranmoor Cliffe Road 270
Ranmoor Crescent 270
Ranmoor Grange 270
Ranmoor Hall (Snaithing Brook)
  273–4
Ranmoor House 271
Ranmoor Inn 270
Ranmoor Park Road 270
Ranmoor Road 270
Redvers House 100
Regent Court, Bradfield Road 32, **291**
Regent Court, Portobello 87
Regent Terrace 129
Revenue Buildings 132
Rivelin Valley Catholic Cemetery
  278–9
River Don Navigation 12
River Don Works *194*, 195, *196*
Riverdale 267
Riverside Court Hotel (Lion Hotel)
  155
Riverside Exchange 42, **174**
Robens Building *161*

Rockingham Street 14, 123
Rollestone 243, 245, 246
Royal Bank of Scotland, Church
  Street 109
Royal Exchange Buildings 28, **154**,
  **155**
Royal Hallamshire Hospital 39, 247,
  **248–9**
Royal Hospital *see* Public Dispensary
Royal Infirmary (Heritage Park) 16,
  26, **283**
Royal Plaza 132
Royal Sheffield Institution for the
  Blind 131
Royal Victoria Buildings 154
Royal Victoria Station Hotel
  (Holiday Inn) 157
Rundle Road 232
Ruskin House 281–2
Ruskin Museum 74, 241
Ruth Square *18*
Rutland Arms 143
Rutland Hall 172–3
Rutland Park 252
Rutland Road 172–3
Rutland Works 172
Rydal 30, **274**
Ryegate Centre 254–5

St Aidan, City Road 31, **217–18**
St Andrew, Psalter Lane 232–3
St Andrew Primitive Methodist
  Church, Heeley 238
St Andrew Scottish Presbyterian
  Church 256
St Augustine, Brocco Bank 263
St Barnabas, London Road 223
St Barnabas Road 222
St Bartholomew, Burgoyne Road
  279–80
St Catherine R.C. Church,
  Burngreave Road 31, *179*
St Catherine of Siena 36
St Cecilia House 262
St Charles Borromeo 196
St Charles Street 196
St Cuthbert, Firvale 27, *182*
St George, St George's Square 14,
  **88**
St George's Museum 74
St George's Square 28, 40, 78, 79,
  **86–8**
St Hilda, Windmill Lane 31, *188*
St James, St James Street 188
St James Presbyterian Church Hall
  176
St James' Row 108–9, 114–15
St James' Street 115, 188
St John, Bernard Street 213

St John, Crookesmoor (Wesleyan Chapel) 286
St John, Ranmoor 23, 25, 110, **267**, *268*
St John, Sharrow Lane (Methodist Church) 225
St John the Baptist, Penistone Road 291
St Joseph, Heavygate Road 280
St Joseph's School 280–1
St Luke, Crookes 27, **276**, **277**
St Luke, Hollis Croft 55
St Luke's National Schools 15, **160**
St Marie *see* cathedral (R.C.)
St Marie's Presbytery *120*
St Mark, Broomhill 36, **249**, *250*
St Mark, Malin Bridge 293
St Mark's Crescent 249
St Mary, Bramall Lane 14, **220**, **221**
St Mary, Howard Road 279
St Mary's Road 36
St Mary's Sunday School, Matilda Lane 139
St Matthew, Carver Street 27, **124**, *125*
St Paul, Pinstone Street *8*, 56, 95
St Paul, Wordsworth Avenue 36, *37*
St Paul and St James 14
St Paul's National School 137
St Paul's Parade 96
St Peter, Ellesmere Road 181
St Peter and St Paul *see* cathedral
St Polycarp, Malin Bridge 31, **293**
St Silas, Broomhall 257
St Stephen, Fawcett Street 285
St Thomas, Nairn Street 277–8
St Timothy, Slinn Street 27, **278**
St Vincent R.C., Crofts 159, **162**
St Vincent R.C., Pickmere Road 278
St Vincent's Presbytery (Provincial House) 161
St Vincent's Schools 162
Sale memorial Vicarage 214
Salvation Army Citadel, Cross Burgess Street 97
Salvation Army Citadel, Psalter Lane 233
Sanderson's Works 166
Sandygate Road 272–3
Saunders Building 260
Savile Street (Savile Street East) 16, *191*, *192*, **193**
School of Art 23, 110
School for the Blind 254
School Board offices 117, *118*
School Road Wesleyan Chapel 278
Science and Technology Park 197
Scotia Works 140
Scotland Street 160–7
Scott Road 176

Sellers Wheel 138–9
Shalesmoor 14, **168–70**
shambles 15
Sharrow *219*, 220–30
Sharrow Head House 228
Sharrow Lane 224–5
Sharrow Snuff Mills **228**, **229**, 261
Sharrow Vale Road 228–9
Sharrow Vale Road Wesleyan Reform Chapel 229
Sheaf Brewery 225–6
Sheaf Quay 158
Sheaf Square 140
Sheaf Street 22, 89–92, **152–3**
Sheaf Works 12, **158**, 271
Sheffield, Ashton-under-Lyne and Manchester Railway, 22
Sheffield Co-operative Society Department Store *see* Castle House
Sheffield College, Granville Road 35, **215–16**
Sheffield College, Sharrow Lane *224*, 225
Sheffield College, Walkley Centre 279
Sheffield Hallam University 35–6, 40, **89–92**, 260
    Adsett's Centre 40, 92
    Atrium *91*, 92
    Eric Mensforth Building 90
    Harmer Building 90
    Howard Building 90
    Nelson Mandela Building 90
    Norfolk Building 90
    Owen Building 89–90
    Science Park 136, 140–1
    Sheaf Building 90
    Stoddart Building 92
    Surrey Building 90
Sheffield and Hallamshire Bank
    Norfolk Street 104–5
    Sharrow Lane 224
    Wicker 156
Sheffield High School for Girls 252
Sheffield Hospital for Women 112
Sheffield Institute for the Blind 132
Sheffield Mail Centre 195
Sheffield Medical Institution 117
Sheffield Metal Co. Works *164*
Sheffield and Rotherham Railway 13, 16, 191
Sheffield and Tinsley Canal 145
Sheffield Transport Interchange 152
Sheffield Union Bank, London Road 225
Sheffield Union Workhouse and Infirmary 183
Sheffield Waterworks Co. Offices *123*
Sheffield Wednesday Football Ground 292

Western Bank  40, 78, 79, *80*, **81–6**
Westfield Terrace  127
Weston Park  286
west.one  42, **128**
Wharncliffe Fireclay Works  **128**, 197
Wharncliffe House  112
Wharncliffe Road  258
Wharncliffe Works  170–1
Wheats Lane  113
White Building  17, 28, 110, **150**, *151*
White Croft  159
White Gate  270
White House Buildings  285
White Lion  240
Wicker  **154–6**
Wicker Arches  *156*
Wicker Congregational Church  25
Wicker Iron Works  180–1
Wicker Station  191
Wilkinson Street  123, **256**
William Street  255
Williamson Road  233
Wilson Carlile College of Evangelism  128
Wilson Place  5, **238**
Wilson Road  262–3
Wilton Place  260
Wincobank  26, *181*, **185–6**
Wincobank Avenue  186

Winter Garden  39, 42, **74–5**, *76*, 96, 103
Winter Street  84
Wisewood estate  29, **293**
Wisewood Lane  293
Woodseats  6
Woodside estate  35, **178–9**
Woodthorpe estate  29, 33
Woodvale Flats  265
Woodville Hall  260
Woofinden Convalescent Home  263
Worksop Road  198
Workstation  140
Wright Memorial Church Room  257

Ye Olde Hole in the Wall  191
Yemeni Community Centre  198
YMCA  119
York City & County Bank  28, **145**
Yorkshire Bank, Commercial Street  149
Yorkshire Bank, Fargate  119
Yorkshire Cable/Telewest offices  197
Yorkshire House  97–8
Yorkshire Penny Bank, Attercliffe  26, **197**
YWCA  30, **127**

Zeenat Restaurant  198

# Illustration Acknowledgements

Every effort has been made to contact or trace all copyright holders. The publishers will be glad to make good any errors or omissions brought to our attention in future editions. We are grateful to the following for permission to reproduce illustrative material:

John Donat: 56
English Heritage (NMR): 2, 5, 8, 14, 22, 23, 28, 29, 30, 31, 32, 33, 35, 37, 40, 42, 43, 54, 55, 57, 58, 61, 63, 64, 68, 69, 77, 78, 83, 84, 85, 87, 88, 89, 92, 93, 94, 95, 96, 98, 100, 101, 104, 106, 110, 114, 116, 118, 120, 124, 125, 128, 129, 130, 132, 133, 135, 138, 139, 140, 142, 145, 146, 147, 150, 152, 154, 155, 156, 157, 158, 159, 161, 162, 166, 169, 170, 171
Alan Fagan: 9 (courtesy of Sheffield Industrial Museums Trust), 49, 99 (courtesy of English Heritage), 122
David Grandorge: 24
Ruth Harman: 11, 62, 65, 66, 113, 115, 117
Roger Harper: 41

Elain Harwood: 121, 151
Canon Nick Howe: 27
John Minnis: 10, 13, 15, 16, 17, 19, 20, 70, 71, 72, 73, 74, 75, 79, 91, 107, 109, 131, 149, 163, 164
Joy Minnis: 21
Sheffield Archives: 6, 26, 60, 112, 136, 167
Sheffield City Council, Design and Print Service: 3, 36, 38, 39, 53, 80
Sheffield City Council, Architects Services : 123, 143
Sheffield Hallam University (Linda Bussey): 50, 51
Sheffield Local Studies Library: 4, 7, 12, 18, 34, 82, 103, 108, 126, 165
The Smithson Family Collection: 45
Touchmedia: 1, 25, 44, 52, 59, 67, 76, 81, 86, 90, 97, 102, 105, 111, 119, 127, 134, 137, 141, 144, 148, 153, 160, 168
The University of Sheffield: 46, 47, 48

A special debt of gratitude is owed to English Heritage and its photographer, Keith Buck, who took the majority of the photographs for this volume.